LOGIC AND DATA BASES

LOGIC AND DATA BASES

Edited by

Hervé Gallaire
Centre d'Etudes et de Recherches de Toulouse
Toulouse, France

and

Jack Minker
University of Maryland
College Park, Maryland

PLENUM PRESS · NEW YORK AND LONDON

Library of Congress Cataloging in Publication Data

Symposium on Logic and Data Bases, Centre d'études et de recherches de Toulouse, 1977.
Logic and data bases.

Includes indexes.

1. Data base management – Congresses. 2. Logic, Symbolic and mathematical – Congresses. I. Gallaire, Hervé. II. Minker, Jack. III. Title.
QA 76.9.D3S97 001.6'42 78-14032
ISBN 0-306-40060-X

The content of this volume is based on the proceedings of the Symposium on Logic and Data Bases held at the Centre d'Etudes et de Recherches de L'Ecole Nationale Supérieure de L'Aéronautique et de L'Espace de Toulouse (C.E.R.T.), Toulouse, France, November 16–18, 1977

A Division of Plenum Publishing Corporation
227 West 17th Street, New York, N.Y. 10011

Printed in the United States of America

FOREWORD

Mathematical logic provides a conceptual framework for many different areas of science. It has been recognized recently that logic is also significant for data bases. To focus on this important topic, a group of researchers met at a workshop in Toulouse, France on November 16-18, 1977. The workshop was held at the Centre d'Etudes et de Recherches de L'Ecole Nationale Supérieure de L'Aéronautique et de L'Espace de Toulouse (C.E.R.T.). We are pleased to acknowledge the financial support received from the Direction des Recherches, Etudes et Techniques d'Armenent (D.R.E.T) and from C.E.R.T. Without this support the workshop would not have been possible. We particularly wish to thank our friend and colleague Jean Marie Nicolas for handling much of the organization of the workshop.

This book is a collection of substantially revised versions of the majority of the papers presented at the workshop. Every paper was reviewed carefully by at least two reviewers. Many thanks are due to our reviewers for their detailed reading of the papers and their constructive comments.

The book provides, for the first time, a comprehensive description of the interaction between logic and data bases. It will be seen that logic can be used as a programming language, as a query language, to perform deductive searches, to maintain the integrity of data bases, to provide a formalism for handling negative information, to generalize concepts in knowledge representation, and to represent and manipulate data structures. Thus, logic provides a powerful tool for data bases that is accomplished by no other approach developed to date. It provides a unifying mathematical theory for data bases. In our introductory article we describe the important concepts of logic and relational data bases that are needed for the remaining chapters, and provide an overview of the major ideas set forth by the authors.

We believe that the book can be used as the basis for a graduate course in computer science. For this purpose, the student should have a firm background in mathematical logic. It would be desirable, but not essential, that the student have a first course in data base systems and in heuristic methods.

Although we have included some background in our introductory article, the instructor will want to expand slightly on the fundamentals of resolution theorem proving and the relational data base model. This can be accomplished in the first few weeks of the semester.

The chapters in the book are presented in a preferred sequence. In addition to the introductory chapter there are five major sections in the book. The first section discusses how data bases may be viewed in the framework of mathematical logic. The second section discusses the use of mathematical logic to represent knowledge and to perform deduction. How one can deal with negative information is described in the third section and in the section, "Data Bases Viewed Through Logic", in articles by Reiter and by Nicolas and Gallaire. Logic and data base integrity is the subject of the fourth section. Finally, some applications and a description of how existing query languages relate to logic is described in the last section. The instructor can select individual chapters from the book for reading depending upon the topics he wishes to stress.

We wish to express our grateful appreciation to Mrs. Pat Young for her work and devotion to the book. She handled all correspondence with the authors and referees, typed the entire book and helped to organize the index.

H. GALLAIRE
J. MINKER
August 1978

CONTENTS

FOREWORD

INTRODUCTION

An Overview and Introduction to Logic and Data Bases, H. Gallaire, J. Minker, and J. M. Nicolas 3

DATA BASES VIEWED THROUGH FORMAL LOGIC

Data Base: Theory vs. Interpretation, J. M. Nicolas and H. Gallaire 33

On Closed World Data Bases, R. Reiter 55

Logic for Data Description, R. Kowalski 77

KNOWLEDGE REPRESENTATION AND DEDUCTION

An Experimental Relational Data Base System Based on Logic, J. Minker 107

Deductive Question-Answering on Relational Data Bases, R. Reiter 149

Deductive Planning and Pathfinding for Relational Data Bases, C. Kellogg, P. Klahr, and L. Travis 179

DEDUCE 2: Further Investigations of Deduction in Relational Data Bases, C. L. Chang 201

Nondeterministic Languages Used for the Definition of Data Models, M. Colombetti, P. Paolini, and G. Pelagatti 237

An Axiomatic Data Base Theory, S-Å. Tärnlund 259

NEGATIVE INFORMATION AND DATA BASES

Negation as Failure, K. L. Clark 293

LOGIC AND DATA BASE INTEGRITY

Integrity Checking in Deductive Data Bases, J. M. Nicolas and K. Yazdanian 325

QUERY LANGUAGES AND APPLICATIONS

The Application of PROLOG to the Development of QA and DBM Systems, I. Futó, F. Darvas, and P. Szeredi 347

The Predicate Calculus-Language KS as a Query Language, W. Dilger and G. Zifonun 377

High Level Data Base Query Languages, A. Pirotte 409

AUTHOR INDEX 437

SUBJECT INDEX 441

List of Referees 455

Addresses of Contributing Authors 457

INTRODUCTION

AN OVERVIEW AND INTRODUCTION TO LOGIC AND DATA BASES

Herve Gallaire[1], Jack Minker[2] and Jean Marie Nicolas[1]

ONERA-CERT, Toulouse, France[1]

University of Maryland, College Park, Maryland[2]

ABSTRACT

In this introductory chapter we provide both an overview of mathematical logic and relational data base concepts that serve as background for the book, as well as an introduction to the major ideas discussed in the individual chapters. The first section of this paper is devoted to a description of first order logic, while the second describes the relational data base model. The next sections summarize the five major units of chapters.

The theme of this collection is that mathematical logic provides a conceptual framework for data base systems. The first unit demonstrates this, showing explicitly how data base concepts can be analyzed in terms of formal logic, and provides a characterization of the hypothetical worlds on which data base systems work. The second analyzes knowledge representation and how it relates to the process of deduction; alternate approaches are described and their advantages and limitations are noted. The third considers how logic may be used to express constraints on a data base and to maintain data base integrity. A similar approach proves useful in dealing with the fourth topic - meaning assigned to answers when negative questions are posed. The last demonstrates how logic provides a unifying framework for query language.

INTRODUCTION

Mathematical logic has been applied to many different areas, including that of data bases. The material presented in this book shows how logic can be used to express and to solve many fundamentally difficult problems, and for understanding data bases. The chapters are grouped into broad classes corresponding to the five main topics treated in this book.

The first set of papers focuses on the analysis of data base concepts in terms of formal logic, and provides a characterization of the hypothetical worlds on which data base systems work. The second considers knowledge representation as it relates to the process of deducing facts implicit in the data base; alternate approaches and their limitations are presented. The third describes how logic may be viewed so as to express and to maintain data base integrity. A similar view proves useful in dealing with the fourth topic, namely describing how meaning can be assigned to answers to negative questions. The final topic studies existing and proposed query languages for relational data base systems, demonstrating how logic provides a unifying framework for such languages.

LOGICAL SYSTEMS

The material in this section provides a brief overview of logic as it relates to this book. The reader who would like a more detailed description should refer to the books by Chang and Lee [1973] and by Mendelson [1964].

A logical system can be defined from two different, but equivalent viewpoints: the _semantic view_, and the _syntactic view_. Both approaches are founded upon first defining a language - a collection of symbols and of rules for building well-formed formulas (_wffs_).

The Language of First Order Logic - Syntax

The language used throughout the book is that of the first order predicate calculus. The language consists of the following primitive symbols:

- variable and constant symbols which will be denoted by lowercase letters taken from the end of the alphabet for variable symbols, and from the beginning of the alphabet for constant symbols;

- function symbols denoted by lower case symbols f, g, and h;

- predicate symbols which will be denoted by uppercase letters;

- two logical connectives: $\neg$ (negation); $\rightarrow$ (implication); and;

- the universal quantifier: $\forall$ (for all).

Using the above symbols, the objective is to specify the well-formed formulae (wffs) that constitute the legal statements in the language. The rules for building wffs in the language require that _terms_ and _atomic formulae_ be defined first.

The _terms_ are defined recursively as follows:

(1) a constant is a term;

(2) a variable is a term;

(3) if f is a function symbol of n arguments and if $t_1,\ldots,t_n$ are terms, then $f(t_1,\ldots,t_n)$ is a term;

(4) There are no other terms.

Terms form the arguments of atomic formulae.

The _atomic formulae_ are defined as follows:

- if P is a predicate letter of n arguments ($n \geq 0$) and if $t_1,\ldots,t_n$ are terms, then $P(t_1,\ldots,t_n)$ is an atomic formula.

When n=0, the atomic formula is called a proposition. An atomic formula or the negation of the atomic formula will be referred to as a _literal_.

Well-formed formulae are defined using atomic formulae, parentheses, the logical connectives and the universal quantifier as follows:

(1) atomic formulae are wffs;

(2) if A is a wff and x is an individual variable, then $(\forall x)A$ is a wff;

(3) if A and B are wffs, then $\neg(A)$, $(A) \rightarrow (B)$ are wffs;

(4) the only wffs are those obtainable by finitely many applications of (1), (2), and (3).

Example: $(\forall x)P(x)) \rightarrow ((\forall x)Q(x))$ is a wff.

From primitive connectives and quantifiers listed above, it is possible to introduce abbreviations:

$A \wedge B$ for $\neg(A \rightarrow \neg B)$, $\exists xA$ for $\neg(\forall x \neg A)$,

$A \vee B$ for $(\neg A \rightarrow B)$, $A \leftrightarrow B$ for $(\neg A \vee B) \wedge (A \vee \neg B)$

That is, the logical and ($\wedge$), the logical or ($\vee$), the existential quantifier ($\exists x$), and logical equivalence ($\leftrightarrow$), can be constructed from the primitive symbols. A wff in which all variables are quantified, i.e., no variable is free, is called a closed wff (otherwise it is open). Most of the work in logic (proof theory, ...) deals only with closed wffs. For example, to prove that a formula ϕ is a theorem, it is necessary and sufficient to show that its universal closure, $\overline{\phi}$, which is ϕ universally quantified on all its free variables, is a theorem too. This is not quite the case in our use of logic for data bases. A query to a data base is formulated as an open wff where free variables are placeholders for elements of answers.

Semantics

In the propositional calculus there are no terms. An interpretation is an assignment of truth values to atomic formulas. From these truth values one can calculate the truth value of a well-formed formula in propositional calculus. Since first-order predicate logic contains variables, the definition of an interpretation must be modified. To define an interpretation of a wff in first-order logic it is necessary to define a domain and an assignment to constants, function symbols, and predicate symbols in the wff.

An interpretation consists of a non-empty domain E, and an assignment of "values" to each constant, function symbol occurring in the wff as follows:

(1) To each constant symbol assign an element in E.

(2) To each n-place function symbol, assign a mapping from E^n to E. (E^n is defined as, $E^n = \{(x_1,\ldots,x_n) \mid x_1 \in E,\cdots,x_n \in E\}$.)

(3) To each n place predicate symbol, assign a mapping from E^n to $\{T,F\}$, where by T we denote "true", and by F, "false".

In a first-order logic we are dealing with closed wffs. Thus, in a given interpretation, a closed wff is either true or false (no matter which value is assigned to its variables). We will have occasion to use the following definitions in this book.

- An interpretation of a set of wffs $\mathbb{W}$ is called a model of $\mathbb{W}$ iff every wff of $\mathbb{W}$ is true in that interpretation.

- A wff W is a logical consequence of a set of wffs $\mathbb{W}$ iff W is true in all models of $\mathbb{W}$. The notation $\mathbb{W} \models W$ is used in this instance.

- A wff W is satisfiable if it has a model, otherwise it is unsatisfiable.

- A wff W is valid if it is true in all possible interpretations (a wff which is not valid may well be satisfiable i.e., true in some interpretations).

Syntax - Theory

Given a language, a theory can be defined on this language as follows.

Predicate calculus consists of axiom schemas called logical axioms, and two rules of inference; Modus Ponens and Generalization. These rules can be stated as:

From P and P $\rightarrow$ Q infer Q(Modus Ponens), and

From P infer $(\forall x)P$ (Generalization).

From axioms one can deduce theorems by using rules of inference. If additional axioms are defined one obtains a formal system called a first order theory. These new axioms are called proper (non-logical) axioms.

A theorem W deducible from the axioms of a theory T is denoted by,

$$\vdash_T W \ .$$

A wff is a consequence of a set of wffs $\mathbb{W}$ if W is derivable from the axioms of theory T and formulas in $\mathbb{W}$, and is denoted by:

$$\mathbb{W} \vdash_T W \ .$$

A model of a theory T is an interpretation in which all axioms of T are true. A theorem derivable from a set of axioms is true in every model of the set of axioms.

Soundness - Completeness

The syntactic and semantic approaches represent two different methods of performing reasoning. In the syntactic approach the proof of a formula is constructed, while in the semantic approach the validity of a formula is being tested. It has been shown by Gödel [1930] that the two approaches are equivalent to one another. Thus, either the syntactic or the semantic method of reasoning can be used. The Gödel relationship is referred to as the completeness and soundness result. The completeness result states that if a formula W is true in all models of the set of axioms $\mathcal{W}$, then W can be proved from the hypotheses $\mathcal{W}$. This is denoted by formula (1).

$$\mathcal{W} \models W \quad \underset{(2)}{\overset{(1)}{\rightleftarrows}} \quad \mathcal{W} \vdash W$$

The soundness result, (2), states that if the formula W is provable from the hypothesis $\mathcal{W}$, then it implies that the formula W is true in all models of $\mathcal{W}$.

Theorem Proving

Given a wff one can ask whether it is a theorem of a given theory. In general, this is an unsolvable problem as no procedure is guaranteed to terminate in a finite amount of time if the given wff is not a theorem. In trying to determine if a wff is a theorem, one can continually apply deduction rules to axioms in all possible ways. This process is guaranteed to terminate in a finite amount of time if there are only a finite number of deductions that are possible, or in the event that the given formula is indeed a theorem (thus the problem is said to be semi-decidable).

Instead of blindly applying deduction rules to axioms so as to derive all possible theorems, it is possible to define purely syntactic procedures in order to check whether the given wff is a theorem. These syntactic procedures are based on semantic properties such as satisfiability or unsatisfiability. Thus, instead of using the syntactic operators for inference (Modus Ponens and Generalization) one can, in view of the soundness and completeness results, use new operators derived from notions such as satisfiability of wffs. Rather than attempting to deduce W, one can show that $\neg$ W, in conjuction with the given set of axioms, is unsatisfiable. Instead of having to try all possible interpretations, one can use syntactic procedures which derive new wffs from $\neg$ W and the given set of axioms, which are guaranteed to preserve satisfiability. Consequently, if they derive an obviousely unsatisfiable formula, the empty formula denoted by $\square$, then $\neg$ W together with the axioms is unsatisfiable. (Observe that since if

$\vdash (\forall x)W$ then $\vdash W$ (and conversely), it is sufficient to deal only with closed wffs.)

Such procedures in which the empty formula is derived from the negation of the formula, i.e., (theorem to be tested) and the set of axioms are called refutation procedures. They do not yield a formal proof, but a result, namely that the formula W is a theorem. The proof procedure derives the null formula when the negation of W is a theorem. Embedded in the derivation is a formal proof which can be extracted. The best known refutation proof procedure is based on the resolution principle of Robinson (Robinson [1965]). It can be applied to wffs after they are put in a standard normal form (and then called clauses) in which all variables are implicitly universally quantified. A clause is a disjunction of literals. Every set of wffs can be transformed to clause form. The transformation is satisfiability preserving.

Example of a clause: $P(x,y) \vee Q(x,z,t) \vee \neg R(z,t)$.

Resolution as developed by Robinson can be defined simply for the propositional calculus (i.e., the first order language without quantifiers and terms) as follows: if the set of clauses $\{p \vee q, \neg p \vee r\}$ is satisfiable, then so is the set $\{p \vee q, \neg p \vee r, q \vee r\}$. The clause $q \vee r$ is derived from the clauses $p \vee q$ and $\neg p \vee r$ by using the resolution principle which deletes the complementary propositions (p and $\neg p$) from the two clauses and forms the disjunction of the remaining parts. At the propositional level the resolution principle acts as a cancellation law which, given two clauses with complementary literals forms a new derived clause. The literals in the respective two clauses on which the cancellation law is applied are referred to as the resolved literals, while the newly found clause is called the resolvent.

Consider the set of clauses $\{p \vee q, \neg q\}$, which may be thought of as the axioms of a system. If one wants to determine if p is a theorem, one negates p and combines it with the set of axioms to obtain the set $\{\neg p, p \vee q, \neg q\}$. Applying the cancellation law to the above set, one obtains the new set $\{\neg p, p \vee q, \neg q, p, q\}$. The clause p is derived from $\neg p$ and $p \vee q$, while q is derived from $\neg q$ and $p \vee q$. Applying the same rule again to the derived set, one obtains $\{\neg p, p \vee q, \neg q, p, q, \Box\}$. The empty clause, $\Box$, is derived from the complementary literals p and $\neg p$. Since the $\Box$ clause denotes always false, and hence is unsatisfiable, the set including the negated theorem ($\neg p$) must be unsatisfiable. Hence, p must be a theorem relative to the axioms.

The derivation of the empty clause, $\Box$, can be envisioned in graphical form as shown in the refutation graph of Figure 1.

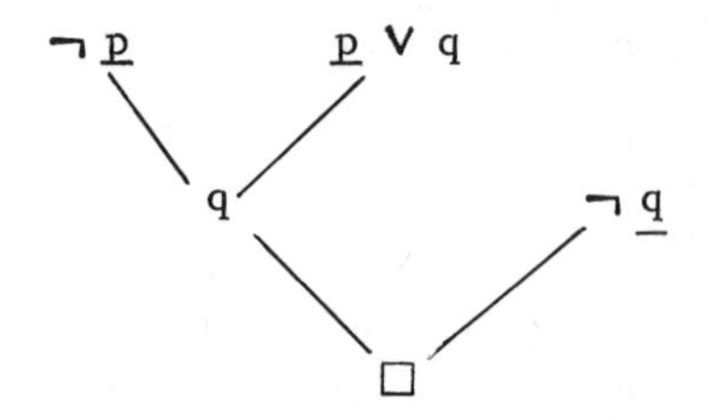

Figure 1. Refutation Graph

Underlined literals in the graph are resolved upon literals. A node of a graph is a resolvent of the two present clauses.

Resolution applied to first-order theories has to handle atomic formulae which contain terms. The process is, however, approximately similar, but requires an additional step called unification, which acts as a pattern match on arguments of predicates. Unification is explained briefly in the following example.

Example: If $\{P(x,z,b) \vee Q(f(x), z), \neg P(t,a,u) \vee R(t,u)\}$ is satisfiable,

then so is $\{P(x,z,b) \vee Q(f(x), z) \neg P(t,a,u) \vee R(t,u), \vee Q(f(t), a) \vee R(t,b)\}$,

i.e., $Q(f(t),a) \vee R(t,b)$ is derived by deleting complementary literals after they have been "unified". That is, consider the literals $\{P(x,z,b), P(t,a,u)\}$, which are the atomic forms of the literals in the two clauses that appear complemented. If a substitution is found which makes the literals identical, then one can cancel the complemented literals from the two clauses, form the disjunction of the literals remaining in the two clauses, and apply the unifying substitution to the newly formed clause. In the above example, a unifier for the set is:

$$x \leftarrow t$$

$$z \leftarrow a$$

$$u \leftarrow b ,$$

where $\psi \leftarrow \varphi$ denotes that ψ is to be replaced by φ. The notation φ/ψ is also used in the book to mean the replacement of ψ by φ .

In addition to binary resolution of two clauses illustrated above, one must also have factoring of a clause. At the propositional level, factoring corresponds to a clause which has a repeated literal. Thus, from $p \vee q \vee p$, one can derive the clause $p \vee q$. At the level of first-order clauses, one must be able to find a unifier for clauses that have the same predicate letter to derive a new clause. For example, given the clause $\{P(f(x),a,z) \vee Q(x,z) \vee P(f(g(t)),w,h(t)\}$, the clause $P(f(g(t)),a,h(t)) \vee Q(g(t),h(t))$ can be derived because

$$x \leftarrow g(t)$$
$$w \leftarrow a$$
$$z \leftarrow h(t)$$

is a unifier for $\{P(f(x),a,z),\ P(f(g(t)),w,h(t))\}$, and the unifier applied to the given clause permits the derivation to be made.

To apply the resolution principle devised by Robinson, the negation of the alleged theorem P, or the clausal form of $W \wedge \neg P$, where W is the logical "anding" ($\wedge$) of all proper axioms of the theory, is formed. Binary resolution and factoring are applied respectively to pairs of clauses or individual clauses. The process is iterated until the □ clause is generated, in which case P is indeed a theorem. If P is not a theorem, the process does not terminate in general.

This process cannot be executed in a practical way without a strategy (called a <u>search strategy</u>). A strategy should be complete, i.e., it should be able to derive □ from the negation of every theorem. Although an inference system such as binary resolution and factoring may be complete, the manner in which it is applied by a search strategy may result in its <u>not</u> being complete. Many strategies have been defined, but it is out of the scope of this paper to present them. However, in the framework of this book, an important distinction is made between the so-called bottom-up and top-down strategies. Bottom-up strategies first apply resolution to clauses which arise from the axioms, while top-down strategies first apply resolution to clauses arising from the negation of the alleged theorem.

Top-down search has also been referred to as backward chaining. It starts from the theorem to be proved and works backward from the theorem to show that it can be derived from the given axioms. Bottom-up search has been referred to as forward chaining and works forward from the hypotheses (given set of axioms) to derive the theorem.

As will be discussed further in this and later chapters, a category of clauses central to data base applications is the class of Horn clauses. A <u>Horn clause</u> is one that has <u>at most</u> one positive literal. Horn clauses lend themselves to a ready interpretation. Three different interpretations may be made as follows depending respectively on whether the Horn clause consists of a single positive literal, all negative literals, or negative plus one positive literal.

$P(x)$ is a Horn clause that asserts $P(x)$;

$\neg Q \vee \neg R$ is a Horn clause that denotes a goal to be proven (since the negation of the clause, $Q \wedge R$ is the theorem to be proved);

$P \vee \neg Q \vee \neg R$ is a Horn clause, equivalent to $(Q \wedge R) \rightarrow P$, and can be regarded as a procedure P whose body is a call to procedures Q and R. The left hand portion of the implication is referred to as the antecedent, and the right hand to the consequent. A bottom-up viewpoint will denote that if Q and R are known, then P is knows, top down denotes that to solve P, solve Q and solve R.

DATA BASES

Defining a data base is subordinate to defining a conceptual model which lays the ground for the logical representation (as opposed to physical) of information. Three main approaches have been used to specify a conceptual model for data base systems. These are the hierarchical, network, and relational approaches. Because it is through the relational model of data that interconnections between mathematical logic and data bases are evident, we consider here only the relational approach.

Although Levien and Maron [1967] used (binary) relations to represent data, credit for formalizing the relational model for data base management is given to Codd [1970]. Since Codd's article, the relational model of data has been studied and discussed extensively. For detailed surveys readers are referred to Date [1977], Tsichritzis and Lochovsky [1977], Chamberlin [1976] and Cadiou [1976]. (The latter provides a very nice formal presentation of the relational data model.) In this section only the main notions of the relational model are described.

In the relational model, data are organized as a collection of relations. A relation is defined mathematically as follows:

Let $D_1,\ldots,D_n$ be n domains (not necessarily distinct) of elements. A relation defined on $D_1,\ldots,D_n$, is a subset of the cartesian product $D_1 \times \ldots \times D_n$.

A relation is, therefore, a set of tuples, where a tuple $(d_1,\ldots,d_n)$ has as its ith component the element $d_i \in D_i$. Because a relation is a set, all the tuples in a relation are distinct and the order of tuples is immaterial. Obviously, the order of the components in a tuple is meaningful. But instead of referring to arguments of relations by their relative positions, they are usually referred to by (distinct) names called columns or attributes. The attribute values in a relation consist of all the elements in the components in the tuples that correspond to the attribute name. An attribute (or a collection of attributes) such that each value unambiguously identifies a tuple is called a key for the relation.

For example, in the relation PRODUCT presented below, NAMES, REFPRO, and MW (Molecular weight) are attribute names and the attribute "NAMES" is a key.

PRODUCT

(REFPRO.	NAMES	MW)
ENN236	ANILIN	93.12
ENN236	AMINOPHEN	93.12
ENN330	TETRAFINOL	154

Normal Form of Relations

In an application, the same data can be represented through different collections of relations. However, each representation does not necessarily provide the same properties with regard to data manipulation. For example, the same data as those given above with the relation PRODUCT, can be represented by means of the following two relations:

PN

(REFPRO.	NAMES)
ENN236	ANILIN
ENN236	AMINOPHEN
ENN330	TETRAFINOL

PMW

(REFPRO.	MW)
ENN236	93.12
ENN330	154

It happens that when the data is represented with the relation PRODUCT, the molecular weight of a given product occurs as many times as this product has different names. Now suppose that (due to an error) the molecular weight of the product ENN236 has to be updated. To correctly carry out this update all tuples in which ENN236 appears must be found and changed. Because in the relation PMW the molecular weight of a given product occurs only once, such a problem is avoided when relations PN and PMW are used to represent these data.

In order to characterize relations which have "good" data manipulation properties, normalized relations have been defined. In fact, starting from the so-called first normal form (1NF), three other normal forms have been defined: 2NF, 3NF(BCNF) and 4NF. Each normal form is an improvement of the preceding one for avoiding data manipulation anomalies. We do not describe the differences between these normal forms as they are not required for the material presented in this book. A relation is in first normal form, if components of tuples are atomic elements. Whether a relation is under another normal form is bound to the concept of dependencies which may exist between its attributes. For example, one type of dependency which is termed a functional dependency. In a relation, an attribute B functionally depends on an attribute A ($A_{|} \rightarrow B$) if and only if to each value of A there corresponds only one value of B.

Data Manipulation Languages

Data manipulation languages within the relational model provide facilities for entering, deleting, updating and retrieving (querying) data. Because of the predominance of querying they are often all called query languages.

Queries on a data base are of two types: closed and open. A "closed query" requires a YES/NO response and is a statement for which it is asked whether or not it is satisfied on the data base. For example, a closed query is "does the ABC corporation manufacture DEFs?" An "open query" asks for a set of tuples as answers."List all products manufactured by the ABC corporation." is an example of an open query. Thus, an open query consists of a formula which defines a new relation from stored relations.

Several kinds of data manipulation languages have been defined for the relational model. Most of them have the common property thay they are (to various degrees), more assertional then procedural languages. That is, they enable one to characterize target data by stating their properties, instead of describing how they are to be retrieved. Three main families of languages can be distinguished: languages based on the relational algebra, predicate calculus oriented languages, and mapping oriented languages.

The relational algebra consists of a family of operators which enable relations of the data base to be combined to obtain derived relations. An answer to an open query is a relation to be derived from the given data base relations. Apart from the standard set operations (union, intersection...), other operators are provided (e.g., selection, projection, join,...). For example, the join operator, applied to two relations R_1 and R_2, builds a third relation R_3 whose tuples are obtained from those of R_1 and R_2 by concatenation whenever some specified condition holds.

The predicate calculus language has been used as a basis for the second family of query languages (e.g., relational calculus of Codd [1972]). In these languages, queries are expressed as logical formulas specifying conditions that data must satisfy to be retrieved. Such formulas are built with logical connectives (e.g., AND, OR,...), and quantifiers ("for all", "there exist").

In mapping oriented languages, the basic block consists in a mapping which transforms, using some relations, some known attributes into attributes whose values are asked for. Such blocks can be nested in order to build complex queries. For example, given a relation R and two attributes A_1 and A_2, in the language SEQUEL (Chamberlin et al. [1974]) a mapping is expressed as:

SELECT A_1

FROM R

WHERE A_2 = value

Views and Integrity Constraints

Apart from the data manipulation facilities mentioned above, other facilities are provided by data base languages. Two of them are: view definitions and integrity constraint assertions.

A _view_ is a relation (or set of relations) not stored explicitly in the data base, but which is introduced through defining expressions. Such a definition expression consists of a correspondence between the defined relation and a (open) formula of the query language involving stored relations and other views. After a view has been defined it can be used in the query language in the same way as any other relation (except for insertions, deletions, and updates which raise some problems).

An _integrity constraint_ is a condition which has to be satisfied on the data base. Broadly, it corresponds to a (closed) formula of the query language which is asserted. When a request for updated data is made, the update is accepted or rejected depending on whether the integrity constraints are satisfied.

DATA BASES VIEWED THROUGH FORMAL LOGIC

The first set of chapters is concerned with the analysis of data bases in terms of formal logic. The goal of such an analysis is to provide a better understanding of data bases, and consequently to be able to use tools and results from formal logic in the context of data bases.

However, before proceeding, some additional vocabulary elements have to be made precise.

Defining a relation as the set of tuples (elementary facts) which satisfy it (i.e., by its _extension_) is only one way to define it. A relation can be defined _intensionally_ as a set of general laws expressed as well-formed formulae in the first-order predicate calculus in which it is involved. In most of the chapters, a data base is considered as a collection of relations, some of which are defined extensionally and some intensionally, and some partially extensionally and partially intensionally. In some chapters, the set of relational tuples is referred to as the _extensional data base_ (_EDB_) whereas the set of general laws is called the _intensional data base_ (_IDB_).

In the chapter by Nicolas and Gallaire, several approaches for formalizing data base concepts in first order logic are presented and compared. They argue that in fact the more adequate approach consists of considering the set of elementary facts that consist of the extensional data as an interpretation of a first order theory whose proper axioms are the general laws. Furthermore, they point out that some general laws serve better as integrity rules used to test data being input to a data base, whereas others are used more appropriately as derivation rules to deduce the extension of relations defined by general axioms. Some broad criteria for helping to make a choice between the two possibilities are presented. In the different approaches the problems raised by unknown information and negative information are treated. _Negative information_ is a specific statement that a particular fact does not hold. For example, the ABC Corporation does _not_ manufacture DEF. Listing all of the negative facts relating to an item would be tedious, if not a waste of space. However, if one does not specify a negative piece of information one cannot determine, in general, whether the lack of a specific fact means that whether or not it pertains is true or false, or that it is false. Nicolas and Gallaire show that when derivation rules are restricted to a particular case of Horn clauses, some problems dealing with negative information are alleviated. They further show how their proposed formalization can be used for the particular case of general laws which are functional and multivalued dependency statements. A multivalued dependency statement $Y \to\to Z$ is defined as follows. Let $R(X_1,\ldots,X_n)$ be an n-ary relation. Let Y and Z be two subsets of $\{X_1,\ldots,X_n\}$ and T be the complement in $\{X_1,\ldots,X_n\}$ of $\{Y \cup Z\}$. The multivalued dependency statement $Y \to\to Z$ holds for R iff R is the natural join of its projection R[YZ] and R[YT]. (See Beeri et al. [1977].)

Reiter, in his chapter, "Closed World Data Bases" focuses on evaluating answers to queries in a deductive context under two assumptions, referred to as the _open world assumption_ (_OWA_) and the _closed world assumption_ (_CWA_). Under the OWA a negative literal is true if and only if (iff) a proof of it exists, whereas under the CWA a negative literal is assumed to be true if no proof of the corresponding positive one exists. The CWA is similar to what is referred to as the convention for negative information representation discussed by Nicolas and Gallaire. After defining a predicate calculus oriented query language, Reiter formally defines open world and closed world answers. An answer in the relational data base system case is always definite. That is, an answer consists of the conjunction of tuples that satisfy the condition. However, there are data base problems for which it is known that more than one possibility exists, but the conjunction of the possibilities does not necessarily pertain. Thus, for example, one might wish to state that ' "A" is located in "B" or "C" '. This statement cannot be entered into a conventional relational data base, but can be expressed in predicate calculus as LOC(A,B) V LOC(A,C). Reiter refers to such data as indefinite. He extends the usual notion of answer by including non-definite answers. Such data and responses can be obtained from the predicate calculus data bases.

Furthermore, it is shown that closed world evaluation of queries can be decomposed into open world evaluation of atomic formulae in conjunction with some operators of the relational algebra. Reiter further shows that the CWA with respect to answering negative type questions can lead to inconsistencies. However, he proves that for data bases dealing only with Horn clauses such inconsistencies cannot occur even under the CWA. He further shows that specifying negative information in such a data base is irrelevant.

The last chapter in this unit, by Kowalski, has as its main thesis that there is no clear cut distinction between data bases and programs, and that only logic is suitable for both. Attention is focused on the characteristics of logic that allow data to be defined not only by means of specific (or elementary) facts as given by relational tuples, but also by general rules as given by well-formed formulae. Kowalski disagrees with the concept of separating explicitly defined relations (extensional data) from implicitly (intensional data) defined ones and states, "a typical relation needs to be defined both by specific assertions and by general laws." As far as querying is concerned, Kowalski notes two drawbacks of the relational calculus language. First, there may be more natural ways of using logic for querying than those provided by the relational calculus, and second, relational calculus lacks recursion. From this lack of recursion, he concludes that the relational completeness result described by Codd [1970] is misleading. Completeness as defined by Codd provides a "standard language" in which one can express statements. A language is then considered complete if it can perform all of the operations described by Codd. This definition of completeness is shallow in contrast to the concept of completeness as described in logic in the section entitled Soundness - Completeness. Thus, the term completeness as it has been used in relational data base contexts is totally different from the concept used in logic.

On another plane, the use of logic for knowledge representation has been criticized by advocates of frame theory. Minsky [1975] defined a frame as, "...a data structure for representing a stereotyped situation, like being in a certain kind of living room, or going to a child's birthday party." Kowalski addresses some of these criticisms by showing that a frame can be expressed in predicate logic. Finally, Kowalski extols the virtues of binary relations over that of n-ary relations.

KNOWLEDGE REPRESENTATION AND DEDUCTION

A dominant theme in this book is that of representing knowledge in logic. A primary reason for doing so is that the language of logic can be used to represent knowledge, data structures and programs. Hence, it achieves a uniformity of representation and provides a firm mathematical basis for data base development.

In some chapters, a particular first order logic, called many-sorted logic, is used while in others semantic networks are discussed. Understanding these concepts is necessary for the discussion of representation and knowledge.

Many-Sorted Logic

A many-sorted logic assumes that there is a non-empty set I, whose members are called sorts. For each sort i, there are variables v_1^i, v_2^i,... that belong to sort i; for each sort i there is a set (possibly empty) of constant symbols of sort i; for each $n > 0$ and each (n+1)-tuple $< i_1,\dots,i_n, i_{n+1}>$ of sorts there is a set (possibly empty) of n-place function symbols, each of which is said to be of sort $< i_1,\dots,i_n, i_{n+1} >$; for each $n > 0$ and each n-tuple $< i_1,\dots,i_n>$ of sorts, there is a set (possibly empty) of n-place predicate symbols each of which is said to be a sort of $< i_1,\dots,i_n>$; for each sort i there is a universal and existential quantifier, $\forall_i$ and $\exists_i$. As in predicate calculus, one can form well-formed formulae. The predicate calculus contains only one sort, and hence permits statements such as "the blue ate the green", which would be prohibited in a many-sorted logic by requiring that only an animate object that is alive can eat. Many-sorted logic has been used as a means to represent knowledge in the chapters by Chang, Dilger and Zifonun, Kellogg et al, Minker and Reiter. A many-sorted logic can be embedded in first order predicate calculus, and therefore does not have any more power (Enderton [1972]).

Semantic Networks and Data Structures

A semantic network represents concepts expressed by natural language words and phrases as nodes connected by a set of arcs called semantic relations. Quillian [1968] was the first proponent of the use of semantic networks for linguistic understanding and QA systems. In a semantic net, nodes represent human verbal concept structures and semantic relations represent the linguistic processes of thought that are used to combine semantic nodes into natural language description of events. Its graph can be regarded as a labeled directed network, where the labels on arcs represent binary relations.

Deliyanni and Kowalski [1977] note that simple semantic networks as defined above can express only collections of variable-free assertions. Using binary relations only they define an extended form of semantic network which can be regarded as a variant syntax of the clausal form of logic. One of the consequences of their extension is that semantics for semantic networks is defined implicitly. McSkimin and Minker [1977,1978] have also shown how to generalize semantic networks using n-ary relations and are not restricted to binary relations. Their semantic network consists of a semantic graph which relates sorts to one another in a hierarchic type relationship, contains facts, general axioms, a dictionary and a semantic form space. The use of a many-sorted logic is also inherent in their work. Minker, in his chapter, briefly outlines the semantic network and describes an operational system, MRPPS 3.0, which embodies the various concepts described in McSkimin and Minker [1977,1978] and McSkimin [1976]. Kellogg et al. in their chapter have also implemented a semantic network similar in many ways to that described by Minker.

As evidenced by work described in this book, efforts in the area of logic and data bases are using a many-sorted logic. In particular, predicate calculus languages discussed by Chang, Dilger and Zifonun, Kellogg et al., Minker, and Reiter are evidence of this trend. Minker and Reiter use a many-sorted logic to avoid sentences such as "the blue ate the green". Furthermore, in performing deductive searches, it is faster to determine that an argument in a predicate is in a particular sort, than to retain general axioms which serve the same purpose and require time consuming proofs.

One of the classical problems of computer science is data-modeling. This is particularly true in the data base field where arguments still arise concerning the best conceptual or physical data model. Logic does not escape this problem as was first pointed out by Kowalski [1974]. In his chapter on logic for data description, Kowalski envisions modeling data through assertions. Tarnlund, on the other hand, models data by considering them as terms. In order to see the difference between both approaches one can think of a list either as a set of assertions, each of which deals with an element of the list (thus providing for a direct access to each element), or as a true list which must be scanned in order to access particular elements. The point made by Tarnlund in his chapter concerns efficiency of representation and algorithms he shows that for a large set of data structures (including trees, ordered k-dimensional trees) axiomatic theories can be specified in which algorithms (such as update, order,...) are just instances of proofs of theorems from the axioms. The efficiency of the algorithms is tightly related to the length of the proof. The logic algorithms he develops are shown to be both efficient and correct. This type of work relates directly to the abstract data types programming approach (Goguen [1976]).

Although not directed towards the same goal as Tarnlund, the chapter by Colombetti et al. is a step toward axiomatizing data bases. They try to formalize conceptual models, rather than the physical models of Tarnlund. Apart from this difference the techniques are similar and are cast into an abstract data types programming approach. A conceptual model is specified through axioms, expressed in a language like PROLOG (Roussel [1975]), which allows the model to be tested. Another point of interest developed is the question of what is needed to describe a data model. That is, which axioms must be given in order to express what is called the signature of the model. This rather formal point is exemplified partially on binary relations.

Deductive Approach Taken by Minker

Managing the search in a system that contains general axioms can become cumbersome. In this book, several different approaches to handling deductive search in a relational data base are described.

The approach to deduction taken by Minker is to treat the extensional and intensional data bases as one file. That is, no distinction is made between the EDB (extensional data base) and the IDB (intensional data base). The apparent reason for this is that the facts in the EDB may be viewed as extensions of the intensional axioms in the IDB. This is consistent with the view of logic and data bases as expounded by Nicolas and Gallaire in their chapter, and the approach by Kowalski. That is, that the extensional data base is an interpretation of a first order theory whose proper axioms are the general laws.

Given a Boolean AND condition consisting of literals to be answered, Minker describes an artificial intelligence approach to answering such questions. The Boolean AND condition is negated to form a clause. Heuristics, based upon semantic information in the data base are used to select a literal to be solved in the query clause. A top-down goal tree is generated with a query clause as start node. Once a selected relation is specified in this clause, a search of the EDB/IDB is made to retrieve the set of all possible matches with the specified literal. An EDB entry that matches the specified literal can be considered to have solved the literal. Thus, one must solve the remaining literals in the query. Each IDB clause that has a literal that matches the query literal adds new literals to the query literals and forms a new branch of a search or goal tree. The system control structure manages the goal tree and determines which literal to search for in the EDB/IDB. Heuristics are used to determine which node to expand next. The search stops when at least one solution to the query occurs. The system can be extended to find all answers to a query assuming that there are only a finite number of answers possible. The system is complete in the sense that if there is a solution to a query, it will be found.

Deduction Approach Taken by Reiter

Reiter in his approach to deduction assumes that the EDB is considerably larger than the IDB. This is a realistic assumption. He further separates the deduction mechanism from that of the retrieval operations. His objective is to use an existing relational data base system to search the EDB.

A query consisting of AND conditions that enters the system searches the IDB for consequents that match the relations in the AND conditions. For each match, the relation matched is replaced by the antecedents of the IDB axiom. This forms a new query for each match. The process is continued until there are no more consequents that match. Assuming that there are no recursively defined axioms, the process terminates. The end result is a set of AND conditions that must now be sent to the EDB. In every AND condition all of the resulting relations must appear in the EDB. Retrieving all of the AND queries through the EDB retrieves all responses to the original query. The first step in the Reiter approach uses a theorem prover to operate upon the query using the axioms to achieve a new set of queries. The second step is to use a conventional relational data base to answer the set of queries.

Using the Reiter approach a query can be compiled so that a conventional relational data base system may be used. In the Minker approach, the query is interpreted with search guided by a control structure. The Minker work is oriented towards finding a single answer to a query, while the Reiter approach finds all answers. To improve his technique, when the set of AND conditions is to be searched, Reiter will have to determine which one to search first and will have to optimize the accessing of the EDB entries. Both approaches are equivalent to one another when there are no recursive axioms in the IDB. The Minker approach, although not restricted by recursion is, in practice, limited by the machine storage capacity. In handling recursion, Reiter will have to specify a cut-off limit on the size of the AND conditions when recursion exists. However, it is not clear that one should permit recursive axioms in the IDB for realistic problems. When recursion exists in the IDB, the search is, in general, not complete in that all solutions may not be found.

Both Minker and Reiter permit relations to be defined partially in the the EDB and partially in the IDB. The Minker and Reiter search strategies and inference systems are complete and sound thus assuring that every answerable query will, indeed, be answered.

Deductive Approach Taken by Kellogg, Klahr, and Travis

Kellogg et al, like Reiter, separate the EDB from the IDB. Axioms in the IDB are stored in a connection graph. That is, if two clauses exist, where, in one clause a literal unifies with a literal in another clause (with a negated predicate letter), a connection is made between the clauses and the unifying substitution is saved.

Deductive pathfinding is centered around a process called middle-term chaining. The predicate connection graph is used to find implication chains from assumptions and goals. Queries are considered to consist of assumptions and goals. At an elementary level one may ask a question of the form: does $A_1 \wedge A_2 \ldots \wedge A_n \rightarrow B_1 \wedge B_2 \ldots \wedge B_m$. The A_i are considered to be assumptions, while the B_j are considered to be goals. Middle-term chaining combines the process of forward chaining from assumptions in a query to backward chaining from goals in that query. When no assumptions exist, backward chaining is used to solve the query.

Search-compute plans are generated, and searches are then made part of the data base. The approach is similar to Reiter's in that the IDB is used to generate the search plan partially during the initial stages. It is also similar to the Minker approach since the plans are not fully developed and control is handled by the system to determine the direction of the search process. The search process, however, might not be complete.

Deductive Approach Taken by Chang

Chang has developed a query language termed DEDUCE 2 for relational data bases. The query language allows one to state queries, axioms, and heuristics. Relations in the EDB are called _base relations_ whereas relations defined by the axioms in the IDB are called _virtual relations_. The approach taken by Chang for deductive relational data bases centers around evaluation of queries. In a manner similar to Reiter, a query is evaluated in two steps. First, the axioms of the IDB are used to transform the query into one having only base relations. Second, the transformed query is evaluated by a conventional data base system. Unlike Minker and Reiter, Chang insists that a relation be either in the EDB or the IDB, but not in both.

The process used to transform queries is based upon a technique developed by Chang for theorem proving, and termed the rewriting rules method. Chang considers an optimization problem for achieving efficient retrieval of AND conditions when access paths to data are known in advance.

NEGATIVE INFORMATION AND DATA BASES

Negative information corresponds to the fact that a given tuple does not satisfy a relation and may be represented by a _negative ground literal_ (a literal is ground if it contains no variables). In logical systems, negative information is treated in the same way as positive information both in representation and manipulation. Yet, in some applied domains, especially in data bases (for reasons specific to these domains), negative information is represented implicitly. More precisely, a negative ground literal $\neg L$ is assumed to be true if L fails to be proved.

This implicit representation has several terminologies. It is called "convention for negative information representation" by Nicolas and Gallaire, the "closed world assumption (CWA)" by Reiter, and "interpreting negation as failure" as discussed in the chapter by Clark.

In general, negative information raises many complications. However, it raises no problems under the CWA if as Reiter states, "there are no gaps in the knowledge". Furthermore, when only ground literals are dealt with, as in classical data bases, the CWA produces no inconsistencies; but this is not always the case when general laws are taken into account and a deduction process is involved.

The chapter by Clark is chiefly concerned with interpretation of negation as failure (to be introduced below). Problems raised by negative information are addressed in the chapters by Nicolas and Gallaire and by Reiter (in the section of the book, Data Bases Viewed Through Formal Logic).

Nicolas and Gallaire, have shown a way to alleviate problems raised by the "convention for negative information representation". Namely, one should retain as derivation rules only general laws corresponding to a particular case of Horn clauses. These clauses, referred to as regular clauses contain precisely one positive literal. A similar result is proved more formally by Reiter who shows that inconsistencies can occur under the CWA. He further proves that data bases, with only definite clauses (identical to regular clauses), are always consistent under the CWA.

The interpretation of negation as failure amounts to considering $\neg P$ as true providing we fail to prove P. Clark examines how this interpretation of negation relates to the usual truth functional semantics of negation. By making precise the notion of a query on a data base of clauses and their evaluation, he defines the completed data base C(B) from a given data base B. A clause in B is assumed to be the "if part" of an "if and only if" definition of a relation. Then, broadly speaking, the completed data base C(B) is obtained by adding to B those axioms corresponding to the "only if parts", and axioms which express constants with different names are different. Clark shows that every failed attempt to prove a formula P in B is, in effect, a proof of $\neg P$ in C(B). Therefore, negation as failure applied to a data base, constitutes a sound inference rule for deductions from a completed data base. Although his approach is, in general, not complete, Clark provides conditions under which completeness will be satisfied.

INTEGRITY AND DATA BASES

Integrity constraints are general statements that data must obey. Some kinds of integrity constraints have been isolated in the relational model, but in fact, all the power of the (data manipulation) language can be used to express such statements. As examples, consider those which impose constraints on components of tuples in a relation (e.g., they must belong to a given domain), or some special constraint which ties attributes in the same relation to one another and called (functional and multivalued) dependencies.

Particular integrity constraints of the first type are taken into account in a straightforward way when a many-sorted logic is used. Although not discussed in their chapters they are considered in Minker (McSkimin and Minker [1977,1978]) and Reiter [1977]. As for dependency constraints, Nicolas and Gallaire propose ways of expressing them in first-order logic and show the utility of such a formulation.

With regard to more general statements, Nicolas and Gallaire also note that some may be viewed as integrity constraints, while others may be used as derivation rules. That is, there are two ways in which one may interpret general statements. Furthermore, they provide some broad criteria enabling one to choose how to best interpret a given statement.

The paper by Nicolas and Yazdanian is essentially devoted to integrity checking. They present different methods of handling integrity constraints concurrently with axioms. They also consider a special type of integrity constraint called transition laws, which relate information on different states of a data base. A state may be considered to be an instance of time. For example, a person may be married in one state and divorced or single in other states. By introducing special purpose relations, called action relations, they provide a formulation of transition laws, as first order logic expressions. Such a formulation enables one to handle transition laws in the same way as state laws.

Chang allows integrity constraints to be any formula that can be expressed in DEDUCE 2, in particular, those using numerical quantifiers of DEDUCE 2. Integrity constraints normally used to check the integrity of data in the extensional data base are shown to apply also to the query evaluation process to test the validity of queries.

Kowalski deals with the integrity (consistency) of data by introducing a special purpose predicate: INCONSISTENT. Such a constraint is handled by an implicational statement such that its consequence is precisely the predicate INCONSISTENT, and the premise (antecedent), a formula expressing the negation of the constraint the data must obey. When an inconsistency occurs in the data base the predicate INCONSISTENT is derivable from the integrity constraints. Hence, checking data integrity can be performed in the same way as querying - by using a predicate INCONSISTENT.

LANGUAGES

Most papers appearing in this book deal with language issues. The focus of work described here is with language facilities for querying on an especially high level as opposed to a lower procedural level. The former languages guarantee better data independence, one of the assets of the relational model.

At least three basic approaches to query languages can be taken: relational calculus languages, relational algebra languages, and mapping oriented languages. The last two language types are not non-procedural. These language types are discussed in the section Data Manipulation Languages.

The choice between these language types is both a theoretical issue and a very important one for the user. This section deals with some aspects of both problems.

The chapter by Pirotte shows that logic is again as powerful a framework for a query language as any other approach. He presents a unifying theory based on predicate calculus for most languages of relational systems, showing how to express constructs similar to that of other approaches in the relational calculus. This is not meant to say that relational calculus is the best language to use. Rather one should focus on what appears to be essential issues of concern to the user.

A major distinction is to be made between tuple oriented languages and domain oriented languages. Tuple-oriented languages use variables to represent tuples of relations, as well as to express the traditional record notion of data models. Domain-oriented languages used domain variables more closely related to the semantics of data, while allowing a direct handling of attributes (rather than using projections of relations).

Pirotte gives a predicate calculus unifying formalism for both tuple-oriented and domain-oriented languages. He also considers reducing the range of these variables (domain or tuples variables) to obtain meaningful queries: typing variables or range restriction of variables connected to a discipline assures that range restrictions are used properly. It appears that tuple variables are usually not typed but rather, "range restricted". As such, they convey most of the expressions of the relational calculus and some of the expression of mapping oriented languages. Domain variables can be typed as well as range restricted (as in mapping languages which are basically domain oriented although not typed).

Apart from above, for which a unifying predicate calculus formalism is presented, it is believed that one of the constraints of predicate calculus can be removed, namely the use of quantifiers. Pirotte shows how to eliminate quantifiers so as to obtain set oriented versions of the languages he defines, and also how to eliminate variables which are often implicit in natural languages (simulated by pronouns, textual contiguity,...) achieving constructs identical to those of nested mappings.

Based on this chapter, it appears that only logic provides a uniform treatment of all needed concepts in query languages.

Other aspects of query languages have not been covered in this discussion. In particular, definition of views specific to users, or of integrity constraints. Some of the chapters in other sections deal with these problems (Reiter, and Chang, for instance). A final problem is covered in this section, one which is a very important issue for the future users of data base systems, namely that of developing a natural language query.

The chapter by Dilger and Zifonun provides for an intermediate step in achieving natural language query capability. Their aim is to give the user a language sufficiently close to but not having the full power of natural language. The language KS presented by them is part of the system termed PLIDIS, aimed at using German as an interactive language. KS is capable of handling not only queries as presented up to now, but also yes-no queries. It is a typed domain-oriented language. It is possible to eliminate quantifiers, and when this is done, KS then becomes a set oriented language. However, quantifiers are seen as a normal tool for natural language queries, and the paper discusses their treatment in arbitrary queries.

In addition to its use as a query language, predicate logic has an additional feature - it can be used as a programming language. That the first order predicate calculus can be used as a programming language was noted first by Kowalski [1974]. His language is restricted to Horn Axioms. The consequent of a Horn Axiom is a single literal which is interpreted as a procedure. Kowalski and van Emden [1976] have shown how one can interpret various methods of programming language semantics (operational, Scott-Stratchey) in first-order logic. A predicate calculus language has been developed by Colmerauer and his group at the University of Marseilles. Their development, PROLOG, is based on Kowalski's results. Details concerning the language may be found in Roussel [1975]. PROLOG includes automatic backtracking. Warren [1977] has developed a compiled version of PROLOG which permits fast operation times - comparable to that obtained with LISP programs. A number of data base systems have been developed using PROLOG (Dahl [1977] and Futó [1977]).

In their chapter, Futó et al. describe enhancements to the PROLOG language implemented at Budapest (such as file handling, symbolic input, fast look up of data) and provide examples of the use of PROLOG for applications in areas such as prediction and retrieval of drug interactions. These applications, although limited in size, are real life applications and demonstrate the feasibility of using PROLOG in well-defined fields.

SUMMARY

We have, in this introduction, set the stage for material provided in the chapters to follow. It will be seen that logic is a powerful tool for relational data bases. It can be used as a query language, a programming language, to prove the correctness of programs, perform deductive searches, maintain the integrity of a data base, provide a formalism for handling negation, generalize the concept of semantic networks, and represent and manipulate data structures. Thus, more than any other approach, logic provides a unifying framework for data bases.

There are many issues that remain to be resolved. For example, should one permit recursion in data base systems? Should functions be permitted to appear in relations? Are there classes of data bases that should be studied? The use of recursive axioms implies that, in general, it is not possible to determine whether or not all answers to a query have been found. However, it is conceivable that there are special ways that permit some recursive axioms to be handled. With regard to functions, we have the problem of handling equality (e.g., one function is equal to another function) for which no computationally efficient method has been found. Reiter, in his chapters, touches upon some of these problems.

Data base problems that relate to business-type applications generally do not have functions and have limited or no recursion. However, data base problems related to robotics require functions and recursion. Hence, defining a data base to be free of functions and recursion would be too restrictive. Considering different classes of data bases to determine how complex they might become (relative to the so-called business data base problems) would be of considerable interest.

The chapters in this book are but a beginning contribution to an important field - logic and data bases. We believe that through efforts such as described in this book, data base systems will be placed in a formal mathematical context.

ACKNOWLEDGMENTS

The authors would like to thank Barry Jacobs, Rita Minker and Guy Zanon for their helpful comments on this paper.

The work was supported by the DRET with a contribution from the CNRS. It was also supported by the NSF under Grant GJ-43632 and by NASA under Grant 21-002-270.

REFERENCES

1. Beeri, C., Fagin, R. and Howard, H. J. [1977] A Complete Axiomatization for Functional and Multivalued Dependencies in Data Base Relations, *Proceedings of ACM SIGMOD Conference*, Toronto, Canada, August 1977, 47-61.

2. Cadiou, J. M. [1976] On Semantic Issues in the Relational Model of Data, In *Mathematical Foundations of Computer Science*, (A. Mazurkiewiz, Ed.), Vol. 45, Springer-Verlag, 1976, 23-28.

3. Chamberlin, D.D., Boyce, R. F. [1974] SEQUEL: A Structured English Query Language, *Proc. ACM SIGMOD Workshop on Data Description, Access and Control*, May 1974, 249-264.

4. Chamberlin, D. D. [1976] Relational Data Base Management Systems, *Computing Surveys 8* (1976), 43-66.

5. Chang, C. L. and Lee, R.C.T. [1973] *Symbolic Logic and Mechanical Theorem Proving, Computer Science and Applied Mathematics,* Series of Academic Press, Inc., New York, 1973.

6. Codd, E. F. [1970] A Relational Model of Data for Large Shared Data Banks, *CACM 13,* 6 (June 1970), 377-387.

7. Codd, E. F. [1972] Relational Completeness of Data Base Sublanguages, In *Data Base Systems* (R. Rustin, Ed.), Prentice-Hall, Englewood Cliffs, N.J., 1972, 65-98.

8. Dahl, V. [1977] Some Experiences on Natural Language Question-Answering Systems, *Proceedings of the Workshop on Logic and Data Bases,* Toulouse, November 1977.

9. Date, C. J. [1977] *An Introduction to Database Systems 2nd Ed.,* Addison-Wesley Publishing Co., Reading, Mass., 1977.

10. Deliyanni, A. and Kowalski, R. A. [1977] Logic and Semantic Networks, Department of Computing and Control Research Report, Imperial College, London, June 1977. Also *Proceedings of the Workshop on Logic and Data Bases,* Toulouse, November 1977.

11. Enderton, H. B. [1972] *A Mathematical Introduction to Logic,* Academic Press, New York, 1972.

12. Futó, I., Darvas, F., and Cholnoky, E. [1977] Practical Application of an AI Language, II, *Proceedings of the Hungarian Conference on Computing,* Budapest, 1977, 385-400.

13. Gödel, K. [1930] Die Vollstandigkeit der Axiome des logischen Funktionenkalkiu, *Monatshefte für Mathematik und Physik 37,* (1930), 349-360. Also, The Completeness of the Axioms of the Functional Calculus of Logic, In *From Frege to Gödel* (J. van Heijenoort, Ed.), Harvard University Press, Cambridge, Mass., 1967, 582-591.

14. Goguen, J. G., Thatcher, C. W. and Wagner, E. G. [1976] An Initial Algebra Approach to the Specification, Correctness, and Implementation of Abstract Data Types, In *Current Trends in Programming Methodology, Vol. 3, Data Structuring* (R. Yeh, Ed.), Prentice Hall, Englewood Cliffs, N.J., 1976.

15. Kowalski, R. A. [1974] Logic for Problem Solving, *Memo No. 75,* Department of Computational Logic, University of Edinburgh, Edinburgh, 1974.

16. Kowalski, R. A. and van Emden, M. [1976] The Semantics of Predicate Logic as a Programming Language, *JACM 23* (October 1976), 733-742.

17. Levien, R. and Maron, M. E. [1967] A Computer System for Inference Execution and Data Retrieval, *CACM 10,* 11 (Nov. 1967), 715-721.

18. McSkimin, J. R. [1976] "The Use of Semantic Information in Deductive Question-Answering Systems," Ph.D. Thesis, Department of Computer Science, University of Maryland, College Park, Maryland, 1976.

19. McSkimin, J. R. and Minker, J. [1977] The use of a Semantic Network on a Deductive Question-Answering System, *Proceedings IJCAI-77,* Cambridge, Mass., 1977, 50-58.

20. McSkimin, J. R. and Minker, J. [1978] A Predicate Calculus Based Semantic Network for Question-Answering Systems, In *Associative Networks - The Representation and Use of Knowledge in Computers* (N. Findler, Ed.), Academic Press, New York, in press.

21. Mendelson, E. [1964] *Introduction to Mathematical Logic,* Van Nostrand, New York, 1964.

22. Minsky, M. [1975] A Framework for Representing Knowledge, In *The Psychology of Computer Vision* (P. Winston, Ed.), McGraw-Hill, New York, 1975, 211-280.

23. Quillian, M. R. [1968] Semantic Memory, In *Semantic Information Processing* (M. Minsky, Ed.), M.I.T. Press, Cambridge, Mass., 1968, 216-270.

24. Reiter, R. [1977] An Approach to Deductive Question-Answering, *BBN Report No. 3649,* Bolt, Beranek and Newman, Inc., Cambridge, Mass., Sept. 1977.

25. Robinson, J. A. [1965] A Machine Oriented Logic Based on the Resolution Principle, *JACM 12* (Jan. 1965), 25-41.

26. Roussel, P. [1975] PROLOG: Manuel de Reference et d'Utilisation, Groupe d'Intelligence Artificielle, U.E.R., de Luminy, Universite d'Aix-Marseille, Sept. 1975.

27. Tsichritzis, D. C. and Lochovsky, F. H. [1977] *Data Base Management Systems,* Academic Press, New York, 1977.

28. Warren, D. [1977] Implementing PROLOG - Compiling Predicate Logic Programs, Dept. of AI, *No. 39,* Edinburgh, 1977.

DATA BASES VIEWED THROUGH FORMAL LOGIC

DATA BASE: THEORY vs. INTERPRETATION

J. M. Nicolas and H. Gallaire

ONERA-CERT

Toulouse, France

ABSTRACT

This paper is concerned with the formalization of data bases in terms of first order logic concepts. Two approaches to such a formalization are first considered. In the first approach the elementary facts as well as the general statements are considered as the proper axioms of a first order theory, whereas in the second one the elementary facts are considered as defining an interpretation of a first order theory whose proper axioms are the sole general statements. These two approaches are discussed and contrasted with regard to the representation of negative information, querying and integrity checking. Both of them impose a uniform use of general statements; so, a third approach, which is an extension of the second one, is proposed. It enables one to use some general statements as derivation rules while others are used as integrity rules. Finally, due to their importance in relational data bases, some results specific to functional and multivalued dependency statements are stated.

INTRODUCTION

Mathematical logic has been used as a formal conceptual framework for question answering systems since the early 1960s. In the data base area, especially with the advent of relational systems, predicate calculus based languages have been introduced with, we believe, a positive effect on the field.

Formalizing, with logic, many more data base concepts will yield other improvements, especially by taking into account results from proof theory and model theory.

Although QA systems and DBM systems are both concerned with representation of information which must be operated on, logic must not be used in a similar way for both types of systems; the main reason for this is due to the difference in the worlds they handle.

In this paper we first present a short introduction to the QA systems approach and shown in what respect this approach is not directly applicable to DBM systems; next, two approaches, one an extension of the other, are detailed and we show why, they are a better fit to DBMS requirements. Finally, due to the importance, in relational DBMS, of dependency statements (both functional and multivalued ones) we state some results specific to them; it should be noted that these results are attained easily through the proposed formalization.

This paper is a somewhat revised version of Nicolas et al. [1976] and the last section is closely related to the short note by Nicolas and Demolombe [1977]. It consists of five sections. The first one presents the various types of information that are relevant to this study. The next three sections deal respectively with each of the above mentioned approaches. Finally, the next section is concerned with dependency statements. The concepts of first order logic which are used in this paper are basic ones and the reader is assumed to be aware of them. However, if needed he is referred to the introductory paper by Gallaire, Minker and Nicolas, or to a standard text such as Kleene [1968].

CONCISE DESCRIPTION OF A WORLD

Different Types of Information

A world, or rather a state in this world, can be envisioned as a set of elements linked together by relations and functions. Since a function is just a particular case of a relation*, we shall consider only relations in the remainder of this paper. Information in a state of the world is the knowledge of the truth-value (True/False) of a statement which can be either an elementary fact as in "Peter is John's father" or a general law as in "a father of a father is a grandfather". Expressed in a predicate calculus language these statements are closed wffs (i.e., formulas with no free variables), in particular elementary facts are just ground literals.

In a state of the world, statements have a well-defined truth-

* $y = f(x)$ is equivalent to $F(x,y)$ together with the axiom

$$\forall x\ \forall y\ \forall z\ ((F(x,y) \wedge F(x,z)) \rightarrow (y=z)) .$$

value, however, their truth value is known only for some of them in general; all others can be considered as having the "unknown" value. Hence three values: True, False, Unknown are needed in the perceived world which is in fact the only one that can be represented.

Elementary facts, together with general laws, constitute only a subset of information on the perceived world. We call them explicit information as opposed to implicit information which can be derived from the explicit ones and which can as well be redundant with them. This redundancy can be more or less important, depending on the properties of the world being considered. Elementary facts attached to a False value are usually called negative information; they can be expressed in many different ways:

i) explicitly by asserting a negative ground literal
e.g. $\neg R(a_1,\ldots,a_n)$

ii) implicitly by stating laws which allow them to be derived, as for example:

- uniqueness laws:

  $\neg$ Birthyear (John, 1950) can be derived from the assertion Birthyear (John, 1948) and the general law: "Everybody has a unique birth year".

- completeness* laws which express that for a given relation (in every interpretation) every fact not true is false. This means that no unknown value is associated to facts supported by this relation. A very simple example of such a law would be:

  $$\forall x\ (P(x) \rightarrow (x=a) \vee (x=b))$$

  which asserts that any fact P(.) other than P(a) or P(b) is false (e.g. $\neg P(c)$). We must mention that here constants which have different names are assumed to be different (i.e., $a \neq c$, $b \neq c$, $a \neq b$).

Different World Properties

It is clear that world properties will influence choices of information representations. A world can be finite or infinite, closed or open. Finiteness (respectively infiniteness) of a world is trivially bound to the finiteness (respectively infiniteness) of the set of its elements. As we consider only a state of the world,

* We chose this qualifier by analogy with one of the meanings of "completeness" in logic; namely, a theory is complete if for all wffs W either W or $\neg$W is provable. (See Mendelson [1964].)

a world can be finite and evolving. Finiteness is an inherent property of the world, while being closed or open depends on how we perceive it. A closed world is defined as being one in which for every relation $R(x_1,\ldots,x_n)$ and n-tuple $< a_1,\ldots,a_n >$, either $R(a_1,\ldots,a_n)$ is true or $\neg R(a_1,\ldots,a_n)$ is true; hence, a world in which for every relation there is a completeness law is closed. A world not closed is open.

Usually DBMS worlds are finite but may be open or closed. However, whether they are open or closed, they are in fact implicitly assumed to be closed in their standard representation (hierarchical, network, relational). And then, as explained in the section entitled The Data Base, unknown facts (if any) are confused with negative ones as discussed in Demolombe and Nicolas [1976]. As quoted by Nicolas and Syre [1974], such an assumption does not raise problems as long as only explicit information is handled, but implies special caution for implicit information handling. This point will be detailed in the section entitled Negative Information.

We shall now discuss different approaches - all of them using logic as a framework - for representing a perceived world.

FIRST APPROACH: THE PERCEIVED WORLD AS A FIRST ORDER THEORY

Representation

This approach is essentially that commonly used in Question Answering Systems. It amounts to representing the perceived world as a first order theory (with equality). Thus, one only represents statements known to be true or to be false; more precisely, the theory (T) is defined as follows:

- its set of constants (respectively predicate names) is the set of elements (respectively relations) appearing within information.

- its set of proper axioms is the set of well formed formulae (wffs) associated with explicit information (i.e. elementary facts and general laws) in the following way: if the statement is known to be true, then the wff is an axiom and if it is known to be false then the negation of the wff is an axiom.

According to this construction, implicit information are the theorems of T and the world is an interpretation of it. But, whether it is a model (i.e., an interpretation in which the axioms are true) or not cannot be verified since this depends on how well the perceived world fits the world, and the world is known only through the perceived world. One can only try to prove the consistency or inconsistency* of this theory. Only when it is inconsistent can we conclude negatively as then T cannot have any model.

Query Formulation and Evaluation

As when stating laws, we shall use predicate calculus oriented languages for querying. But a few remarks are first in order. We shall distinguish two cases: closed queries and open queries.

Closed Queries. Closed queries call for a yes/no answer; hence, they correspond to closed wffs when expressed in the language of the predicate calculus. Let W be a closed wff to be answered. To do so one must try to derive W. If W is a theorem, then the answer is "yes"; else try to derive $\neg W$. If $\neg W$ is a theorem, the answer is "no", else the answer is "don't know".

Example: With respect to the relations introduced in Table 1, some closed queries can be:

Is P6 a component of P2? : COMPON(P6,P2)?
Does P2 have a component? : $\exists x$ COMPON(x,P2)?
Does M1 make parts which are of type T3? :
$\exists x\ (\exists y\ \text{MANU}(M1,x,y) \land \exists z\ \exists t\ \text{PC}(x,z,t,T3))$?

Notice that in such an approach, objects of the perceived world are seen as a set of constants in a theory and not as a domain in an interpretation. Hence, the finiteness property does not bear any influence on the decidability (or undecidability)** of whether a given wff is a theorem (the world can itself be infinite).

Open Queries

An open query calls for a set of objects or of tuples as answers, which satisfy some conditions stated in the query. For example, "Which are the components of P2?", "What are the characteristics of type T3 parts made by M1?".

One can express such questions by wffs with the writing convention of using free variables for the elements to be retrieved. The above questions can then be expressed as COMPON(x,P2) and $\exists y\ \text{MANU}(M1,x,y) \land \text{PC}(x,z,t,T3)$. The answer to the first of these

* A theory is inconsistent iff there is a wff W such that both W and $\neg W$ are theorems of it; otherwise, it is consistent.

** In the first section we ruled out functions, choosing relations instead. But notice that in wffs, expressions of laws and of queries, existential quantifiers can appear in the scope of universal quantifiers - expressing functional links (SKOLEM functions) between variables.

Table 1. Relations Definitions

COMPON(x,y): its intended meaning is defined by

$COMPON(a_1,a_2)$ is true iff "part referenced by a_1 is a component of part referenced by a_2".

PC(x,y,z,t): its intended meaning is defined by

$PC(a_2,b_2,c_2,d_2)$ iff "part referenced by a_2 is called b_2, has weight c_2, and type d_2".

MANU(x,y,z): its intended meaning is defined by

$MANU(a_3,b_3,c_3)$ iff "factory referenced by a_3 makes a part referenced by b_3 and sells it \$ c_3".

will be a set of a_i's; the second will,return triples $< x=a_i, z=b_i, t=c_i >$.

One might inquire how to evaluate the answers so as to get the semantic meaning of such open wffs. If $F(x_1,\ldots,x_n)$ is a wff which only has $x_1,\ldots,x_n$ as free variables, it is irrelevant to try and prove $F(x_1,\ldots,x_n)$; rather one must find all formulas $F(a_{i_1},\ldots,a_{i_n})$ which are theorems. This is equivalent to finding all proofs to the existential closure of F, i.e. to $\exists x_1\ldots\exists x_n \; F(x_1,\ldots,x_n)$.

How well does this fit data base context?

Such an approach allows one to take into account among others, laws which only have infinite models; however, it is not clear whether this is an advantage considering worlds specific to data base context. Further, it allows one to handle disjunctive informations as in "Smith teaches mechanics or physics". TEACH(Smith, mechanics) $\vee$ TEACH(Smith, physics). This type of information is most often not available in classical DBMS, and when it is available, it is handled in a rather cumbersome way.

Usually, the volume of information, in particular elementary facts, is huge, and this prohibits using standard proof methods which would be too inefficient on such an amount of data. This approach must be adapted to data base context in several ways:

- specific representation and handling of elementary facts. Access to elementary facts must interfere as little as possible with the deductive process. Furthermore, they must be stored in such a way that efficient data retrieval techniques can be used (see Nicolas and Syre [1974], Chang [1976] and Reiter [1977]).

- better data semantic treatment; in particular, identify unary relations and manipulate them as semantic classes as it is done by McSkimin and Minker[1977,1978] and by Reiter [1977].

- more appropriate proof search methods for <u>open</u> queries - essentially a no-backtrack algorithm is needed, as in Nicolas and Syre [1974] and more nicely in Fishman and Minker [1975] - or develop quite specific methods as in Kellogg et al. [1976].

However, with regard to data base management, two major drawbacks remain.

The first one has to do with the fact that this approach makes it compulsory to explicitly or implicitly represent negative information. But worlds to be considered in data base applications are generally finite and "weakly" open, i.e. support few unknown information. It is not possible then to make explicit all negative information; not only because there are too many of them, but also because a user does not usually see the need for making them explicit. It is possible to exhibit two solutions which rely both upon an implicit representation of negative facts - either by introducing completeness laws for each relation, although such laws must be modified each time there is an updating of the information - or by using globally, as Nicolas and Syre [1974], a representation convention for negative information, namely: $\neg A$ is a theorem iff A is not a theorem, for all ground literals A. This convention is similar to the so called closed world assumption of Reiter [1977]. In both cases there is a merging between unknown* and negative informations. In order not to derive non sensible information one is led to constrain the syntax of general laws. This last point will be made precise in the section entitled Negative Information.

The second drawback is related to verifying the integrity of information. Such a verification is fundamental in data base management. In usual DBM systems it consists in verifying whether

---

* What has been called here unknown information is different from the unknown value in standard data base manipulation as will be explained in the next section.

elementary information obeys what are usually called integrity constraints. Integrity constraints are nothing more than general laws, but they are interpreted and used in a different way (as integrity rules, see the following sections) than in this approach.

The drawback of this approach is precisely due to the fact that it imposes a uniform use of all general laws as derivation rules (i.e. they are all used to derive implicit information), forbidding using some of them as integrity rules. However, we shall note that when unary relations are distinguished and treated as semantic classes (or more formally as "sorts"), the laws which bind the arguments of a relation to their sorts (e.g., $\forall x \forall y$ (OWNER(x,y) $\rightarrow$ PERSON(x) $\wedge$ CAR(y)), are in fact, handled as integrity rules (no matter how they are represented). But, in the data base context other laws than the above ones have to be used in a similar way as this will be examplified later. If it is not the case, verifying the validity of the information relies only upon verifying the consistency of a first order theory. Because all information is considered as being the proper axioms of a first order theory, each time an information is added, updated or suppressed this amounts to modifying the proper axioms, hence to being in a different theory whose consistency has to be checked. But, from a practical point of view that would not be acceptable in the data base context. Kowalski [1976] avoids such a problem by the introduction of a special purpose relation "INCONSISTENT" whose proof is tried out when one wants to test the consistency.

Finally, we will now see, with an example, that some laws are used better as integrity rules than as derivation rules as the present approach would impose it.

Let us consider two relations. The relation "OWNER(x,y)" whose intended meaning is that person x owns car y, and the relation "LICENCE(x,y)" whose intended meaning is that person x has the driving licence number y. Let us also consider the general law: "Every car's owner must have a driver licence"; its corresponding wff is "$\forall x$ ($\exists y$ OWNER(x,y) $\rightarrow$ $\exists z$ LICENCE(x,z))". Interpreted as an integrity rule such an existential law will allow one to detect the cases where for a given fact "OWNER(p,c)" there is not a fact of the kind "LICENCE(p,n)". This interpretation seems to fit better the meaning of the law than an interpretation as a derivation rule. In this latter case it would only allow one to infer that person p has a driving Licence but would be useless to determine answers to queries asking for licence numbers of some persons.

SECOND APPROACH: THE SET OF ELEMENTARY INFORMATION AS AN INTERPRETATION OF A FIRST ORDER THEORY

The set of elementary information considered as an interpretation of a first order theory is the approach which is in fact implicitly followed in relational data base systems. Usually, however, the link with logic has only been exploited for query language purposes, except by Florentin [1974]. We will see that results from logic can be exploited for other purposes.

This approach consists in giving a preferential place to elementary information. The world assumed to be well perceived, so that the extensions of relations are known explicitly, independently from the general laws. This means that using the latter as derivation rules, will produce redundant information.

So, the perceived world is divided into two parts. The first one is composed of general laws. The second one is composed of elementary information and constitutes the data base.

The Data Base

For semantic reasons, unary relations are considered apart from other relations. Unary relations define semantic classes of elements; the fact that an element belongs to a particular class is generally less interesting for queries than for providing a bound on the range of variables in other relations. This is the reason why, in relational systems, unary relations are distinguished from others and exploited by means of the notion of domains.

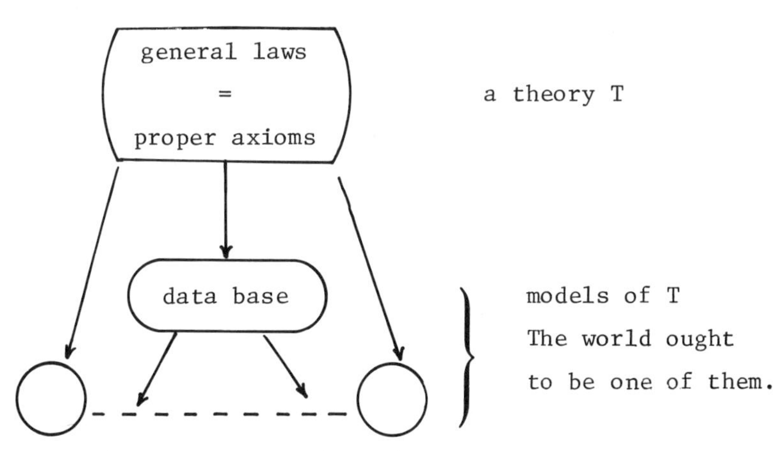

Figure 1. Data Base Theory

Then, in this approach, the data base appears as a necessarily finite set of elements subdivided into domains on which relations are defined. These relations are given through their extensions.

Although in the perceived world elementary facts can be true, false, or unknown, only true facts are represented (up to a few exceptions) and then, false facts and unknown ones are blended together. Indeed, a special value called the "unknown" value, can occur as a component of a tuple in a relation, but it is not allowed to occur for components belonging to the primary key; furthermore when it occurs it does not necessarily represent an unknown fact. Some examples will explain this point.

Let us consider two relations in third normal form (see Codd [1974]). The first relation is

CD (EMPLOYEE NUMBER, DEGREE)

Notice first that the "unknown" value is not allowed to appear in a tuple component which belongs to the primary key. Then, when a given tuple, like < C1, Ph.D > does not appear in the extension of CD, it may mean that either "C1 did not receive a Ph.D" or "it is unknown whether he received it"; there is no way to know which of the two holds. Here, unknown and false are blended together. The second relation is

CN (EMPLOYEE NUMBER, NAME, WIFE's NAME)

If a tuple such as < C2, SMITH, "unknown" > appears in the extension of CN, that may mean either that "C2 has a wife but her name is unknown" or that "C2 has no wife", i.e., $\exists x$ CN (C2,SMITH,x) or $\neg \exists x$ CN (C2,SMITH,x). Then all facts like CN (C2,SMITH,x_i) are implicitly represented as unknown facts in the first case, and as negative facts in the second one. The only time a difference can be made is when, for example, it is known that every employee has a wife.

As in the first approach, queries can be stated in a predicate calculus oriented language. However, formulas are not to be interpreted as theorems to be proved, but have to be evaluated by means of "truth tables" in the interpretation of the theory which is the data base. In fact, as shown in Figure 1, the data base is not exactly one interpretation but covers several ones which are obtained from the data base by substituting particular values to "unknown" ones. As the evaluation of queries is applied to a finite set, even when corresponding formulas contain universal or existential quantifiers, their evaluation can effectively be carried out. But, one should note that, while evaluating answers to queries, a convention for negative information is made. It is implicitly assumed that a tuple which does not appear in the extension of a relation does not satisfy it. Thus the answer to a query like $\forall x\ (P(x) \rightarrow Q(x))$ is given from the state of the extensions of the two relations P and Q, and not from some general law that can be known on the universe. As an example, consider the two relations given below:

MN (Company,	Product)
C11	P3
C11	P5
C13	P2
C11	P6

RP (Agent,	Product)
A6	P3
A6	P2
A6	P5
A6	P6
A7	P2
A7	P6

In the example, an agent represents products from several companies but not necessarily all products from a given company. The answer to the query "Does A6 represent all products manufactured by C11" (i.e., $\forall x\ (MN(C11,x) \rightarrow RP\ (A6,x))$ will be "yes". It is clear that this answer, which is valid with regard to the data base, is also valid with regard to the world iff all the products manufactured by M11 and all the products represented by A6 are known. Let us finally notice that information such as "$P(a) \vee Q(a)$" cannot be expressed in this approach.

General Information

In what way can general information be exploited in this approach?

They can be used for determining whether a relation has a given property; for example whether it is in a certain normal form (e.g., 3NF, 4NF). Normal forms have been introduced in the relational data "model" in order to avoid some data manipulation anomalies which occur with unnormalized relations (see Date [1977]). The property for a relation to be in a given normal form cannot be determined (as for any property) from its extension at a given time; but this must be done from general laws which defined its intension. In fact, in this case, only some particular general laws are useful. They are called functional and multivalued dependency statements. In the section Some Comments on Functional and Multivalued Dependency Statements, such laws will be considered more thoroughly.

In a more general way, general laws may be used as integrity rules, in verifying whether the data base is actually a model of the theory T. This will be the case, if these laws are all true expressions on the data base. The reader is referred to Table 2 (in the next section) where an example is presented: all the laws are true when evaluated on the data base. Now, every operation on the data base (adding, suppressing, updating an elementary information) corresponds to a change of interpretation. In order that the new interpretation be also a model of the theory T, the operation will have to be such that the laws remain true. For a given operation, only some of the laws might be falsified and thus have to be evaluated on the new interpretation. The problem to determine which laws are concerned is addressed by Nicolas and Yzadanian [1978].

The world ought to be a model of the theory T. How can this be ensured? In fact there is no way to ensure this. The only thing that can be done is to verify the consistency of the theory. If it is not consistent, no model of it exists and so, the world cannot be one model either.

Verifying that the theory is consistent can be time consuming. However, for an application, general rules are rather permanent and so procedures to test the consistency, would have to be run only a few times. Furthermore, every first order theory which admits a model is consistent. Hence, when the data base is a model of the theory (which is easier to verify), the theory is thus necessarily consistent and one needs not run procedures to determine this fact.

General laws can also be used, in this approach, in a way other than as integrity rules. They can be used to corroborate the perennial character of the answer to some questions. Let us make this point more precise.

Every theorem of the theory T, namely every formula provable from general laws, is true in every model of T (Completeness theorem); thus, it is true in the data base. But conversely, a formula which is true on the data base is not necessarily a theorem. This means that the answer to a query which is only evaluated on the data base, is valid only in the context of this interpretation.

On the contrary, if the formula is confirmed as a theorem of T, it will stay valid whatever are the modifications on the data base, provided the data base remains a model of T. For some queries it may be important to make the difference.

As an example let us consider the last question we already stated: "Does A6 represent all products manufactured by C11?" The questioner may want to know if the answer "yes" results from an induction from elementary facts (tuples of the extension of relations) or from the existence of an agreement (general law) between A6 and C11.

Table 2. Typical Data Base

1. ELEMENTARY INFORMATION

CIVIL STATUS (SS number, Age, Sex)

SS number	Age	Sex
I1	20	Male
I3	45	Fem
I2	50	Fem
I9	15	Male
I5	70	Male
I6	68	Fem
I7	25	Male
I8	80	Male
I4	10	Male

LIVE(S.S. NB, Town)

S.S. NB	Town
I1	New York
I2	Paris
I3	Paris
I6	Syracuse
I4	Paris
I8	Los Angeles
I5	Syracuse
I7	Geneva
I9	Washington

FATHER (father, son)

father	son
I2	I1
I2	I4
I5	I2

GF(grandfather, grandson)

grandfather	grandson
I8	I9
I5	I1*
I5	I4*

BROTHER (Brother, Brother)

Brother	Brother
I4	I7
I1	I4*
I1	I7*

MARRIED (husband, wife)

husband	wife
I2	I3
I5	I6

2. GENERAL INFORMATION

G1: $\forall x \forall y\ (\exists z (\text{FATHER}(x,z) \wedge \text{FATHER}(z,y)) \rightarrow \text{GF}(x,y))$

The father of a father is a grandfather.

G2: $\forall x \forall y\ (\exists z (\text{BROTHER}(x,z) \wedge \text{BROTHER}(z,y)) \rightarrow \text{BROTHER}(x,y))$

The brother of a brother is a brother.

G3: $\forall x \forall y \forall z\ (\text{FATHER}(z,x) \wedge \text{FATHER}(z,y) \wedge (x \neq y) \rightarrow \text{BROTHER}(x,y))$

Two children of the same father are brothers.

G4: $\forall x \forall y (\text{MARRIED}(x,y) \rightarrow \exists z\ \text{CIVIL STATUS}(x,z,\text{Male}) \wedge \exists t\ \text{CIVIL STATUS}(y,t,\text{Fem}))$

In any married couple the husband is a male and the wife is a female.

G5: $\forall y\ (\exists x \exists z\ \ \text{CIVIL STATUS}(x,y,z) \rightarrow (y < 150))$

An age is less than 150.

G6: $\forall x \forall y \forall z\ (\text{MARRIED}(x,y) \wedge \text{LIVE}(x,z) \rightarrow \text{LIVE}(y,z))$

A wife lifes in the same town as her husband.

G7: $\forall x \forall y \forall z\ (\text{LIVE}(x,y) \wedge \text{LIVE}(x,z) \rightarrow (y=z))$

Anybody lives in only one town.

G8: $\forall x\ (\exists y \exists z\ \text{CIVIL STATUS}\ (y,x,z) \rightarrow \text{AGE}(x))$

The second argument of the relation "CIVIL STATUS" is an age.

* tuples quoted by an asterisk will be referred to in section on Derivation Rules.

A THIRD APPROACH: AN EXTENSION OF THE SECOND APPROACH

In each of the previous two approaches, general laws are considered globally: all are used as derivation rules in the first approach and all are used as integrity rules in the second one. This emphasizes that, for a given law to be an integrity rule or derivation rule, is not an inherent property, but depends on the interpretation we have of it.

We will discuss criteria which will allow one to decide whethera general law is more appropriate to be used in either one of the two ways.

In Table 2, following the second approach, laws are interpreted as integrity rules. The reader could verify that all of them are true on the data base. Let us consider law G1. It allows one, among other things, to verify every time a new 2-tuple is introduced in the extension of the relation "FATHER (x,y)", that this updating is compatible with the extension of the relation "GF (x,y)". But, rather than verifying that it is true, it could be introduced in the data base and assumed to be true, contributing in this way to the definition of the relation "GF (x,y)". This would lead one to consider that the extension of this relation consists not only in an explicit part, but also in an implicit part obtained by evaluating the expression, "∃z (FATHER (x,z) ∧ FATHER (z,y))". So, used as a derivation rule, this law would avoid storing explicitly the 2-tuples: < I5, I1 > and < I5, I4 > . Furthermore, all the modifications that could occur in the extension of the relation "FATHER (x,y)" would be compatible by definition of "GF (x,y)" with its extension.

Can the same reasoning be applied to all the general laws? Let us consider law G5. It would allow one to deduce implicit information such as "20 is less than 150". This information seems to have almost no interest in the data base context, and leads us to think that this law would be more useful as an integrity rule. This point is detailed in the following section.

Integrity Rules

What peculiarities does the relation "LESS (x,y)" present when compared to "GF (x,y)", which can explain the difference we have just mentioned? The answer is that (in the data base context) an axiomatic definition of the relation "LESS (x,y)" does not yield anything more, because the whole extension* of this relation can be

* In fact, we do not have exactly an extension in the data base but an algorithm which determines whether a given 2-tuple does belong or not to this extension.

known in the data base by means of an algorithm. This relation constitutes an example of what we shall call primitive relations. We shall keep among other (e.g., see existential laws in the section entitled How well does this fit data base context?) integrity rules, the laws such that if they were used as derivation rules they would allow one to infer information on primitive relations.

We will see that the property of a relation being primitive comes from a choice, and that this choice can be made at different levels. At the system level, the choice is to retain unary relations as "domains", and to retain relations that can be defined by an algorithm independently from other relations (e.g., "Less than", "greater than", "equal" ...). At the user level, where the user (or more precisely the administrator) decides to define as primitive a relation, because, depending on his application, he considers that he must (and he can) explicitly specify its extension.

In Table 2, laws G5, G7, G8, and G4 will be used as integrity rules; G5, G7 and G8 because they are concerned with system primitive relations ($<$, = and Age) and G4 because it is concerned with a user primitive relation (CIVIL STATUS). Laws connecting relation arguments with "domains", like G8, which have been made explicit here for presentation clarity, can be implicitly taken into account when defining relations.

We wish to point out that laws other than those dealing with primitive relations, can be considered as potential integrity rules. In the same way as it is supposed that a primitive relation extension is entirely defined by its explicit part, it can be assumed that for another relation its extension is entirely defined by an explicit part and a given set of derivation rules. So that, any other law dealing with this relation will, as derivation rule, produce redundant implicit informations and will thus be used better as an integrity rule. The above stated criterion is intuitive and can certainly be refined.

Derivation Rules

Using laws G1, G2, G3, and G6 as derivation rules will allow one to suppress from the explicit extensions of relations the tuples quoted with an asterisk. Though this is not very significant in Table 2, it can be seen to save storage space, and could be significant. But another more important advantage of this approach is that it gives one the opportunity to express some general knowledge perceived on the world without having to split it into elementary information.

How can these laws, which define extensions of relations in terms of extensions of other ones, be exploited? Two solutions can be explored.

The first one consists in considering two kinds of relations: on one hand, base relations, the extensions of which are entirely defined at the explicit level; on the other hand, derived relations, the extensions of which are only implicit. Each derived relation is defined from base relations (or from other derived relations) by means of a query language expression, called its definition expression.

The extension of a derived relation is produced by evaluating on the data base the expression of base relations obtained as followed: substitute to the derived relation its definition expression, and repeat this process for every derived relation which appears until there are only base relations. This is similar to the standard treatment of views.

The second solution consists in considering the extension derivation as the deduction of facts which are tuples, associated with the relation they satisfy. So, in order to get the extension of an n-ary relation $R(x_1,\ldots,x_n)$, all the n-tuples $<a_{i_1},\ldots,a_{i_n}>$ such that $R(a_{i_1},\ldots,a_{i_n})$ is provable, have to be retrieved. This can be done in the same way as stated in the first approach, namely by proving the formula $\exists x_1 \ldots \exists x_n R(x_1,\ldots,x_n)$ provided strategies are used which allow one to obtain all the proofs of this formula. As pointed out in the section entitled How well does this fit data base context?, negative information raises a problem with regard to derivation of facts. This problem is discussed in the next section.

This latter solution presents different advantages over the former.

First, it enables one to manipulate relations such that their extensions are defined both explicitly and implicitly. An example will help clarify this point. Let us consider the relation GF (x,y) of Table 2. It may be known that "I8 is the Grandfather of I9" without knowing who is the father or the mother of I9, because the first knowledge results from a local observation. So, this information could not be obtained from any rules which contribute to the relation "GF (x,y)" as defined in the general laws. The only way to represent it, is in giving it explicitly.

A second advantage is that, laws which define only partially relations can be used as derivation rules. An example of such a law is: "A5 represents all products manufactured by C11".

A third advantage lies in the fact that it enables one to take into account recursive laws like G2. But we must notice that the proposal made by Chang [1976], although close to the first solution given here, allows recursive laws too. This is essentially due to the fact that his formalism includes laws with a variable number of literals.

Negative Information

As in the second approach, it will be assumed here that each tuple which does not belong to the extension (explicit and implicit) of a relation does not satisfy it. But, if this convention is acceptable at the explicit level, we have to be careful so that wrong information is not introduced in the implicit extensions. Namely, because negative information is not positively sure, we have to forbid the derivation of positive information from negative information. This can be done by forbidding some forms of derivation rules.

We shall consider now formulas put into clausal form:

$$A_1 \wedge \ldots \wedge A_n \rightarrow B_1 \vee \ldots \vee B_p$$

where all A_i and B_j are positive literals. For each B_j a clause can be interpreted as the derivation rule:

$$A_1 \wedge \ldots \wedge A_n \wedge \neg B_1 \ldots \wedge \neg B_{j-1} \wedge \neg B_{j+1} \ldots \wedge \neg B_p \rightarrow B_j \quad .$$

In order to avoid derivation from negative information, only formulae such that p=1 should be accepted as derivation rules. We note that this form of clauses is a particular case of Horn clauses called "regular" clauses by Colmerauer [1975].

Query Language and Knowledge Expression Language

The constraint imposed on the form of derivation rules exhibits the difference there is between the query language and the language in which derivation rules are expressed. There is not such a restriction on the expression of the query language, nor on integrity rules, which are in fact closed queries which must be evaluated "true". A query is not a formula to be proved but, as in the second approach, a formula to be evaluated in an interpretation, with extensions which are both defined explicitly and implicitly.

SOME COMMENTS ON FUNCTIONAL AND MULTIVALUED DEPENDENCY STATEMENTS

We now consider the topic of functional and multivalued dependency statements. All results presented here are implicitly contained in the last two sections and more thoroughly detailed by

Nicolas and Demolombe [1977].

Dependency statements are but a particular case of general laws which is of prime importance in the decomposition process and normalization of relations. This is why people have looked for a definition, for example, as Beeri et al. [1977], of valid and complete formal systems which allow their formalization. We argue that, due to the analysis carried out in approaches two and three above, logic with equality is adequate for formalizing dependency statements. Before showing how they can be expressed by wffs, let us recall the meaning of functional and multivalued dependency statements.

Let $R(X_1,\ldots,X_n)$ be an n-ary relation, Y and Z two subsets of $\{X_1,\ldots,X_n\}$, then the functional dependency statement $Y \rightarrow Z$ holds for R iff whenever two tuples of R agree on Y then they also agree on Z.

Let $R(X_1,\ldots,X_n)$ be an n-ary relation. Let Y and Z be two subsets of $\{X_1,\ldots,X_n\}$ and T be the complement in $\{X_1,\ldots,X_n\}$ of $\{Y \cup Z\}$. The multivalued dependency statement $Y \twoheadrightarrow Z$ holds for R iff R is the natural join of its projection R[YZ] and R[YT]. (See Beeri et al. [1977].)

i) functional dependency statements expressed as wffs

Let $R(X_1,\ldots,X_n)$ be an n-ary relation, $F: X_1X_3X_4 \rightarrow X_3X_6$ be a functional dependency statement, and WF be the following wff:

$$\text{WF:}\quad \forall x_1,\ldots,\forall x_n, \forall x_2', \forall x_5', \forall x_6',\ldots,\forall x_n' \; [(R(x_1,x_2,\ldots,x_n) \wedge R(x_1,x_2',x_3,x_4,x_5',x_6',\ldots,x_n')) \rightarrow (x_3{=}x_3) \wedge (x_6{=}x_6')]$$

Given the evaluation rules of a wff on an interpretation, WF is true in an interpretation iff, in the extension of R, any n-tuple coinciding on the 1st, 3rd and 4th element also coincide on the 3rd and 6th element. In other words, WF is true in an interpretation iff the extension of R (in that interpretation) satisfies the statement F.

ii) multivalued dependency statements expressed as wffs

Now let us define a relation $P(Y_1,\ldots,Y_m)$, a multivalued dependency statement: $M : Y_1Y_3Y_4 \twoheadrightarrow Y_3Y_6$, and the wff:

$$\text{WM:}\quad \forall_{y_1} \forall_{y_2} \ldots \forall_{y_m} \; [\exists y_2' \exists y_5' \exists y_7' \ldots \exists y_m' \; P(y_1,y_2',y_3,y_4,y_5',y_6,y_7',\ldots,y_m') \wedge \exists y_6' \; P(y_1,y_2,y_3,y_4,y_5,y_6',y_7,\ldots,y_m)) \rightarrow P(y_1,y_2,\ldots,y_m)]$$

<u>Proposition</u>: WM is true in an interpretation iff the extension of P in that interpretation contains ($\supseteq$) the natural join, on $Y_1Y_3Y_4$, of the projections $P[Y_1Y_3Y_4Y_6]$ and $P[Y_1 \ldots Y_5\ Y_7 \ldots Y_m]$. While it is out of the scope of this paper to give the proof of the preceding proposition, we shall make a few remarks:

i) In a given interpretation, only those p-tuples which, once substituted to $< x_1, \ldots, x_p >$ in " $\exists x_{p+1}, \ldots, \exists x_n\ Q(x_1, \ldots, x_p, \ldots x_n)$" lead to a true formula, are also the p-tuples of the projection of the Q relation extension on the first p attributes; and vice-versa.

ii) In a given interpretation, only those (q+p+r)-tuples which, once substituted to x_i, y_j, z_l ($\forall i,j,l$) in "$S(x_1, \ldots, x_q, y_1, \ldots, y_p) \wedge S2(x_1, \ldots, x_q, z_1, \ldots, z_r)$", lead to a true formula, are also the (q+p+r)-tuples of the natural join on the first q attributes of the extensions of S1 and S2; and vice versa.

Form the preceding proposition, from the fact that a relation extension is always contained ($\subseteq$) within the natural join of a couple of its projections, and finally from the definition of multivalued dependency statements previously given, if follows that: WM is a true wff in an interpretation iff the extension of P satisfies the multivalued dependency statement M.

When one is concerned with the derivation of the logical consequences from a set of dependency statements it is, in fact, more interesting to use a formal system derived from logic for closed wffs, namely the clause language with resolution and paramodulation inference rules (see Chang and Lee [1973]).

The interest of a logic formalization here, is twofold. On the one hand its validity and completeness have already been shown. On the other hand, it accounts for more general statements. This last point is rather important because it is a fact that dependency statements can be a logical consequence ($\models$) of a set of dependency statements together with more general ones (which have no equivalent dependency statements).

A last remark is in order. Dependency statements, expressed in clausal form, lead to clauses without Skolem functions. Such sets of clauses are trivially decidable. So all dependency statements which are logical consequences of a given set of dependency statements can be <u>effectively</u> derived. From a practical standpoint algorithms which carry out this task are then very simple to write in programming languages based on logic, as in the language PROLOG (see Roussel [1975]).

CONCLUSION

It is clear that a study of links between formal logic and data bases must go further than a simple analogy at the language level. In this paper we have shown how it is possible to use results from proof theory and model theory in a well adapted formalization.

Three approaches have been detailed. The first one merely consists of interpreting the whole collection of information perceived on the world as a set of axioms in a first order theory. In the other two approaches, the elementary facts are, on the contrary, separated from general laws. The collection of information can be looked at as a model of a first order theory which has general laws as axioms. The difference between the last two approaches is not a fundamental one; it depends only on how elementary information is defined, i.e. in a strictly explicit way or as a mixture of explicit and implicit information.

ACKNOWLEDGMENTS

The authors would like to thank the referees for their helpful comments on this paper.

This work was supported by the DRET with a contribution from the CNRS.

REFERENCES

1. Beeri, C., Fagin, R., and Howard, H.J. [1977] A Complete Axiomatization for Functional and Multivalued Dependencies in Data Base Relations, *Proceedings of ACM SIGMOD Conference,* Toronto, Canada, August 1977, 47-61.

2. Chang, C. L. and Lee, R.C.T. [1973] *Symbolic Logic and Mechanical Theorem Proving, Computer Science and Applied Mathematics,* Series of Academic Press, Inc., New York, N.Y., 1973.

3. Chang, C. L. [1976] Deduce: A Deductive Language for Relational Data Bases, In *Pattern Recognition and Artificial Intelligence* (C. H. Chen, Ed.), Academic Press, New York, N.Y., 1976, 108-134.

4. Codd, E. F. [1974] Recent Investigation in Relational Data Base Systems, *Proceedings of IFIP Congress 74,* Stockholm, Sweden, August 1974, 1017-1921.

5. Colmerauer, A. [1975] Les grammaires de mêtamorphose, *T.R. Groupe d'Intelligence Artificielle*, Marseille, France, Nov. 1975.

6. Date, C. J. [1977] *An Introduction to Database Systems* (Second Edition), Addison-Wesley Publishing Company, Reading, Massachusetts, 1977.

7. Demolombe, R. and Nicolas, J. M. [1976] Knowledge Representation and Evolutivity in Data Base Management Systems, *T. Report CERT - LDB - 76/5*, Toulouse, France, Nov. 1976.

8. Fishman, D. H. and Minker, J. [1975] Π-Representation. A Clause Representation for Parallel Search, *Artificial Intelligence 6*, 2 (1975), 103-127.

9. Florentin, J. J. [1974] Consistency Auditing of Data Bases, *The Computer Journal 17*,1 (Feb. 1974), 52-58.

10. Kellogg, C., Klahr, P., and Travis, L. [1976] A Deductive Capability for Data Base Management, *Proceedings of 2nd Int. Conference on VLDB*, Brussels, Belgium, Sept. 1976, 181-196.

11. Kleene, S. C. [1968] *Mathematical Logic*, John Wiley and Sons, Inc., New York, 1968.

12. Kowalski, R. A. [1976] Logic and Data Bases, *Logic Programming Meeting*, Imperial College, London, May 1976.

13. McSkimin, J.R. and Minker, J. [1978] A Predicate Calculus Based Semantic Network for Question-Answering Systems, In *Associative Networks - The Representation and Use of Knowledge in Computers* (N. Findler, Ed.), Adacemic Press, New York, N.Y., 1978 (in press).

14. McSkimin, J. R. and Minker, J. [1977] The Use of a Semantic Network in a Deductive Question-Answering System, *Proceedings IJCAI-77*, Cambridge, Massachusetts, 1977, 50-58.

15. Mendelson, E. [1964] *Introduction to Mathematical Logic*, D. Van Nostrand, New York, 1964.

16. Nicolas, J.M. and Syre, J.C. [1974] Natural Question Answering and Automatic Deduction in the System Syntex, *Proceedings of IFIP Congress 1974*, Stockholm, Sweden, August 1974, 595-599.

17. Nicolas, J.M., Demolombe, R. and Yazdanian, K. [1976] Contribution of Predicate Logic to Data Bases, *T. Report CERT - LBD 76/1*, Toulouse, France, Sept. 1976.

18. Nicolas, J. M. and Demolombe, R. [1977] A short note on the use of first order logic in the formalization of functional and multivalued dependencies, *T. Report CERT - LBD 77/1*, Toulouse, France, Sept. 1977.

19. Nicolas, J.M. and Yazdanian, K. [1978] Integrity Checking in Deductive Data Bases, In *Logic and Data Bases* (H. Gallaire and J. Minker, Eds.), Plenum Press, New York, N.Y., 1978, 325-344.

20. Reiter, R. [1977] An Approach to Deductive Question-Answering, *BBN Report No. 3649*, Cambridge, Mass., Sept. 1977.

21. Roussel, P [1975] PROLOG - Manuel de référence et d'utilisation, *Groupe d'Intelligence Artificielle*, Marseille, France Sept. 1975.

ON CLOSED WORLD DATA BASES

Raymond Reiter

The University of British Columbia

Vancouver, British Columbia

ABSTRACT

Deductive question-answering systems generally evaluate queries under one of two possible assumptions which we in this paper refer to as the open and closed world assumptions. The open world assumption corresponds to the usual first order approach to query evaluation: Given a data base DB and a query Q, the only answers to Q are those which obtain from proofs of Q given DB as hypotheses. Under the closed world assumption, certain answers are admitted as a result of failure to find a proof. More specifically, if no proof of a positive ground literal exists, then the negation of that literal is assumed true.

In this paper, we show that closed world evaluation of an arbitrary query may be reduced to open world evaluation of so-called atomic queries. We then show that the closed world assumption can lead to inconsistencies, but for Horn data bases no such inconsistencies can arise. Finally, we show how for Horn data bases under the closed world assumption purely negative clauses are irrelevant for deductive retrieval and function instead as integrity constraints.

INTRODUCTION

Deductive question-answering systems generally evaluate queries under one of two possible assumptions which we in this paper refer to as the open and closed world assumptions. The open world assumption corresponds to the usual first order approach to query evaluation: Given a data base DB and a query Q, the only answers to Q are those which obtain from proofs of Q given DB as hypotheses. Under the closed world assumption, certain answers are admitted as a result of failure to find a proof. More specifically, if no proof of a positive ground literal exists, then the negation of that literal is assumed true. This can be viewed as equivalent to implicitly augmenting the given data base with all such negated literals.

For many domains of application, closed world query evaluation is appropriate since, in such domains, it is natural to explicitly represent only positive knowledge and to assume the truth of negative facts by default. For example, in an airline data base, all flights and the cities which they connect will be explicitly represented. Failure to find an entry indicating that Air Canada flight 103 connects Vancouver with Toulouse permits one to conclude that it does not.

This paper is concerned with closed world query evaluation and its relationship to open world evaluation. In the section, Data Bases and Queries, we define a query language and the notion of an open world answer to a query. The section called The Closed World Assumption formally defines the notion of a closed world answer. The section, Query Evaluation Under the CWA, shows how closed world query evaluation may be decomposed into open world evaluation of so-called "atomic queries" in conjunction with the set operations of intersection, union and difference, and the relational algebra operation of projection. In the section, On Data Bases Consistent with the CWA, we show that the closed world assumption can lead to inconsistencies. We prove, moreover, that for Horn data bases no such inconsistencies can arise. Also, for Horn data bases, the occurrence of purely negative clauses is irrelevant to closed world query evaluation. By removing such negative clauses one is left with so-called definite data bases which are then consistent under both the open and closed world assumptions. Finally, in the section, The CWA and Data Base Integrity, we show that these purely negative clauses, although irrelevant to deductive retrieval, have a function in maintaining data base integrity.

In order to preserve continuity we have relegated all proofs of the results in the main body of this paper to an appendix.

DATA BASES AND QUERIES

The query language of this paper is set oriented, i.e. we seek all objects (or tuples of objects) having a given property. For example, in an airline data base the request "Give all flights and their carriers which fly from Boston to England" might be represented in our query language by:

$$< x/\text{Flight},\ y/\text{Airline} \mid (Ez/\text{City})\text{Connect } x,\text{Boston},z \wedge \text{Owns } y,x \wedge \text{City-of } z,\text{England} >$$

which denotes the set of all ordered pairs (x,y) such that x is a flight, y is an airline and

$$(Ez/\text{City})\text{Connect } x,\text{Boston},z \wedge \text{Owns } y,x \wedge \text{City-of } z,\text{England}$$

is true. The syntactic objects Flight, Airline and City are called types and serve to restrict the variables associated with them to range over objects of that type. Thus, (Ez/City) may be read as "There is a z which is a city".

Formally, all queries have the form

$$< x_1/\tau_1,\ldots,x_n/\tau_n \mid (Ey_1/\theta_1)\ldots(Ey_m/\theta_m)W(x_1,\ldots,x_n,y_1,\ldots,y_m) >$$

where $W(x_1,\ldots,x_n,y_1,\ldots,y_m)$ is a quantifier-free formula with free variables $x_1,\ldots,x_n,y_1,\ldots,y_m$ and moreover W contains no function signs. For brevity we shall often denote a typical such query by $< \vec{x}/\vec{\tau} \mid (E\vec{y}/\vec{\theta})W >$. The τ's and θ's are called <u>types</u>. We assume that with each type τ is associated a set of constant signs which we denote by $|\tau|$. For example, in an airline data base, |City| might be {Toronto, Boston, Paris,...,}. If $\vec{\tau} = \tau_1,\ldots,\tau_n$ is a sequence of types we denote by $|\vec{\tau}|$ the set $|\tau_1| \times\ldots\times |\tau_n|$.

A <u>data base</u> (DB) is a set of clauses containing no function signs. For an airline data base, DB might contain such information as:

"Air Canada flight 203 connects Toronto and Vancouver."

Connect AC203, Toronto, Vancouver

"All flights from Boston to Los Angeles serve meals."

(x/Flight)Connect x,Boston,LA ⊃Meal-serve x

Let $Q = < \vec{x}/\vec{\tau} \mid (E\vec{y}/\vec{\theta})W(\vec{x},\vec{y}) >$ and let DB be a data base. A set of n-tuples of constant signs $\{\vec{c}^{(1)},\ldots,\vec{c}^{(r)}\}$ is an <u>answer</u> to Q (with respect to DB) iff

1. $\vec{c}^{(i)} \in |\vec{\tau}|$ $i = 1,\ldots,r$ and

2. $DB \vdash \bigvee_{i \le r} (E\vec{y}/\vec{\theta})W(\vec{c}^{(i)},\vec{y})$

Notice that if $\{\vec{c}^{(1)},\ldots,\vec{c}^{(r)}\}$ is an answer to Q, and $\vec{c}$ is any n-tuple of constant signs satisfying 1. then so also is $\{\vec{c}^{(1)},\ldots,\vec{c}^{(r)},\vec{c}\}$ an answer to Q. This suggests the need for the following definitions:

An answer A to Q is minimal iff no proper subset of A is an answer to Q. If A is a minimal answer to Q, then if A consists of a single n-tuple, A is a definite answer to Q. Otherwise, A is an indefinite answer to Q. Finally define $||Q||_{OWA}$ to be the set of minimal answers to Q. (For reasons which will become apparent later, the subscript OWA stands for "Open World Assumption".) Notice the interpretation assigned to an indefinite answer $\{\vec{c}^{(1)},\ldots,\vec{c}^{(r)}\}$ to Q: $\vec{x}$ is either $\vec{c}^{(1)}$ or $\vec{c}^{(2)}$ or...or $\vec{c}^{(r)}$ but there is no way, given the information in DB, of determining which. Instead of denoting an answer as a set of tuples $\{\vec{c}^{(1)},\ldots,\vec{c}^{(r)}\}$ we prefer the more suggestive notation $\vec{c}^{(1)}+\ldots+\vec{c}^{(r)}$, a notation we shall use in the remainder of this paper.

Example 1.

Suppose DB knows of 4 humans and 2 cities:

$$|Human| = \{a,b,c,d\} \quad |City| = \{B,V\}$$

Suppose further that everyone is either in B or in V:

$$(x/Human)Loc\ x,B \vee Loc\ x,V$$

and moreover, a is in B and b is in V:

$$Loc\ a,B \quad Loc\ b,V$$

Then for the query "Where is everybody?"

$$Q = < x/Human, y/City \mid Loc\ x,y >$$

we have

$$||Q||_{OWA} = \{(a,B),(b,V),(c,B)+(c,V),(d,B)+(d,V)\}$$

i.e. a is in B, b is in V, c is either in B or V and d is either in B or V.

Since it is beyond the scope of this paper, the reader is referred to Reiter [1977] or Reiter [1978] for an approach to query evaluation which returns $||Q||_{OWA}$ given any query Q.

THE CLOSED WORLD ASSUMPTION

In order to illustrate the central concept of this paper, we consider the following purely extensional data base (i.e., a data base consisting of ground literals only):

$|\text{Teacher}| = \{a,b,c,d\}$

$|\text{Student}| = \{A,B,C\}$

Teach		
	a	A
	b	B
	c	C
	a	B

Now consider the query: Who does not teach B?

$$Q = < x/\text{Teacher} \mid \overline{\text{Teach}}\ x,B >$$

By the definition of the previous section, we conclude, counter-intuitively, that

$$||Q||_{OWA} = \phi\ .$$

Intuitively, we want $\{c,d\}$ i.e. $|\text{Teacher}| - || < x/\text{Teacher} | \text{Teach}\ x,B > ||_{OWA}$. The reason for the counterintuitive result is that first order logic interprets the DB literally; all the logic knows for certain is what is explicitly represented in the DB. Just because $\overline{\text{Teach}}$ c,B is not present in the DB is no reason to conclude that $\overline{\text{Teach}}$ c,B is true. Rather, as far as the logic is concerned, the truth of Teach c,B is unknown! Thus, we would also have to include the following facts about Teach:

$\overline{\text{Teach}}$		
	a	C
	b	A
	b	C
	c	A
	c	B
	d	A
	d	B
	d	C

Unfortunately, the number of negative facts about a given domain will, in general, far exceed the number of positive ones so that the requirement that all facts, both positive and negative, be explicitly represented may well be unfeasible. In the case of purely extensional data bases there is a ready solution to this problem. Merely explicitly represent positive facts. A negative fact is implicitly present provided its positive counterpart is not explicitly present. Notice, however, that by adopting this convention, we are making an assumption about our knowledge about the domain, namely, that we know everything about each predicate of the domain. There are no gaps in our knowledge. For example, if we were ignorant as to whether or not a teaches C, we could not permit the above implicit representation of negative facts. This is an important point. The implicit representation of negative facts presumes total knolwedge about the domain being represented. Fortunately, in most applications, such an assumption is warranted. We shall refer to this as the closed world assumption (CWA). Its opposite, the open world assumption (OWA), assumes only the information given in the data base and hence requires all facts, both positive and negative, to be explicitly represented. Under the OWA, "gaps" in one's knowledge about the domain are permitted.

Formally, we can define the notion of an answer to a query under the CWA as follows:

Let DB be an extensional data base and let $\overline{EDB} = \{\overline{P\vec{c}} \mid P$ is a predicate sign, $\vec{c}$ a tuple of constant signs and $P\vec{c} \notin DB\}$ Then $\vec{c}$ is a CWA answer to $< \vec{x}/\vec{\tau} \mid (E\vec{y}/\vec{\theta})W(\vec{x},\vec{y}) >$ (with respect to DB) iff

1. $\vec{c} \in |\vec{\tau}|$ and

2, $DB \cup \overline{EDB} \vdash (E\vec{y}/\vec{\theta})W(\vec{c},\vec{y})$

For purely extensional data bases, the CWA poses no difficulties. One merely imagines the DB to contain all negative facts each of which has no positive version in the DB. This conceptual view of the DB fails in the presence of non ground clauses. For if $P\vec{c} \notin DB$, it may nevertheless be possible to infer $P\vec{c}$ from the DB, so that we cannot, with impunity, imagine $\overline{P\vec{c}} \in DB$. The obvious generalization is to assume that the DB implicitly contains $\overline{P\vec{c}}$ whenever it is not the case that $DB \vdash P\vec{c}$.

Formally, we can define the notion of an answer to a query under the CWA for an arbitrary data base DB as follows:

Let

$\overline{EDB} = \{\overline{P\vec{c}} \mid P$ is a predicate sign, $\vec{c}$ a tuple of constant signs and $DB \not\vdash P\vec{c}\}$

Then $\vec{c}^{(1)} + \ldots + \vec{c}^{(r)}$ is a CWA answer to

$< \vec{x}/\vec{\tau} \mid (E\vec{y}/\vec{\theta})W(\vec{x},\vec{y}) >$ (with respect to DB) iff

1. $\vec{c}^{(i)} \in |\vec{\tau}|$ i=1,...,r and

2. $DB \cup \overline{EDB} \vdash \bigvee_{i \leq r} (E\vec{y}/\vec{\theta})W(\vec{c}^{(i)},\vec{y})$

This definition should be compared with the definition of an answer in the previous section. We shall refer to this latter notion as an OWA answer. As under the OWA, we shall require the notions of minimal, indefinite and definite CWA answers. If Q is a query, we shall denote the set of minimal CWA answers to Q by $||Q||_{CWA}$.

Example 2.

We consider a fragment of an inventory data base.

1. Every supplier of a part supplies all its subparts.

(x/Supplier)(yz/Part)Supplies x,y $\wedge$ Subpart z,y $\supset$ Supplies x,z

2. Foobar Inc. supplies all widgets.

(x/Widget)Supplies Foobar,x

3. The subpart relation is transitive.

(xyz/Part)Subpart z,y $\wedge$ Subpart y,x $\supset$ Subpart z,x

Assume the following type extensions:

|Supplier| = {Acme, Foobar, AAA}

$|\text{Widget}| = \{w_1,w_2,w_3,w_4\}$

$|\text{Part}| = \{p_1,p_2,p_3,w_1,w_2,w_3,w_4\}$

Finally, assume the following extensional data base:

Supplies	x	y
	Acme	p_1
	AAA	w_3
	AAA	w_4

Subpart	x	y
	p_2	p_1
	p_3	p_2
	w_1	p_1
	w_2	w_1

Then $\overline{EDB}$ is:

Supplies	x	y
	Acme	w_3
	Acme	w_4
	AAA	p_1
	AAA	p_2
	AAA	p_3
	AAA	w_1
	AAA	w_2
	Foobar	p_1
	Foobar	p_2
	Foobar	p_3
	p_1	Acme
	p_1	AAA
	p_1	Foobar
	p_1	p_1
	p_1	p_2
	p_1	p_3
	p_1	w_1
	etc.	

Subpart	x	y
	p_1	p_1
	p_1	p_2
	p_1	p_3
	p_1	w_1
	p_1	w_2
	p_1	w_3
	p_1	w_4
	p_2	p_2
	p_2	p_3
	p_2	w_1
	p_2	w_2
	p_2	w_3
	p_2	w_4
	p_3	p_3
	p_3	w_1
	p_3	w_2
	p_3	w_3
	p_3	w_4
	etc.	

The notion of a CWA answer is obviously intimately related to the negation operators of PLANNER (Hewitt [1972]) and PROLOG (Roussel [1975]) since in these languages, negation means "not provable" and the definition of $\overline{EDB}$ critically depends upon this notion. Clark [1978] investigates the relation between this notion of negation as failure and its truth functional semantics. The need for the CWA in deductive question-answering systems has been articulated in Nicolas and Syre [1974].

Notice that under the CWA, there can be no "gaps" in our knowledge about the domain. More formally, for each predicate sign P and each tuple of constant signs $\vec{c}$, either DB $\vdash P\vec{c}$ or $\overline{EDB} \vdash \overline{P\vec{c}}$ and since, under the CWA the data base is taken to be DB $\cup$ $\overline{EDB}$, we can always infer either $P\vec{c}$ or $\overline{P\vec{c}}$ from DB $\cup$ $\overline{EDB}$. Since there are no "knowledge gaps" under the CWA, it should be intuitively clear that indefinite CWA answers cannot arise, i.e. each minimal CWA answer to a query is of the form $\vec{c}$. The following result confirms this intuition.

Theorem 1.

Let $Q = \langle \vec{x}/\vec{\tau} \mid (E\vec{y}/\vec{\theta})W(\vec{x},\vec{y})\rangle$. Then every minimal CWA answer to Q is definite.

There is one obvious difficulty in directly applying the definition of a CWA answer to the evaluation of queries. The definition requires that we explicitly know $\overline{EDB}$ and, as Example 2 demonstrates, the determination of $\overline{EDB}$ is generally non trivial.

In any event, for non toy domains, $\overline{EDB}$ would be so large that its cxplicit representation would be totally unfeasible. Fortunately, as we shall see in the next section, there is no need to know the elements of $\overline{EDB}$ i.e. it is possible to determine the set of closed world answers to an arbitrary query Q by appealing only to the given data base DB.

QUERY EVALUATION UNDER THE CWA

It turns out that the CWA admits a number of significant simplifications in the query evaluation process. The simplest of these permits the elimination of the logical connectives $\wedge$ and $\vee$ in favour of set intersection and union respectively, as follows:

Theorem 2.

1. $\| < \vec{x}/\vec{\tau} \mid (E\vec{y}/\vec{\theta})(W_1 \vee W_2) > \|_{CWA} = \| < \vec{x}/\vec{\tau} \mid (E\vec{y}/\vec{\theta})W_1 > \|_{CWA} \cup$

$$\| < \vec{x}/\vec{\tau} \mid (E\vec{y}/\vec{\theta})W_2 > \|_{CWA}$$

2. $\| < \vec{x}/\vec{\tau} \mid W_1 \wedge W_2 > \|_{CWA} = \| < \vec{x}/\vec{\tau} \mid W_1 > \|_{CWA} \cap \| < \vec{x}/\vec{\tau} \mid W_2 > \|_{CWA}$

Notice that in the identity 2, the query must be quantifier free. Notice also that the identities of Theorem 2 fail under the OWA. To see why, consider the following:

Example 3

$|\tau| = \{a\}$

DB: Pa $\vee$ Ra

$Q = < x/\tau \mid Px \vee Rx >$

$\|Q\|_{OWA} = \{a\}$

but

$\| < x/\tau \mid Px > \|_{OWA} = \| < x/\tau \mid Rx > \|_{OWA} = \phi$

Example 4

$|\tau| = \{a,b\}$

DB: Pa $\vee$ Pb, Ra, Rb

$Q = < x/\tau \mid Px \wedge Rx >$

$$\|Q\|_{OWA} = \{a+b\}$$

but

$$\|< x/\tau \mid Px >\|_{OWA} = \{a+b\}$$

$$\|< x/\tau \mid Rx >\|_{OWA} = \{a,b\}$$

One might also expect that all occurrences of negation can be eliminated in favour of set difference for CWA query evaluation. This is indeed the case, but only for quantifier free queries and then only when DB $\cup$ $\overline{EDB}$ is consistent.

Theorem 3.

If W, W_1 and W_2 are quantifier free, and DB $\cup$ $\overline{EDB}$ is consistent, then

1. $\|< \vec{x}/\vec{\tau} \mid \overline{W} >\|_{CWA} = |\vec{\tau}| - \|< \vec{x}/\vec{\tau} \mid W >\|_{CWA}$

2. $\|< \vec{x}/\vec{\tau} \mid W_1 \wedge \overline{W}_2 >\|_{CWA} = \|< \vec{x}/\vec{\tau} \mid W_1 >\|_{CWA} - \|< \vec{x}/\vec{\tau} \mid W_2 >\|_{CWA}$

To see why Theorem 3 fails for quantified queries, consider the following:

Example 5

$|\tau| = \{a,b\}$

DB: Pa,a

Then $\overline{EDB} = \{\overline{P}a,b,\ \overline{P}b,a,\ \overline{P}b,b\}$

Let $Q(P) = < x/\tau \mid (Ey/\tau)Px,y >$

$Q(\overline{P}) = < x/\tau \mid (Ey/\tau)\overline{P}x,y >$

Then $\|Q(P)\|_{CWA} = \{a\}$

$\|Q(\overline{P})\|_{CWA} = \{a,b\} \neq |\tau| - \|Q(P)\|_{CWA}$

Notice also that Theorem 3 fails under the OWA.

By an atomic query we mean any query of the form $< \vec{x}/\vec{\tau} \mid (E\vec{y}/\vec{\theta})Pt_1,\ldots,t_n >$ where P is a predicate sign and each t is a constant sign, an x, or a y.

Theorems 2 and 3 assure us that for quantifier free queries, CWA query evaluation can be reduced to the Boolean operations of set intersection union and difference applied to atomic queries. However, we can deal with quantified queries by introducing the following projection operator (Codd [1972]):

Let $Q = < \vec{x}/\vec{\tau}, z/\psi | W >$ where W is a possibly existentially quantified formula, and $\vec{x}$ is the n-tuple $x_1,\ldots,x_n$. Then $||Q||_{CWA}$ is a set of (n+1)-tuples, and the projection of $||Q||_{CWA}$ with respect to z, $\pi_z ||Q||_{CWA}$, is the set of n-tuples obtained from $||Q||_{CWA}$ by deleting the (n+1)st component from each (n+1)-tuple of $||Q||_{CWA}$. For example, if $Q = < x_1/\tau_1, x_2/\tau_2, z/\psi | W >$ and if

$$||Q||_{CWA} = \{(a,b,c),(a,b,d),(c,a,b)\}$$

then

$$\pi_z ||Q||_{CWA} = \{(a,b),(c,a)\}$$

Theorem 4.

$$||< \vec{x}/\vec{\tau} | (E\vec{y}/\vec{\theta})W >||_{CWA} = \pi_{\vec{y}} ||< \vec{x}/\vec{\tau}, \vec{y}/\vec{\theta} | W >||_{CWA}$$

where $\pi_{\vec{y}}$ denotes $\pi_{y_1}\pi_{y_2}\cdots\pi_{y_m}$

Corollary 4.1

1. $||< \vec{x}/\vec{\tau} | (E\vec{y}/\vec{\theta})\overline{W}>||_{CWA} = \pi_{\vec{y}} ||< \vec{x}/\vec{\tau}, \vec{y}/\vec{\theta} | \overline{W} >||_{CWA}$

$$= \pi_{\vec{y}}(|\vec{\tau}| \times |\vec{\theta}| - ||< \vec{x}/\vec{\tau}, \vec{y}/\vec{\theta} | W >||_{CWA})$$

2. $||< \vec{x}/\vec{\tau} | (E\vec{y}/\vec{\theta})W_1 \wedge W_2 >||_{CWA} = \pi_{\vec{y}}(||< \vec{x}/\vec{\tau}, \vec{y}/\vec{\theta} | W_1 >||_{CWA}$

$$\cap\ ||< \vec{x}/\vec{\tau}, \vec{y}/\vec{\theta} | W_2 >||_{CWA})$$

Thus, in all cases, an existentially quantified query may be decomposed into atomic queries each of which is evaluated under the CWA. The resulting sets of answers are combined under set union, intersection and difference, but only after the projection operator is applied, if necessary.

Example 6.

$$||< x/\tau | (Ey/\theta)Px,y \vee Qx,y\ Rx,y >||_{CWA}$$

$$= ||< x/\tau | (Ey/\theta)Px,y||_{CWA} \cup \pi_y(||< x/\tau, y/\theta | Qx,y >||_{CWA}$$

$$\cap\ ||< x/\tau, y/\theta | Rx,y >||_{CWA})$$

$$\| < x/\tau | PxQx \vee \overline{R}x > \|_{CWA} = \| < x/\tau | Px > \|_{CWA}$$

$$\cap \| < x/\tau | Qx > \|_{CWA} \cup [|\tau| - \| < x/\tau | Rx > \|_{CWA}]$$

$$\| < x/\tau | (Ey/\theta) Px,y \vee Qx,y \overline{R}x,y > \|_{CWA}$$

$$= \| < x/\tau | (Ey/\theta) Px,y > \|_{CWA} \cup \pi_y (< x/\tau, y/\theta | Qx,y > \|_{CWA}$$

$$- \| < x/\tau, y/\theta | Rx,y > \|_{CWA})$$

In view of the above results, we need consider CWA query evaluation only for atomic queries.

We shall say that DB is <u>consistent with the CWA</u> iff DB $\cup$ $\overline{EDB}$ is consistent.

<u>Theorem 5.</u>

Let Q be an atomic query. Then if DB is consistent with the CWA, $\|Q\|_{CWA} = \|Q\|_{OWA}$.

Theorem 5 is the principal result of this section. When coupled with Theorems 2 and 3 and the remarks following Corollary 4.1 it provides us with a complete characterization of the CWA answers to an arbitrary existential query Q in terms of the application of the operations of projection, set union, intersection and difference as applied to the OWA answers to atomic queries. In other words, CWA query evaluation has been reduced to OWA atomic query evaluation. A consequence of this result is that we need never know the elements of $\overline{EDB}$. CWA query evaluation appeals only to the given data base DB.

<u>Example 7.</u>

We consider the inventory data base of Example 2. Suppose the following query:

$$Q = < x/Supplier | (Ey/Widget) Supplies\ x,y \wedge Subpart\ y,p_1 \wedge \overline{Supplies}\ x,p_3 >$$

Then

$$\| Q \|_{CWA} = \pi_y (\| Q_1 \|_{OWA} \cap \| Q_2 \|_{OWA}) \cap (|Supplier| - \| Q_3 \|_{OWA})$$

where

$$Q_1 = < x/Supplier, y/Widget | Supplies\ x,y >$$

$Q_2 = <$ x/Supplier, y/Widget | Subpart y,p_1 $>$

$Q_3 = <$ x/Supplier | Supplies x,p_3 $>$

It is easy to see that

$\|Q_1\|_{OWA}$ = {(Foobar,w_1), (Foobar,w_2), (Foobar,w_3), (Foobar,w_4), (AAA,w_3), (AAA,w_4), (Acme,w_1), (Acme,w_2)}

$\|Q_2\|_{OWA}$ = {(Acme,w_1), (Acme,w_2), (AAA,w_1), (AAA,w_2), (Foobar,w_1), (Foobar, w_2)}

$\|Q_3\|_{OWA}$ = {Acme}

whence

$\pi_y(\|Q_1\|_{OWA} \cap \|Q_2\|_{OWA})$ = {Foobar,Acme}

and

|Supplier| $-$ $\|Q_3\|_{OWA}$ = {Foobar,AAA}

Hence

$\|Q\|_{CWA}$ = {Foobar}.

ON DATA BASES CONSISTENT WITH THE CWA

Not every consistent data base remains consistent under the CWA.

Example 8.

DB: Pa $\vee$ Pb

Then, since DB $\not\vdash$ Pa and Db $\not\vdash$ Pb , $\overline{\text{EDB}} = \{\overline{\text{Pa}}, \overline{\text{Pb}}\}$ so that DB $\cup$ $\overline{\text{EDB}}$ is inconsistent.

Given this observation, it is natural to seek a characterization of those data bases which remain consistent under the CWA. Although we know of no such characterization, it is possible to give a sufficient condition for CWA consistency which encompasses a large natural class of data bases, namely the Horn data bases. (A data base is Horn iff every clause is Horn i.e. contains at most one positive literal. The data base of Example 2 is Horn.)

Theorem 6

Suppose DB is Horn, and consistent. Then DB $\cup$ $\overline{EDB}$ is consistent i.e., DB is consistent with the CWA.

Following van Emden [1977] we shall refer to a Horn clause with exactly one positive literal as a definite clause. If DB is Horn, let Δ(DB) be obtained from DB by removing all non definite clauses i.e., all negative clauses. The following Theorem demonstrates the central importance of these concepts:

Theorem 7

If $Q = \langle \vec{x}/\vec{\tau} \mid (E\vec{y}/\vec{\theta})W \rangle$ and DB is Horn and consistent, then $\|Q\|_{CWA}$ when evaluated with respect to DB yields the same set of answers as when evaluated with respect to Δ(DB). In other words, negative clauses in DB have no influence on CWA query evaluation.

Theorem 7 allows us, when given a consistent Horn DB, to discard all its negative clauses without affecting CWA query evaluation. Theorem 7 fails for non Horn DBs, as the following example demonstrates:

Example 9

DB: $\overline{P}a \vee \overline{R}a$, Ra $\vee$ Sa, Pa

Then DB $\vdash$ Sa

But Δ(DB) = {Ra $\vee$ Sa, Pa} and Δ(DB) $\nvdash$ Sa.

Let us call a data base for which all clauses are definite a definite data base.

Theorem 8

If DB is definite then DB is consistent.

Corollary 8.1

If DB is definite then

(i) DB is consistent

(ii) DB is consistent with the CWA.

Corollary 8.1 is a central result. It guarantees data base and CWA consistency for a large and natural class of data bases. Since the data base of Example 2 is definite we are assured that it is consistent with the CWA.

In van Emden [1977], he addresses, from a semantic point of view, the issues of data base consistency under the CWA. He defines the notion of a "minimal model" for a data base as the intersection of all its models. If this minimal model is itself a model of the data base, then the data base is consistent with the CWA. Van Emden goes on to point out some intriguing connections between minimal models and Scott's minimal fixpoint approach to the theory of computation, results which are elaborated in van Emden and Kowalski [1976].

THE CWA AND DATA BASE INTEGRITY

Theorem 7 has an interesting consequence with respect to data base integrity. In a first order data base, both intensional and extensional facts may serve a dual purpose. They can be used for deductive retrieval, or they can function as integrity constraints. In this latter capacity they are used to detect inconsistencies whenever the data base is modified. For example, if the data base is updated with a new fact then logical consequences of this fact can be derived using the entire data base. If these consequences lead to an inconsistency, the update will be rejected.

In general, it is not clear whether a given fact in a data base functions exclusively as an integrity constraint, or for deductive retrieval, or both (Nicolas and Gallaire [1978]). However, if the data base is both Horn and closed world, Theorem 7 tells us that purely negative clauses can function only as integrity constraints. Thus the CWA induces a partition of a Horn data base into negative and non-negative clauses. The latter are used only for deductive retrieval. Both are used for enforcing integrity.

SUMMARY

We have introduced the notion of the closed world assumption for deductive question-answering. This says, in effect, "Every positive statement that you don't know to be true may be assumed false". We have then shown how query evaluation under the closed world assumption reduces to the usual first order proof theoretic approach to query evaluation as applied to atomic queries. Finally, we have shown that consistent Horn data bases remain consistent under the closed world assumption and that definite data bases are consistent with the closed world assumption.

ACKNOWLEDGMENT

This paper was written with the financial support of the National Research Council of Canada under grant A7642. Much of this research was done while the author was visiting at Bolt, Beranek and Newman, Inc., Cambridge, Mass. I wish to thank Craig Bishop for his careful criticism of an earlier draft of this paper.

APPENDIX

Proofs of Theorems

Theorem 1.

Let $Q = < \vec{x}/\vec{\tau} \,|\, (E\vec{y}/\vec{\theta})W(\vec{x},\vec{y}) >$. Then every minimal CWA to Q is definite.

The proof requires the following two lemmas:

Lemma 1

Let $W_1,\ldots,W_r$ be propositional formulae. Then

$DB \cup \overline{EDB} \vdash W_1 \vee \ldots \vee W_r$

iff $DB \cup \overline{EDB} \vdash W_i$ for some i.

Proof: The "only if" half is immediate.

With no loss in generality, assume that the set of W's is minimal, i.e., for no i do we have

$$DB \cup \overline{EDB} \vdash W_1 \vee \ldots \vee W_{i-1} \vee W_{i+1} \vee \ldots \vee W_r .$$

Suppose W_1 is represented in conjunctive normal form, i.e. as a conjunct of clauses. Let $C = L_1 \vee \ldots \vee L_m$ be a typical such clause. Then $DB \cup \overline{EDB} \vdash L_i$ or $DB \cup \overline{EDB} \vdash \overline{L_i}$, i=1,...,m. Suppose the latter is the case for each i, $1 \leq i \leq m$. Then $DB \cup \overline{EDB} \vdash \overline{C}$ so that $DB \cup \overline{EDB} \vdash \overline{W_1}$. Since also $DB \cup \overline{EDB} \vdash W_1 \vee \ldots \vee W_r$, then $DB \cup \overline{EDB} \vdash W_2 \vee \ldots \vee W_r$ contradicting the assumption that the set of W's is minimal. Hence, for some i, $1 \leq i \leq m$, $DB \cup \overline{EDB} \vdash L_i$ so that $DB \cup \overline{EDB} \vdash C$. Since C was an arbitrary clause of W_1, $DB \cup \overline{EDB} \vdash W_1$ which establishes the lemma.

Lemma 2

$DB \cup \overline{EDB} \vdash (E\vec{y}/\vec{\theta})W(\vec{y})$ iff there is a tuple $\vec{d} \in |\vec{\theta}|$ such that $DB \cup \overline{EDB} \vdash W(\vec{d})$.

Proof: The "only if" half is immediate.

Since $DB \cup \overline{EDB} \vdash (E\vec{y}/\vec{\theta})W(\vec{y})$ then for tuples $\vec{d}^{(1)},\ldots,\vec{d}^{(r)} \in |\vec{\theta}|$

$$DB \cup \overline{EDB} \vdash \bigvee_{i \leq r} W(\vec{d}^{(i)})$$

The result now follows by Lemma 1.

Proof of Theorem 1:

Suppose, to the contrary, that for $m \geq 2$, $\vec{c}^{(1)}+\ldots+\vec{c}^{(m)}$ is a minimal CWA answer to Q. Then

$$DB \cup \overline{EDB} \vdash \bigvee_{i \leq m} (E\vec{y}/\vec{\theta})W(\vec{c}^{(i)},\vec{y})$$

i.e.,

$$DB \cup \overline{EDB} \vdash (E\vec{y}/\vec{\theta}) \bigvee_{i \leq m} W(\vec{c}^{(i)},\vec{y})$$

so by Lemma 2 there is a tuple $\vec{d} \in |\vec{\theta}|$ such that

$$DB \cup \overline{EDB} \vdash \bigvee_{i \leq m} W(\vec{c}^{(i)},\vec{d})$$

By Lemma 1, $DB \cup \overline{EDB} \vdash W(\vec{c}^{(i)},\vec{d})$ for some i whence $\vec{c}^{(i)}$ is an answer to Q, contradicting the assumed indefiniteness of $\vec{c}^{(1)}+\ldots+\vec{c}^{(m)}$.

Theorem 2.

1. $$\|\langle \vec{x}/\vec{\tau} \,|\, (E\vec{y}/\vec{\theta})(W_1 \vee W_2)\rangle\|_{CWA} = \|\langle \vec{x}/\vec{\tau} \,|\, (E\vec{y}/\vec{\theta})W_1\rangle\|_{CWA} \cup \|\langle \vec{x}/\vec{\tau} \,|\, (E\vec{y}/\vec{\theta})W_2\rangle\|_{CWA}$$

2. $$\|\langle \vec{x}/\vec{\tau} \,|\, W_1 \wedge W_2\rangle\|_{CWA} = \|\langle \vec{x}/\vec{\tau} \,|\, W_1\rangle\|_{CWA} \cap \|\langle x/\tau \,|\, W_2\rangle\|_{CWA}$$

Proof: 1. follows from Lemmas 1 and 2 and Theorem 1. The proof of 2. is immediate from Theorem 1.

Theorem 3.

If W, W_1 and W_2 are quantifier free, and $DB \cup \overline{EDB}$ is consistent, then

1. $$\|\langle \vec{x}/\vec{\tau} \,|\, \overline{W}\rangle\|_{CWA} = |\vec{\tau}| - \|\langle \vec{x}/\vec{\tau} \,|\, W\rangle\|_{CWA}$$

2. $$\|\langle \vec{x}/\vec{\tau} \,|\, W_1 \wedge \overline{W}_2\rangle\|_{CWA} = \|\langle \vec{x}/\vec{\tau} \,|\, W_1\rangle\|_{CWA} - \|\langle \vec{x}/\vec{\tau} \,|\, W_2\rangle\|_{CWA}$$

Proof: 1. The proof is by structural induction on W. Denote $\|\langle \vec{x}/\vec{\tau} \,|\, W\rangle\|_{CWA}$ by Q(W).

We must prove

$$Q(\overline{W}) = |\vec{\tau}| - Q(W) .$$

Case 1: W is $Pt_1,\ldots,t_m$ where P is a predicate sign and $t_1,\ldots,t_m$ are terms.

Suppose $\vec{c} \in Q(\overline{W})$. Let $\Pi(\vec{c})$ be $Pt_1,\ldots,t_m$ with all occurrences of x_i replaced by c_i. Then $DB \cup \overline{EDB} \vdash \overline{\Pi}(\vec{c})$. Since $DB \cup \overline{EDB}$ is consistent, $DB \cup \overline{EDB} \not\vdash \Pi(\vec{c})$, i.e. $\vec{c} \notin Q(W)$. Since $\vec{c} \in |\vec{\tau}|$, then $\vec{c} \in |\vec{\tau}| - Q(W)$, so that $Q(\overline{W}) \subseteq |\vec{\tau}| - Q(W)$. Now suppose $\vec{c} \in |\vec{\tau}| - Q(W)$. Then $\vec{c} \notin Q(W)$ so $DB \cup \overline{EDB} \not\vdash \Pi(\vec{c})$. But then $DB \cup \overline{EDB} \vdash \overline{\Pi}(\vec{c})$, and since $\vec{c} \in |\vec{\tau}|$, then $\vec{c} \in Q(\overline{W})$, so that $|\vec{\tau}| - Q(W) \subseteq Q(\overline{W})$.

Case 2: W is $U_1 \wedge U_2$.

Assume, for i=1,2 that $Q(\overline{U_i}) = |\vec{\tau}| - Q(U_i)$.

$$
\begin{aligned}
\text{Then } Q(\overline{W}) &= Q(\overline{U_1 \wedge U_2}) \\
&= Q(\overline{U}_1 \vee \overline{U}_2) \\
&= Q(\overline{U}_1) \cup Q(\overline{U}_2) \quad \text{by Theorem 2} \\
&= [|\vec{\tau}| - Q(U_1)] \cup [|\vec{\tau}| - Q(U_2)] \\
&= |\vec{\tau}| - [Q(U_1) \cap Q(U_2)) \\
&= |\vec{\tau}| - Q(U_1 \wedge U_2) \quad \text{by Theorem 2} \\
&= |\vec{\tau}| - Q(W)
\end{aligned}
$$

Case 3: W is $U_1 \vee U_2$.
The proof is the dual of Case 2.

Case 4: W is $\overline{U}$.

Assume that $Q(\overline{U}) = |\vec{\tau}| - Q(U)$. Since $Q(U) \subseteq |\vec{\tau}|$, it follows that $Q(U) = |\vec{\tau}| - Q(\overline{U})$. i.e. $Q(\overline{W}) = |\vec{\tau}| - Q(W)$.

$$
\begin{aligned}
Q(W_1 \wedge \overline{W}_2) &= Q(W_1) \cap Q(\overline{W}_2) \quad \text{by Theorem 2} \\
&= Q(W_1) \cap [|\vec{\tau}| - Q(W_2)] \text{ by 1.} \\
&= Q(W_1) - Q(W_2) \quad \text{since } Q(W_1) \subseteq |\vec{\tau}|.
\end{aligned}
$$

Theorem 4.

$$\|\langle \vec{x}/\vec{\tau} \,|\, (E\vec{y}/\vec{\theta})W(\vec{x},\vec{y})\rangle\|_{CWA} = \pi_{\vec{y}}\|\langle \vec{x}/\vec{\tau}, \vec{y}/\vec{\theta} \,|\, W(\vec{x},\vec{y})\rangle\|_{CWA}$$

where $\pi_{\vec{y}}$ denotes $\pi_{y_1}\pi_{y_2}\ldots\pi_{y_m}$

Proof:

Suppose $\vec{c} \in \| < \vec{x}/\vec{\tau} | (E\vec{y}/\vec{\theta})W(\vec{x},\vec{y}) > \|_{CWA}$

Then by definition

$$DB \cup \overline{EDB} \vdash (E\vec{y}/\vec{\theta})W(\vec{c},\vec{y})$$

whence by Lemma 2 there is a tuple $\vec{d} \in |\vec{\theta}|$ such that

$$DB \cup \overline{EDB} \vdash W(\vec{c},\vec{d})$$

i.e., $\vec{c},\vec{d} \in \| < \vec{x}/\vec{\tau}, \vec{y}/\vec{\theta} | W(\vec{x},\vec{y}) > \|_{CWA}$

i.e., $\vec{c} \in \Pi_{\vec{y}} \| < \vec{x}/\vec{\tau}, \vec{y}/\vec{\theta} | W(\vec{x},\vec{y}) > \|_{CWA}$

Now Suppose $\vec{c} \in \Pi_{\vec{y}} \| < \vec{x}/\vec{\tau}, \vec{y}/\vec{\theta} | W(\vec{x},\vec{y}) > \|_{CWA}$

Then for some tuple $\vec{d} \in |\vec{\theta}|$

$$\vec{c},\vec{d} \in \| < \vec{x}/\vec{\tau}, \vec{y}/\vec{\theta} | W(\vec{x},\vec{y}) > \|_{CWA}$$

so that $DB \cup \overline{EDB} \vdash W(\vec{c},\vec{d})$

i.e., $DB \cup \overline{EDB} \vdash (E\vec{y}/\vec{\theta})W(\vec{c},\vec{y})$

i.e. $\vec{c} \in \| < \vec{x}/\vec{\tau} | (E\vec{y}/\vec{\theta})W(\vec{x},\vec{y}) > \|_{CWA}$

Theorem 5.

Let Q be an atomic query. Then if DB is consistent with the CWA, $\|Q\|_{CWA} = \|Q\|_{OWA}$.

Proof: The proof requires the following:

Lemma 3

If DB is consistent with the CWA then every atomic query has only definite OWA answers.

Proof:

Let $Q = < \vec{x}/\vec{\tau} | (E\vec{y}/\vec{\theta})P(\vec{x},\vec{y}) >$ be an atomic query where $P(\vec{x},\vec{y})$ is a positive literal. Suppose, on the contrary, that Q has an indefinite OWA answer $\vec{c}^{(1)} + \ldots + \vec{c}^{(m)}$ for $m \geq 2$. Then

$$DB \vdash \bigvee_{i \leq m} (E\vec{y}/\vec{\theta})P(\vec{c}^{(i)},\vec{y}) \qquad (1)$$

and for no i, $1 \leq i \leq m$, is it the case that $DB \vdash (E\vec{y}/\vec{\theta})P(\vec{c}^{(i)},\vec{y})$.

Hence, for all $\vec{d} \in |\vec{\theta}|$, $DB \not\vdash P(\vec{c}^{(i)},\vec{d})$ i=1,...,m.

Thus $\overline{P}(\vec{c}^{(i)},\vec{d}) \in \overline{EDB}$ for all $\vec{d} \in |\vec{\theta}|$, i=1,...,m.

Hence, $DB \cup \overline{EDB} \vdash \overline{P}(\vec{c}^{(i)},\vec{d})$ for all $\vec{d} \in |\vec{\theta}|$, i=1,...,m and from

(1), $DB \cup \overline{EDB} \vdash \bigvee_{i \leq m} (E\vec{y}/\vec{\theta})P(\vec{c}^{(i)},\vec{y})$

i.e. $DB \cup \overline{EDB}$ is inconsistent, contradiction.

Proof of Theorem 5:

Let $Q = \langle \vec{x}/\vec{\tau} \,|\, (E\vec{y}/\vec{\theta})P(\vec{x},\vec{y}) \rangle$ where $P(\vec{x},\vec{y})$ is a positive literal. By Lemma 3 $\|Q\|_{OWA}$ consists only of definite answers. Now

$$\vec{c} \in \|Q\|_{OWA} \text{ iff } \vec{c} \in |\vec{\tau}| \text{ and } DB \vdash (E\vec{y}/\vec{\theta})P(\vec{c},\vec{y})$$
$$\vec{c} \in \|Q\|_{CWA} \text{ iff } \vec{c} \in |\vec{\tau}| \text{ and } DB \cup \overline{EDB} \vdash (E\vec{y}/\vec{\theta})P(\vec{c},\vec{y})$$

Hence $\|Q\|_{OWA} \subseteq \|Q\|_{CWA}$.

We prove $\|Q\|_{CWA} \subseteq \|Q\|_{OWA}$. To that end, let $\vec{c} \in \|Q\|_{CWA}$. Then $DB \cup \overline{EDB} \vdash P(\vec{c},\vec{d})$ for some $\vec{d} \in |\vec{\theta}|$.

If $DB \vdash P(\vec{c},\vec{d})$, then $\vec{c} \in \|Q\|_{CWA}$ and we are done.

Otherwise, $DB \not\vdash P(\vec{c},\vec{d})$ so that $\overline{P}(\vec{c},\vec{d}) \in \overline{EDB}$

i.e. $DB \cup \overline{EDB} \vdash P(\vec{c},\vec{d})$ and $DB \cup \overline{EDB} \vdash \overline{P}(\vec{c},\vec{d})$

i.e. DB is inconsistent with the CWA, contradiction.

Theorem 6.

Suppose DB is Horn, and consistent. Then $DB \cup \overline{EDB}$ is consistent, i.e. DB is consistent with the CWA.

Proof: Suppose, on the contrary, that $DB \cup \overline{EDB}$ is inconsistent. Now a theorem of Henschen and Wos [1974] assures us that any inconsistent set of Horn clauses has a positive unit refutation by binary resolution in which one parent of each resolution operation is a positive unit. We shall assume this result, without proof, for typed resolution*. Then since $DB \cup \overline{EDB}$ is an inconsistent

*Because all variables are typed, the usual unification algorithm (Robinson [1965]) must be modified to enforce consistency of types. Resolvents are then formed using typed unification. For details, see (Reiter [1977]).

Horn set, it has such a (typed) positive unit refutation. Since all clauses of $\overline{EDB}$ are negative units, the only occurrence of a negative unit of $\overline{EDB}$ in this refutation can be as one of the parents in the final resolution operation yielding the empty clause. There must be such an occurrence of some $\overline{U} \in \overline{EDB}$, for otherwise $\overline{EDB}$ does not enter into the refutation in which case DB must be inconsistent. Hence, DB $\cup \{\overline{U}\}$ is unsatisfiable, i.e. DB $\vdash$ U . But then $\overline{U}$ cannot be a member of $\overline{EDB}$, contradiction.

Theorem 7.

If $Q = < \vec{x}/\vec{\tau} \mid (E\vec{y}/\vec{\theta})W >$ and DB is Horn and consistent, then $\|Q\|_{CWA}$ when evaluated with respect to DB yields the same set of answers as when evaluated with respect to Δ(DB). In other words, negative clauses in PB have no influence on CWA query evaluation.

Proof: By Theorems 2, 3, and 4 CWA query evaluation is reducible to OWA evaluation of atomic queries whenever DB is consistent. Hence, with no loss in generality, we can take Q to be an atomic query. Suppose then that $Q = < \vec{x}/\vec{\tau} \mid (E\vec{y}/\vec{\theta})P(\vec{x},\vec{y}) >$, where $P(\vec{x},\vec{y})$ is a positive literal. Denote the value of $\|Q\|_{CWA}$ with respect to DB by $\|Q\|^{DB}_{CWA}$. Similarly, $\|Q\|^{\Delta(DB)}_{CWA}$, $\|Q\|^{DB}_{OWA}$, $\|Q\|^{\Delta(DB)}_{OWA}$. We must prove $\|Q\|^{DB}_{CWA} = \|Q\|^{\Delta(DB)}_{CWA}$. Since DB is consistent and Horn, so also is Δ(DB) so by Theorem 6, both DB and Δ(DB) are consistent with the CWA. Hence, by Theorem 5, it is sufficient to prove $\|Q\|^{DB}_{OWA} = \|Q\|^{\Delta(DB)}_{OWA}$. Clearly $\|Q\|^{\Delta(DB)}_{OWA} \subseteq \|Q\|^{DB}_{OWA}$ since $\Delta(DB) \subseteq DB$. We prove $\|Q\|^{DB}_{OWA} \subseteq \|Q\|^{\Delta(DB)}_{OWA}$. To that end, let $\vec{c} \in \|Q\|^{DB}_{OWA}$. Then DB $\vdash (E\vec{y}/\vec{\theta})P(\vec{c},\vec{y})$. Hence, as in the proof of Theorem 6, there is a (typed) positive unit refutation of DB $\cup \{\overline{P}(\vec{c},\vec{y})\}$. Since DB is Horn and consistent, $\overline{P}(\vec{c},\vec{y})$ enters into this refutation, and then only in the final resolution operation which yields the empty clause. Clearly, no negative clause other than $\overline{P}(\vec{c},\vec{y})$ can take part in this refutation i.e. only definite clauses of DB enter into the refutation. Hence we can construct the same refutation from $\Delta(DB) \cup \{\overline{P}(\vec{x},\vec{y})\}$ so that $\Delta(DB) \vdash P(\vec{c},\vec{y})$ i.e. $\vec{c} \in \|Q\|^{\Delta(DB)}_{OWA}$.

Theorem 8.

If DB is definite, then DB is consistent.

Proof: Every inconsistent set of clauses contains at least one negative clause.

REFERENCES

1. Clark, K.L. [1978] Negation as Failure, In *Logic and Data Bases* (H. Gallaire and J. Minker, Eds.), Plenum Press, New York, N.Y., 1978, 293-322.

2. Codd, E.F. [1972] Relational Completeness of Data Base Sub-languages, In *Data Base Systems* (R. Rustin, Ed.), Prentice-Hall, Englewood Cliffs, N.J., 1972, 65-98.

3. Henschen, L. and Wos, L. [1974] Unit Refutations and Horn Sets, *JACM 21*, 4 (October 1974), 590-605.

4. Hewitt, C. [1972] Description and Theoretical Analysis (Using Schemata) of PLANNER: A Language for Proving Theorems and Manipulating Models in a Robot, *AI Memo No. 251*, MIT Project MAC, Cambridge, Mass., April 1972.

5. Nicolas, J.M. and Gallaire, H. [1978] Data Bases: Theory vs. Interpretation, In *Logic and Data Bases* (H. Gallaire and J. Minker, Eds.), Plenum Press, New York, 1978, 33-54.

6. Nicolas, J. M. and Syre, J.C. [1974] Natural Question Answering and Automatic Deduction in the System Syntex, *Proceedings IFIP Congress 1974*, Stockholm, Sweden, August, 1974.

7. Reiter, R. [1977] An Approach to Deductive Question-Answering, *BBN Report No. 3649*, Bolt, Beranek and Newman, Inc., Cambridge, Mass., Sept. 1977.

8. Reiter, R. [1978] Deductive Question-Answering on Relational Data Bases, In *Logic and Data Bases* (H. Gallaire and J. Minker, Eds.), Plenum Press, New York, N.Y., 1978, 149-177.

9. Robinson, J. A. [1965] A Machine Oriented Logic Based on the Resolution Principle, *JACM 12*, (January 1965), 25-41.

10. Roussel, P. [1975] PROLOG: Manuel de Reference et d'Utilisation, Groupe d'Intelligence Artificielle, U.E.R. de Luminy, Universite d'Aix-Marseille, Sept. 1975.

11. van Emden, M. H. [1977] Computation and Deductive Information Retrieval, Dept. of Computer Science, University of Waterloo, Ont., Research Report CS-77-16, May 1977.

12. van Emden, M.H. and Kowalski, R.A. [1976] The Semantics of Predicate Logic as a Programming Language, *JACM 23*, (Oct. 1976), 733-742.

LOGIC FOR DATA DESCRIPTION

Robert Kowalski

Imperial College

London, England

ABSTRACT

Logic is useful both for describing static data bases as well as for processing data bases which change. Both the static and dynamic management of data bases depends upon the form of definitions: whether data is defined by means of complete if-and-only-if definitions or only by means of the if-halves, whether the only-if half of an if-and-only-if definition is stated explicitly or is assumed implicitly, and whether the only-if assumption is understood as a statement of the object language (in the data base) or as a statement of the meta-language (about the data base). Similar considerations apply to the processing of computer programs. When logic is used to describe information, the conventional distinction between data bases and programs no longer applies.

INTRODUCTION

Taking the relational view of data (Codd [1970]) as our point of departure, we shall compare the n-ary relation representation of n-column tables with the representation by means of binary relations. We shall argue for the utility, even in conventional data bases, of using logic to describe data by means of general laws.

We shall investigate the role of deduction in the processing of new information. In general, new information

(1) may be ignored, if it is already implied by the existing data;

(2) may replace existing data, if they are implied by it;

(3) may be added to the data base if it is independent from the existing data; or

(4) may contradict the data base, in which case consistency can be restored either by abandoning or suitably restricting some sentence which participates in the derivation of contradiction.

The last case is the most interesting. It is the case which applies both when data violate consistency constraints and when exceptions contradict general rules.

We shall argue that both the static and the dynamic management of a data base depends on whether the data is defined by full if-and-only-if definitions or only by the if-halves of the definitions. It depends also on whether the only-if half

A only-if B

of an if-and-only-if definition

A if-and-only-if B

is expressed in the object language

$A \rightarrow B$

or in the meta language

"The <u>only</u> way the conclusion B can be established is by using the sentence $A \leftarrow B$."

When logic is used to represent information, the distinction between data bases and programs disappears. General laws which describe the data function as programs which compute the data when it is required. The relational representation of data in data bases applies with similar benefits to the representation of data structures in programs. The same problem-solving techniques can be used both for data retrieval and program execution, for verifying data base integrity constraints and proving program properties, for updating and modifying data bases and developing programs by successive refinement.

Throughout this paper, except for if-and-only-if definitions, we restrict our attention to the use of Horn clauses. A compact introduction to clausal form and logic programming can be found in other papers (Gallaire et al. [1978]) in this volume.

DATA DESCRIPTION

In relational data bases (Codd [1970]), tables are regarded as relations. For each column of the table, there is a component in the corresponding relation. Thus to an n-column table there corresponds an n-ary relation. Rows of the table are n-tuples of the relation.

As a first approximation, tables and their corresponding relations can be represented in logic by means of assertions. The table

Course	Number	Name	Teacher	Level
	103	Programming	SJG	B.Sc.1
	1.4	Logic	RAK	M.Sc.

for example, can be represented by the assertions

Course(103,Programming,SJG,B.Sc.1)←

Course(1.4,Logic,RAK,M.Sc.)←

In this representation the n-ary relation is named by an n-ary predicate symbol.

An alternative representation, which is suggested by a comparison of logic and semantic networks (Deliyanni and Kowalski [1978]), uses binary predicate symbols.

Isa(103, Course)←

Name(103, Programming)←

Teacher(103, SJG)←

Level(103,B.Sc.1)←

Isa(1.4, Course)←

Name(1.4, Logic)←

Teacher(1.4, RAK)←

Level(1.4, M.Sc.)←

In this representation, each row of the table is named by a constant symbol (e.g. 103 or 1.4) which uniquely identifies the row. The entry i in column C, row r is represented by the assertion

C(r,i)←

Membership of a row r in the table T is also expressed by an assertion

Isa(r,T)←

We shall call the representation of tables by binary relations the binary representation, for short. The representation of n-column tables by n-ary relations will be called the n-ary representation. Notice that, in this terminology, the binary and n-ary representations are always different - even when n equals two.

It has been argued (Deliyanni and Kowalski [1978]) that the binary representation offers several advantages over the n-ary representation. Particularly important for data base applications are that unknown information can be more easily ignored and additional information can be more easily added. It can be argued, moreover, that binary relations offer a better model of data tables. Both binary and n-ary relations formalize the property of tables that the order of rows does not matter. In both cases, different ways of ordering the rows of a table correspond to different ways of ordering assertions. However, binary, but not n-ary, relations capture the additional property of tables that the order of columns does not matter. In the case of binary relations, interchanging the columns of a table corresponds to reordering assertions - which does not affect their meaning. In the case of n-ary relations, interchanging columns corresponds to interchanging components of the relation. The new n-ary relation is generally different from the original one.

Interchanging the last two columns of the Course-table, for example, gives rise to the same set of assertions in the binary representation but to different assertions

Course(103,Programming,B.Sc.1,SJG)←

Course(1.4,Logic,M.Sc.,RAK)←

in the n-ary representation.

More important, from a practical point of view, is that the binary representation is more useful than the n-ary representation for describing data by means of general laws. The direct translation into logic of the general rule

"RAK teaches all logic courses"

for example, is the statement

Teacher(x,RAK ← Name(x,Logic)

"If a course is a logic course than RAK teaches it"

in the binary representation. It can be shown that the same rule cannot be expressed by means of Horn clauses using the n-ary Course-predicate.

The argument in favour of binary relations is an oversimplification. The Marks-table

Marks	Student#	Course#	Grade

and the Plus relation

Plus(x,y,z)   x plus y is z

for example, are more naturally expressed by ternary relations than they are by binary ones. Reconciling these examples with the argument in favour of the binary representation is a problem for which we do not yet have a satisfactory solution. It is related to the problem of defining suitable normal forms for relational data bases (Codd [1970]).

The relational data base model views data as explicitly presented in tables. It provides no facilities for expressing general rules or for representing data computationally. The emphasis on explicit representation of data may be attributable in part to the unsuitability of the n-ary representation for expressing general laws. It may also be due to a belief that conventional data bases do not often conform to general rules. Our own empirical observations lead us to the opposite conclusion.

Conventional tables of data give direct access to information and are easy to read. Like abstract data structures in programming, they provide an abstract view of the data which does not go into the details of its derivation. It does not follow, however, that there are no general rules underlying the data or that making such rules explicit would not be useful. Tables of logrithms, interest tables, the periodic table of the elements, tyre pressure tables, tables of parts and their costs, tables of predicted astronomical phenomena are obvious examples of data tables which are governed by general rules. Depending upon the size of the tables and the complexity of the derivations, such data might be represented more efficiently by means of general rules which compute them when they are necessary rather than by means of tables which store them explicitly.

That general laws are not more apparent in conventionally presented data bases is a consequence, in part, of the computational difficulty of recognising patterns of data and of proposing general laws to account for them. Discovering general laws underlying explicitly presented data is the problem of induction. It is easier to avoid problem-solving altogether and to define the data by menas of general rules in the first place. It is easier, for example, to rule that

> "All compulsory, third year, undergraduate courses are held in room 145."
>
> "Radiators, with surface area ≤ 20 square feet, cost £ 2.50 per square foot."
>
> "Front tyre pressure, for the Renault 4, under normal driving conditions, is 18 psi for all brands of tyre, except Sempervite, for which it is 19 psi."
>
> "The university bookstore has a standing order of 10 copies per month of 'Sky and Telescope' magazine for every month of the academic year."

than it is to discover such laws in the unorganized, explicit form of the data. Moreover, if the data base system is able to understand both general laws and specific facts, then there is a positive incentive to organize the data by means of general rules. Using a general rule, instead of many specific facts, has the advantage that the data

is easier to input,
occupies less space, and
is easier to change.

What happens when the data is defined by means of both general laws and their exceptions will be treated later when we discuss the dynamic aspects of data bases.

Perhaps it is less surprising that conventional data base systems are unable to process general laws when we reflect that they are troublesome for administrators as well. The general rule

RAK requires an overhead projector for all his lectures

is an administrator's headache. It is easier to deal with tables of specific room-time-equipment requirements than it is to apply general rules. It is more convenient for the administrator if RAK constructs hiw own entries in the table and keeps the general rules to himself.

A number of proposals (Chang [1976], Kellogg et al. [1978] and Reiter [1978b]) have been made to extend the expressive power of conventional data bases by using logic to define part of the data implicitly while using the conventional data base system to store the rest explicitly. In some cases (Chang [1976]), the restriction is imposed that the implicitly defined relations be distinct from those which are explicitly stored. This restriction simplifies interfacing with the existing data base system, but it imposes unnatural constraints on the data. A typical relation needs to be defined both by means of specific facts and general laws. For example

"Course 203 is held in room 139."

"All compulsory third year undergraduate courses are held in room 145."

DATA QUERY LANGUAGES

The relational view of data provided by the relational data base model is intended more for data query languages than it is for data description. Although logic has been used to describe data and data base queries (Darlington [1969], Minker [1975], and Nicolas and Syre [1974]) independently of the relational data base model, until recently, the relational calculus was the only relational query language to be explicitly formulated in logic. Since then, van Emden [1979] has shown how query-by-example as developed by Zloof [1975] can be expressed in logic in a manner compatible with the n-ary representation of tables. Moreover, Pirotte [1978], using logic as a uniform formalism, has shown how to classify and construct a variety of relational query languages.

Although the relational model views tables as n-ary relations, it can be argued that the relational calculus treats them as binary relations. Given, for example, the tables

Course	Number	Name	Teacher	Level

Lecturer	Number	Name	Group	Office

the query

"What courses do theory group lecturers teach."

can be formulated in both the n-ary and the binary representations

```
←Ans(x)

 Ans(x) ← Course(x,y,u,v),Lecturer(z,u,theory,w)

 Ans(x) ← Isa(x,course),Teacher(x,u),Isa(z,lecturer),
          Name(z,u),Group(z,theory)
```

As van Emden [1979] argues, the n-ary representation is like the query-by-example formulation. The binary representation, on the other hand, is like the relational calculus formulation. The relational calculus would use unary type predicates instead of Isa-predicates and unary function symbols instead of binary predicates, i.e.,

```
Ans(x) ← Course(x), teacher(x) = u,
         Lecturer(z), name(z) = u,
         group(z) = theory
```

or more compactly

```
Ans(x) ← Course(x), teacher(x) = name(z),
         Lecturer(z), group(z) = theory .
```

The difference between the binary relations and the unary functions, however, is more syntactic than semantic.

INTEGRITY CONSTRAINTS

The use of logic to express integrity constraints on data is analogous to the use of logic to express properties of programs. There is no difference in principle between the integrity constraint

"All computer laboratories are held in the afternoons"

and the program property

"All permutations of a list have the same length as the list."

It is uneconomical to develop separate strategies for solving what is essentially the same problem: verifying integrity constraints in data bases and proving properties of programs.

Nicolas and Gallaire [1978] observe that the same general law can be used either as part of the definition of the data or as an integrity constraint. A similar remark holds for programs. When the program property is a specification of the program which can be executed efficiently then it can be used as a program itself.

Otherwise it serves as a property with respect to which a more efficient program needs to be consistent.

A DEPARTMENTAL DATA BASE

At Imperial College we are developing a general purpose logic programming system which we intend to use for data base purposes as well as for other programming tasks. The system accepts Horn clause programs including negative procedure calls. The procedure call

not - P

succeeds if all attempts (using Horn clauses) to execute P fail. Clark [1978] has shown that such an interpretation of negation is consistent with interpreting the Horn clauses which define the predicate symbol of P as the if-half of an if-and-only-if definition. The implementation uses PROLOG (Roussel [1975]), data structures but avoids its extralogical language features. Like PROLOG, it executes procedure calls top-down. However, it coroutines procedure calls, automatically tests for loops and, when failure occurs, analyzes bindings of variables in order to control backtracking more intelligently.

Below is a fragment of the data base we are designing to describe our department. A part of the data base concerned with the timetable of courses has been run as a pilot project by David Smith, an undergraduate in our department.

We use function symbols to construct names of individuals. For example, given the two-argument function symbol lect, the constant symbol RAK and the constant symbol 323, the expression lect(RAK,323) names that part of course 323 which consists of RAK's lectures. Similarly stgp(RAK,323) names the part which consists of RAK's study groups. In relational data bases, only integers and character strings are allowed as data objects. There are no data structures corresponding to those constructed using function symbols.

In order to increase readability, we use infix notation for relation symbols. For example, we write $(x \leq y)$ instead of $\leq(x,y)$. Similarly, we write

(x is occupied in y) instead of Occupied(x,y), etc.

(1) (x is occupied in y) ← (x teaches y)

(2) (x is occupied in y) ← (x attends y)

(3) (x is occupied in y) ← (x is member of committee y)

(4) (x teaches lect(x,y))←

(5) (x teaches stgp(x,y))←

(6) (the hour of lect(RAK,323) is 9:30)←

(7) (the hour of lect(RH,323) is 11:30)←

(8) (the hour of stgp(x,323) is 15:30)←

(9) (the day of lect(RAK,323) is MON)←

(10) (the day of lect(RH,323) is WED)←

(11) (the day of stgp(x,323) is MON)←

(12) (the term of x is II) ← (x is part of 323)

(13) (lect(x,y) is part of y)←

(14) (stgp(x,y) is part of y)←

(15) (the room of lect(x,323) is 139)←

(16) (the room of stgp(x,y) is 222) ← (Year of y is 3)

(17) (the building of x is Huxley) ← (x is part of y),(Dept of y is CCD)

(18) (Year of 323 is 3)←

(19) (Dept of 323 is CCD)←

(20) (AM attends lect(RAK,323))←

(21) (JCA attends lect(RH,323))←

(22) (x attends 323) ← (x is 3rd year student)

(23) (x attends lect(RH,323)) ← (x is M.Sc. student)

(24) (x attends y) ← (x attends z), (y is part of z)

(25) (Capacity of 139 is 50)←

(26) (Capacity of 222 is 25)←

(27) (total of 17 attend lect(RAK,323))←

(28) (total of 39 attend lect(RH,323))←

(29) (total of 16 attend stgp(x,323))←

We intend to use the system to test integrity constraints by defining conditions under which the data base would be inconsistent; for example, if an activity x is held in a room whose capacity is less than the number of people who attend it.

Inconsistent(x) ← (the room of x is y), (total of u attend x),
(capacity of y is v), (v < u)

The system can check for inconsistencies by periodically asking itself to find inconsistent activities via the query

←Inconsistent(x)

To make an appointment with RAK at 16.30 on Thursday in term II, a user of the data base might pose the query

← (RAK is occupied in x), (the hour of x is 16.30),
(the day of x is Thurs), (the term of x is II)

DATA BASES AND PROGRAMS

Conventional data base systems compensate for their inability to express general laws by interfacing with a conventional programming language. The programming language is host to the data base system and provides the possibility of defining data procedurally.

Logic, in contrast, serves as a single uniform language which can be used both for expressing data definitions, queries and integrity constraints, as well as for defining programs. Indeed, when both data bases and programs are formulated in logic, the distinction between them disappears. When logic is used to describe data bases, the general laws behave as procedures. If the procedures are executed bottom-up, then they generate explicit assertions corresponding to conventional tables of data. If the procedures are executed top-down, they compute the data when it is needed. Bottom-up and top-down execution are different but equivalent ways of using the same information (Kowalski [1976]).

When logic is used to define programs, procedures are represented by means of relations which hold between the input and the output. A given input-output relation might be defined both by assertions and by general laws. The general laws are often recursive and the assertions serve as the bases of the recursions. A logic program for symbolic integration, for example, like the one written in PROLOG by Bergman and Kanoui [1973], defines the relationship between a function and its integral both by means of assertions, such as

sin(x) is the integral of cos(x)
with respect to x

and by general laws, such as,

u+v is the integral of u'+v'
with respect to x
if u is the integral of u' with respect to x
and v is the integral of v' with respect to x.

The symbolic integration program is a clear example of a program which can also be regarded as a data base.

The distinction between data bases and programs becomes less distinct when we use assertions and procedures instead of terms as data structures. Instead of representing the sequence

a,c,b,a

by a term

cons(a,cons(c,cons(b,cons(a,nil))))

as in LISP, we can give it a name, say A, and represent it by the assertions

Item(A,o,a)←

Item(A,1,c)←

Item(A,2,b)←

Item(A,3,a)←

Length(A,4)←

where Item(x,y,z) means that

z is the yth item of x

and Length(x,y) means that

y is the length of x.

Instead of writing a conventional recursive program to reverse a sequence, for example,

Rev(x,y) ← Rev*(x,nil,y)

Rev*(nil,y,y)←

Rev*(cons(u,x),z,y) ← Rev*(x,cons(u,z),y)

we can write a non-recursive one. Here rev(x) names the sequence which is the reverse of x.

Item(rev(x),u,y) ← Item(x,v,y), Length(x,w),(u+v=w)

Length(rev(x),y) ← Length(x,y)

Programming with data represented by relations is programming at a higher level than with data represented by terms. It is especially suitable for representing data structures such as graphs. A program of this sort was written and run on our logic system at Imperial College by a high school student, Jacob Foguel, during the summer of 1977. The program systhesises organic compounds by searching for appropriate sequences of reactions. Chemical compounds are described by defining the atoms which belong to them and by defining the bonds between atoms. The information that

The bond b of strength s holds between the atoms a_1 and a_2 in the compound c

might be expressed by a single n-ary relationship

Bond(b,s,a_1,a_2,c)←

or by several binary relationships

(b belongs to c)←

(b bonds a_1)←

(b bonds a_2)←

(b has strength s)←

The initial compound is defined by means of assertions; the goal compound, by a goal statement; and compounds which result from chemical reactions, by general laws. The resulting data-base-program has the same structure as our formulation of the plan-formation problem in Kowalski [1974]. The initial and goal compounds correspond to initial and goal states. Chemical reactions correspond to actions which transform one state into another. Like actions, they are described by specifying (1) the preconditions which must hold true of a compound in order for the reaction to take place, (2) the new bonds which the reaction introduces and (3) the old bonds which the reaction destroys. A frame axiom is necessary to express that bonds which are not destroyed are retained in the new compound. As in plan-formation, the frame axiom states that most of the facts which hold true of a given situation remain true of the new situation which results from performing an action.

Similar to the chemistry program, but more important commercially, are the drug analysis programs written in PROLOG at the ministry of Heavy Industry in Budapest (Futo et al. [1978]). Those programs typically employ binary rather than more general n-ary relations because much of the information about a given drug might be unavailable.

The relational data base community is beginning to feel the need for programming languages which interface with data bases more smoothly than existing programming languages. The design of a programming language by Zloof [1977] based on query-by-example is a significant development in this direction. It is worth observing, however, that logic programming shows how to extend <u>any</u> query language to a programming language:

Simply add a procedure head P to a query $\leftarrow Q$

in order to turn it into a procedure $P \leftarrow Q$.

P consists of the name of a relation together with components which normally occur already in Q . In such a manner, for example, we can turn the query

"What is the number y of hours per year that teacher x teaches?"

into the definition

"The teaching load of x is y if y is the number of hours per year that teacher x teaches."

which behaves as a program for computing teaching loads, when it is interpreted top-down.

The extension of query languages to programming languages permits the definition of recursive procedures, since the same relation can be named in both the procedure head and the procedure body. The ability to pose queries of recursively defined relations is absent in the relational data base query languages, but is present in the programming languages which extend them. The inclusion of recursively defined relations remedies an incompleteness in the original query language (Codd [1972]).

THE DYNAMICS OF EVOLVING DATA BASES

Complex programs and data bases change with time. New information becomes available. Old information is refined. Inconsistencies appear and are resolved.

It is a common misconception to assume that a data base formulated in logic changes only monotonically by expanding its information content. The monotonicity assumption is the basis of Minsky's (Minsky [1975]) criticism of logic for representing human knowledge.

In general the attempt to assimilate new information into an existing data base can give rise to one of four situations.

(1) The existing data base already implies the new information. The implied information need not be added explicitly to the data base.

(2) The new information, together with part of the information in the data base, implies information in the other part of the data base. The implied information can be replaced by the new information.

(3) The new information is independent from the existing data. It is simply added to the data base.

(4) The new information is inconsistent with the existing data base. Consistency can be restored either by abandoning, or by suitably restricting some sentence which participates in, and is indispensible for, the proof of inconsistency.

In the first three cases the data base changes monotonically. In the first case the new data base has the same information content as the original one. In the second case it includes the information in the original data base. In the third case it necessarily contains more information.

It is the fourth case which is most interesting. It includes both the case in which the new data violates existing integrity constraints as well as the case in which it is an exception which contradicts existing general rules. When the data violates an integrity constraint, consistency is maintained by rejecting the data. When the data is an exception which contradicts a general rule, the data is added to the data base and consistency is preserved by adding the exception as an extra condition which restricts the application of the general rule.

The accommodation of exceptions to general rules in an evolving data base provides further support for the thesis that it is easier to construct general rules than it is to discover them. It is easy to add an exception to a general rule, transforming, for example,

(the room of lect(x,y) is 145) ← (Year of y is 3),
(y is compulsory)

into

(the room of lect(x,302) is 139)←

(the room of lect(x,y) is 145) ← (Year of y is 3),
(y is compulsory),
(y is different from 302).

It is more difficult to discover the restricted rule and its exceptions by analyzing the explicit form of the data.

Interactive timetabling is a potentially useful application of the dynamic evolution of a data base which describes the activities of a university department. Early versions of the timetable might be defined by ambitiously general laws.

"All 1st year lectures are held in room 314."

"All lectures with more than 50 students are held in room 145."

Conflicts which arise as inconsistencies among the general rules and the integrity constraints would be reconciled by abandoning or restricting the general rules. The search space of possible timetables defined by general rules and their exceptions would be more manageable than the conventional search space of all possible activity-time-place relations defined explicitly, without general rules.

THE MONTONICITY CRITICISM RECONSIDERED

Minsky's monotonicity criticism can be countered by drawing attention to the importance of reconciling inconsistency as a method of nonmonotonically changing a logic data base. The situation is somewhat complicated, however, by the fact that the statement which needs to be abandoned or restricted may be one which is neither explicitly stated nor logically implied by the original data base.

To illustrate the complications, suppose that we have a data base containing <u>only</u> the information

"A and B teach programming and are both professors."

Suppose that we change the data base by adding the new information

"C, who is different from A and B, also teaches programming."

It can be argued, at the informal, natural language level, that the statement

"Everyone who teaches programming is a professor."

holds in the original data base but not in the new one. Addition of the new information nonmonotonically alters the information content of the data base.

Let us see what happens when we try to formalize the argument in logic. If we assume, as we have until now, that the initial data base is represented by means of Horn clauses

Teaches(A,programming)←

Teaches(B,programming)←

Professor (A)←

Professor (B)←

then the statement

Professor(x) ← Teaches(x,programming)

is not a logical consequence of the data base and consequently is not invalidated by the new information

Teaches(C,programming)←

← C = A

← C = B

In order to justify the informal argument, it is necessary to assume that the only information there is to know about the Teaches-relation is the information given in the original data base. We need, at least, to add to the original data base the assumption

"Only A and B teach programming"

x = A, x = B ← Teaches(x,programming)

The statement that everyone who teaches programming is a professor is now a logical consequence of the augmented data base. The new information that C teaches programming is inconsistent with the data base and behaves as an exception to a general rule. Consistency is restored by adding the new information to the data base and by modifying the general rule, replacing it by the more restricted rule.

$$x = A,\ x = B,\ x = C \leftarrow \text{Teaches}(x,\text{programming})$$

The revised formulation in logic justifies the informal natural language argument. It makes explicit two considerations which are not stated in the informal argument: (1) the assumption that the only people who teach programming are those we know about in the data base, and (2) the automatic, consistency restoring, modification of the assumption, when we learn that another individual teaches programming.

In general, Minsky's monotonicity criticism of logic can be answered (1) by making explicit the assumption that all the information there is to know is already present in the data base and (2) by recognising that the acquisition of knowledge involves more than simply adding new statements to a data base.

THE IF-AND-ONLY-IF FORMULATION OF DEFINITIONS

The preceding discussion of the monotonicity criticism has brought out a potential difficiency in the use of Horn clauses to express definitions. Horn clauses typically express only the if-halves of definitions, which are completely expressed by using if-and-only-if. The clauses

$$\text{Teaches}(A,\text{programming}) \leftarrow$$

$$\text{Teaches}(B,\text{programming}) \leftarrow$$

for example, are only the if-half of the if-and-only-if definition

$$\text{Teaches}(x,\text{programming}) \leftrightarrow [x = A \lor x = B]$$

of the "who teaches programming" relation.

It is not always clear whether it is the full if-and-only-if definition or only the Horn clause if-half which is required for a given relation. This is largely because the if-half alone is sufficient for most useful purposes. It is sufficient, in particular, for computing, in the sense of logic programming, all instances of the relation. The only-if half of the definition may be needed, however, for proving properties of the relation or for answering queries containing universal quantifiers. For example, simply to determine

"Who teaches programming?"

the if-half of the if-and-only-if definition is sufficient. But to answer in the affirmative

"Are all the people who teach programming professors?"

the only-if half is necessary. The fact that the if-half of a definition is sufficient for computing instances of a relation, whereas the only-if half is necessary for proving properties, has been used by Clark and Tarnlund [1977] in their techniques for proving properties of Horn clause logic programs in first-order logic.

There are occasions when only the if-half of a definition is justified. Reiter [1978a] calls the assumption that the data base contains all the information there is to know the closed world assumption. The assumption that there may be more to know is called the open world assumption. Our proposal is to identify the closed world assumption with if-and-only-if definitions and the open world assumption with the if-halves. This has the advantage that the closed world and open world assumptions can be mixed in the same data base, applied to different relations or to different instances of the same relation. Reiter makes an interesting alternative proposal to formalize the closed world assumption by expressing that the individuals named in the data base are the only individuals there are.

Distinguishing whether it is the full if-and-only-if definition or only the if-half which is required is complicated by the fact that in natural language it is common to assert only the if-halves of definitions whether or not the only-if-halves are also intended Even logicians have sanctioned the unstated only-if assumption in the case of inductive definitions. When a logician gives the inductive definition of natural number, for example

(N1) o is a natural number

(N2) if x is a natural number then the successor of x is a natural number

if it is not explicitly stated that

(N3) the only natural numbers are those given by conditions (1) and (2)

it is none-the-less implicitly assumed.

Natural language carries the unstated only-if assumption to the extreme. The classical fallacy of logic is probably an example of this. Assume, for example,

B ← A .

Now suppose

B ←

We may safely conclude

A ←

if we assume that

A is the only condition under which B holds

that is, it was the if-and-only-if definition of B which was intended

B if-and-only-if A

when only the if-half was stated.

It is curious that natural language should be so careless about specifying whether or not the unstated only-if assumption is to be applied. This may be a consequence, in part, of the awkwardness of the if-and-only-if syntax. In data bases, the definition of a relation may be scattered in several places, intermingled with the definition of other relations. In such cases, an if-and-only-if expression at the head of the definition is not appropriate. A more convenient syntax might be one which follows the last clause of the definition and which states that no other clause of the definition follows - an explicit

"and that is all there are"

statement, for example.

AMBIGUITY OF ONLY-IF

The considerations we have just outlined are further complicated by the fact that the only-if assumption is ambiguous.

A if-and-only-if B

can be expressed wholely in the object-language

$A \leftarrow B$

$A \rightarrow B$

or the if-half can be expressed (using Horn clauses) in the object language

$A \leftarrow B$

and the only-if-half can be expressed in the meta-language

"The sentence 'A ← B' states the only conditions under which A holds."

The inductive definition of natural number is a simple example. The only-if-half can be expressed in the object language

$\mathrm{Numb}(x) \rightarrow \{x = o \vee \exists x' \; [x = \mathrm{succ}(x') \wedge \mathrm{Numb}(x')]\}$

or it can be expressed in the meta-language

"Sentences (N1) and (N2) state the only conditions under which x is a number."

An important practical consequence of the ambiguity is that arguments which need to appeal to the only-if-halves of definitions can be formalized either in the object language or in the meta-language. Proving properties of logic programs is one example. Constructing answers to queries containing negation or universal quantifiers is another.

Consider, for example, the Horn clause logic program which defines the Append relation on lists.

(A1) $\mathrm{Append}(\mathrm{nil}, x, x) \leftarrow$

(A2) $\mathrm{Append}(\mathrm{cons}(x,y), z, \mathrm{cons}(x,y')) \leftarrow \mathrm{Append}(y,z,y')$.

Here the expression Append(u,v,w) is to be read as expressing that the list w results from appending the list v to the list u.

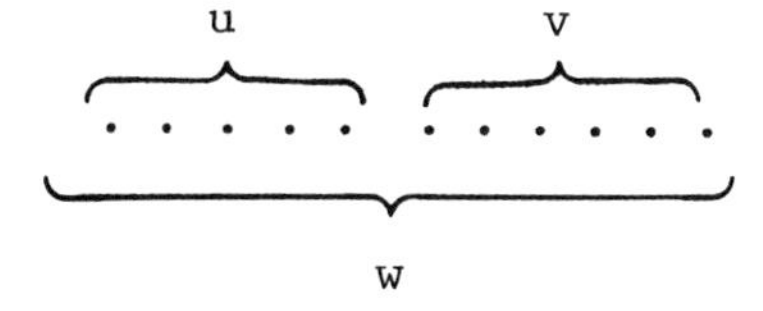

the property that

Append(x,nil,x) holds for all lists x

can be proved either in the object-language or in the meta-language.

The object-level proof is the one constructed by the method of Clark and Tarnlund [1977]. It expresses, in the object language, both the only-if-half of the definition

$$\text{Append}(u,v,w) \rightarrow \{[u = \text{nil} \wedge v = w] \vee \exists x,y,y'[u = \text{cons}(x,y) \wedge w = \text{cons}(x,y') \wedge \text{Append}(y,v,y')]\}$$

as well as the appropriate axiom schema for lists.

The alternative method is to prove the property in the meta-language. Assume that (A1) and (A2) are the only methods for establishing that the Append relation holds among lists. Suppose that A is any list. We need to demonstrate that

(A3) Append(A,nil,A)←

can be proved using only (A1) and (A2). The demonstration is by induction on the structure of A. If A is nil, then there is a one-step proof of (A3) using (A1) alone. If A is cons(B,A'), then by the induction hypothesis there is some n-step proof of

Append(A',nil,A')←.

By adding an extra step to the proof, using (A2), we obtain an n+1 step proof of

Append(cons(x,A'),nil,cons(x,A'))←

for any x and therefore a proof of (A3) in particular.

The object-level and meta-level proofs are similar. They contain similar steps and employ a similar induction on the structure of lists. Their logical status, however, is quite different.

Similar observations apply when the only-if assumption is necessary for answering data base queries. For example, given the Horn clause data base

Teaches(A,programming)←

Teaches(B,programming)←

Professor(A)←

Professor(B)←

the only-if assumption is necessary to justify a positive answer to the question

"Is everyone who teaches programming a professor?"

When the only-if assumption is expressed in the object-language, a typical goal-directed theorem prover reasons backward, trying to establish the goal both by asserting that some individual, say I, teaches programming and by trying to show that I is a professor. Reasoning forward from the assumption that I teaches programming, it uses the only-if assumption to conclude that I is A or I is B. Considering each case in turn, it uses the definition of the Professor relation to show that I is a professor in any case.

When the only-if assumption is expressed in the meta-language, the meta-level theorem prover uses the Horn clause if-half of the definition of the Teaches-relation in order to find all answers to the question

"Who teaches programming?"

$\leftarrow$ Teaches(x,programming)

for each x=i in the set of all solutions, it uses the Horn clauses defining the Professor-relation to show that

i is a professor

$\leftarrow$ Professor(i) .

If it succeeds in doing so, it concludes that everyone who teaches programming is a professor.

The two proofs have in common that they both show that everyone who teaches programming is a professor by finding all individuals who teach programming and showing that each of them is a professor. The object-level proof uses the only-if half of the definition to derive a nonHorn clause disjunction which identifies all the individuals who teach programming

$$I = i_1 \vee I = i_2 \vee \ldots \vee I = i_n \ .$$

The meta-level proof uses the Horn clause if-half of the definition to find the set of all solutions to the problem of finding an individual who teaches programming

$$\{i_1, i_2, \ldots, i_n\} \ .$$

Both proofs use the Horn clause if-half of the definition of the Professor-relation to show that each i_j (who teaches programming) is a professor.

Given the Horn clause if-half of a relation, the only-if assumption is necessary to show that some instance P of the relation does not hold

$\leftarrow$ not-P .

The proof can be carried out at the object-level by using the only-if half of the relation to show that none of the conditions which might imply P hold. Or it can be carried out at the meta-level by showing that the search space, determined by all the ways of using the Horn clause definition of the relation to establish P, contains no solutions. Clark [1978] has shown that for any meta-level proof of not-P, of a sufficiently simple kind (using no induction, for example), there exists a structurally similar object-level proof using the object-level only-if half of the definition. Presumably, Clark's proof can be generalized to cover situations requiring induction. If the meta-level proof uses an induction argument to show that an infinite search space contains no solutions, the corresponding object-level proof would use an induction axiom stated in the object language.

CONCLUSIONS

The use of logic for data description abolishes the distinction between data bases and programs. The same techniques apply to problems in both fields. Strategies which apply to the execution of programs apply also to the retrieval of answers to data base queries. Methods for proving properties of programs apply both to verification of integrity constraints and to retrieval of answers to queries involving negation and universal quantifiers. Procedures for maintaining dynamically evolving data bases apply to the evolutionary development and modification of programs.

The need for a single uniform formalism for describing both data bases and programs becomes unarguable once we recognize the existence of a continuum with deterministic programs and explicitly described data bases on opposite extremes. Programs for symbolic integration, synthesis of organic compounds, drug analysis and natural language understanding lie at intermediate positions along the continuum. Conventional formalisms may be suitable for conventional data bases; but logic is useful both for conventional data bases and programs as well as for the computational data bases which lie between the extremes.

ACKNOWLEDGMENTS

I am grateful for the useful discussions I have had with Keith Clark, Bernard Marsh and Marek Sergot. This research was supported by the Science Research Council and aided, in its later stages, by a visiting appointment at the University of Syracuse.

REFERENCES

1. Bergman, M. and Kanoui, H. [1973] Application of Mechanical Theorem Proving to Symbolic Calculus, *Third International Symposium on Advanced Computing Methods in Theoretical Physics*, C.N.R.S., Marseille, June 1973.

2. Chang, C. L., [1976] DEDUCE: A Deductive Query Language for Relational Data Bases, In *Pattern Recognition and Artificial Intelligence* (C. H. Chen, Ed.), Academic Press, Inc., New York, 1976, 108-134.

3. Clark, K. L., Tarnlund, S. A. [1977] A First Order Theory of Data and Programs, *Proceedings IFIP 77*, North-Holland, 1977, 939-944.

4. Clark, K. L. [1978] Negation as Failure, In *Logic and Data Bases* (H. Gallaire and J. Minker, Eds.), Plenum Press, New York, 1978, 293-322.

5. Codd, E. F. [1970] A Relational Model for Large Shared Data Bases, *CACM 13*, 6 (June 1970), 377-387.

6. Codd, E. F. [1972] Relational Completeness of Data Base Sublanguages, In *Data Base Systems* (R. Rustin, Ed.), Prentice-Hall, Englewood Cliffs, N.J., 1972, 65-98.

7. Darlington, J. L. [1969] Theorem Proving and Information Retrieval, In *Machine Intelligence 4* (B. Meltzer and D. Michie, Eds.), American Elsevier Publishing Co., Inc. New York, 1969.

8. Deliyanni, A. and Kowalski, R. A. [1977] Logic and Semantic Networks, Department of Computing and Control Research Report, Imperial College, London, June 1977. Also *Proceedings of the Workshop on Logic and Data Bases*, Toulouse, November 1977.

9. Futó, I., Szeredi, P., and Darvas, F. [1977] Some Implemented and Planned PROLOG Applications, *Workshop of Logic and Data Bases*, Toulouse, November 1977.

10. Gallaire, H., Minker, J. and Nicolas, J.M. [1978] An Overview and Introduction to Logic and Data Bases, In *Logic and Data Bases* (H. Gallaire and J. Minker, Eds.), Plenum Press, New York, 1978, 3-30.

11. Gallaire, H. and Minker, J., Editors [1978] *Logic and Data Bases*, Plenum Press, New York, 1978.

12. Green, C. [1969] Theorem-Proving by Resolution as a Basis for Question Answering Systems, In *Machine Intelligence 4* (B. Meltzer and D. Michie, Eds.), American Elsevier Publishing Co., Inc., New York, 1969, 183-205.

13. Kellogg, C., Klahr, P., Travis, L. [1978] Deductive Planning and Pathfinding for Relational Data Bases, In *Logic and Data Bases* (H. Gallaire and J. Minker, Eds.), Plenum, N.Y., 179-200.

14. Kowalski, R. A. [1974] Logic for Problem-Solving, *Memo No. 75*, Department of Computational Logic, University of Edinburgh, 1974.

15. Kowalski, R. A. [1976] Algorithm = Logic + Control, Research Report, Department of Computing and Control, Imperial College, London, 1976.

16. Minker, J. [1975] Performing Inferences over Relational Data Bases, *Proceedings of 1975 ACM SIGMOD International Conference on Management of Data*, 1975, 79-91.

17. Minsky, M. [1975] A Framework for the Representation of Knowledge, In *The Psychology of Computer Vision* (P. Winsont, Ed.), McGraw Hill, New York, 1975, 211-280.

18. Nicolas, J. M. and Syre, J. C. [1974] Natural Question Answering and Automatic Deduction in the System SYNTEX, *Proceedings IFIP Congress 1974*, North Holland Publishing Co., Stockholm, Sweden, August 1974.

19. Nicolas, J. M. and Gallaire, H. [1978] Data Base: Theory vs. Interpretation, In *Logic and Data Bases* (H. Gallaire and J. Minker, Eds.), Plenum Press, New York, 1978, 33-54.

20. Pirotte, A. [1978] High Level Data Base Query Languages, In *Logic and Data Bases* (H. Gallaire and J. Minker, Eds.), Plenum Press, New York, 1978, 409-436.

21. Reiter, R. [1978] On Closed World Data Bases, In *Logic and Data Bases*(H. Gallaire and J. Minker, Eds.), Plenum Press, New York, 1978, 55-76.

22. Reiter, R. [1978] Deductive Question-Answering on Relational Data Bases, In *Logic and Data Bases* (H. Gallaire and J. Minker, Eds.), Plenum Press, New York, 1978, 149-177.

23. Roussel, P. [1975] PROLOG: Manuel de Reference et d'Utilisation, Groupe d'Intelligence Artificielle, U.E.R. de Luminy, Universite d'Aix-Marseille, Sept. 1975.

24. van Emden, M. H. [1979] Computation and Deductive Information Retrieval, In *Formal Description of Programming Concepts* (E. Neuhold, Ed.), North-Holland, to be published.

25. Zloof, M. M. [1975] Query-by-Example, *Proceedings AFIPS 1975 NCC, Vol 44,* AFIPS Press, Montvale, N. J., 1975, 431-348.

26. Zloof, M. M. and deLong, S. P. [1977] The System for Business Automation (SBA): Programming Language, *CACM 20,* 6 (June 1977), 385-396.

KNOWLEDGE REPRESENTATION AND DEDUCTION

AN EXPERIMENTAL RELATIONAL DATA BASE SYSTEM BASED ON LOGIC

(Or Clause Encounters of a Logical Kind)

Jack Minker

University of Maryland

College Park, Maryland

ABSTRACT

An experimental relational data base system whose design is based upon logic is described. Logic was chosen as the design principle since it is a useful way in which to represent knowledge, and it forms a mathematical basis both for reasoning with data and for maintaining the integrity of a data base. The latter is a needed capability of data base systems as one wants to derive new facts from facts listed explicitly in the data base.

The system is designed to handle large data bases and for general problems in theorem proving. The data base aspect of the work is emphasized in this paper.

Queries to the system consist of well-formed formulae in the predicate calculus. Knowledge in the system is stored in a semantic network. The semantic network consists of explicit facts stored in the extensional data base; general axioms, which permit new facts to be derived, and are stored in the intensional data base, the semantic graph which provides information sometimes represented as unary relations; the dictionary which defines constant symbols; and the semantic form space used for integrity constraints and testing inputs.

A description is provided of the system. The manner in which the extensional and intensional data bases are accessed, how deductive search is controlled, and the manner in which written and spoken natural language output is achieved are described in the paper.

INTRODUCTION

A comprehensive, integrated data base system based on mathematical logic has been developed and is described in this paper. The rationale for the system and the reason for basing the work on logic is described.

A major objective of the work was to develop a system from which one could deduce facts that are implicit within the data base. It is, in general, not practical or even possible to make explicit all relationships that might exist within a system. Doing so might take an inordinate amount of storage for answering queries that arise infrequently. It is natural that when one is deducing facts from a system, that logic be used. A great deal is known about logic and how it can be used to perform deductive searches. This work can be carried over to data base systems.

The system developed and described in this paper is termed MRPPS 3.0 (Maryland Refutation Proof Procedure System). It is implemented on the UNIVAC 1108 in a structured programming language SIMPL (Basili and Turner [1976]). Queries to the system can be any well-formed formula in the predicate calculus. The system is an outgrowth of MRPPS 2.0, which has been described by Minker et al. [1973,1974], and by McSkimin and Wilson [1974]. The current system is a major modification of the previous work so as to make it more useful for handling large data bases.

The system described in this paper differs from the MRPPS 2.0 system in three distinct ways. Whereas the first system is based on a one-sorted logic, the current system is based on a many-sorted logic. Facts and general axioms are grouped together in sets in what is referred to as Π-σ notation, rather than retaining facts and general axioms as individual statements. Finally, two inference mechanisms which have been shown to be useful for data base deductive searches are used, whereas MRPPS 2.0 had many inference mechanisms.

BACKGROUND

Many-Sorted Logic

In the first-order predicate calculus, one is dealing with predicates that can take on arguments. The arguments can be arbitrary terms, where a term is defined recursively to consist of a variable, a constant, or a function whose arguments are terms. The language of the predicate calculus consists of well-formed formulae, formed by combining predicates with the logical symbols of conjunction ($\wedge$), disjunction ($\vee$), negation ($\sim$), implication ($\rightarrow$), and equivalence ($\leftrightarrow$), and by quantifying over these formulae using the symbols $\exists$ (there exists) and $\forall$ (for all). In such a language there is a single domain. Hence, first order predicate calculus is a one-sorted logic. A precise definition of first-order logic may be found in Enderton [1972]. Typical statements in such a language are:

$$(\forall x,y,z,w,t)(\text{MANUFACTURES}(x,y,z) \wedge \text{USES}(w,y,t) \rightarrow (\text{SUPPLIES}(x,w,y))$$

$$(\forall x,y)(\text{PARENT}(x,y) \rightarrow \text{MALE}(x) \vee \text{FEMALE}(x))$$

$$(\forall x,y)(\text{FATHER}(x,y) \rightarrow (\exists z)\text{MOTHER}(z,y)) \; .$$

Semantically anomalous sentences can be formed in first-order logic which have no basis in the real world. Thus, for example, if the color blue is a term and the fruit banana is a term, a well-formed formula could be

FATHER(BLUE,BANANA),

which states that "blue is the father of banana."

One can avoid such anomalies by considering a many-sorted logic. In such a logic, predicates and terms can belong to different universes. Quantifiers can be restricted to range over these different universes. Thus, if one wanted to restrict the arguments of MANUFACTURES to companies, items manufactured, and the location of the company, and the arguments of USES to the name of the company, the item used, and the location of the company, then one could write

$$(\forall x_c)(\forall y_I)(\forall z_L)(\forall w_c)(\forall t_L)(\text{MANUFACTURES}(x_c,y_I,z_L) \wedge \text{USES}(w_c,y_I,t_L) \rightarrow \text{SUPPLIES}(x_c,w_w,y_I)),$$

where x_c and w_c range over names of companies, y_I ranges over items, and z_L and t_L range over names of locations.

In addition to eliminating many nonsense sentences, restricting arguments of predicates to belong to specified sorts constrains deductive search by not allowing formulae to interact as freely as they might in a one-sorted logic. McSkimin and Minker [1977] describe how interactions are constrained, and this paper does not expand upon this use of a many-sorted logic. It should be noted, however, that everything that can be done using a many-sorted logic can be done using a one-sorted logic (Enderton [1972]). The MRPPS 3.0 System is based on a many-sorted logic.

Clause Form

In first order logic one has the logical connectives and quantifiers as defined in the previous section. It is possible to transform a well-formed formula into another formula in prenex normal form. The transfomation is described in Chang and Lee [1973], and is truth preserving. Prenex-normal form can be written as, QM , where Q consists of all of the quantifiers in the formula ($\exists$ and $\forall$), while M is quantifier-free and only contains the logical connectives $\wedge$, $\vee$, $\sim$ and $\rightarrow$.

By introducing what have been called Skölem functions, one can eliminate existential quantifiers. The resulting formula is then only universally quantified. One can eliminate the universal quantifiers since all variables are known to be universally quantified. Note that in a many-sorted logic, universally quantified variables can be thought of as ranging over some non-empty domain corresponding to the sort of the variable. For example, the formula

$$(\forall x)(\forall y)(\exists z)(P(x,y) \wedge (Q(y,x) \rightarrow R(z,x,y))$$

may be written as

$$(\forall x)(\forall y)(P(x,y) \wedge Q(y,x) \rightarrow R(f(x,y),x,y)),$$

and finally as

$$P(x,y) \wedge Q(y,x) \rightarrow R(f(x,y),x,y).$$

The function f(x,y) is termed a Skölem function and provides the value of z whose existence is assured by x and y . Although the system described in this paper accommodates Skölem functions, we do not need them for its description in this paper.

It is further convenient to transform the quantifier free form into a conjunction of clauses. Let $\mathcal{D}(x_1,\cdots,x_n)$ be a conjunction of literals, and $\mathcal{C}(x_1,\cdots,x_m)$ be a disjunction of literals, then by a <u>clause</u> it is meant an expression of the form

$$\mathcal{D}(x_1,x_2,\cdots,x_n) \rightarrow \mathcal{C}(x_1,\cdots,x_m) .$$

Thus,

$$(1) \quad P(x,y) \wedge Q(y,z) \wedge R(x,y,z) \rightarrow M(x,z) \vee T(z,y)$$

is a clause. This form can be written equivalently as a disjunction of literals,

(2) $\sim P(x,y) \vee \sim Q(y,z) \vee \sim R(x,y,z) \vee M(x,z) \vee T(z,y,x)$.

Expressions (1) or (2) are referred to as clauses. A clause consisting of a disjunction of literals in which there is only one positive literal is termed a Horn clause. Most applications of data bases contain only Horn clauses. The positive literal in a Horn clause may be considered to be defined by the negative literals. In the implication form of a Horn clause, the negative literals become positive literals and are on the left hand side of the implication, while the positive literal remains a positive literal and is on the right hand side of the implication. Hence, the left hand literals imply a single positive literal. In the non-Horn clause case, the disjunction of several positive literals appear on the right hand side. Hence, literals on the left of the implication imply the disjunction of several literals, and ambiguities may arise. In conventional data bases one does not expect such ambiguities, as one generally knows the rules by which one can derive a single positive literal.

As will be noted in the section Relations and Π-σ Notation, the MRPPS 3.0 system assumes a particular form of clauses termed Π-σ notation. We defer this particular notation to the description of the system.

Relations and Virtual Relations

A relation is a set of n-tuples whose arguments belong to different domains. In a relational data base, relations can be explicit and may be thought of as being stored in tables. However, it is not always possible to list all of the n-tuples for a relation. Consider the relation ISANINTEGER . This relation consists of a infinite set $\{\cdots,-2,-1,0,1,2,\cdots\}$, and cannot be stored in a finite table.

One can _partially_ specify a relation, by listing only some n-tuples, while others can be generated in some fashion. We shall refer to such relations as _virtual relations_. Following Carnap [1958], we refer to the set of all n-tuples of a relation to be the _extension_ of the relation. Such n-tuples are stored in what shall be referred to as the _extensional data base_ (EDB). Entries in the EDB are unit, fully instantiated clauses. An n-tuple will be referred to as a relational statement. A relation is a _virtual relation_ if it is not an extensional relation, and appears unnegated in a clause (form (2), section - Clause Form). The clause therefore specifies the rules by which virtual relations may be made explicit. That is, how one may determine their extension. Virtual relations are also defined by clauses and are stored in what shall be referred to as _intensional data base_ (IDB). A clause that defines a virtual relation may contain constants and variables in the terms of the arguments of the relations in the clause.

ELEMENTS OF THE MRPPS 3.0 SYSTEM

MRPPS 3.0 is a comprehensive system intended for experimental work with deduction for relational systems. It has in input language, a definition capability, a deductive mechanism, an index structure to access extensional relations and virtual relation definitions, and can provide natural language answers and reasons in written or spoken form.

The current version of MRPPS 3.0 is outlined in Figure 1. Only the major elements of the system are depicted there. In this section a brief description of the role of each block is provided. In subsequent sections, portions of the system are described in further detail. As will be noted in the text, other papers have been written which provide descriptions of portions of the system.

Eight major blocks are depicted in Figure 1. Although there are a number of different input types permitted in the system, only three types are described in the figure. Relational statements are specified to the system as assertions and are entered as shown in Block 1. Virtual relation definitions are specified by clauses and are also entered in Block 1. A relational statement is also a clause as defined in the Background Section. Inputs to the system from Block 1 are, therefore, clauses.

Assertions are stored in the extensional data base (EDB) while clauses which define virtual relations are stored in the intensional data base (IDB). Before this can be done, they must be tested to determine if they are well-formed with respect to the model of the knowledge stored in the Semantic Network (Block 6). If they are not well-formed, they are rejected and the user is informed of the reason for the rejection. Testing for well-formedness is accomplished in the processing associated with Block 3. An assertion such as MANUFACTURES(BANANAS,LATHES,MARYLAND) would be rejected from the system if the model required that the first argument of the specified relation be a company and it is known that BANANAS is a fruit.

Queries to the system consist of a conjunction of clauses. It is assumed that the user has trnasformed the input to clause form. Query clauses are also tested against the model of knowledge contained in the Semantic Network to determine if they are well-formed before an attempt is made to answer tham. Thus, if the query asks for an individual who is both the father and the mother of a particular person, and the model specifies that such an individual cannot exist, it will be rejected since an individual cannot be both a male and a female. A query may not satisfy the model, but, if suitably modified it could. When this arises, the system automatically makes the changes. Thus, if the query is "who is the father of ABLE", and a sort has not been provided for the argument corresponding to the father of ABLE in the relational statement, then the system will automatically restrict the argument to be from the domain of male individuals.

The Deductive Search Mechanism is depicted in Block 4. Its primary function is to control the search for an answer to a query. Queries may contain requests for relational statements that are explicit and are stored in the EDB, or for relational statements that are virtual and whose definitions are in the IDB. The deductive search mechanism is described in the section entitled Deductive Search Mechanism.

All knowledge within the system is contained in the Semantic Network shown in Block 6. Relational statements, in the form of assertions are contained in the network as well as definitions of virtual relations. In addition it contains a dictionary which defines elements in the system; a semantic graph which defines semantic categories and how they interrelate (semantic categories represent the sorts in the system); and a semantic form space which provides rules to determine the well-formedness of inputs. A description of the Semantic Network is provided in the section - The Semantic Network.

Access to the Semantic Network is through the Knowledge Base Index shown in Block 5. The Knowledge Base Index permits rapid access to entries in the EDB, the IDB, and the semantic form space. An overview of the index structure is provided in the section - Knowledge Base Index.

The Deductive Search Mechanism concludes its search when an answer to a query is found. However, the precise answer to the query or the reasons for the answer are embedded in the proof graph produced. Answers to queries and reasons may be provided to the user in three forms: symbolic, natural language written statements or natural language spoken output. The symbolic output is obtained by an answer/reason algorithm and is discussed in the section entitled Proof Tree in Symbolic Form. The written and spoken translation of the answer and reasons is discussed in the sections Natural Language Proof and Reason Output and Voice Proofs and Reasons, respectively.

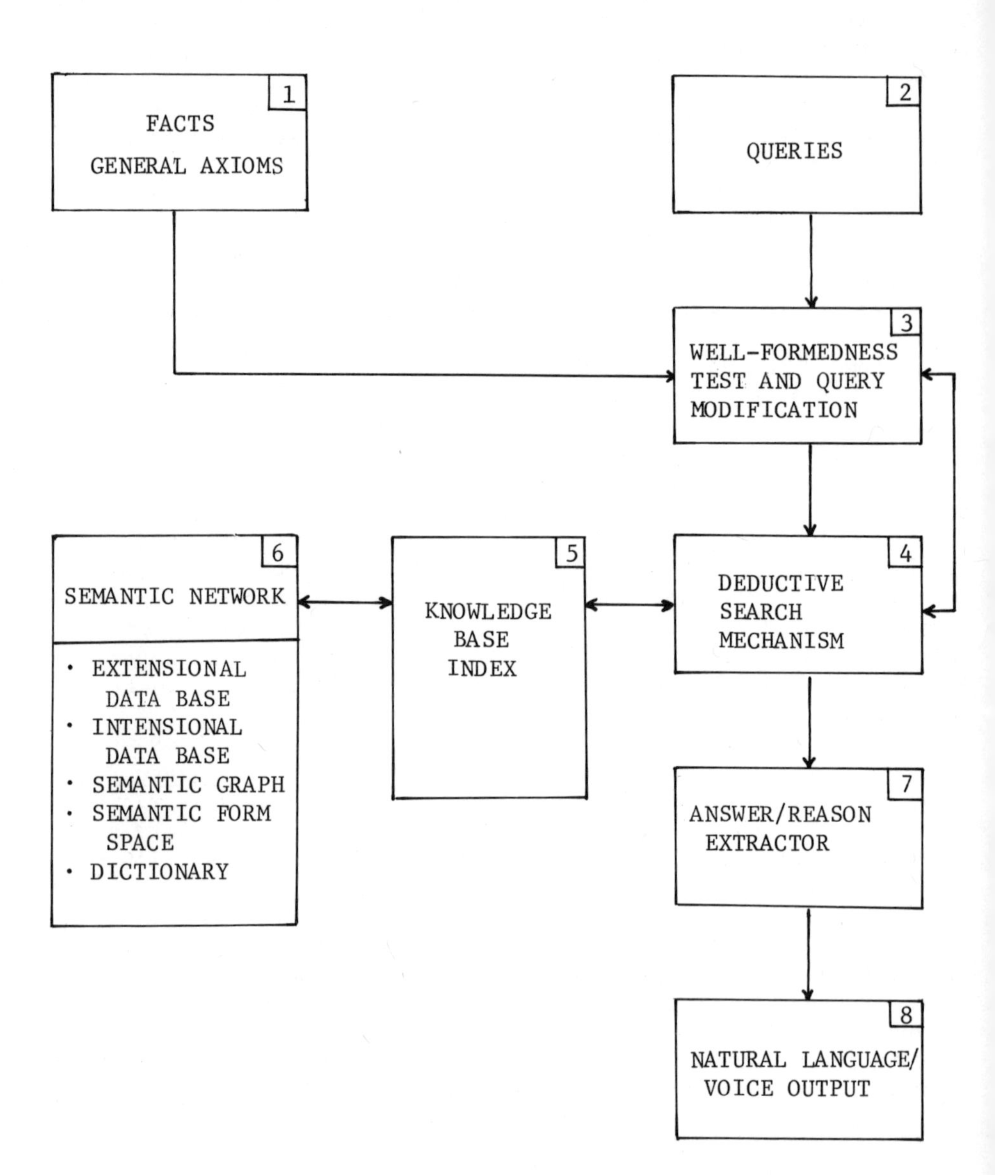

Figure 1. Block Diagram of the Elements of the MRPPS 3.0 System

SEMANTIC NETWORK

Relations and Π-σ Notation

To better comprehend the Semantic Network, it will be well to describe Π-σ clauses. Consider the relation MANUFACTURE given in Table 1.

It should be noted that if several relational statements were combined, there would be a saving of space. That is, the relational table could be written as is Table 2.

Table 1. MANUFACTURE Relation

ABC	SHOVELS	Maryland
ABC	SCREWDRIVERS	Maryland
ABC	PLIERS	Maryland
ABC	WRENCHES	Maryland
ABC	HAMMERS	Maryland
ABC	PITCH FORKS	Maryland
ACME	RESISTORS	Virginia
ACME	CAPACITORS	Virginia
ACME	SWITCHES	Virginia
ACME	SCOPES	Virginia

Table 2. Condensed Form of MANUFACTURE Relation

ABC	HAMMERS, PITCH FORKS, PLIERS, SCREWDRIVERS, SHOVELS, WRENCHES	MARYLAND
ACME	CAPACITORS, RESISTORS, SCOPES, SWITCHES	VIRGINIA

Within the system a form similar to that depicted in Table 2 is used. For EDB data the form consists of an ordered pair, (template, Π-σ sets). The template for the MANUFACTURES relation is (α, x_1, x_2, x_3) where α represents a relation placeholder, and the x_i, i=1,2,3 are the argument placeholders of the relation. The Π-σ substitution sets are forms of the following kind: $\{S_0/\alpha, S_1/x_1, \ldots, S_n/x_n\}$, where the S_i are either sets of constants or a boolean combination of categories. Thus Table 2 would be represented as:

$((\alpha, x_1, x_2, x_3)$, {{[MANUFACTURES]/α, [ABC]/x_1, [HAMMERS, PITCHFORKS, PLIERS, SCREWDRIVERS, SHOVELS, WRENCHES]/x_2, [MARYLAND]/x_3} ,

[MANUFACTURES]/α, [ACME]/x_1, [CAPACITORS, RESISTORS, SCOPES, SWITCHES]/x_2, [VIRGINIA]/x_3}}).

General axioms may also be placed in the form (template, Π-σ set). A template, now is like a clause of the type described in the section - Background. Thus, formula (1) may be written as,

$((\alpha,x,y,z) \wedge (\beta,u,y,w) \rightarrow (\gamma,x,u,y)$, {{[MANUFACTURES]/$\alpha$, <u>companies</u>/x, <u>inventory item</u>/y, <u>location</u>/z, <u>location</u>/w, <u>companies</u>/u, [USES]/β, [SUPPLIES]/γ}}).

Bracketed items represent sets of constants, and underlined items represent categories.

A more precise description of the notation, termed Π-σ notation is given in the following section. The notation coalesces similar relational statements into a compact form. If, for example, the ABC company manufactures the same items in two states, say MARYLAND and CALIFORNIA, formula (2) need only be modified to place CALIFORNIA in the same set as MARYLAND.

Elements of the Semantic Network

Knowledge within the system is contained in a semantic network (McSkimin and Minker [1977]) which consists of four major components: (1) the <u>semantic graph</u> which specifies set-theoretic relationships between categories; (2) the data base of assertions stored in the EDB, and inference rules (or general axioms) stored in the IDB; (3) the dictionary of constants, function names, and categories in the system, and; (4) the semantic form space which defines the semantic constraints placed on arguments of predicates.

The Semantic Graph. In a many-sorted logic, the universe consists of many different domains. Each domain is called a semantic category. It may happen that different semantic categories relate to one another. A semantic category could be a geographical area, or it could be a specific geographical area such as a country. Relationships among semantic categories are specified in a graph which can represent disjointness, inclusion, or overlap. A typical semantic graph which shows these relationships is given in Figure 2.

The semantic graph represents relationships among semantic categories. The set of all elements in a particular category represents a unary relation. Thus, if FIDO is a dog, one could represent this as the unary relation DOG(FIDO) . To determine that FIDO is also an animal and a mammal would require the two clauses,

$$DOG(x) \rightarrow ANIMAL(x)$$

$$ANIMAL(y) \rightarrow MAMMAL(y) \ .$$

To find that FIDO is a mammal in the MRPPS 3.0 system, FIDO is accessed in the dictionary and it is found that it points to the semantic category for DOG. The entry for DOG points to ANIMAL which, in turn leads to MAMMAL. To avoid having to traverse the semantic graph, the transitive closure of the graph is obtained and stored in the system. In effect, all relationships among unary relations are precompiled in advance. To determine that FIDO is a mammal requires essentially a table look-up. Precompilation is particularly useful when one has transitive relationships among unary relations that are needed frequently. It is also useful for n-ary relations as discussed in the section entitled Related Developments.

A boolean combination ($\cap, \cup, \sim$) of semantic categories can be expressed in the system. Thus, judge $\cap$ lawyer , senator $\cap$ male $\cap$ $\sim$liberal are examples of categories, referred to as a Boolean Category Expression (BCE).

Data Base. The data base consists of assertions (unit fully instantiated clauses stored in the EDB, and clauses stored in the IDB. The form in which these are represented was outlined in the section on Relations and Π-σ Notation. More formally, a Π-σ clause is an ordered pair $\mathfrak{C} = (T, \Phi)$, where T is a clause template , and Φ a set of Π-σ (substitution) sets. T is a constant-free clause as defined in the Clause Form section. However,

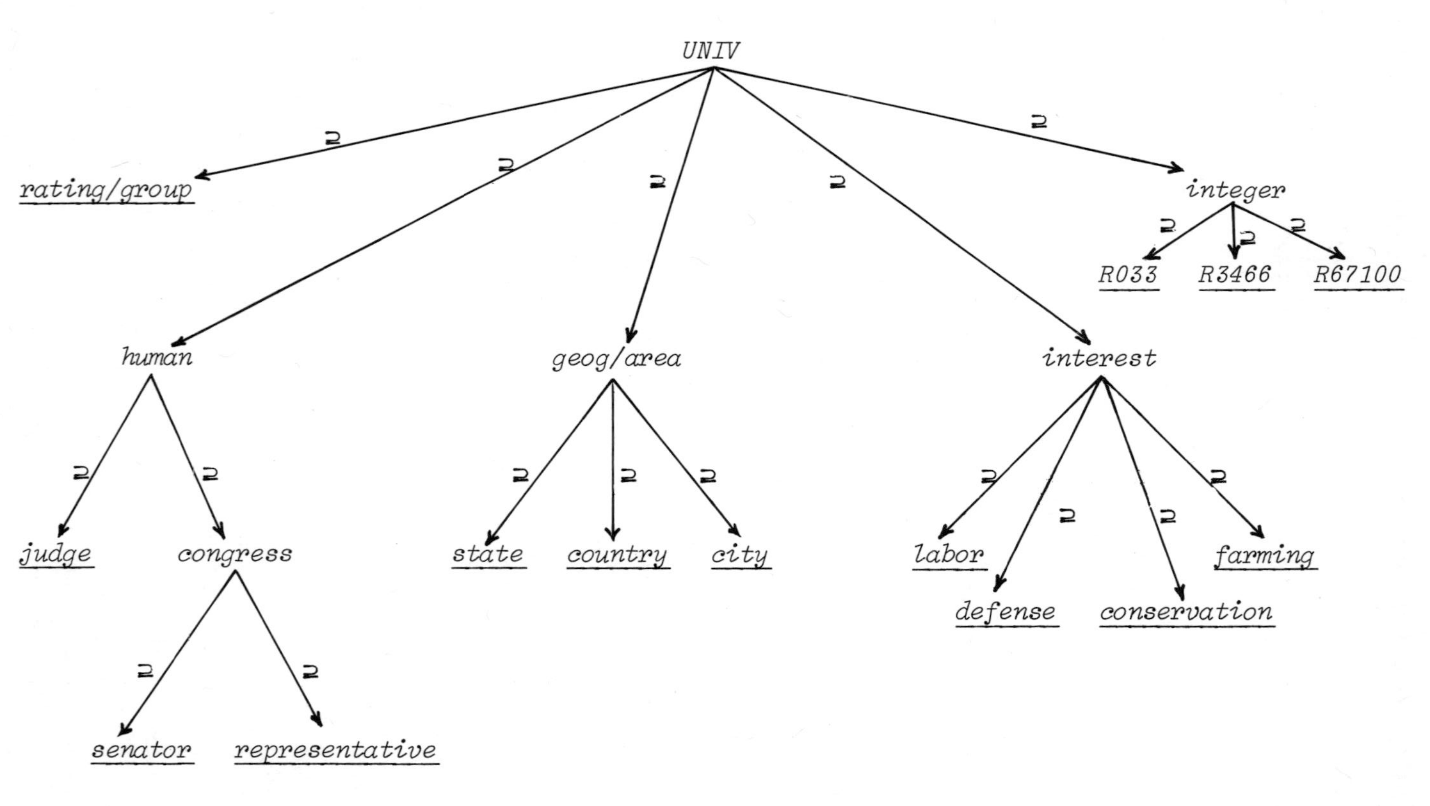

Figure 2. Semantic Graph (Only superset arcs shown - Primitive categories underlined)

literals in a clause have their predicate letters replaced by a variable, and the variable is made part of an n+1-tuple. Thus, if one had the literal $P(x,y)$, it would be replaced by (α,x,y), with the placeholder α designating the name of the predicate P. The second part of the ordered pair is a finite set of Π-σ (substitution) sets $\Phi = \{\varphi_1,\ldots,\varphi_n\}$ where φ is the form $\{S_1/v_1,\ldots,S_m/v_m\}$, and where a Π-substitution component is an expression of the form $S/v = ([D^E,D^X],D^I)/v$. D^E is a possibly empty finite set of constants explicitly included in S; D^X is a possibly empty finite set of constants explicitly excluded in S; D^I is a possibly empty set of constants represented as a BCE and implicitly included in S; v is a placeholder variable, or simply a variable. The following conditions are required to hold (1) $D^E \cap D^I = \emptyset$; (2) $D^X \subseteq D^I$.

A Π-σ substitution component indicates that v is universally quantified over the set $D^E \cup (D^I \cap \sim D^X)$. The ordered pair provides a compact notation that represents the set of relational statements and axioms that would be represented in the system were the entries in a Π-σ set applied to the template form, to obtain individual relational statements.

Dictionary. The dictionary lists the semantic category for each relation, constant, or function name in the system. It also lists the names of the semantic categories. Items that would be listed in the dictionary are, for example, the relation names MANUFACTURE, SUPPLIES, and USES; the constant names, ACME, MARYLAND, CAPACITORS and RESISTORS; and the semantic categories COMPANY, STATE, and ITEM. A function name might be ADD, which given two arguments returns the sum of the two arguments.

Semantic Form Space. The semantic form space defines semantic constraints that are to be imposed upon the predicate name and on each argument of the predicate. The semantic form space consists of ordered pairs of the form (T,Φ), where T is a clause with a distinguished literal, and Φ is a Π-σ set. The distinguished literal is the one upon which constraints are placed. Associated with each Π-σ set are two types of counting information. For each counting relation the number of entries that could appear in the extension of the relation is specified. Thus, given a three place relation R, it might be known that the extension of R contains exactly n three-tuples. The second type specifies counting information on arguments of a relation. Thus, it might be known further that the set of all tuples of R which have constants in the first and third arguments is a constant, n_1. Certainly, if one had the relation PARENT, and a second argument of a tuple in this set is a constant, then the first argument can be satisfied by only two individuals. Such semantic information is useful for directing a search as described in McSkimin and Minker [1977].

Knowledge Base Index

One can proceed in a number of ways in developing a system with an inferential capability. It is possible to separate the EDB from the IDB. This could be done particularly if there is a relational data base system with which one could interface. The relational data base could be used to access base relations on peripheral devices. The IDB entries, which in general, are substantially smaller than the EDB entries could be stored in primary memory, and thereby accessed directly. An alternate approach taken here is to combine the two structures, the EDB and the IDB into one structure.

All n-ary relational statements with the same template may be stored together or separately at the discretion of the user. Thus, given a binary relation, FATHER and another binary relation, MOTHER, where the FATHER relation is given by

a	b
a	c

, and the MOTHER relation is given by

d	e
d	f
d	g

, the data may be stored as one template with two substitution sets,

$$((\alpha,x,y),\{\{[\text{FATHER}]/\alpha,\ [a]/x,\ [b,c]/y\},\ \{[\text{MOTHER}]/\alpha,\ [d]/x,\ [e,f,g]/y\}\}),$$

or as two templates each having a single substitution set. The statements specify that a is the father of b and c , and that d is the mother of e, f, and g . Horn clauses that define virtual relations that have the same structures can also be stored together or separately. Thus, the virtual relation GRANDFATHER is defined by the Horn Clause

$$((\alpha,x,y) \wedge (\beta,y,z) \rightarrow (\gamma,x,z),\{\{[\text{FATHER}]/\alpha,\ [\text{FATHER}]/\beta,\ [\text{GRANDFATHER}]/\gamma,\ \underline{\text{male}}/x,\ \underline{\text{male}}/y,\ \underline{\text{human}}/z\},\ \{[\text{FATHER}]/\alpha,\ [\text{MOTHER}]/\beta,\ [\text{GRANDFATHER}]/\gamma,\ \underline{\text{male}}/x\ \underline{\text{female}}/y,\ \underline{\text{human}}/z\}\}),$$

and, stored in the IDB, or it may be aplit into two templates each with a single substitution set and stored in the IDB.

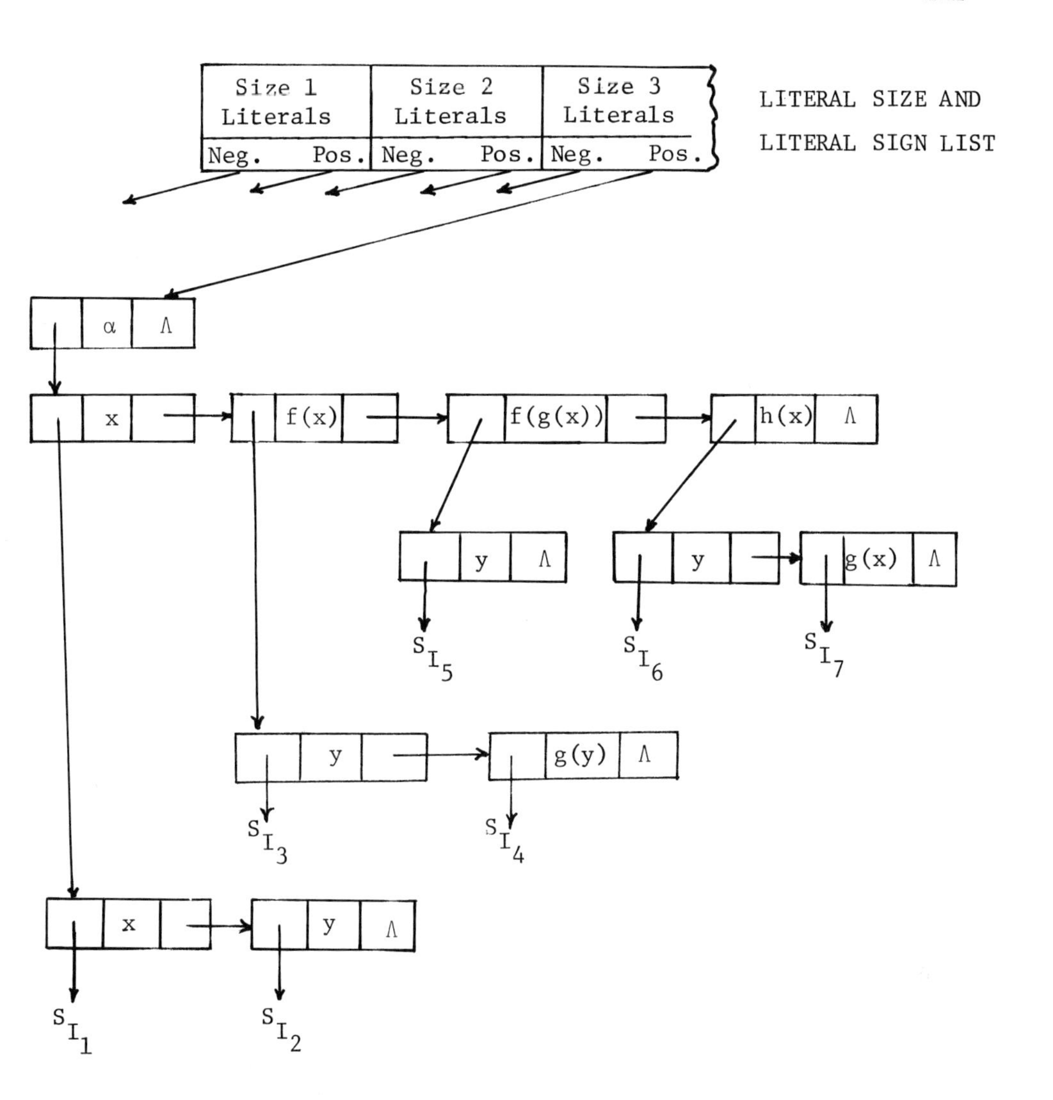

Literals Represented:

(α,x,x)	(α,f(g(x)),y)
(α,x,y)	(α,h(x),y)
(α,f(x),y)	(α,h(x),g(x))
(α,f(x),g(y))	

Figure 3. Knowledge Base Index Structure - Literal Template Tree Structure

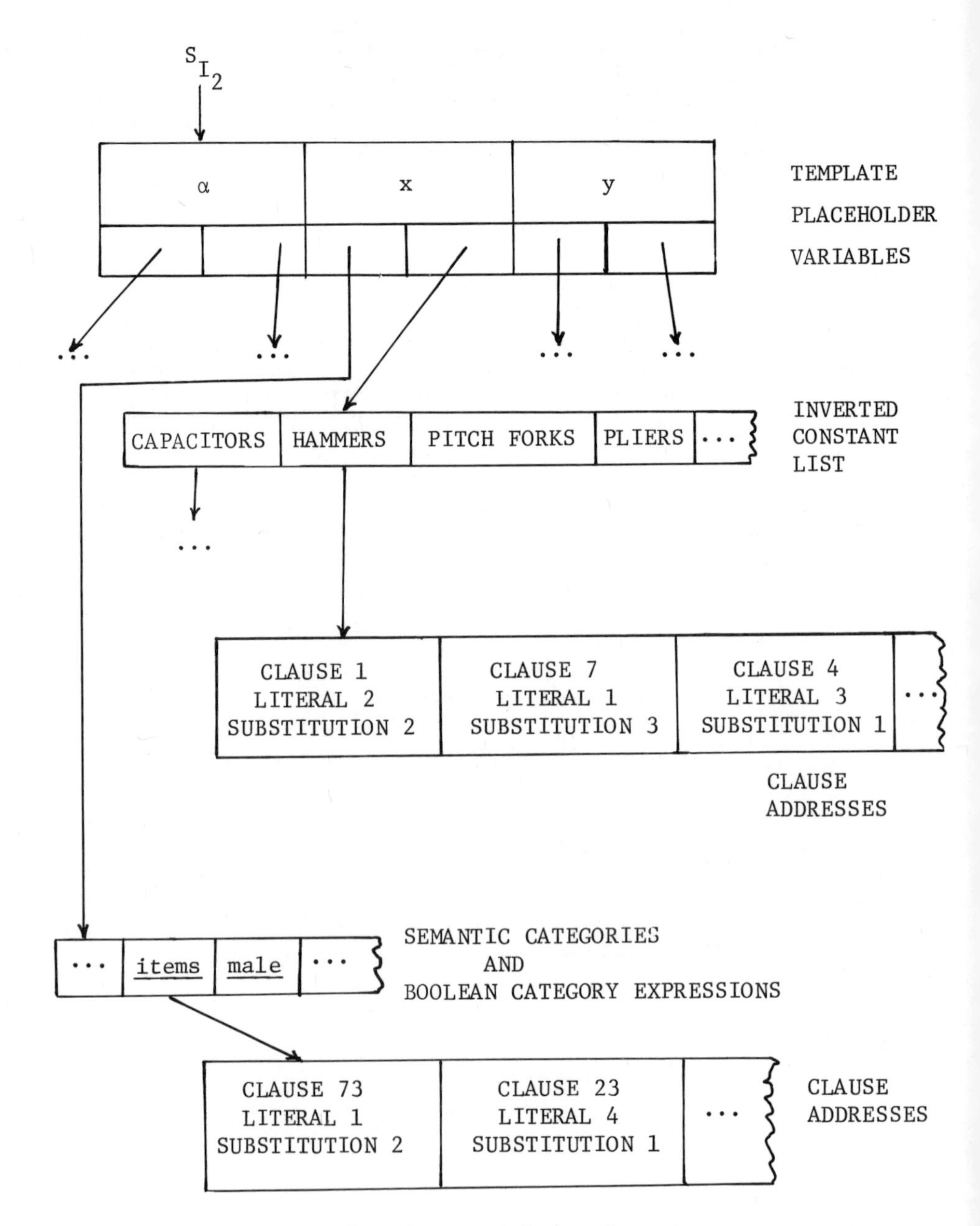

Figure 4. Inverted Index Structure

Knowledge Base Index Structure. Entries in the EDB/IDB must be accessed through the index structure termed the Knowledge Base Index. The index structure is in essence an inverted file in which one can access a relational statement in the EDB or a Horn clause in the IDB on any argument position. The design of the MRPPS 3.0 Knowledge Base Index Structure is due to Wilson [1976]. For details concerning the structure and an analysis of the utility of the representation, the reader is referred to Wilson [1976].

The Knowledge Base Index Structure, shown in Figure 3, consists of:

(1) a literal size and literal sign list,
(2) a literal template tree structure, and
(3) an inverted index file.

The literal size and literal sign list points to where the template tree structure for a literal of a particular size and a particular sign is stored. The literal template tree structure is stored as a binary tree. The root of the tree contains the predicate placeholder name of the literal template. At a depth of one below the root, in separate nodes, is contained each term of the first argument of a relation with the specified size and sign in some clause in the EDB/IDB. At a level k below the root where we define level for the binary tree counting left nodes that must be passed through to reach the node, are the terms that may appear in the kth argument of a relational statement. It should be noted that terms in templates and in the literal template tree structure are free of constants, and contain placeholder names and function constants. If one proceeds down a branch of a literal template tree structure, one obtains the form of a literal template that is stored in either the EDB or the IDB.

The terminal node of each branch of the literal template tree structure points to the list of placeholders associated with the literal template described by the branch of the tree. Thus, as shown in Figure 4, the placeholder names associated with a branch are α, x, and y. For example, S_{I_2} in Figure 3 might point to this list. Each placeholder name contains two pointers - a left-pointer and a right-pointer. The right-pointer points to a list of constants associated with the placeholder name. Each constant, in turn, points to a list which contains the location of the clause (or relational statement), the literal within the clause, and the substitution set in the clause which contains the constant. Thus, every clause in the system that has the constant in the particular literal template argument is found in one pass of the Knowledge Base Index Structure. The left branch associated with the placeholder name contains a pointer to each boolean category expression associated with it. This, in turn points to a list which contains the clause, the literal within the clause, and the substitution set that contains the boolean category expression.

Pattern-Matching and the Knowledge Base Index Structure. Given a Π-σ literal consisting of a literal template and a Π-σ set, all clauses in the EDB/IDB which can match a given Π-σ literal are found at once by matching the Knowledge Base Index. This is accomplished by a pattern-matching operation described in Wilson [1976]. The pattern-match is an adaptation of the Robinson unification algorithm.

An outline of how the pattern matching works is sketched by the following example. Let the Π-σ literal be searched for $((\beta,h(u),v),\{\{[F]/\beta,\ UNIV/y,\ [a]/v\}\})$. Turning to Figure 3, an attempt is made to find all branches of the template literal tree structure that can be made to match $(\beta,h(u),v)$. The root α can be made to be the same as β by the substitution $\{\alpha/\beta\}$. Then, at a level of depth one, $\{h(u)/x\}$ can be made to match and also $\{u/x\}$ in the last node at depth one. Hence, two template substitutions are possible up to this point: $\{\alpha/\beta,\ h(u)/x\}$ and $\{\alpha/\beta,u/x\}$. Proceeding to the next level of the tree, the following matches can be made through the branches labeled

S_{I_1} with substitution $\{\alpha/\beta,\ h(u)/x,\ h(u)/v\}$

S_{I_2} with substitution $\{\alpha/\beta,\ h(u)/x,\ y/v\}$

S_{I_6} with substitution $\{\alpha/\beta,\ u/x,\ y/v\}$

S_{I_7} with substitution $\{\alpha/\beta,\ u/x,\ g(u)/v\}$

Now, the actual substitution sets associated with each matching branch and the given Π-σ literal must be compatible for there to be a match. In S_{I_1}, α must have an [F] associated with it. If not, the pattern match fails. Assume that it does not fail, then all clauses that match are retained. Since the substitution $h(u)$ for x is made, the placeholder x must not be a constant, and must have a category compatible with that of $h(u)$. Assume that this is satisfied, by some clauses. The two sets of clauses found (for the two arguments) must match. Assuming that this set is not null, then the third argument is considered in the same manner as the previous arguments. A failure results from paths S_{I_1} and S_{I_7} since a function can be substituted for a placeholder variable only if it represents a semantic category. The placeholder variable v represents the constant symbol [a]. Hence, the only templates that can be made to match are those represented by the branches S_{I_2} and S_{I_6}. The results of the search yields the substitution sets and matching literals of <u>all</u> clauses in the EDB/IDB that match the specified pattern.

Finding all patterns that match at once is a powerful tool and provides much flexibility for the control structure in the choice that can be made to direct the search. This aspect will be discussed in the section on Subproblem Selection.

DEDUCTIVE SEARCH MECHANISM

Proof Procedure System

The MRPPS 3.0 is a proof procedure system consisting of an inference mechanism and a search strategy. The inference mechanism is used to deduce a new clause from two given clauses. The search strategy is used to determine which two clauses to select for deducing a new clause. A wide number of choices exist for both the inference mechanism and the search strategy of a proof procedure system.

MRPPS 3.0 is a refutation proof procedure system. That is, it starts with the negation of the question to be answered and tries to find a contradiction. There are a number of resolution-based inference mechanisms that can be chosen. Whichever inference mechanism is chosen, it is desirable that it be _complete_ and _sound_. In the context of a Question-Answering system, an inference mechanism is _complete_ if, when the negated question is applied to the set of clauses and the question can be answered, then a contradiction will result. An inference mechanism is _sound_ if, given the question, and it is not known that the question can be answered, and the negated question is shown to be contradictory, the question must have been answerable. Whether or not a proof procedure system is complete depends on both the inference mechanism and the search strategy control structure.

Based on research by Fishman [1973] on MRPPS 2.0 it was decided to implement two inference systems in MRPPS 3.0: SL-resolution and LUSH-resolution. SL-resolution (linear resolution with unrestricted selection function) is complete and sound for arbitrary sets of clauses, however LUSH-resolution (linear resolution with unrestricted selection function for Horn clauses) is complete only for Horn clauses. SL-resolution was developed independently by Kowalski and Kuehner [1971], Loveland [1969], and Reiter [1971]. LUSH-resolution was devised by Kowalski and described by Hill [1974].

The search strategy in MRPPS 3.0 can be either complete, or not complete depending upon parameters chosen by the user. Even when the search strategy is not complete, an answer may be obtained. This will occur if the search strategy fortuitously directs the search along a branch of the proof graph that has a solution.

Description of Inference Mechanisms for Horn Clauses

The inference mechanisms of SL-resolution and LUSH-resolution are closely related. The case in which Horn clauses exist is considered below for both inference mechanisms. If Horn clauses do not exist, then SL-resolution must be used. We do not describe the non-Horn clause case in this paper. When Horn clauses exist, SL-resolution is a particular case of LUSH-resolution.

Let the query be specified, and be transformed to prenex normal form. The negation of the query is formed, and is then transformed to clause form. For the negation of the query to be a set of Horn clauses, they must be of the form

(1) $\sim L_1 \vee \cdots \vee \sim L_n$ or

(2) $\sim L_1 \vee \cdots \vee \sim L_v \vee M$,

where the $L_i, i=1,2,\cdots,n$ and M are positive literals. For simplicity, query clauses of the form (1) are considered below. Query clauses of the type (2) are handled in a manner similar to the discussion that follows.

Let the negated query clause be of the form (1). To solve the query in clause form one proceeds as follows with either of the two inference systems, SL-resolution or LUSH-resolution. From among the n negated literals, one of the literals is selected to be solved. When it is selected, it is moved to the right-most position in the clause. Without loss of generality, assume $\sim L_n$ is the literal selected to be solved. Two cases may pertain. First, the unnegated literal L_n is a base relation. That is, it has relational statements in the EDB. Second, if it is not a base relation, then there might be a clause in the IDB with the same relation name as L_n . If neither of these cases apply, the query cannot be answered.

Assume that the first case pertains. Then, an attempt is made to match L_n from the query against all L_n' in the EDB in which both have the same relation name. If there is a match, then what remains to be solved is

(3) $(\sim L_1 \vee \cdots \vee \sim L_{n-1})\Theta$,

where Θ is a substitution required to make L_n and L_n' match. To solve (1) it is now sufficient to solve (3).

If on the other hand, L_n is a virtual relation, and there is a Horn clause

(4) $\sim M_1 \vee \sim M_2 \vee \cdots \vee \sim M_r \vee L_n'$

in the IDB such that L_n and L'_n have the same relation name and can be made to match, then to solve (3) it is sufficient to solve,

$$(5) \quad (\sim L_1 \vee \cdots \vee \sim L_{n-1} \vee \boxed{\sim L_n} \vee \sim M_1 \vee \cdots \vee \sim M_r)\, \theta_1 \ .$$

The entry $\boxed{\sim L_n}$ is retained in (5) as a bookkeeping device. It never interacts with EDB or IDB entries again. Now, one must solve (5) to solve (1). One proceeds to select a literal in (5) to be solved as was done in (1). The choice of which literal to select depends upon whether SL-resolution or LUSH-resolution is the inference mechanism. If SL-resolution is employed, one can select only from the most recently introduced literals. That is, from among the $M_i, i=1,\ldots,r$. In all descendant clauses, the M_i must be solved before any of the $L_j, j=1,\ldots,n-1$ are solved.

However, in LUSH-resolution one can select from either the $L_j, j=1,\cdots,n-1$ or from the $M_i, i=1,\ldots,r$. LUSH-resolution, in the context of Horn-clauses provides greater flexibility than does SL-resolution. Since most data base problems consist of Horn-clauses, one should use LUSH-resolution over SL-resolution for such problems.

Search Strategy Controller

The Search Strategy Controller provides the control component of the system. Its major role is to guide the search towards a solution to a query. The current version of the Search Strategy Controller in MRPPS 3.0 is described in detail in Minker [1977], so that only its functions are outlined in this section. Reference will be made to the eight modules of the Block Diagram of the Search Strategy Controller shown in Figure 5.

(1) Search Strategy Controller Executive

(2) Workspace Controller

(3) Syntactic Filtering

(4) Semantic Actions and Lemma Formation

(5) Subproblem Selection

(6) Node Generation

(7) Pattern-Directed Search (Unification Algorithm)

(8) Inference Mechanism

The eight modules are independent of one another, and a new module can be substituted simply by assuring that the interface is maintained. Initial versions of all modules except for (3), Syntactic Filtering, and the Semantic Actions of (4), have been implemented in MRPPS 3.0.

Every query can be transformed into the problem of solving a set of conjunctions of literals, where the solution to any one conjunct solves the problem. In the following it is assumed that the query has been so transformed, and since the query is negated to be solved, a set of clauses is formed. Each clause is passed to the Search Strategy Controller Executive through which all data pass. A synopsis of the sequence of steps that takes place in the Search Strategy Controller is shown in Figure 6. The reader should review this figure before reading the brief description of each module that follows. The numbers in each box relate to the blocks in Figure 5.

Search Strategy Controller Executive. The Search Strategy Controller Executive (SSCE) controls the search process in the system. It initiates transfers between five of the seven modules shown. Each clause from the negation of the query is passed initially to the Search Strategy Controller Executive and then

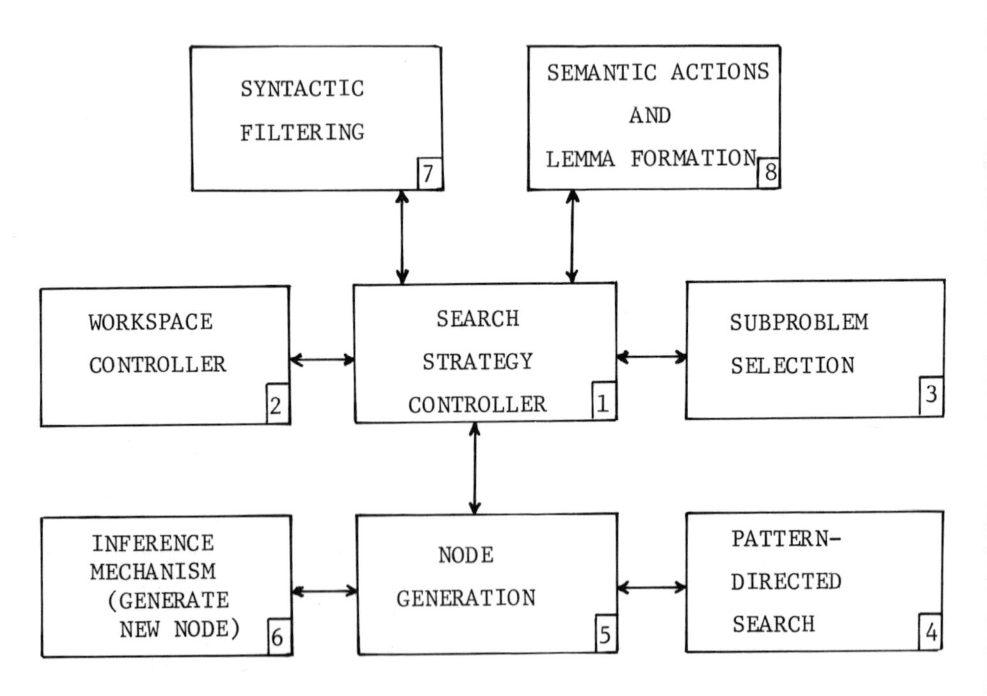

Figure 5. MRPPS 3.0 - Block Diagram of Search Strategy Controller

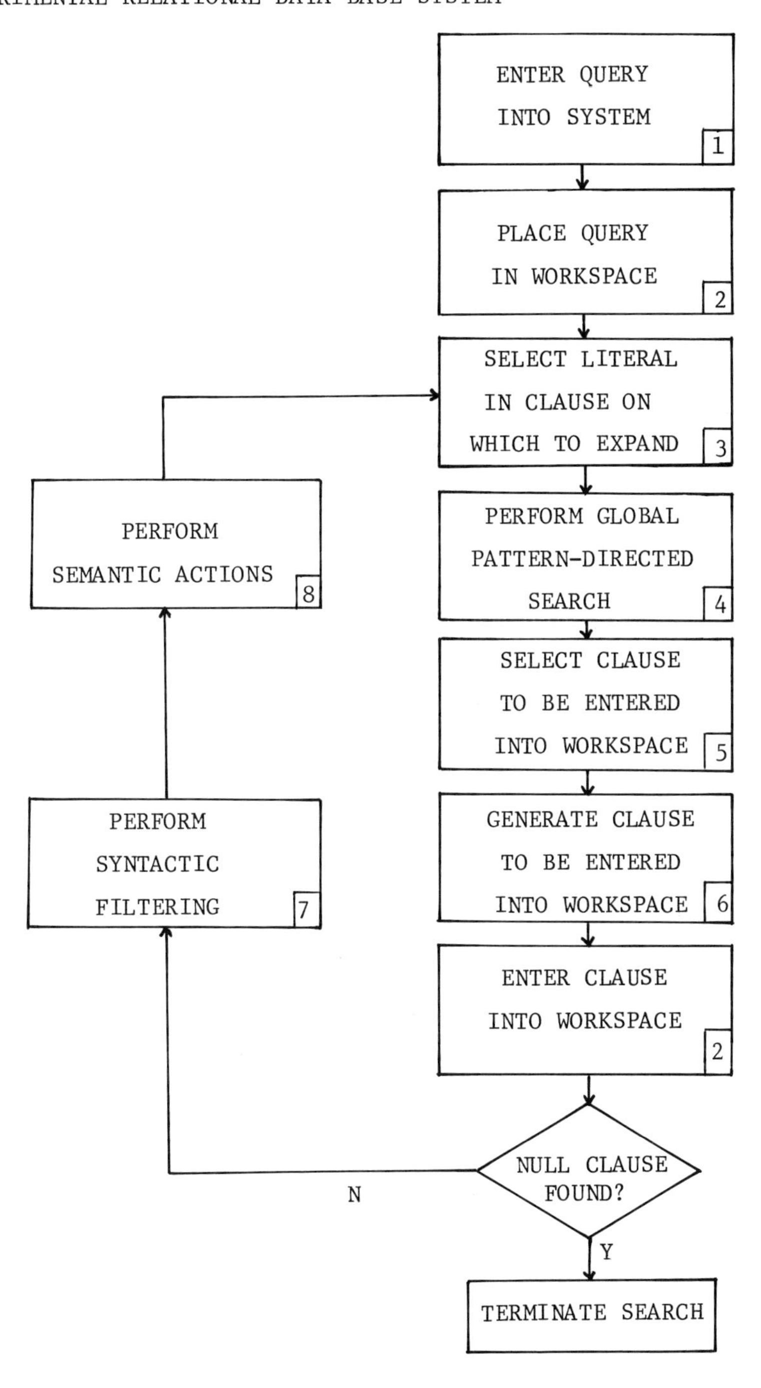

Figure 6. Synopsis of Search Strategy Controller Processing

passed to the Workspace Controller for entry into the search space. Clauses developed during the deduction process in the node-generation module are transferred to the workspace by the SSCE. Other functions of the Search Space Controller Executive are described in conjunction with the description of each module.

Workspace Controller. The Workspace Controller places clauses from the negation of the query, and clauses derived from these clauses in the workspace. Every descendant clause is linked to its immediate parent. A dynamic storage allocator assigns space to each clause. A query clause has no parent clause and is the root node of a problem solving graph started in the workspace. The workspace contains the template structure for each clause and a pointer to its Π-σ sets. When the Workspace Controller is completed, it returns control to the Search Strategy Controller Executive which initiates the next step in the search process.

Syntactic Filtering. The SSCE calls upon Syntactic Filtering when a clause is eligible to be entered in the workspace. Entries in the problem solving graph in the Workspace Controller area may be eligible for deletion by Syntactic Filtering. This can happen when the clause template just entered, except for a change of variables, is identical to another clause template in the workspace, and the Π-σ set of the newly entered Π-σ clause is contained within a Π-σ clause already stored. In this case, the newly entered clause is deleted. A second form of deletion arises when there are Π-σ clauses that form tautologies. That is, both a Π-σ literal and the negation of the Π-σ literal appear in the same clause. In this case the entire Π-σ clause is deleted.

Semantic Actions and Lemma Formation. Whenever a literal of a conjunct is solved, Semantic Actions and Lemma Formation is initiated. The inference mechanisms of SL-resolution and LUSH-resolution provide bookkeeping functions which permit one to detect when a literal has been solved (Minker [1978]). The Workspace Controller stores the clauses containing the literal that has been solved, performs the appropriate linking of clauses in the workspace, and transfers control to the SSCE which invokes Semantic Actions and Lemma Formation.

When a literal has been solved information may have been learned. Thus, if one is searching for the parents of an individual, and two parents have been found, then one wants to cease searching for additional parents of the individual. Semantic Actions detects when this occurs, and performs the steps needed to accomplish the actions (McSkimin [1976], McSkimin and Minker [1977]).

Lemma Formation arises when a literal that was defined as a virtual relation has been solved partially. That is, some implicit facts have been made explicit. When this arises it might be advantageous to the search process to store the relational statements found in the EDB. Then, in subsequent processing the relational statements can be accessed directly from the EDB rather than having to solve for them again. The user would have to specify criteria to permit the automatic storing of derived data in the EDB.

Subproblem Selection. Given a clause that has been entered into the workspace, and has passed through Syntactic Filtering and through Semantic Actions and Lemma Formation, the SSCE sends the clause to Subproblem Selection. A choice is made here to determine which literal to solve next. From the set of literals eligible for selection, the Subproblem Selection module uses the following criteria:

(1) Select a literal whose relation name appears as a base relation in the EDB over those that are exclusively virtual relations and stored in the IDB.

(2) From among those literals that have corresponding base relations, select the one that is more fully instantiated than others (i.e., has more arguments that are constants rather than variables).

(3) From among those literals that are virtual relations, select those that are more fully instantiated than others.

The reason for the above choice is that in the case of base relations, the more instantiated the literal is, the smaller the number of matches one will have when pattern-matching the literal against the EDB. This is desirable since one wants to work with the smallest possible sets when one is trying to answer a query, as this will minimize the work. A similar consideration pertains to virtual relations. Notice that even when a set of literals from which one can select all have corresponding base relations, one wants to access the relations in a sequence such that the least amount of work is performed. The determination of which literal to solve first is the function of a search controller.

Node Generation. Once a literal has been selected, a decision must be made as to the next clause to be entered into the workspace. This is the function of the Node Generation Module. It is achieved by managing three lists and selecting the best clause on the Operator List. The lists are:

(1) Specification List (SPECLIST) - a list of all literals selected which have not yet been matched against the EDB/IDB and are waiting to be matched.

(2) Operator List (OPLIST) - a list of all literals that have have been matched against the EDB/IDB, but have not yet been entered into the workspace. Each literal on the Operator list points to a list of <u>all</u> extensional and intensional clauses that can be made to match the given literal. The unifier that causes the match to be made is also retained. The list of clauses pointed to by the literal can interact with the clause in the workspace from which the literal on the operator list comes as described in the section on Description of Inference Mechanisms for Horn clauses. The clause that would result if this interaction took place is called the best projected merit of the clause pointed to by the literal on the Operator list. The best projected merit is calculated by $f(n) = g(n)+h(n)$, where $g(n)$ is the depth of the clause in the workspace from the root of the proof tree + 1 , and $h(n)$ is the number of literals of the clause in the workspace + the number of literals in the operator clause - 2 . The depth of a clause from the negation of the query is defined to be zero.

(3) Closed List (CLOSED) - a list of all literals that come from clauses in the workspace to which all operators have been applied. Hence, the clause in the workspace cannot be expanded further by clauses in the EDB or the IDB.

The relationships between the lists are shown diagrammatically in Figure 7. Literals are first entered into the (SPECLIST) where they are subsequently unified against the EDB/IDB. When this occurs, the literal and pointers to the list of clauses with which it unifies is placed on the OPLIST . When the literal on the OPLIST no longer points to any clause (because they have been entered into the workspace), the literal is removed from this list and placed on CLOSED. When a literal is selected in the Subproblem Selection module, it is transferred to the Node Generation Module. After it is placed on the SPECLIST, a determination is made as to which literal to attempt to solve next in the workspace. The first entry on the OPLIST is accessed. A search is then made of the SPECLIST to determine if a possible match of a literal on this list against the EDB/IDB may result in a better operator. If it can, then transfer is given to the Pattern-Matching process. If it cannot, then transfer is given to the Inference Mechanism to derive a new clause based on the best operator on the OPLIST. The resulting clause is removed from the OPLIST and transferred to the Search Strategy Controller Executive to be entered into the workspace.

Pattern-Directed Search. Pattern-Directed Search is the algorithm which takes a literal template Π-σ set pair in the SPECLIST, and matches it against the data base using the Knowledge Base Index structure to find all clauses in the EDB/IDB that it matches, as described in the Pattern-Matching and the Knowledge Base Index Structure section. Since a relation name in the system may be both a base relation and a virtual relation, the search of the Knowledge Base Index returns the list of all base relations in the EDB, and virtual relations in the IDB that match the given literal template.

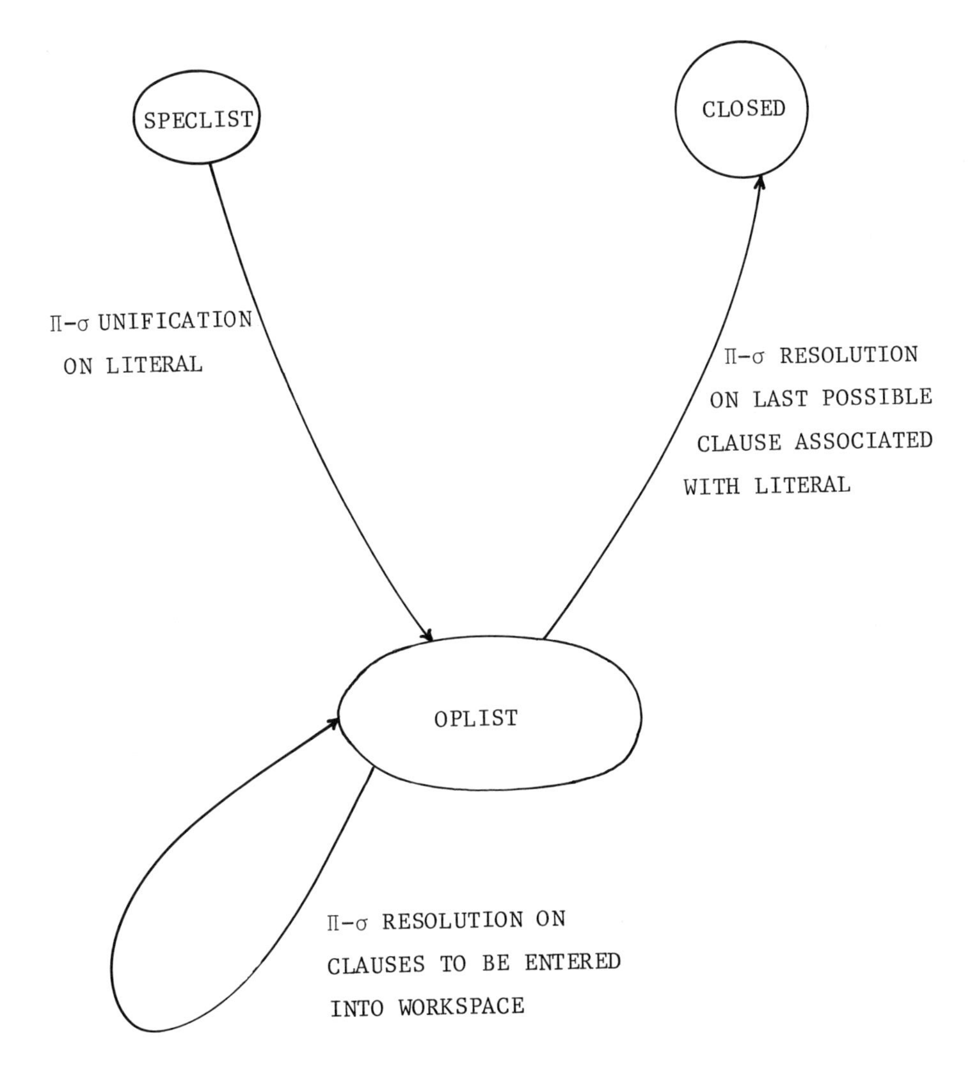

Figure 7. Relationships Between Lists in Node Generation Module

The Pattern-Directed Search may be performed in two modes. In the first mode only syntactic matches are made. In the second mode, termed semantic pattern-directed match, advantage is taken of the many-sorted logic and tests are made to determine if a match can be made. The modifications needed to do this and how semantic pattern-directed search is expected to help in the search process is described in detail in McSkimin and Minker [1977].

Inference Mechanism. The Inference Mechanism module is separate from the pattern-matching (unification) module. It takes a clause from the workspace, and an EDB or IDB entry, applies the unifier found by the pattern matcher to form a new clause. The new clause is then passed to the Search Strategy Controller Executive, to be entered into the workspace. The inference mechanism performs all the bookkeeping as specified by SL-resolution or LUSH-resolution.

The process described above terminates either when an answer is found, or the system runs out of time or space. The current system terminates when one or more solutions to a problem are found. Because of the Π-σ notation used, all solutions which have the same proof tree and template structure, except for changes in constants, are found at the same time. This is one of the advantages of Π-σ notation. This is in contrast to finding all solutions. One could find all solutions by continuing the process until there are no more literals on either the SPECLIST or OPLIST. That is, all proof trees would be found. In case there is recursion in axioms, it might not be possible to find all solutions, but only those within a specified depth from the root clause could be found.

ANSWER COMPREHENSION

The search for a proof terminates when all of the literals in the negation of the query have been solved. Thus, when one terminates the proof, it is known that an answer exists. The answer is the set of bindings made to the variables from the query-clause to solve all the literals. Hence, one must find these bindings. An algorithm to do so was developed first by Green [1969], and subsequently generalized by Luckham and Nilsson [1971]. When some of the relations in the query-clause are virtual relations, it is important that not only the answer, but the reasoning that led to the answer be available to the user. The reason steps are the clauses in the EDB/IDB that are used in the resulting proof tree. When using either SL-resolution or LUSH-resolution, Minker [1978] and Powell [1977] have shown how the reasons can be listed in the MRPPS 3.0 system. The reader is referred to these two papers for details.

The user can obtain three different forms for the answer and proof tree which contains the reasons. These are:

(1) symbolic form,

(2) natural language form, and

(3) voice output form.

A description of the output module of MRPPS 3.0 is contained in Powell and Thompson [1978]. A brief description of each form is provided below using the following example. The system has two base relations: MANUFACTURE and USES. The MANUFACTURE relation is given in Table 1 (Relations and Π-σ Notation section) and the USES relation is given in Table 3, following.

In addition, it has the virtual relation SUPPLIES defined in the IDB by,

MANUFACTURES(u,v,w) $\wedge$ USES(r,v,s) $\rightarrow$ SUPPLIES(u,r,v)

Proof Tree in Symbolic Form

The output for the question ($\exists$x)SUPPLIES(ACME,RADIO,x)? is shown in Figure 8. The question asks, "What does the ACME company supply the RADIO company?".

The MRPPS 3.0 system prints the proof steps as shown in Figure 8, and following the proof steps, the symbolic output for the proof is presented as shown in Figure 9. The user who has experience with these forms has no problem in understanding the answer and the reason steps.

Table 3. USES Relation

POOK	SCREWDRIVERS	DELAWARE
POOK	PLIERS	DELAWARE
RADIO	RESISTORS	NEW YORK
RADIO	CAPACITORS	NEW YORK
RADIO	SCOPES	NEW YORK

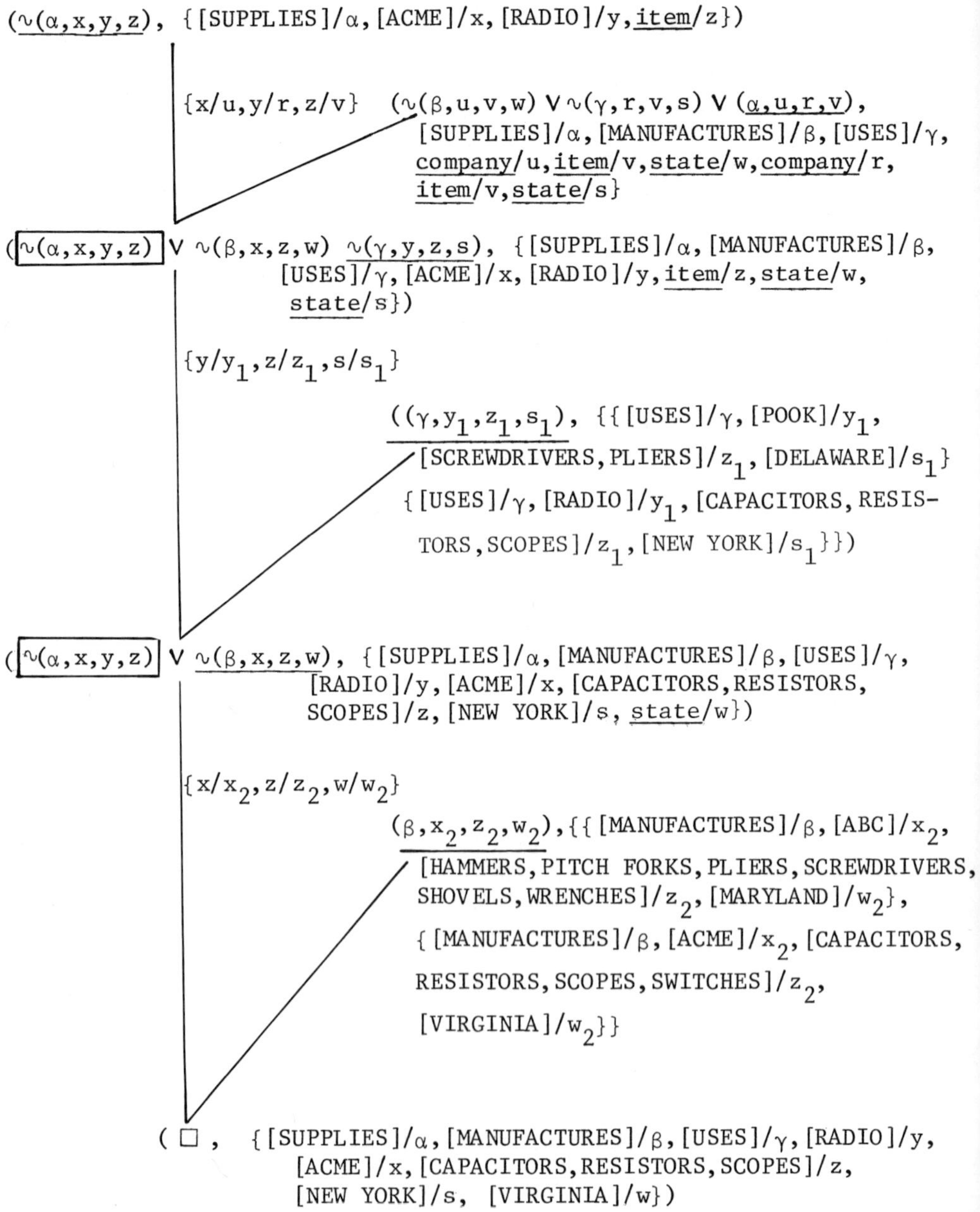

(∿(α,x,y,z), {[SUPPLIES]/α,[ACME]/x,[RADIO]/y,item/z})

{x/u,y/r,z/v} (∿(β,u,v,w) ∨ ∿(γ,r,v,s) ∨ (α,u,r,v),
[SUPPLIES]/α,[MANUFACTURES]/β,[USES]/γ,
company/u,item/v,state/w,company/r,
item/v,state/s}

(∿(α,x,y,z) ∨ ∿(β,x,z,w) ∿(γ,y,z,s), {[SUPPLIES]/α,[MANUFACTURES]/β,
[USES]/γ,[ACME]/x,[RADIO]/y,item/z,state/w,
state/s})

{y/y_1,z/z_1,s/s_1}

((γ,y_1,z_1,s_1), {{[USES]/γ,[POOK]/y_1,
[SCREWDRIVERS,PLIERS]/z_1,[DELAWARE]/s_1}
{[USES]/γ,[RADIO]/y_1,[CAPACITORS,RESIS-
TORS,SCOPES]/z_1,[NEW YORK]/s_1}})

(∿(α,x,y,z) ∨ ∿(β,x,z,w), {[SUPPLIES]/α,[MANUFACTURES]/β,[USES]/γ,
[RADIO]/y,[ACME]/x,[CAPACITORS,RESISTORS,
SCOPES]/z,[NEW YORK]/s, state/w})

{x/x_2,z/z_2,w/w_2}

(β,x_2,z_2,w_2),{{[MANUFACTURES]/β,[ABC]/x_2,
[HAMMERS,PITCH FORKS,PLIERS,SCREWDRIVERS,
SHOVELS,WRENCHES]/z_2,[MARYLAND]/w_2},
{[MANUFACTURES]/β,[ACME]/x_2,[CAPACITORS,
RESISTORS,SCOPES,SWITCHES]/z_2,
[VIRGINIA]/w_2}}

(□, {[SUPPLIES]/α,[MANUFACTURES]/β,[USES]/γ,[RADIO]/y,
[ACME]/x,[CAPACITORS,RESISTORS,SCOPES]/z,
[NEW YORK]/s, [VIRGINIA]/w})

Figure 8. Proof Graph

Natural Language Proof and Reason Output

It is inconvenient for individuals who are not familiar with the system notation to understand the symbolic outputs. For this purpose, a relatively straightforward natural language output is provided which was designed and implemented by Klein [1976] for the MRPPS 3.0 system. A brief description of how natural language is generated is provided here.

Each relation name within the system has associated with it a pattern specifying the skeleton of a sentence. The pattern consists of a character string that contains constants and special symbols.

1. ANSWER

   SUPPLIES(ACME,RADIO,{CAPACITORS,RESISTORS,SCOPES})

2. GENERAL RULE

   MANUFACTURE(ACME,{CAPACITORS,SCOPES,RESISTORS},VIRGINIA)

   $\wedge$ USES(RADIO,{CAPACITORS,RESISTORS,SCOPES},NEW YORK)

   $\rightarrow$ SUPPLIES(ACME,RADIO,{CAPACITORS,RESISTORS,SCOPES})

3. ASSERTION

   USES(RADIO,{CAPACITORS,RESISTORS,SCOPES},NEW YORK)

4. ASSERTION

   MANUFACTURE(ACME,{CAPACITORS,SCOPES,RESISTORS},VIRGINIA)

Figure 9. Symbolic Answer and Reason Output

Consider the ordered pair of template and Π-σ set:

$$((\alpha, x_1, x_2, x_3),\ \{[\text{MANUFACTURE}]/\alpha,\ [\text{ACME}]/x_1,\ [\text{CAPACITORS, RESISTORS, SCOPES, SWITCHES}]/x_2,\ [\text{VIRGINIA}]/x_3\}).$$

The pattern associated with the template structure might be:

@x_1 @SI MANUFACTURES @PI MANUFACTURE @x_2 IN THE STATE OF @x_3

This would provide the following output:

ACME MANUFACTURES CAPACITORS, RESISTORS, SCOPES, AND SWITCHES IN THE STATE OF VIRGINIA .

The pattern interpretation going from left to right is that the @ symbol refers to some variable in the substitution set which immediately follows the symbol. The substitution corresponding to this is found and replaces the symbol. Thus, the first two symbols @x_1 refer to the set of constants ACME in the substitution set associated with the variable x_1 . The next symbol is scanned. The symbol @ is followed by the special symbol SI which denotes that if there were a single constant in the preceding set, then the singular form which follows has to be used. Since there is only one company, MANUFACTURES is printed. Since the singular is printed, the plural form is not needed, and is skipped. The symbols @x_2 specify that the substitution set for x_2 is to be printed. Since there are several entries in the substitution set, a comma is placed between each constant, and the word AND printed before the last constant in the list. The string 'IN THE STATE OF' is then printed as it is listed since it is not preceded by the symbol @ . Finally, the substitution set associated with the variable x_3 is printed. The natural langauge form associated with the symbolic output of Figure 9 is given in Figure 10.

Voice Proofs and Reasons

There are many situations where it is desirable to have a voice output specifying the answer and reason steps. Voice output, like natural language output is a vastly simpler problem than that of voice input.

In developing the voice output for the system there were two major objectives:

1. <u>ANSWER</u>

   THE ACME ORGANIZATION SUPPLIES CAPACITORS, RESISTORS, AND SCOPES TO THE RADIO ORGANIZATION.

2. <u>GENERAL RULE</u>

   BECAUSE THE ACME ORGANIZATION MANUFACTURES CAPACITORS, SCOPES, AND RESISTORS IN VIRGINIA, AND THE RADIO ORGANIZATION USES CAPACITORS, RESISTORS, AND SCOPES IN NEW YORK, IT CAN BE CONCLUDED THAT THE ACME ORGANIZATION SUPPLIES CAPACITORS, RESISTORS, AND SCOPES TO THE RADIO ORGANIZATION.

3. <u>ASSERTION</u>

   THE RADIO ORGANIZATION IS LOCATED IN NEW YORK AND USES CAPACITORS, RESISTORS, AND SCOPES.

4. <u>ASSERTION</u>

   THE ACME ORGANIZATION IS LOCATED IN VIRGINIA AND MANUFACTURERS CAPACITORS, RESISTORS, AND SCOPES.

Figure 10. Natural Language Output

(1) the translator should not require a large amount of core memory, and

(2) the voice output should not be restricted to a particular voice synthesizer.

To satisfy the first criterion the voice translator uses only letter-to-sound rules to generate outputs. Thus, there are no dictionary look ups for exceptions to rules or for common words. Instead, a context sensitive grammar is used to generate sound output given a string of words. The approach used in MRPPS 3.0 was developed by Elovitz et al. [1975] at the Naval Research Laboratory (NRL). Thompson [1976] has modified the NRL grammar slightly and reorganized it to be more efficient.

To satisfy the second criterion, a two pass translator has been developed. In the first pass the English sentence is translated to International Phonetic Alphabet (IPA) using the NRL grammar. The second pass translates IPA output into the phonemes for the particular device used in the system - the Votrax voice synthesizer.

Details concerning the voice output are beyond the scope of this paper. The reader is referred to the Elovitz, Thompson, and Powell and Thompson papers for details. The user of the MRPPS 3.0 system can select any combination of output modes desired.

RELATED DEVELOPMENTS

Having described the MRPPS 3.0 System, it would be well to relate it to other work in the field. The use of mathematical logic as the basis of a data base system has been recognized by others. Darlington [1962] was, perhaps, the first individual who implemented a data base system based on logic. Green and Raphael [1968] recognized the importance of the work by Robinson [1965] in mathematical theorem proving as it relates to data base problems. The work on MRPPS 3.0 builds upon that work and provides a comprehensive system not previously developed. The SYNTEX system developed by Nicolas and Syre [1974] also uses logic as a basis for deduction as does the system developed by Kellogg, Klahr and Travis [1977]. They built a comprehensive system including an input and output language, and their work bears many relationships to the work of MRPPS 3.0.

The use of mathematical logic provides a powerful extension of the relational algebra and relational calculus described by Codd [1971]. Whereas Codd's work does not account for recursively defined relations, such relations are natural within mathematical logic and easily handled. Relational systems were proposed so as to simplify the specifications of queries to a data base. One can improve upon this simplification by the use of mathematical logic. The concept of a virtual relation stored as a definition in the IDB permits the user to ask questions directly about the relation, and not to be concerned about how to construct the relation from other relations in a system and to then have to express the query in a language.

Semantic networks and predicate calculus logic are compatible with one another as outlined in this paper and more thoroughly in McSkimin and Minker [1977]. This compatibility is also clearly demonstrated by Deliyanni and Kowalski [1977], who extend the concept of a semantic network. Whereas Deliyanni and Kowalski consider binary relations as the basis of their semantic network, the MRPPS 3.0 system handles n-ary relations. Others who have used semantic networks for data base systems are Shapiro [1971,1977], Woods [1975], and Mylopoulous et al. [1973]. A survey of work on semantic networks may be found in Schubert [1976].

It has been noted that virtual relations are defined by clauses in the IDB. These clauses may interrelate with one another. Thus, for example, consider the clauses

(1) $FATHER(x,y) \wedge MOTHER(z,y) \rightarrow HUSBAND(x,z)$

(2) $FATHER(u,v) \wedge HUSBAND(v,w) \rightarrow FATHER\text{-}IN\text{-}LAW(u,w)$

Let the FATHER and MOTHER relations be base relations in the EDB, and let HUSBAND and FATHER-IN-LAW be virtual relations defined by (1) and (2) in the IDB. Whereas HUSBAND is defined exclusively by base relations, FATHER-IN-LAW is defined in terms of both a virtual relation and a base relation. One can replace (2) by the new definition,

(3) $FATHER(u,v) \wedge FATHER(v,y) \wedge MOTHER(w,y) \rightarrow FATHER\text{-}IN\text{-}LAW(u,w)$,

where, now, FATHER-IN-LAW is defined exclusively in terms of base relations. Except when one has recursively defined virtual relations, it is possible to interrelate Horn clauses so that virtual relations are defined exclusively in terms of base relations. When a query clause contains a virtual relation, its definition is then found in the IDB and consists exclusively of base relations. In applying all of the interrelationships possible, one will generally obtain a larger set of clauses in the IDB. On the other hand, the modest amount of preprocessing that is required could save much processing time.

When IDB clauses are interacted as described above, a new IDB, called the compiled clauses IDB, is created. Now, when a query enters the system, excluding the case of recursive axioms in the IDB, each literal of the query which matches a literal in the compiled IDB is replaced in the query by literals all of which are base relations.

However, regardless of which set of clauses are in the IDB, i.e., the original or the compiled clauses, the MRPPS 3.0 system requires that the control structure handle the search process and use the Knowledge Base Index to access the data and axioms. Since, in the compiled IDB case, trivial deductions result, the effect is for the system to be interfaced with a relational data base system.

Reiter [1978] and Chang [1977] take a similar, but slightly different approach than that taken in this paper. Their approach is to interface directly with a conventional relational data base. General axioms are stored in the IDB. Reiter, as we do also, permits relations defined in the IDB to appear in the relational data base as well. Chang places the restriction that a relation defined in the IDB does not appear in the EDB.

In the Reiter and Chang approaches, query clauses interact with the IDB at compilation time using a theorem prover. Once the query is compiled, the theorem prover and the IDB are no longer needed. Recursive axioms can be handled by placing a limit on the number of literals in a clause. In this case, and also in MRPPS 3.0, one cannot guarantee retrieving all answers to a query. Each resultant clause, when searched against relations in the EDB achieves a response to a query. The set solutions from all clauses from the query constitute the set of all answers. Although MRPPS 3.0 stops when an answer has been found, there is no reason why all answers (assuming no recursively defined axioms) could not be found. In most data base applications, _all_ answers to a question are needed. If recursively defined axioms exist all answers cannot be found. However, in some cases, when counting information is used, even if recursively defined axioms exist, all answers can be found. How recursively defined axioms should be handled for data base systems is an important problem. However, one of the major advantages of using logic over the approach taken by Codd [1971] is to account for recursion.

Reiter and Chang could, of course, have compiled clauses in the IDB. As before, a compilation of the query against the already compiled clauses would take place using a theorem prover. In this case, the compilation would be faster than using uncompiled general axioms. The resultant compilation would be equivalent to the interpretive approach taken in MRPPS 3.0 in which the control structure would operate on the query clauses with essentially one step deductions on the query literals, using the compiled IDB clauses to obtain clauses all of whose literals appear in the EDB.

The approach described by Kellogg, Klahr and Travis [1977] lies mid-way between the above two approaches. They partly-compile their IDB, and partly control the search through a control structure.

SUMMARY

An experimental data base system, MRPPS 3.0, based on mathematical logic has been described. The major portions of the system that deal with the handling of large data bases, the deductive search and the answer comprehension system have been implemented. The portions that deal with the semantic graph are undergoing testing.

The MRPPS 3.0 system is comprehensive in scope as it integrates an input module, a semantic network, a deductive search mechanism, and an answer comprehension mechanism that includes natural language and spoken output. The system has undergone moderate testing on a relatively small data base that is rich in deductive searches. Attempts have not yet been made to test the system for large data bases.

Experimental work is required to specify which of a number of alternate design approaches should be incorporated into operational systems. In the work described here, greater consideration will have to be given to the heuristics within the search strategy controller, and to counting information.

In developing comprehensive data base systems, it is important that they be constructed using sound principles. Mathematical logic provides a firm foundation for such systems as illustrated in this paper. It plays a fundamental role in the deduction portion of the system, and in other portions of such systems as described in other chapters in this book.

ACKNOWLEDGMENTS

The author would like to particularly thank Alan Aronson, Pat Powell, and Guy Zanon for their constructive comments concerning the paper.

The MRPPS 3.0 System was designed primarily by the author in conjunction with Dr. James McSkimin, Dr. Gerald Wilson and Alan Aronson. A number of students contributed to various parts of the implementation: Pat Powell, Guy Zanon, Jeff Gishen, Steve Small, Mark Klein, Paul Thompson, Roger Gifford, and Mark Rehert.

The work was supported by NASA Grant 21-002-270 and from the NSF GJ-43632.

REFERENCES

1. Basili, V. R. and Turner, A. J. [1976] *SIMPL-T - A Structured Programming Language*, Paladin House, Geneva, Illinois, 1976. Also University of Maryland Computer Science Series, Vol. 2, University of Maryland, College Park, Maryland 20742.

2. Carnap, R. [1958] *Introduction to Symbolic Logic and Its Applications*, Dover Publications, Inc., New York, New York, 1958.

3. Chang, C.L. [1978] DEDUCE 2: Further Investigations of Deduction in Relational Data Bases, In *Logic and Data Bases* (H. Gallaire and J. Minker, Eds.), Plenum Press, N. Y., 1978, 201-236.

4. Chang, C. L. and Lee, R.C.T. [1973] *Symbolic Logic and Mathematical Theorem Proving*, Academic Press, New York, New York, 1973.

5. Codd, E. F. [1971] Relational Completeness of Data Base Sublanguages, Courant Computer Science Symposia 6, May 24-25, 1971. In *Data Base Systems* (R. Rustin, Ed.), Prentice-Hall, Englewood Cliffs, New Jersey, 1972, 65-98.

6. Darlington, J. L. [1962] A COMIT Program for the Davis-Putnam Algorithm, *Res. Lab. Electron.*, Mech. Transl. Grp., M.I.T., Cambridge, Massachusetts, May 1962.

7. Deliyanni, A. and Kowalski, R. A. [1977] Logic and Semantic Networks, Journees d'etudes Logique et bases de donees, Toulouse, France, Nov. 16-18, 1977.

8. Elovitz, H. S. [1975] "Automatic Text Translation to Speech Via Letter-to-Sound Rules," Scholarly Paper, University of Maryland, College Park, Maryland 20742, May 1975.

9. Enderton, H. B. [1972] *A Mathematical Introduction to Logic*, Academic Press, New York, New York, 1972.

10. Fishman, D. H. [1973] "Experiments with a Resolution-Based Deductive Question-Answering System and a Proposed Clause Representation for Parallel Search," Ph.D. Thesis, Department of Computer Science, University of Maryland, College Park, Maryland, 1973.

11. Green, C. C. [1969] Theorem Proving by Resolution as a Basis for Question-Answering Systems, In *Machine Intelligence 4* (B. Meltzer and D. Michie, Eds.), American Elsevier, New York, New York, 1969, 183-205.

12. Green, C. C. and Raphael, B. [1968] The Use of Theorem Proving Techniques in Question-Answering Systems, *Proceedings 1968 ACM National Conference*, Brandon Systems Press, Princeton, New Jersey, 1968, 169-181.

13. Hill, R. [1974] LUSH Resolution and Its Completeness, DCL Memo No. 78, University of Edinburgh, School of Artificial Intelligence, August 1974.

14. Kellogg, C., Klahr, P. and Travis, L. [1978] Deductive Planning and Pathfinding for Relational Data Bases, In *Logic and Data Bases* (H. Gallaire and J. Minker, Eds.), Plenum Press, New York, New York, 1978, 179-200.

15. Klein, M. [1976] "Translating Π-Clauses into English," Scholarly Paper, Department of Computer Science, University of Maryland, College Park, Maryland 20742, 1976.

16. Kowalski R. and Kuehner, D. [1971] Linear Resolution with Selection Function, *Artificial Intelligence 2*, 3/4 (1971), 227-260.

17. Loveland, D. W. [1969] A Simplified Format for the Model Elimination Theorem Proving Procedure, *JACM 16*, 3 (July 1969), 349-363.

18. Luckham, D. and Nilsson, N. [1971] Extracting Information from Resolution Proof Trees, *Artificial Intelligence 2*,1 (1971), 27-54.

19. McSkimin, J. R. [1976] "The Use of Semantic Information in Deductive Question-Answering Systems," Ph.D. Thesis, Department of Computer Science, University of Maryland, College Park, Maryland, 1976.

20. McSkimin, J.R. and Minker, J. [1978] A Predicate Calculus Based Semantic Network for Question-Answering Systems, In *Associative Networks - The Representation and Use of Knowledge in Computers* (N. Findler, Ed.), Academic Press, New York 1978 (in press).

21. McSkimin, J.R. and Minker, J. [1977] The Use of a Semantic Network in a Deductive Question-Answering System, *Proceedings IJCAI-77*, Cambridge, Massachusetts, 1977, 50-58.

22. McSkimin, J.R. and Wilson, G. A. [1974] MRPPS 2.0 User's Manual, CN-15, Computer Science Center, University of Maryland, College Park, Maryland, November 1974.

23. Minker, J. [1978] Search Strategy and Selection Function for an Inferential Relational System, *ACM Transactions on Database Systems 3*,1 (March 1978), 1-31.

24. Minker, J. [1977] Control Structures of a Pattern-Directed Search System, *Proceedings of the Workshop on Pattern-Directed Inference Systems, ACM SIGART Newsletter*, No. 63 (June 1977), 7-14.

25. Minker, J., Fishman, D. H. and McSkimin, J. R. [1973] The Q* Algorithm - A Search Strategy for a Deductive Question-Answering System, *Artificial Intelligence 4*, (1973), 225-243.

26. Minker, J., McSkimin, J. R. and Fishman, D. H. [1974] MRPPS - An Interactive Refutation Proof Procedure System for Question Answering, *J. Computers and Information Sciences 3*, (June 1974), 105-122.

27. Mylopoulos, J., Badler, N., Melli, L. and Roussopoulos, N. [1973] 1 PAK: A SNOBOL-Based Programming Language for Arfiticial Intelligence Applications. *Advance Papers of 3rd Int. Joint Conf. on Artificial Intelligence*, Stanford University, Stanford, California, 1973, 691-696.

28. Nicolas, J. M. and Syre, J. C. [1974] Natural Language Question-Answering and Automatic Deduction in the System SYNTEX, *Proceedings of the IFIP Congress, 1974*, North-Holland Publishing Company, New York, New York, 1974,595-599.

29. Powell, P. [1977] "Answer-Reason Extraction in a Parallel Relational Data Base System," Master's Thesis, Department of Computer Science, University of Maryland, College Park, Maryland 20742, 1977.

30. Powell, P. and Thompson, P. [1978] Natural Language and Voice Output for Relational Data Base Systems, TR-686, Department of Computer Science, University of Maryland, College Park, Maryland 20742, 1978.

31. Reiter, R. [1971] Two Results on Ordering for Resolution with Merging and Linear Format, *JACM 18*,4 (October 1971), 630-646.

32. Reiter, R. [1978] Deductive Question-Answering on Relational Data Bases, In *Logic and Data Bases* (H. Gallaire and J. Minker, Eds.), Plenum Press, New York, New York, 1978, 149-177.

34. Robinson, J. A. [1965] A Machine-Oriented Logic Based on the Resolution Principle, *JACM 12*,1 (January 1965), 23-41.

35. Schubert, L. K. [1976] Extending the Expressive Power of Semantic Networks, *Artificial Intelligence 7*, 2 (1976), 163-198.

36. Shapiro, S. C. [1971] A Net Structure for Semantic Information Storage, Deduction and Retrieval, *Proceedings Inter. Joint Conf. on Artificial Intelligence*, The British Computer Society, London, 1971, 512-523.

37. Shapiro, S. C. [1977] Representing and Locating Deduction Rules in a Semantic Network, *Proceedings of the Workshop on Pattern-Directed Inference Systems, ACM SIGART Newsletter No. 63* (June 1977, 14-18.

38. Thompson, P. [1976] "Rule Precedence within Context-Sensitive Grammars; An Extension of the Letter to Sound Rules Used in Voice Production," Scholarly Paper, Department of Computer Science, University of Maryland, College Park, Maryland 20742, 1976.

39. Wilson, G. [1976] "A Description and Analysis of the PAR Technique - An Approach for Parallel Inference and Parallel Search in Problem Solving Systems," Ph.D. Thesis, Dept. of Computer Science, University of Maryland, College Park, Maryland 20742, 1976. Also Tech. Report TR-464, Department of Computer Science, University of Maryland, 1976.

40. Woods, W. A. [1975] What's in a Link - Foundations for Semantic Networks, In *Representation and Understanding* (D. G. Bobrow and A. Collins, Eds.), Academic Press, New York, 1975, 35-82.

DEDUCTIVE QUESTION-ANSWERING ON RELATIONAL DATA BASES

Raymond Reiter

The University of British Columbia

Vancouver, British Columbia

ABSTRACT

The principal concern of this paper is the design of a retrieval system which combines current techniques for query evaluation on relational data bases with a deductive component in such a way that the interface between the two is both clean and natural. The result is an approach to deductive retrieval which appears to be feasible for data bases with very large extensions (i.e. specific facts) and comparatively small intensions (i.e. general facts). More specifically, a suitably designed theorem prover "sweeps through" the intensional data base, extracting all information relevant to a given query. This theorem prover never looks at the extensional data base. The end result of this sweep is a set of queries, each of which is extensionally evaluated. The union of answers returned from each of these queries is the set of answers to the original query.

One consequence of this decomposition into an intensional and extensional processor is that the latter may be realized by a conventional data base management system. Another is that the intensional data base can be compiled using a theorem prover as a once-only compiler.

This paper is essentially an impressionistic survey of some results which are rigorously treated elsewhere. As such, no proofs are given for the theorems stated, and the basic system design is illustrated by means of an extended example.

INTRODUCTION

The principal concern of this paper is the design of a retrieval system which combines current techniques for query evaluation on relational data bases, e.g. Codd [1972] with a deductive component in such a way that the interface between the two is both clean and natural. The result is an approach to deductive retrieval which appears to be feasible for data bases with very large extensions (i.e. specific facts) and comparatively small intensions (i.e. general facts). More specifically, a suitably designed theorem prover "sweeps through" the intensional data base, extracting all information relevant to a given query. In particular, this theorem prover never looks at the extensional data base. The end result of this sweep is a set of queries, each of which is extensionally evaluated. The union of answers returned from each of these queries is a set of answers to the original query.

There are two important consequences of this decomposition of the question-answering task into a theorem prover computing on the intensional data base, and an extensional processor computing on the extensional data base:

1. The extensional processor can be realized by a conventional data base management system.

2. Because the theorem prover never accesses the extensional data base, the intensional data base can be compiled using the theorem prover as a once-only compiler. This means that at query evaluation time there is no need for a theorem prover, nor are there the usual problems involving search which can plague a theorem proving system.

This paper is essentially a survey of some of the results in Reiter [1977]. As such, it is necessarily impressionistic, so that no proofs are given for the theorems stated, and the basic approach to query evaluation which decouples the theorem prover from the extensional processor is described by means of an extended example. A rigorous presentation is contained in Reiter [1977] to which the interested reader is referred for the painful details.

DATA BASES

The results of this paper apply only to first order data bases with the following properties:

(i) The data base consists of finitely many <u>twffs</u> (typed well-formed formulae). For example, in an inventory domain, such a twff might be

(x/Manufacturer)(y/Part)(z/Part)manufactures x,y
    $\wedge$ Subpart z,y $\supset$ Supplies x,z

i.e., every manufacturer of a part supplies all its subparts. The restricted universal quantifier (y/Part) may be read "for every y which is a Part". The restrictions Manufacturer and Part are called types and are distinguished monadic predicates. If τ is such a type, then $(x/\tau)W$ is an abbreviation for $(x)\tau x \supset W$. We shall later require the notion of a restricted existential quantifier (Ex/τ) which may be read "there is an x in τ". $(Ex/\tau)W$ is an abbreviation for $(Ex)\tau x \wedge W$. We denote by $|\tau|$ the set of all constants which satisfy the type τ. Thus, $|\text{Part}|$ might be {gadget-1, widget-3, bolt-49,...,}. In general, a twff has the form $(x_1/\tau_1)\ldots(x_n/\tau_n)W$ for $n \geq 0$ where W is any quantifier free ordinary first order formula containing no function signs, and $\tau_1,\ldots,\tau_n$ are types. Notice that no existential quantifiers are permitted - all twffs are universally quantified. In the case that the twff has no quantifiers, it is an ordinary ground first order formula.

(ii) There are only finitely many constant signs. Constant signs denote individuals of the data base e.g. bolt-49, Acme-manufacturers, etc.

(iii) Equality is a distinguished predicate. We assume that the data base contains the following equality axioms:

E1. $(x)x=x$

E2. $(x)(y)\ x=y \supset y=x$

E3. $(x)(y)(z)\ x=y \wedge y=z \supset x=z$

E4. For each n-ary predicate sign P

$$(x_1)\ldots(x_n)(x_1')\ldots(x_n')\ x_1=x_1' \wedge\ldots\wedge x_n=x_n' \wedge$$

$$Px_1,\ldots,x_n \supset Px_1',\ldots,x_n'$$

In addition, if $c_1,\ldots,c_p$ are all of the constant signs of the data base, then the following domain closure axiom applies:

DC. $(x)[x=c_1 \vee x=c_2 \vee \ldots \vee x=c_p]$.

The domain closure axiom restricts the universe of discourse to just those individuals denoted by the constant signs of the theory. In the intended interpretation, answers to queries will be formulated exclusively in terms of these finitely many individuals.

Finally, we assume that for each constant sign c, the ground equality literal c=c is in the data base, and for each pair of distinct constant signs c,c' the inequality literal $c \neq c'$ is in the data base. Intuitively, as far as the data base is concerned, two constant signs are treated as equal iff they are identical syntactic objects.

Let DB be a data base as defined above, and let EDB be the set of ground literals of DB. EDB will be called the extensional data base. The intensional data base is defined to be IDB = DB - EDB. Intuitively, the EDB is a set of specific facts like "John Doe teaches Calculus 103", while the IDB is a set of general facts like "All widgets are manufactured by Foobar Inc." or "John Doe teaches Calculus 102 or Bill Jones teaches Calculus 103 (but I don't know which)" together with the equality and domain closure axioms.

QUERIES AND ANSWERS

A query is any expression of the form

$$< x_1/\tau_1,\ldots,x_n/\tau_n \mid (q_1y_1/\theta_1)\ldots(q_my_m/\theta_m)W(x_1,\ldots,x_n,y_1,\ldots,y_m)> \quad (1)$$

where (q_iy_i/θ_i) is (y_i/θ_i) or (Ey_i/θ_i), the τ's and θ's are types, and $W(x_1,\ldots,x_n,y_1,\ldots,y_m)$ is a quantifier-free formula containing no function signs and whose variables are $x_1,\ldots,x_n,y_1,\ldots,y_m$. For brevity, we shall usually denote the typical query (1) by $< \vec{x}/\vec{\tau} \mid (q\vec{y}/\vec{\theta})W(\vec{x},\vec{y})>$.

Intuitively, (1) denotes the set of all n-tuples $\vec{x}$ such that $\vec{x} \in |\vec{\tau}|$* and such that $(q\vec{y}/\vec{\theta})W(\vec{x},\vec{y})$ is true.

As an example, consider an inventory domain and the request "Give those manufacturers who supply all widgets". This might be represented in our query language by

$$<x/Manufacturer \mid (y/Widget)Supplies\ x,y >$$

Formally, let DB be a data base as defined in the previous section, and $Q = < \vec{x}/\vec{\tau} \mid (q\vec{y}/\vec{\theta})W(\vec{x},\vec{y})>$ a query. A set of n-tuples $\{\vec{c}^{(1)},\ldots,\vec{c}^{(r)}\}$ is an answer to Q (with respect to DB) iff

1. $\vec{c}^{(i)} \in |\vec{\tau}| \quad i=1,\ldots,r$ and
2. $DB \vdash \bigvee_{i\leq r} (q\vec{y}/\vec{\theta})W(\vec{c}^{(i)},\vec{y})$

---

* If $\vec{\tau} = \tau_1,\ldots,\tau_n$ is a sequence of types, then $|\vec{\tau}| = |\tau_1| \times\ldots\times |\tau_n|$

Notice that if $\{\vec{c}^{(1)},\ldots,\vec{c}^{(r)}\}$ is an answer to Q and $\vec{c}$ is any n-tuple of constants such that $\vec{c} \in |\vec{\tau}|$ then so also is $\{c^{(1)},\ldots,\vec{c}^{(r)},\vec{c}\}$ an answer to Q. This suggests the need for the following definitions:

A is a _minimal_ answer to Q iff no proper subset of A is an answer to Q. If A is minimal, then if $|A| = 1$, A is a _definite_ answer to Q. Otherwise A is an _indefinite_ answer to Q. Instead of denoting an indefinite answer by $\{\vec{c}^{(1)},\ldots,\vec{c}^{(r)}\}$, we prefer the more suggestive notation $\vec{c}^{(1)}+\ldots+\vec{c}^{(r)}$. Indefinite answers have interpretation:
$\vec{x} = \vec{c}^{(1)}$ or $\vec{x} = \vec{c}^{(2)}$ or...or $\vec{x} = \vec{c}^{(r)}$ but there is not enough information, given DB, to determine which. We shall sometimes refer to expressions of the form $\vec{c}^{(1)} +\ldots+ \vec{c}^{(r)}$ as _disjunctive tuples_. Finally, we denote by $\|Q\|$ the set of minimal answers to Q.

The use of types in deductive question-answering has been independently proposed in McSkimin [1976], McSkimin and Minker [1977], who refer to types as primitive categories. Typically, types are used to block certain unifications, and to maintain data base integrity.

In order to better understand why the possibility of indefinite answers must be entertained, consider the following fragment of a kinship data base:

Example 1

IDB (x/Male)(y/Human)Brother x,y $\supset$ Sibling x,y

(xz/Male)(y/Human)(w/Female)Uncle x,y $\wedge$ Father z,y
$\wedge$ Mother w,y $\supset$ Brother x,z $\vee$ Brother x,w

EDB Uncle a,b Father c,b Mother d,b Brother a,e

Consider the query "Who are all of a's siblings?"

Q = $<$ x/Human|Sibling a,x $>$

Then $\|Q\|$ = {e, c+d}

i.e. e is a sibling of a. Moreover either c is a sibling of a or d is, but there is not enough information available to determine which is the case.

EXISTENTIAL QUERIES AND EQUALITY

Recall that a data base was defined, in part, to contain the equality axioms E1 - E4, and the domain closure axiom DC. The presence of these axioms will clearly prove disastrous for any theorem proving approach to query evaluation. The use of proof procedures with "built in" equality e.g. paramodulation (Robinson and Wos [1969]) will be of little value since the domain closure axiom will still be present and for data bases with a large number of constants, this axiom will inevitably lead to unfeasible computations. Fortunately, for existential queries i.e. queries of the form $<\vec{x}/\vec{\tau} \mid (E\vec{y}/\vec{\theta})W(\vec{x},\vec{y})>$, these axioms turn out to be irrelevant.

Theorem 1

Let E(DB) be the equality and domain closure axioms of a data base DB, and let Q be an existential query. Then A is an answer to Q with respect to DB iff it is an answer to Q with respect to DB - E(DB) i.e. the equality and domain closure axioms are irrelevant to existential query evaluation.

REDUCTION OF ARBITRARY QUERIES TO EXISTENTIAL QUERIES

As we saw in the previous section, equality poses no difficulties for existential queries. Unfortunately, Theorem 1 fails for arbitrary queries. To see why, consider the following data base:

Equality axioms E1 - E4

DC $(x)x=a$

Pa,a

$|\tau| = \{a\}$

i.e., a data base with a single constant a and a single type τ. Then $\|< x/\tau \mid (y/\tau)Px,y> \| = \{a\}$. But $(y/\tau)Pa,y$, i.e., $(y)\tau y \supset Pa,y$ is not provable without the domain closure axiom DC.

The approach which we adopt is to reduce arbitrary queries to existential ones by invoking the "projection" and "division" operators which we now define. Let $Q = < \vec{x}/\vec{\tau}, z/\psi \mid (q\vec{y}/\vec{\theta})W(\vec{x},\vec{y},z) >$. The quotient of $\|Q\|$ by z, $\Delta_z \|Q\|$, is a set of disjunctive tuples and is defined as follows:

$\vec{c}^{(1)} + \ldots + \vec{c}^{(m)} \in \Delta_z \|Q\|$ iff

1. For all $\vec{a} \in |\psi|^m$, $(\vec{c}^{(1)},a_1)+\ldots+(\vec{c}^{(m)},a_m)$ is an answer (not necessaryily minimal) to Q^1 (and hence some sub-disjunctive tuple of $(\vec{c}^{(1)},a_1)+\ldots+(\vec{c}^{(m)},a_m)$ is an element of $||Q||$), and
2. for no i, $1 \leq i \leq m$, does $\vec{c}^{(1)}+\ldots+\vec{c}^{(i-1)}+\vec{c}^{(i+1)}+\ldots+\vec{c}^{(m)}$ have property 1. (There is a slight abuse of notation here. If $\vec{c} = (c_1,\ldots,c_n)$, then $(\vec{c},a)$ is intended to denote $(c_1,\ldots,c_n,a)$.) The operator Δ_z is called the <u>division operator with respect to z</u> and is an appropriate generalization of the division operator of Codd [1972].

<u>The projection of Q with respect to z</u>, $\pi_z ||Q||$, is a set of disjunctive tuples and is defined as follows:

$$\vec{c}^{(1)}+\ldots+\vec{c}^{(m)} \in \pi_z ||Q|| \text{ iff}$$

1. There exist constant signs $a_j^{(i)} \in |\psi|, j=1,\ldots,r_i \; i=1,\ldots,m$ such that $\underset{j \leq r_i \; i \leq m}{+} (c^{(i)}, a_j^{(i)}) \in ||Q||$ and
2. For no i, $1 \leq i \leq m$, does $\vec{c}^{(1)}+\ldots+\vec{c}^{(i-1)}+\vec{c}^{(i+1)}+\ldots+\vec{c}^{(m)}$ have property 1.

The operator π_z is called the <u>projection operator with respect to z</u> and is an appropriate generalization of the projection operator of Codd [1972] .

The following theorem indicates the importance of these operators:

<u>Theorem 2</u>

If $W(\vec{x},y)$ is a (not necessarily quantifier-free) formula with free variables $\vec{x}$ and y , then

1. $||<\vec{x}/\vec{\tau}\,|(y/\theta)W(\vec{x},y)>|| = \Delta_y||<\vec{x}/\vec{\tau},y/\theta\,|W(\vec{x},y)>||$
2. $||<\vec{x}/\vec{\tau}\,|(Ey/\theta)W(\vec{x},y)>|| = \pi_y||<\vec{x}/\vec{\tau},y/\theta\,|W(\vec{x},y)>||$

Using Theorem 2 we can now represent an arbitrary query as the appropriate application of projection and division operators to an existential query. For example,

$$||<x/\tau_1|(Ey/\tau_2)(z/\tau_3)(Ew/\tau_4)W(x,y,z,w)>|| =$$

$$\pi_y\Delta_z||<x/\tau_1,y/\tau_2,z/\tau_3|(Ew/\tau_4)W(x,y,z,w)>||$$

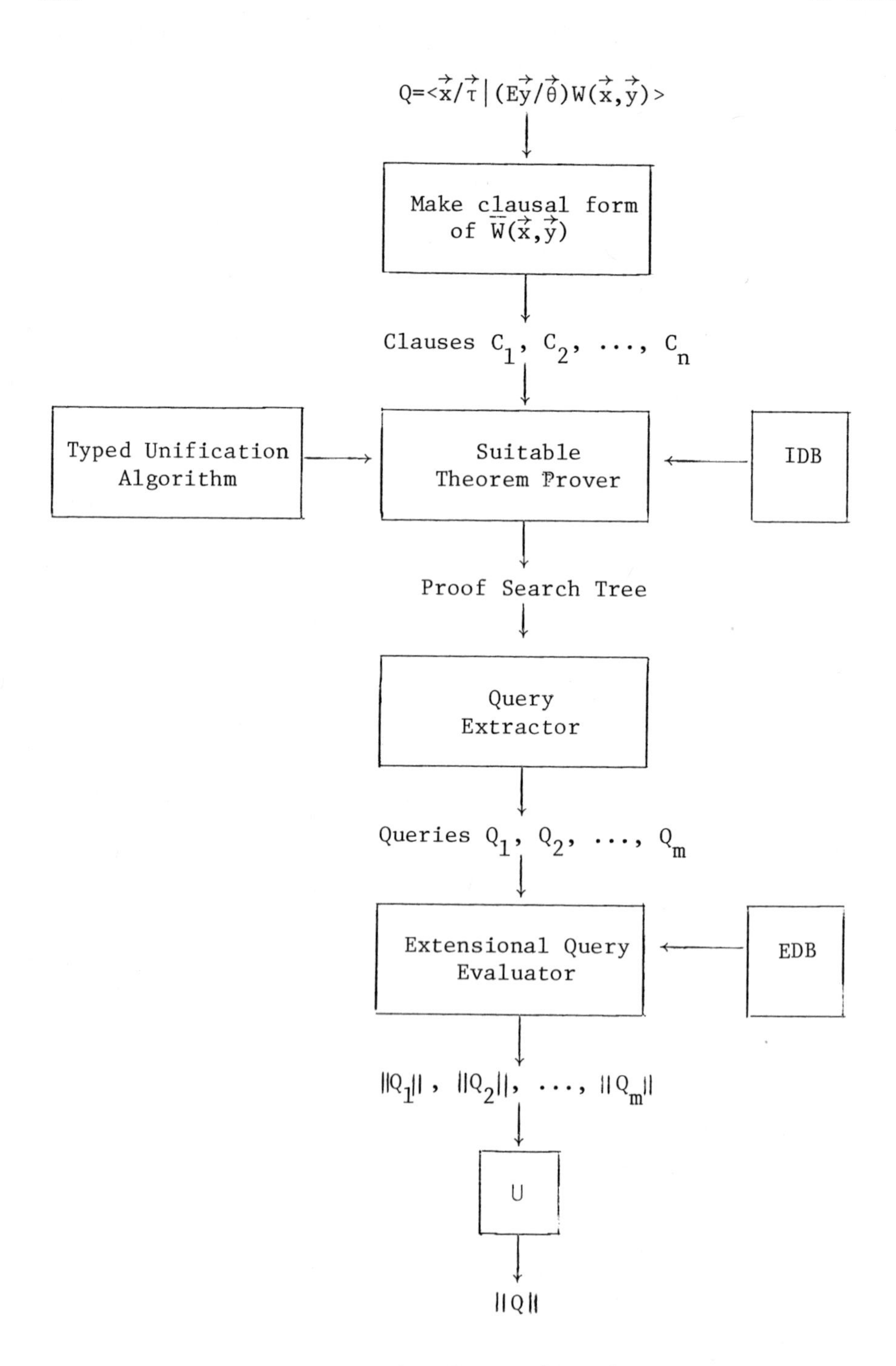

Figure 1. System Overview

In view of Theorem 2 it is sufficient to devise techniques for evaluating existential queries only, in which case, by Theorem 1, we can eliminate the equality and domain closure axioms from the data base.

ANSWERING EXISTENTIAL QUERIES

The approach of this paper is designed for very large data bases in which the vast majority of facts are extensional i.e. $|EDB| \gg |IDB|$ with $|EDB|$ very large. Under these circumstances, conventional theorem proving approaches (e.g., Minker et al. [1972]) are likely to be quite inefficient since the theorem prover is intermingling access to both the IDB and EDB. As an alternative, Figure 1 illustrates our proposed system design. There are several points worth noting:

1. As its name implies, the extensional query evaluator evaluates queries in our query language, but only with respect to the EDB. As such, it need not be a conventional theorem prover.

2. The most significant observation is that the EDB and IDB processors are completely decoupled. The IDB, but not the EDB, is invoked during the theorem proving process. Since, in applications to large data bases, we can expect $|EDB| \gg |IDB|$, the last thing we want is to require of the theorem prover that it have to look at the EDB. Moreover, there are far more efficient non theorem proving techniques for extensional query evaluation, e.g. relational query evaluation (Palermo [1974], Reiter [1976]). In effect, this decoupling of the EDB and IDB processors relegates the search task over the IDB to the theorem prover, and the "search-free computational" task over the EDB to the extensional query evaluator.

3. The result of the theorem proving process is a proof search tree from which a set of queries $Q_1, \ldots, Q_m$ can be extracted. These are extensionally evaluated and the results unioned to obtain the answers to the original query Q.

We cannot in the limited space of this paper, formally describe and justify the approach to deductive question-answering of Figure 1. Instead, we shall try to convey its basic flavour by means of an example. The interested reader is referred to Reiter [1977] for particulars.

Example 2

We consider a simple fragment of an education domain.

IDB (1) A teaches all calculus courses.

(z/Calculus)Teach A,z

(2) B teaches all computer science courses

(y/CS)Teach B,y

(3) If teacher u teaches course v and student w is enrolled in v, then u is a teacher of w.

(u/Teacher)(v/Course)(w/Student)Enrolled w,v $\wedge$ Teach u,v $\supset$ Teacher-of w,u

EDB

Teach	x	y
	A	P100
	B	P200
	C	P300
	D	H100
	D	H200

Enrolled	x	y
	a	C100
	a	P300
	a	CS100
	b	C200
	b	CS200
	b	CS300
	c	H100
	c	C100
	d	H200
	d	P200
	d	P300

|Teacher| = {A,B,C,D}

|Student| = {a,b,c,d}

|Course| = {C100,C200,CS100,CS200,CS300,H100,H200,P100,P200, P300}

|Calculus| = {C100,C200}

|CS| = {CS100,CS200,CS300}

Consider the query "Who are a's teachers?"

Q = < x/Teacher|Teacher-of a,x >

We start by treating (Ex/Teacher)Teacher-of a,x as a theorem to be proved with DB as hypothesis. Using the usual refutation approach, we create the clausal form of its negation i.e. $\overline{\text{Teacher-of}}$ a,x and associate, with the variable x of this clause, the type Teacher. Now consider attempting a linear refutation using $\overline{\text{Teacher-of}}$ a,x as top clause. There are two possibilities:

(i) This top clause could be resolved against a unit of the EDB, or

(ii) It could be resolved against a clause (in this case the clausal form* of (3)) of the IDB.

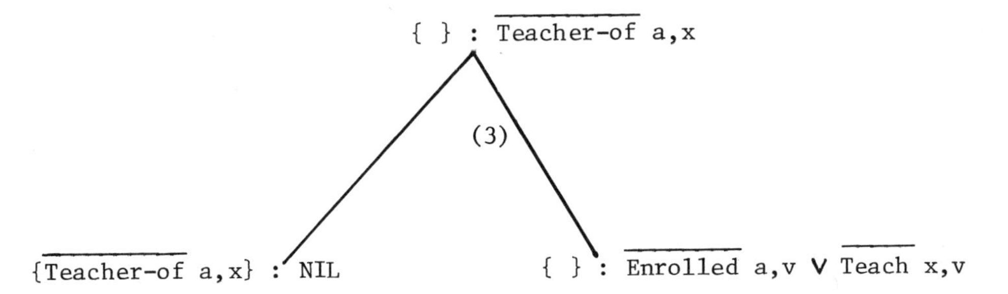

Figure 3. Deduction Step Continued

Our approach is to admit both possibilities, as in Figure 2, but to perform just the second. Literals enclosed in curly brackets represent literals which possibly might have been, but were not, resolved away against the EDB. The label on the right branch of Figure 2 indicates that clause of the IDB against which $\overline{\text{Teacher-of}}$ a,x was resolved. The left branch is unlabeled, indicating that we could have tried to resolve $\overline{\text{Teacher-of}}$ a,x against the EDB, but we have postponed this attempt by instead placing the literal within curly brackets. This left node is now closed, since there are no remaining literals to resolve against the IDB. The right node, with clause $\overline{\text{Enrolled}}$ a,v ∨ $\overline{\text{Teach}}$ x,v remains open. Again there are two possibilities:

(i) Resolve $\overline{\text{Teach}}$ x,v against the EDB, or

(ii) Resolve it against clauses (1) or (2) of the IDB.

Figure 3 represents these possibilities, again postponing the resolution operation against the EDB, as indicated by the unlabeled left branch. The branches labeled (1) and (2) correspond to possibility (ii).

It is clear that we can continue expanding nodes in this way. If

$$N = \{E_1,\ldots,E_k\} : L_1 \vee\ldots\vee L_p$$

is a typical such node, then N will have successors $N_o, N_1, \ldots, N_r$ where

---

* In converting IDB formulae to clausal form, one eliminates the quantifiers. Since all quantifiers are restricted by types, these types must be associated with their corresponding variables in the clausal form.

$$N_o = \{E_1,\ldots,E_k,L_p\} : L_1 \vee \ldots \vee L_{p-1}$$

indicating that we are postponing any attempted resolution of L_p against a unit of the EDB. For $i=1,\ldots,r$

$$N_i = \{E_1\sigma_i,\ldots,E_k\sigma_i\} : R_i$$

where R_i is the resolvent obtained by resolving the clause $L_1 \vee \ldots \vee L_p$ upon its rightmost literal L_p against a clause of the IDB and σ_i is the corresponding unifying substitution. Notice that we are here using a clause ordering linear resolution strategy in which only rightmost literals in a deduction are resolved upon. When suitably formalized, such a strategy can be shown to be complete (Reiter [1971]).

For the example at hand, we can continue expanding nodes until eventually no further expansion is possible. Figure 4 shows the resulting fully expanded tree. The only new feature in this figure is the introduction of an answer literal ANS x (Green [1969]) whose function is to record the substitutions being made for the variable x. Clearly there is a need for this bookkeeping device since any substitution made for x is a possible answer to Q.

Now consider a typical terminal node in Figure 4, say $\{ANS\ x,\ \overline{Enrolled}\ a,v,\ \overline{Teach}\ x,v\} : NIL$. This means that the non answer literals have yet to be resolved away against the EDB. In other words, the query

$$Q_1 = \langle x/Teacher \mid (Ev/Course)Enrolled\ a,v \wedge Teacn\ x,v \rangle$$

when extensionally evaluated yields a set of answers to the original query Q. Similarly, the remaining terminal nodes yield the following queries for extensional evaluation:

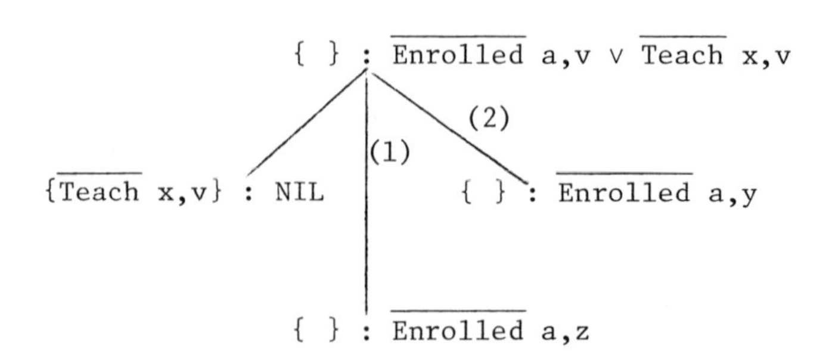

Figure 2. Deduction Step

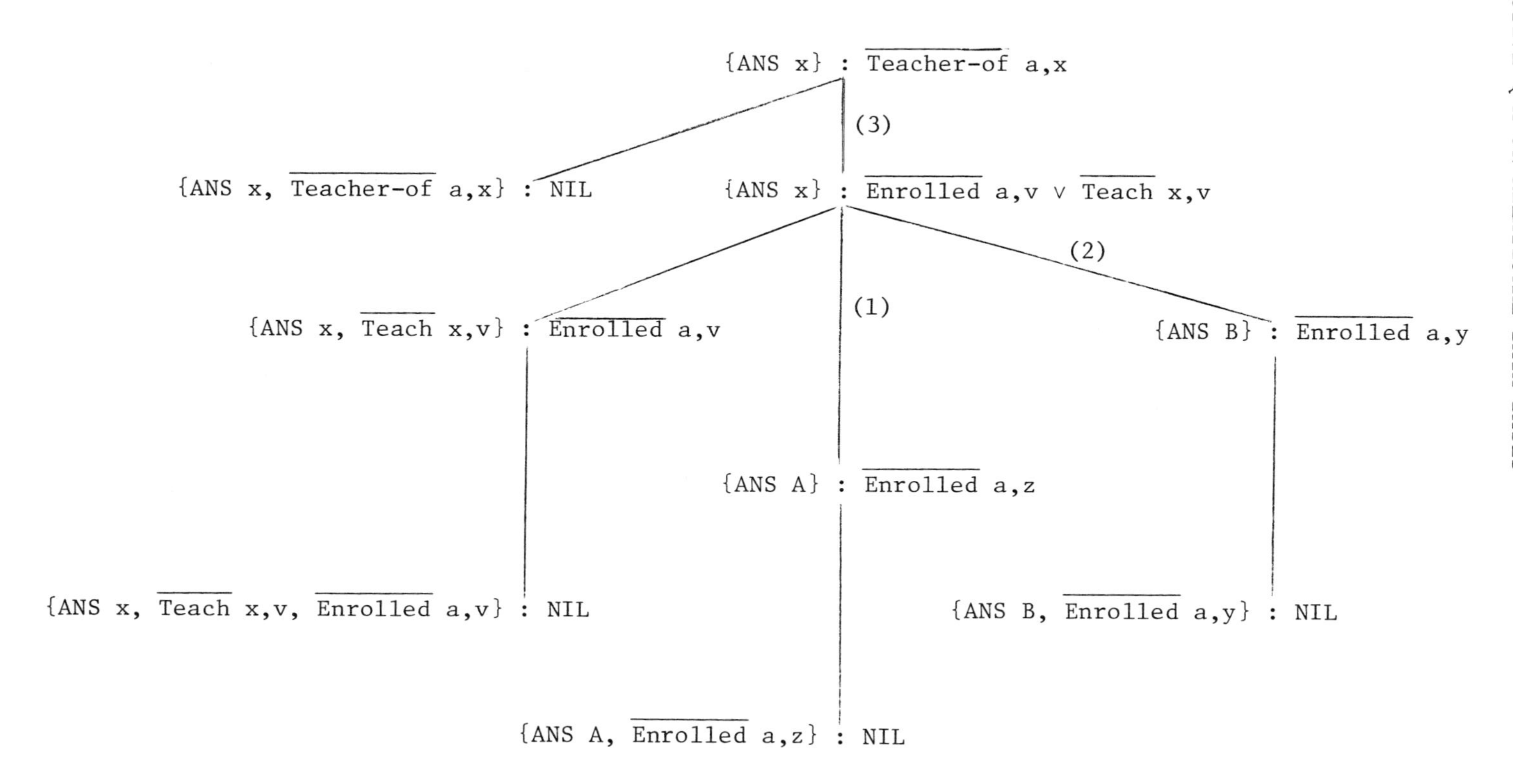

Figure 4. Deduction Steps and Answer Extraction.

Q_2 = < x/Teacher|Teacher-of a,x >

Q_3 = < x/Teacher|(Ez/Calculus)Enrolled a,z ∧ x=A >

Q_4 = < x/Teacher|(Ey/CS)Enrolled a,y ∧ x=B >

These queries have respective extensional values {C}, ϕ, {A}, {B}, the union of which yields

$||Q|| = \{A,B,C\}$

Notice how the intensional and extensional processors are totally decoupled under this approach. Figure 4 represents the first phase of query evaluation. This is the only task allocated to the theorem prover and nowhere in this process does the theorem prover probe the EDB. The second phase requires the extensional evaluation of the queries Q_1, Q_2, Q_3 and Q_4. This can be done by a relational data base management system and is certain to be far more efficient for large EDBs than any theorem proving technique. For an approach to extensional query evaluation designed for the query language of this paper and which optimizes for equality see Reiter [1976].

COMPLETENESS OF THE QUERY EVALUATION PROCESS

As this paper is necessarily impressionistic, we have been deliberately vague in the previous section (Answering Existential Queries) about the nature of the theorem prover that is required. Moreover, there are a number of features which the simple example of that section fails to illustrate:

1. The derivation of indefinite answers.

2. How the types associated with the variables of a clause affect the unification algorithm.

3. The treatment of multiple clauses arising from a query.

In Reiter [1977] all of these issues are made precise. Once this has been done, it is possible to prove the following completeness result:

> Provided the extensional query evaluator returns all and only the answers to a given query and provided an appropriate theorem prover is used for the intensional processing, then the approach of this paper is complete i.e. all and only the answers to a given query will be returned, including indefinite answers should they arise.

In a very real sense, this completeness result must be taken with a grain of salt, for in order to properly make use of it the proof search tree generated by the theorem prover must be finite, as indeed that of Figure 4 is. Clearly we cannot expect finite search trees in the presence of recursive axioms. For example, an axiom defining the transitivity of a relation R

$$(x,y,z/\tau)Rx,y \wedge Ry,z \supset Rx,z$$

will lead to an infinite search tree for the query $< x/\tau, y/\tau\ Rx,y >$. Under such circumstances an heuristic approach could be adopted. For example, the search tree could be truncated at some predefined level bound in which case a set of answers is returned with a warning to the user that some answers might be missing. We favour a different approach, one which guarantees that all search trees will be finite. There are two arguments in favour of this approach:

(i) The user will be assured that all answers to a query will be returned.

(ii) When all search trees are finite, the IDB can be compiled. (See the section on Compiling the IDB below.)

One way of guaranteeing finite search trees is to appropriately *structure* the data base. In Reiter [1978a] an approach to data base structuring is described. Briefly, this first involves characterizing those circumstances under which infinite deductive paths can arise. This can be done in terms of certain sequences, called *cycles*, of IDB formulae. Intuitively, a cycle can be viewed as a possible recursive application of its formulae in the process of searching for a proof. It turns out that cycles can be "cut", and hence infinite deductive paths eliminated, by representing, in the EDB, certain sub-extensions of appropriately designated predicates. In effect, what we are proposing is a criterion by means of which the following question can be answered: In designing a data base, what information should be represented extensionally, and what intensionally? The structuring proposal is to represent enough information extensionally so as to "cut" all of the cycles of the data base, thereby quaranteeing finite search trees.

Although this process of filling in sub-extensions of suitably chosen predicates can always be invoked to cut cycles, this can occasionally be too drastic a remedy. In certain special cases, the particular structure of a cycle can be exploited to prove that it cannot lead to an infinite deduction path, in which case there is no need to enlarge the extensional data base. For example, consider the following recursive intensional fact: "All parts suppliers also provide subparts for those parts."

$$(x,y,z/\text{Part})\text{Subpart } y,z \wedge \text{Supplies } x,y \supset \text{Supplies } x,z$$

Because the Subpart relation is transitive, it is possible to prove that this intension cannot lead to an infinite deductive path. Many other such examples exist.

These last remarks suggest an alternate view of data base structuring. For what they amount to is proving the "correctness" of a data base, where "correct" is taken to mean "all deductive paths will be finite". Under this view, a necessary condition that a data base be well structured is that it has been proved correct. For an elaboration of these ideas, see Reiter [1978a].

COMPILING THE IDB

We have shown that query evaluation may be decomposed into an intensional processor involving a theorem prover which computes only on the IDB, and an extensional processor computing only on the EDB. One very nice feature of this decomposition is that it is now possible to <u>compile</u> the IDB using the theorem prover as a once-only compiler.

The basic idea is quite simple. For each predicate of the data base, say the predicate Teach of the example, determine all "proofs" with top clause Teach x,y as well as with top clause $\overline{\text{Teach}}$ x,y. Notice that these "proofs" involve only clauses of the IDB. Next store all such trees, for all predicates, on an external file, and discard both the IDB and the theorem prover. Then at query evaluation time, read in all of the "proofs" for those signed predicates occurring in the query. These trees can then be appropriately combined to yield all of the "proofs" required by the query.

It turns out that this compilation process together with the resulting query evaluation are considerably simplified under the so-called closed world assumption (CWA). In order to illustrate what is involved we shall assume that the reader is familiar with the material and notation in Reiter [1978b]. In particular, we shall exploit the fact that the set of CWA answers to an arbitrary query can be computed by applying the set operations of union, intersection and difference and the relational algebra operation of projection to the open world assumption (OWA) answers to atomic queries. Thus, CWA query evaluation reduces to OWA evaluation for atomic queries. Now an atomic query has the form

$$Q = < \vec{x}/\vec{\tau} \,|\, (E\vec{y}/\vec{\theta})Pt_1,\ldots,t_n >$$

where each t is an x, a y, or a constant, and P is a predicate sign. Suppose that we had available all "proofs" of the literal

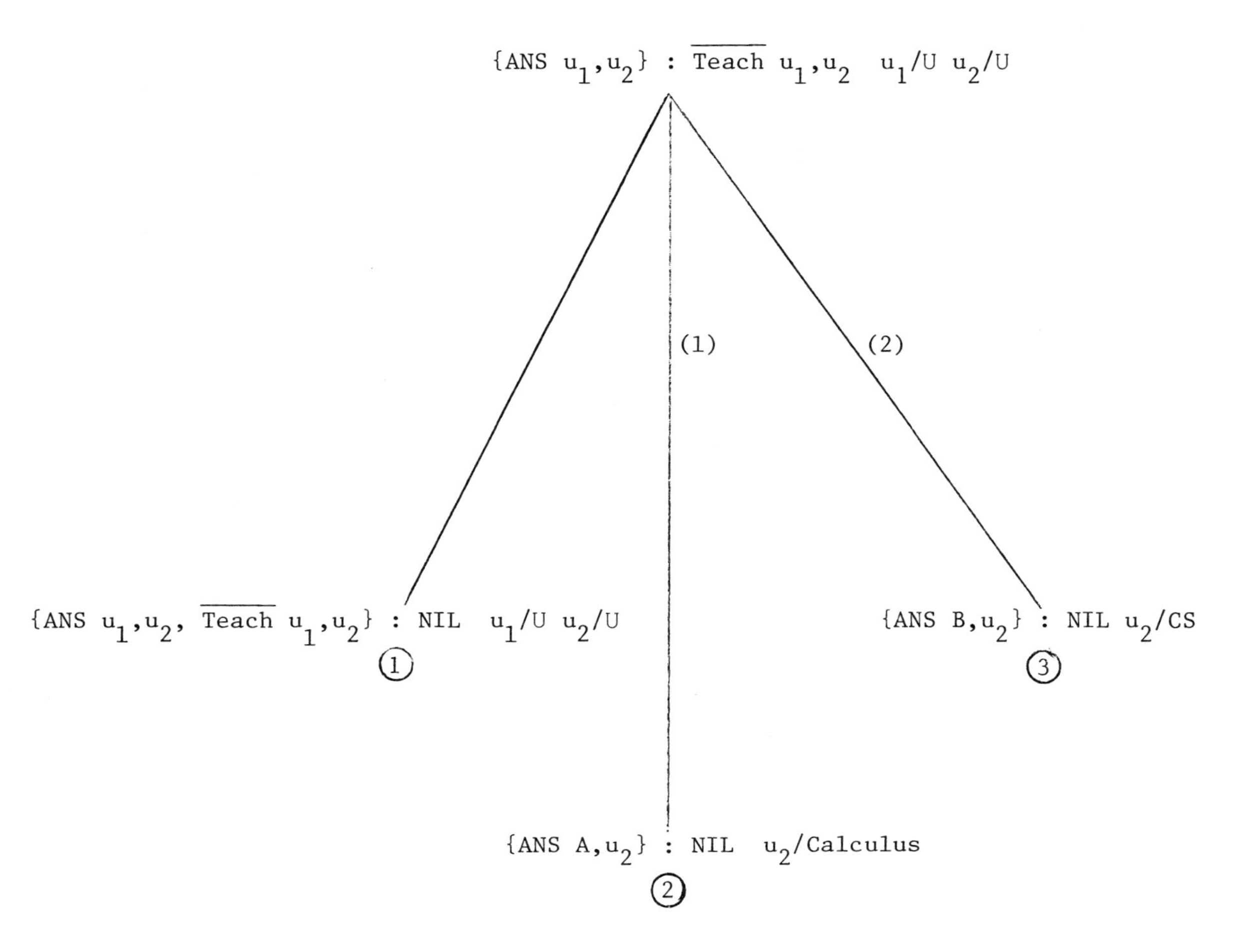

Figure 5. The refutation search tree for Teach.

$Pu_1,\ldots,u_n$ using only the clauses of the IDB, where each variable u_i has type U, the universal type i.e. $|U|$ = the set of all constants. Then to compute $\|Q\|_{OWA}$ simply substitute t_i for u_i in these proofs ensuring that the type of t_i is consistent with the type of u_i. Then, as in the section on Answering Existential Queries, form appropriate queries using the terminal nodes in the resulting proof tree, and extensionally evaluate these queries. The method is best explained by an example.

Example 3

We shall treat the data base of Example 2 in closed world mode. To begin, we compile the predicate Teach i.e. we determine all "proofs" of Teach u_1,u_2 i.e. all "refutations" with top clause $\overline{\text{Teach}}\ u_1,u_2$. Here u_1 and u_2 both have type U. The "refutations" use only the clauses of IDB just as we did in the section on Answering Existential Queries. Figure 5 shows the resulting fully expanded search tree. The types associated with each free variable at a given node are indicated. Now suppose we wish to determine $\|Q\|_{OWA}$ where

$$Q = \langle x/\text{Teacher} \mid \text{Teach } x,\text{CS100} \rangle$$

To do so, substitute x of type Teacher for u_1 and substitute CS100 for u_2 in Figure 5. The substitution of x for u_1 satisfies the type restrictions on u_1 throughout the tree. The substitution of CS100 for u_2 violates the type restriction on u_2 at node 2 since CS100 $\notin$ $|\text{Calculus}|$, so node 2 cannot contribute to the evaluation of Q. Nodes 1 and 3 do contribute, so we form the two queries:

$$Q_1 = \langle x/\text{Teacher} \mid \text{Teach } x,\text{CS100} \rangle$$

$$Q_3 = \langle x/\text{Teacher} \mid x = B \rangle$$

Q_1 and Q_3 extensionally evaluate to ϕ and B respectively, whence $\|Q\|_{OWA} = \{B\}$.

It should be clear that we had no use for the entire tree of Figure 5 - only the terminal nodes were necessary. Moreover, the relevant information contained in these nodes is more succinctly representable by the following three formulae with free variables u_1 and u_2

(i) Teach u_1,u_2 u_1/U u_2/U

(ii) $u_1 = A \wedge u_2 = u_2$ u_1/U $u_2/\text{Calculus}$

(iii) $u_1 = B \wedge u_2 = u_2$ u_1/U u_2/CS

We shall refer to these three formulae as the compiled form of the predicate Teach As a further example consider

$$Q = \langle x/\mathrm{Teacher} \mid (\mathrm{E}y/\mathrm{CS})\mathrm{Teach}\ x,y \rangle$$

Substitute x of type Teacher for u_1 and y of type CS for u_2 in (i), (ii) and (iii) above. This yields a type inconsistency in (ii), so we obtain two queries:

$$Q_1 = \langle x/\mathrm{Teacher} \mid (\mathrm{E}y/\mathrm{CS})\mathrm{Teach}\ x,y \rangle$$

$$Q_3 = \langle x/\mathrm{Teacher} \mid (\mathrm{E}y/\mathrm{CS})x = \mathrm{B} \wedge y = y \rangle$$

These extensionally evaluate to ϕ and {B} respectively, whence $\|Q\|_{OWA} = \{B\}$

Next we compile the predicate Teacher-of. Figure 6 contains the refutation search tree. From its terminal nodes we obtain the following compiled form for Teacher-of:

$\mathrm{Teacher\text{-}of}\ u_1,u_2 \quad u_1/U \quad u_2/U$

$(\mathrm{E}v/\mathrm{Course})\mathrm{Teach}\ u_2,v \wedge \mathrm{Enrolled}\ u_1,v \quad u_1/\mathrm{Student} \quad u_2/\mathrm{Teacher}$

$(\mathrm{E}v/\mathrm{Calculus})\mathrm{Enrolled}\ u_1,v \wedge u_2 = \mathrm{A} \quad u_1/\mathrm{Student}$

$(\mathrm{E}v/\mathrm{CS})\mathrm{Enrolled}\ u_1,v \wedge u_2 = \mathrm{B} \quad u_1/\mathrm{Student}$

Consider evaluating

$$Q = \langle x/\mathrm{Student} \mid \mathrm{Teacher\text{-}of}\ x,\mathrm{B} \rangle$$

Substituting x for u_1 and B for u_2 in the compiled form of Teacher-of yields the following queries for extensional evaluation:

$$Q_1 = \langle x/\mathrm{Student} \mid \mathrm{Teacher\text{-}of}\ x,\mathrm{B} \rangle$$

$$Q_2 = \langle x/\mathrm{Student} \mid (\mathrm{E}v/\mathrm{Course})\mathrm{Teach}\ \mathrm{B},v \wedge \mathrm{Enrolled}\ x,v \rangle$$

$$Q_3 = \langle x/\mathrm{Student} \mid (\mathrm{E}v/\mathrm{Calculus})\mathrm{Enrolled}\ x,v \wedge \mathrm{B} = \mathrm{A} \rangle$$

$$Q_4 = \langle x/\mathrm{Student} \mid (\mathrm{E}v/\mathrm{CS})\mathrm{Enrolled}\ x,v \wedge \mathrm{B} = \mathrm{B} \rangle$$

These extensionally evaluate to ϕ , {d}, ϕ and {a,b} whence $\|Q\|_{OWA} = \{a,b,d\}$.

Finally, consider evaluating the following non atomic query under the CWA:

$$Q = \langle x/\mathrm{Teacher} \mid \mathrm{Teacher\text{-}of}\ a,x \wedge \overline{\mathrm{Teach}}\ x,\mathrm{CS100} \rangle$$

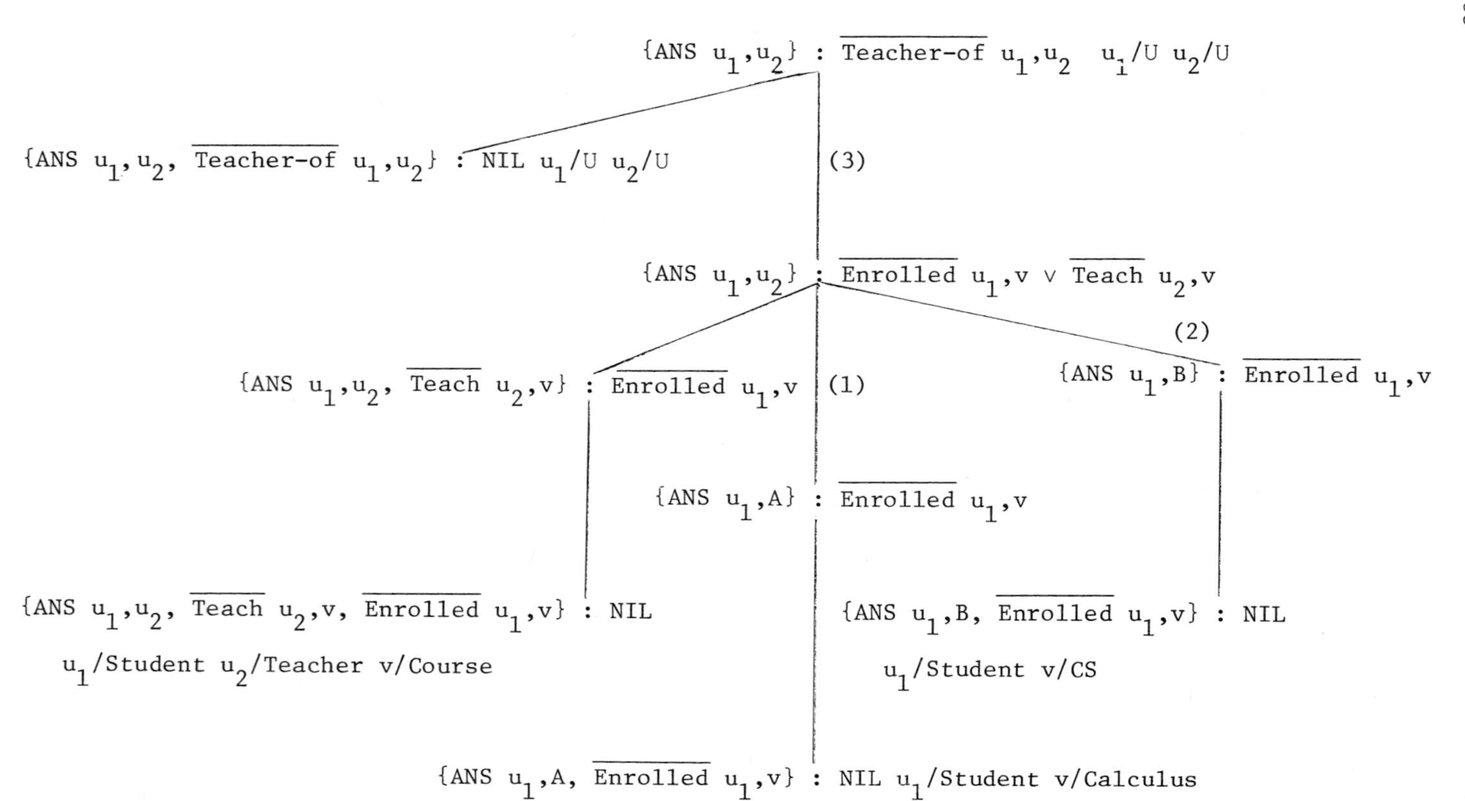

Figure 6. The refutation search tree for Teacher-of.

Then

$$\|Q\|_{CWA} = \|Q_1\|_{OWA} \cap (|Teacher| - \|Q_2\|_{OWA})$$

where

$$Q_1 = < x/Teacher|Teacher\text{-}of\ a,x >$$

$$Q_2 = < x/Teacher|Teach\ x,CS100 >$$

Evaluating Q_1 using the compiled form of Teacher-of yields {A,B,C}. We have already evaluated Q_2 at the beginning of this example, yielding {B}. Hence $\|Q\|_{CWA} = \{A,C\}$.

There are a number of advantages to this approach of compiling the IDB:

(i) The time required for query evaluation is reduced since there is no need to search for all possible proofs.

(ii) Compilation completely eliminates the need for a theorem prover at query evaluation time.

(iii) The compilation process can be effected by a suitably designed interactive theorem prover. This can provide for a far greater measure of control over the deductive mechanism than is currently possible under autonomous theorem proving systems. In particular, the data base designer will be in a position to interactively exploit his or her knowledge of the semantics of the domain to prune fruitless or infinite deduction paths, to apply optimizing transformations, and to recognize redundant or duplicate deductions. Moreover, the design of such an interactive system is far simpler than that of an autonomous theorem prover and requires significantly less code. Finally, since efficiency considerations for such an interactive theorem prover are irrelevant given that it is functioning as a once-only compiler, it's implementation is even further simplified. And of course, once the compilation is completed, the compiler may be expunged from the system.

(iv) The query language of this paper is set oriented i.e. we seek all answers to a given query. Moreover the techniques for query evaluation which we have proposed are specifically directed at computing sets of answers. One might conclude from this that the evaluation of "single answer" queries will require a substantially different approach. By a "single answer" query we mean one whose appropriate answer is "yes", "no" or "I don't know". (This latter cannot arise under the CWA.) For example, "Is A a teacher of b?" i.e. Teacher-of b,A or "Does A teach calculus?" i.e. (Ex/Calculus)Teach A,x.

It should be clear, however, that if the IDB is compiled, it is trivial to evaluate "single answer" queries. Merely instantiate in turn each formula of the appropriate compiled forms of the predicates, and send that formula off to the extensional evaluator to extensionally test its truth value. For example, to evaluate Teacher-of b,A we retrieve the compiled form of Teacher-of and extensionally test each of the following formulae in turn, returning "yes" if and when one of them tests true:

Teacher-of b,A

(Ev/Course)Teach A,v $\wedge$ Enrolled b,v

(Ev/Calculus)Enrolled b,v $\wedge$ A = A

(Ev/CS)Enrolled b,v $\wedge$ B = A

The evaluation of "single answer" queries in the case of "compound" queries is slightly more complicated. By a compound query we mean one with more than one literal. For example, "Is anyone a teacher of both a and b?" i.e.

(Ex/Teacher)Teacher-of a,x $\wedge$ Teacher-of b,x.

In this case one must form all possible conjunctions of pairs of formulae in the compiled form of Teacher-of, and extentionally test each of these in turn. Thus we must test

(Ex/Teacher)Teacher-of a,x $\wedge$ Teacher-of b,x

(Ex/Teacher)Teacher-of a,x $\wedge$ (Ev/Course)Teach x,v
$\wedge$ Enrolled b,v

(Ex/Teacher)Teacher-of a,x $\wedge$ (Ev/Course)Enrolled b,v $\wedge$ x=A

etc.

Of course, the ability to compile the IDB relies upon the absence of recursive axioms. In the section on Completeness of the Query Evaluation Process we argued that the effects of recursive axioms must be neutralized by appropriately structuring the data base in order to guarantee that the theorem prover will return with all answers to a query. Since such a data base can also be compiled, we have a second argument in favour of recursion elimination.

One last point. Notice that the concept of a compiler for the IDB is feasible only under an approach to deductive question-answering which completely decouples the IDB and EDB theorem proving processors, as described earlier (Answering Existential Queries). Any attempt at deductive question-answering by means of a theorem prover which intermingles access to both the IDB and EDB can only run "interpretively" since the set of all possible proofs corresponding to a predicate P will in general be impossibly large in the presence of any sizeable EDB.

DISCUSSION

This paper has addressed a variety of problems that arise in deductive question-answering. It is appropriate at this point to summarize the issues that have been raised, to draw comparisons with other approaches in the literature, and to point out certain difficulties which remain to be resolved.

Indefinite Answers

The possibility of indefinite answers (section on Queries and Answers) has long been recognized in other theorem proving applications (Green [1969]) but seems to have been overlooked or ignored in the deductive question-answering literature. Nevertheless, they are real (see Example 1) and must be taken into account in any proposed theory of deductive retrieval. It is just such answers which make the definitions of the projection and division operators (see Reduction of Arbitrary Queries to Existential Queries) more complicated than their counterparts in relational algebra. Although not described in this paper, there is a satisfactory computational approach to indefinite answers (Reiter [1977]).

As far as I can determine, all current deductive retrieval systems assume only definite answers, and indeed, such answers do make life much simpler. But it seems to me that we need a theory which _guarantees_ that this assumption is warranted. A few such results are known. If the data base is Horn, and the query positive, then no indefinite answers can arise (Reiter [1977]). Moreover, for query evaluation under the closed world assumption, all answers will be definite (Reiter [1978b]).

Interfacing with a Data Base Management System

Both Chang [1977] and Kellogg et al. [1978] have independently proposed interfacing a theorem prover with a data base management system for processing the EDB. Both of these systems use a theorem prover to transform a given query containing virtual relations into one containing only base relations. (A _virtual_ relation has no representation in the EDB, i.e. all of the information about that relation is contained in the IDB. A _base_ relation is one whose total extension is explicitly represented in the EDB. In Example 2, Enrolled is a base relation, Teacher-of is virtual, and Teach is neither.) A data base management system then returns the answers to the transformed query. Since Kellogg, Klahr and Travis are not concerned with returning all answers to a given query, their overall system design differs somewhat from ours. Chang is concerned with retrieving sets of answers and accordingly proposes a similar system architecture. The most significant distinction between our proposal and those of Kellogg et al. and Chang is that we do not require, as they do, that a given relation be either virtual or base, i.e. we permit information about a relation to be contained in both the EDB and IDB. Thus, in Example 2, Teach is neither a virtual nor base relation. In general, this provides for a greater measure of flexibility in representing information about a given domain.

Equality

The whole question of equality in automatic deduction is a thorny one. Although a firm theoretical foundation exists for the treatment of equality (Robinson and Wos [1969]) no feasible computational approach is known for a general first order theory. Nevertheless, there is a definite need for the equality relation in deductive question-answering. For example, the intension "Distinct offspring of the same parent are siblings" cannot be expressed without it:

$$(x,y,z/\text{Human})\text{Parent } y,x \wedge \text{Parent } z,x \wedge y \neq z \supset \text{Siblings } y,z$$

To my knowledge, no work in deductive question-answering has addressed the equality issue. In this paper I have taken what amounts to a first cut at an efficient computational treatment of equality, but at the expense of generality. Specifically, generality is sacrificed in the following ways:

(i) All constants are assumed pairwise distinct i.e. $c_i \neq c_j$ for $i \neq j$.

(ii) More significantly, <u>no function signs are permitted</u> either in the data base or in queries. Since existential quantifiers implicitly lead to function signs (Skolem functions), no intension is permitted to have an existential quantifier in its prenex normal form.

Under these conditions, equality poses no difficulties whatever for existential queries (Theorem 1). If we relax either of conditions (i) or (ii), Theorem 1 fails in which case all of the computational problems associated with equality which plague general purpose theorem provers will arise in the context of deductive question-answering.

What is a Data Base?

An issue which arises as a natural extension of the equality problem has to do with just what is meant by a data base. The definition of a data base in this paper does not admit function signs, in part because of the difficulties they create with respect to equality. There is another compelling reason for adopting a function-free definition of a data base - without some such restriction, any first order theory is a data base. No distinction can be drawn between an inventory domain, and point set topology, despite the fact that reasoning with real world non mathematical domains should not require the full inferential capabilities of a mathematician. The choice of a function-free theory, while not entirely satisfactory, more closely approximates my own intuitive concept of a data base than does an arbitrary first order theory. Perhaps this latter point deserves elaboration. In a function-free theory, answers to queries involve only constants (but not Skolem constants). Another way of expressing this is that all answers are extensional i.e. they involve only known individuals (the constants). This, of course, is in agreement with conventional data base management systems which also treat only extensional entities, so that the concept of a data base defined in this paper can be viewed as an appropriate generalization of these conventional systems. On the other hand, an arbitrary first order theory admits intensional entities i.e. descriptions of new entities in terms of old. Typically, the way such descriptions are formed is by means of functions (usually Skolem functions) whose extensions are not completely known. For example, although we may not know who John's father is, we can nevertheless form the description father(John) - a perfectly respectable, though unknown, individual. It is precisely such intensional entities that lead to all of the problems associated with equality, since different descriptions might denote the same entity. This, in turn, prevents any reasonable notion of the completeness of answer extraction techniques in those cases where all answers to a given query are to be returned, an issue which is further discussed in the following section (Returning All Answers to a Query).

One way that functions might be admitted into the formalism of this paper without opening the door to arbitrary first order theories is to require that the functions so admitted be extensional i.e. we know or can compute their values for all of their arguments. Another is to admit only functions with a free interpretation (Clark [1978]). In the first case, equality of two descriptions reduces to equality of their values. In the second case, two descriptions are equal iff they are syntactically identical. Although such an approach will circumvent the problems associated with equality, it can affect a system's ability to return all answers to a given query in those situations where infinitely many answers arise, an issue which is discussed in the following section.

To my knowledge, all other current research on deductive question-answering (e.g. Minker [1978], Kellogg et al. [1978], Chang [1977]) relies on the concept of a data base as an arbitrary first order theory. What is being argued here is that this concept should be suitably restricted in order to guarantee completeness of the query evaluator, and to provide a computationally feasible treatment of the equality relation.

Returning All Answers to a Query

The approach of this paper, like that of Chang [1977], is designed to return all answers to a given query. In addition, we have a completeness result to the effect that all answers will be returned (section on Completeness of the Query Evaluation Process). It seems to me important that users of a deductive question-answering system be assured, on formal grounds, that all answers to their queries will be returned. Moreover, there are many applications which demand all answers, not simply one or a few. Under these circumstances, systems designed to return single answers (e.g. Kellogg et al. [1978]) or a few answers (e.g. Minker [1978]) can be easily modified to continue searching for more answers once the first has been found. In the case of Kellogg, the underlying proof procedure is incomplete so that we cannot be quaranteed, on a priori grounds, that all answers will be returned. Minker's system does rely on a complete proof procedure and therefore could conceivably be used to return all answers. However, since for both Minker and Chang a data base can be any first order theory, it is difficult to see just what a completeness result for answers might be. For one thing, infinitely many answers are possible. As an example, consider the following data base:

$P0$

$(x)Px \supset Pf(x)$

and the query "Find all x such that Px". The answer set is the infinite set $\{0,f(0),f(f(0)),\ldots,\}$ and this cannot be computed by continuing the search for more answers each time a new answer is found. Clearly, under these circumstances, a deductive Q/A system must be capable of returning set intensions i.e. descriptions of sets, rather than their extensions.

A second, seemingly insurmountable obstacle to the possibility of guaranteeing completeness of answer sets in arbitrary first order theories stems from the equality problem. If by an answer set we mean the set of all distinct answers, then no completeness guarantee is possible, since the question of determining the equality of terms in a general first order theory is recursively undecidable.

The issue of completeness reflects on our earlier discussion of a previous section - What is a Data Base? - i.e. just what should be admitted as a reasonable notion of a data base. It is clear from the above example that if we admit even one function sign, then infinitely many answers are possible, in which case to guarantee completeness we will require a theory of answer extraction which returns set intensions. If we preclude function signs, but admit infinitely many constants, other pathologies can arise. For example, infinitely long indefinite answers may occur (Reiter [1977, Appendix 1]). Moreover, it is not difficult to construct examples with infinite answer sets, so that set intensions must be returned. In general then, it would appear that any natural extension of the concept of a data base beyond that of this paper will require, at the very least, a theory of set intensions whenever sets of answers are to be returned.

Universal Quantification and the Domain Closure Axiom

Recall that in defining the notion of a data base we postulated a domain closure axiom DC which, in essence, states that the only existing individuals are the constants. In the section on Existential Queries and Equality we showed that this axiom is irrelevant for existential query evaluation. For queries with universal quantifiers, however, the presence or absence of DC is crucial. To see why, consider the data base of Example 2 augmented by the type extension $|History| = \{H100,H200\}$, and consider the query "Does D teach all of the history courses?" Since D indeed teaches both H100 and H200, we would intuitively expect the answer to be "yes", corresponding to a successful proof of (x/History)Teach D,x i.e. to a successful proof of (x)History x $\supset$ Teach D,x . But in the absence of a domain closure axiom, no such proof exists! The reason is clear enough - without domain closure there are models of the data base containing additional individuals which are History courses but which are not taught by D. The difficulty can be traced to the semantics of "for all". If the intended interpretation of "(x)" is "for all x that you know about" then the domain closure axiom is required. On the other hand, if we mean "for all x, even those whose possible existence you may not be aware of" then no such axiom is in force.

With the exception of Chang [1977] all of the work that I know of in deductive question-answering does not make the domain closure assumption, in which case their treatment of universally quantified queries may be suspect. Chang, on the other hand, implicitly invokes the domain closure axiom by not skolemizing universally quantified variables in queries or existentially quantified variables in axioms, and by assuming that the underlying data base management system treats the constants as the only existing individuals.

ACKNOWLEDGMENT

This paper was written with the financial support of the National Research Council of Canada under grant A7642.

REFERENCES

1. Chang, C.L. [1978] DEDUCE 2: Further Investigations on Deduction in Relational Data Bases, In *Logic and Data Bases* (H. Gallaire and J. Minker, Eds.), Plenum Press, N.Y., 1978, 201-236.

2. Clark, K. [1978] Negation as Failure, In *Logic and Data Bases* (H. Gallaire and J. Minker, Eds.), Plenum Press, New York, New York, 1978, 293-322.

3. Codd, E. F. [1972] Relational Completeness of Data Base Sublanguages, In *Data Base Systems* (R. Rustin, Ed.), Prentice-Hall, Englewood Cliffs, N.J., 1972, 65-98.

4. Green, C. C. [1969] Theorem Proving by Resolution as a Basis for Question Answering Systems, In *Machine Intelligence, Vol. 4* (B. Meltzer and D. Michie, Eds.), American Elsevier Publishing Co., New York, N.Y., 1969, 183-208.

5. Kellogg, C. Klahr, P. and Travis, L. [1978] Deductive Planning and Pathfinding for Relational Data Bases, In *Logic and Data Bases* (H. Gallaire and J. Minker, Eds.), Plenum Press, New York, N.Y., 1978, 179-200.

6. McSkimin, J. R. [1976] "The Use of Semantic Information in Deductive Question-Answering Systems," Ph.D. Thesis, Department of Computer Science, University of Maryland, College Park, Maryland, 1976.

7. McSkimin, J. R. and Minker, J. [1977] The Use of a Semantic Network in a Deductive Question-Answering System, *Proceedings IJCAI-77*, Cambridge, Massachusetts, 1977, 50-58.

8. Minker, J. [1978] An Experimental Relational Data Base System Based on Logic, In *Logic and Data Bases* (H. Gallaire and J. Minker, Eds.), Plenum Press, New York, New York, 1978, 107-147.

9. Minker, J., Fishman, D. H., and McSkimin, J. R. [1973] The Q* Algorithm - A Search Strategy for a Deductive Question-Answering System, *Artificial Intelligence 4*, (1973), 225-243.

10. Palermo, F. P. [1974] A Data Base Search Problem, In *Information Systems* (J. T. Tou, Ed.), Plenum Press, New York, N.Y., 1974, 67-101.

11. Reiter, R. [1971] Two Results on Ordering for Resolution with Merging and Linear Format, *JACM 18*, 4(October 1971), 630-646.

12. Reiter, R. [1976] Query Optimization for Question-Answering Systems, *Proceedings COLING*, Ottawa, Canada, June 28 - July 2, 1976.

13. Reiter, R. [1977] An Approach to Deductive Question-Answering, *BBN Tech. Report 3649*, Bolt Beranek and Newman, Inc., Cambridge, Mass., Sept. 1977, 161 pp.

14. Reiter, R. [1978a] On Structuring a First Order Data Base, *Proceedings of the Canadian Society for Computational Studies of Intelligence, Second National Conference* (R. Perrault, Ed.), Toronto, July 19-21, 1978.

15. Reiter, R. [1978b] On Closed World Data Bases, In *Logic and Data Bases* (H. Gallaire and J. Minker, Eds.), Plenum Press, New York, N.Y., 1978, 55-76.

16. Robinson, G. A., and Wos, L. [1969] Paramodulation and Theorem Proving in First Order Theories with Equality, In *Machine Intelligence , Vol. 4* (B. Meltzer and D. Michie, Eds.), American Elsevier, New York, N.Y., 1969, 135-150.

DEDUCTIVE PLANNING AND PATHFINDING FOR RELATIONAL DATA BASES

Charles Kellogg[1], Philip Klahr[1], and Larry Travis[2]

System Development Corporation, Santa Monica, California[1]

University of Wisconsin, Madison, Wisconsin[2]

ABSTRACT

Inference planning techniques have been implemented and incorporated within a prototype deductive processor designed to support the extraction of information implied by, but not explicitly included in, the contents of a relationally structured data base. Deductive pathfinding and inference planning are used to select small sets of relevant premises and to construct skeletal derivations. When these "skeletons" are verified, the system uses them as plans to create data-base access strategies that guide the retrieval of data values, to assemble answers to user requests, and to produce proofs supporting those answers. Several examples are presented to illustrate the current capability of the prototype Deductively Augmented Data Management (DADM) system.

INTRODUCTION

Not only are computerized data bases growing in size, number, and complexity, but the number of on-line users is also growing rapidly. The availability of larger and cheaper memories is making it feasible to store vast quantities of data on-line, but this often serves only to increase the frustration of users, who, because of limitations in current data-base retrieval technology, are unable to take full advantage of the information. A major deficiency in present data-base systems is an inability to discover (at the direction of users) implicit relationships among the data items explicitly present.

Deductive logic offers considerable potential for improving on-line access to large, complex data-base domains. The prototype Deductively Augmented Data Management (DADM) system described in this paper has been designed to:

1. Permit a user to pose complex and subtle queries to the system, which, in turn, finds inferential connections linking user-specified concepts to data-base structures.

2. Generate for the user deductively connected evidence chains that he can use in evaluating the utility and credibility of information derived from the data base.*

In particular, user-system interactive techniques have been developed whereby the system creates and displays inference plans and chains of evidence as an integral part of the question-answering process. The user actively participates by supplying advice, refining his queries, and requesting additional plans and evidence as necessary. This interactive cycle continues until the user is satisfied with the quality as well as the quantity of the derived information. Sometimes this entails the provision of evidence both for and against a user's conjecture or working hypothesis. Sometimes the system provides a user with a conditional (yes if...) answer rather than a strictly categorical answer. In all cases, the system permits a user to ask for corroborative evidence by requesting alternative derivations for an answer. (Multiple evidence chains may often reinforce the user's confidence in the value of the information received.)

APPROACH

The design for the deductive processor described in this paper evolved out of research on an English question-answering system called CONVERSE (Kellogg et al. [1971] and Travis et al. [1973]). This system consisted of a language processor (driven by English syntax rules and a semantic network) and a relational data management system that accessed specific facts realized as N-tuple members of predicate (relation) extensions. When analyzing a query such as "Who is mayor of Denver?", the system would use its semantic network to infer that the reference was to the City of Denver, not the County of Denver. The inference was based on the general proposition, represented in the semantic network, that the range of the relation being mayor of includes cities but not counties.

---

* It is important to note that while the deductive processor will be applying rules of strict logical reasoning, the information (the set of general assertions or premises) that is being used to construct evidence chains may range in degree of plausibility from "hard" (strictly true) to "soft" (possibly the cause).

Further, in analyzing more complex queries such as "What cities are in states with a population less than that of the City of Boston?", the system would infer which states possess the property of having a population smaller than that of Boston--an ad hoc property not directly available in the network or data base. While useful, these kinds of inferences are special purpose and limited. We decided that a more general-purpose inferential capability needed to be designed and added to the system for use in many different contexts and for many different purposes (Klahr [1975], Kellogg et al. [1976], Klahr [1978], and Kellogg et al. [1977]).

Two design criteria were crucial in the development of the deductive processor (DP). The first criterion was that the DP would be an independent system yet capable of being "added on" to existing and emerging relational data management systems (RDMSs). This led to a distinct separation between a store of extensional data (specific facts) and a store of intensional data (general statements, premises, rules). The former is accessed by an RDMS, while the latter is accessed by the DP (see Figure 1). (This separation of data is also suggested in a recent proposal by Reiter [1978].) No change is necessary to the RDMS to add on the DP. This same criterion of an RDMS add-on also led to a focus on deduction by exception: user queries not requiring deduction should be identified as such and sent directly to the RDMS.

The second criterion focused on the selection of relevant premises. Premises, or inference rules, are general statements that can be used in making deductions. Given a large number of such premises, a crucial problem arises in controlling the deductive search space. An inference planning process has been designed and implemented to locate potentially relevant premises. This process must be fast and efficient to compensate for the overhead processing involved. But such planning is needed in order to give the system guidance in its deductive searching. Furthermore, the planning process is used to guide and direct relational data-base searching by specifying what facts are needed to support the deductions and proofs found to answer user queries.

ABSTRACTING AND SEMANTICALLY RESTRICTING DEDUCTIVE INTERACTIONS

Processes of abstraction (of deductive interactions) and restriction (of semantic scope) are central to our approach to relevant premise selection. Where possible these abstraction and restriction processes are carried out during premise input in order to minimize processing time during query analysis and deductive question-answering.

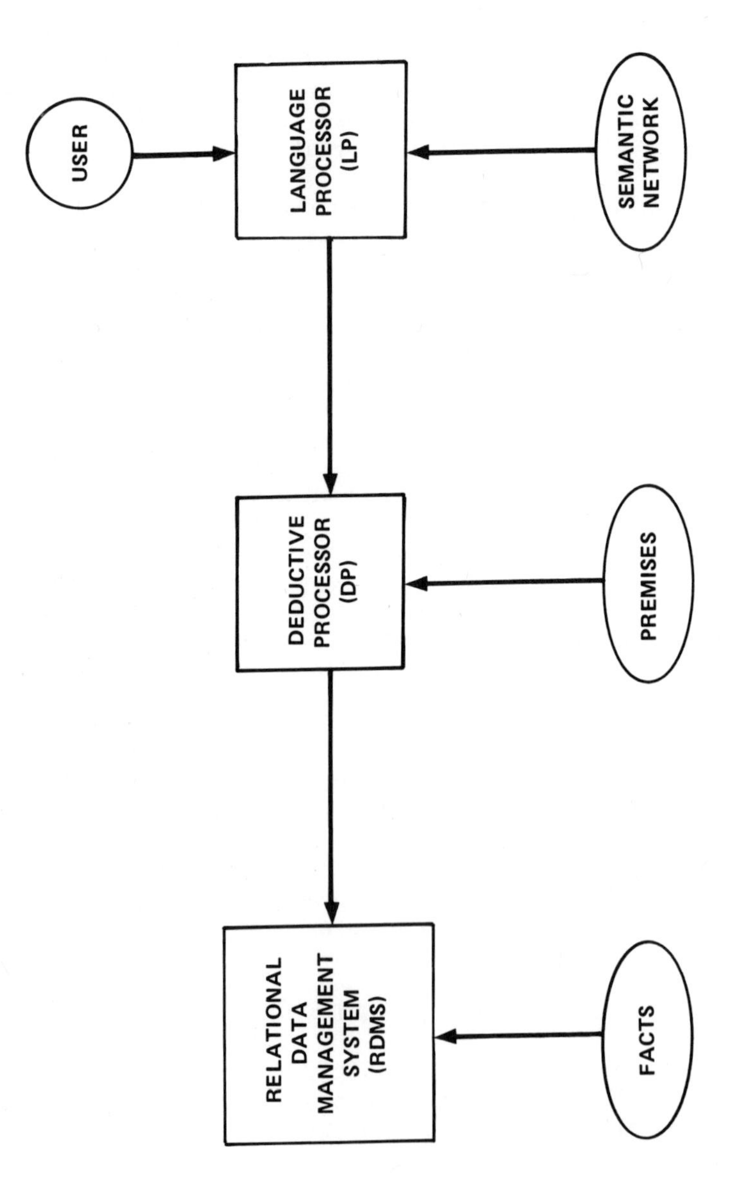

Figure 1. Addition of a Deductive Processor to an English Question-Answering System

Premises and queries are entered into the system as primitive conditional statements (Travis et al. [1973]).* A primitive conditional is a first-order predicate-calculus normal form whose central connective is the implication sign. The antecedent of the implication contains the assumptions of the premise/query and the consequent contains the goals of the premise/query. Assumptions and goals are literals, that is, atomic predicate occurrences or negated atomic predicate occurrences. Within a given antecedent or consequent, literals may be combined either conjunctively or disjunctively. Each predicate occurrence is an instance of a predicate (relation) along with its argument terms (namely variables, constants, or functions). Primitive conditionals are used because they support the introduction of general assertions in a natural way, similar to the way production rules are used in knowledge-based systems; see Davis and King [1975].

Several kinds of information are abstracted from the premises during input and used to create a predicate connection graph (PCG),** as well as other storage structures that promote efficient association of deductive and semantic information (Klahr [1975]). A premise is first converted into a Skolemized, quantifier-free form. The implication (as well as other truth-functional) connections among the predicate occurrences in a premise are encoded into the PCG as a series of deductive dependency Links. Further, the deductive interactions (or unifications--see Robinson [1965]) between predicate occurrences in the new premise and predicate occurrences in existing premises are pre-computed and encoded into the PCG as a series of interpremise associative Arcs. The variable substitutions required for unification are stored elsewhere, for later use in verifying skeletal derivations (i.e., inference or proof) plans.

Semantically restrictive information is introduced in several different forms in order to restrict the logically possible unifications to those that are semantically meaningful for particular application domains.

The variables and constants occurring in premises can be "typed", that is, assigned to specific domain classes. For example, the variable "X" might be assigned the type DOCUMENT, and the constant "Sam" assigned the type SCIENTIST. Then, whenever "X" and "Sam" occur in the same argument position of different instances of a relation, those relation instances will not unify, and they will not be connected in the PCG, due to their semantically

* In an operational system, premises would normally be entered by the data-base administrator.

** See Kowalski [1975] and Sickel [1976] for the use of connection graphs in theorem proving.

incompatible types.

Compound types, consisting of set union, intersection, and difference operations over simple types, may also be used to specify more complex semantic restrictions on predicate domains. A semantic network is used to represent set relationships between types.* Class inclusion paths within this network are used, for example, to permit unification of instances of type SCIENTIST with instances of type MAMMAL. As new premises are entered into the system, this semantic network is automatically updated to reflect new predicate-domain associations.

In addition to this use of semantic information to restrict unification by means of types, unification between multiple occurrences of a predicate within the same premise may sometimes be avoided by restating the premise's assertion by use of logical properties. For example, the predicate "North-of" could be characterized by the premises:

$$\forall x\ \forall y\ (\text{North-of}(x,y)\ \&\ \text{North-of}(y,z) \supset \text{North-of}(x,z))$$

$$\forall x\ \forall y\ (\text{North-of}(x,y) \supset \neg\, \text{North-of}(y,x))$$

$$\forall x\quad (\neg\, \text{North-of}(x,x))$$

The first premise specifies that North-of is transitive. This premise is recursive and can deductively interact with itself and the other premises to cause a rapid expansion of the deductive search space. To help avoid this problem, the DADM system permits binary predicates to be characterized by their logical properties (for example North-of would be assigned the logical properties: transitive, asymmetric, and irreflexive). Computational procedures can then be called to effect special-purpose inferences associated with various groupings of logical properties. Recursive premises describing logical properties of predicates are therefore replaced, where possible, by special-purpose subroutines. Subroutines are being implemented for consistent combinations of the logical properties identified by Elliott [1965].** Future effort will involve other properties such as a relation being hereditary with respect to another relation, e.g., P being hereditary over R in

$$\forall x\ \forall y\ P(x)\ \&\ R(x,y) \supset P(y)$$

---

* See McSkimin and Minker [1977, 1978] for related research on introducing semantic information into a deductive system.

** Properties and examples are: reflexive (equal-to), irreflexive (greater-then), symmetric (equal-to), asymmetric (North-of), transitive (located-in), 1-leader (mother-of), 1-follower (weighs), noregrowth (son-of), and unlooped (mother-of).

Logical properties of binary relations are identified by a user-system dialog that is initiated, as shown below, for the predicate "North-of" (user input is preceded by an asterisk):

* Define (North-of)

Suppose one thing is North-of a second thing that in turn is North-of a third thing. Is the first thing North-of the third?

* Yes

If one thing is North-of a second thing, will it always be the case that the second is North-of the first?

* No

Might it ever be the case?

* No

After the third yes/no response, the system is able to identify "North-of" as a transitive, asymmetric, irreflexive, and unlooped relation.

Variable typing reduces the number of unifications in the PCG by making use of semantic domain restrictions. Logical properties replace some kinds of recursive premises, and their often troublesome unifications, with special-purpose inferencing procedures. A third form of semantic restriction used in the DADM system does not directly eliminate unifications in the PCG, but does limit the selection and use of premises and predicates by means of advice supplied by a data-base administrator or user during query processing.

A data-base administrator enters semantic advice in the form of "Conditions → Recommendations" rules. For example, one could advise that a ship return to its home port if it is damaged by specifying:

(Assumption Damaged(Ship)) → Returns(Ship Ports)

The system would try using premises containing the Returns relation when the Damaged relation occurs as an assumption. Advice rules are stored in an advice file, where they are automatically selected and applied whenever their condition part holds for input queries. In addition to such advice rules, the user could supply advice for a particular query by stating only the advised recommendation for that query.

Advice most typically involves recommendations on the use of particular premises or predicates in finding deductions. For advised premises, the system will try using them whenever possible in the course of constructing a proof. For advised predicates, the system will try chaining through occurrences of them in premises. In the case of negative advice, specified premises and predicates are avoided in proof construction.

INFERENCE PLANNING AND DEDUCTIVE QUESTION ANSWERING

The development, refinement, and execution of inference plans proceeds through a series of phases. These phases are designed to progressively apply a series of increasingly more stringent deductive, semantic, and pragmatic constraints until a user receives his desired information or is convinced that he has explored all reasonable deductive pathways into the data base. These phases are described below.

Deductive Pathfinding

Symbolic queries (in the form of primitive conditionals) are decomposed into a set of assumptions (antecedents of the conditional) and a set of goals (consequents of the conditional). Deductive pathfinding employs a process of middle-term chaining (Klahr [1978]) to be illustrated later. This process uses the predicate connection graph to find chains of middle-term predicates needed to deductively connect assumptions to goals. Middle-term chaining combines the processes of forward chaining from the assumptions in a query and backward chaining from the goals in a query. When a query contains no assumptions, and the system cannot discover plausible ones to use--say, as a result of semantic advice--middle-term chaining defaults to backward chaining. As chaining proceeds, a series of expanding deductive-interaction "wave fronts" are generated from assumptions toward goals and from goals toward assumptions. Intersections are performed on the wave fronts until a non-empty intersection occurs, at which time the system has found an implication chain from an assumption to a goal. Several such implication chains are usually found (shortest chains first) before a user-controlled limit is reached. Middle-term chaining is further constrained by the use of semantic advice and plausibility measures. The plausibility measures are assigned to premises and are used to order the predicate occurrences comprising middle-term chain wave fronts to ensure that the deductive paths involving the most plausible premises are selected first. In a similar fashion, semantic advice obtained from the advice file or from the user is transformed into premise and predicate alert lists that are used to ensure that advised premises and predicates are given priority or avoided, depending upon whether the advice is positive or negative.

The same assumptions may be used to find deductive support for different goals (and subgoals). When assumptions are not supplied in a query, useful assumptions may sometimes be found by following semantic network predicate-domain connections, or by using advised predicates as possible assumptions.

Plan Generation

For each middle-term chain generated, the system extracts the premises whose occurrences are part of the chain. Subgoals resulting from the premises are set up to be resolved either by deductive support through the premises, by data-base search through the relational file, or by procedural computation. Subgoals are added to a proof-proposal tree, which contains the inference plans being formed and developed. Once inference plans have no remaining deductive subgoals, they are available for verification, user review, and instantiation.

Plan Verification

Skeletal plans constructed during plan generation are valid proofs at the truth-functional level. In plan verification, the variable substitutions associated with the unifications in each plan are examined for consistency. If there are no clashes--that is, if no variables are assigned more than one distinct constant value--then verification is successful and instantiation by data-base search may follow. During this stage, classes of variables that must take on the same value are constructed and used to reformulate skeletal derivations into _search-compute plan_ components (i.e., data-base access strategies) and _inference plan_ components (comprising deduced goals, deduced subgoals, and assumptions).

Plan Review, Plan Selection, and Query Refinement

Though on-line interaction may be initiated by the user or prompted by the system at various points during pathfinding and plan generation, most user review and interaction occurs after plan verification. Verified plans are usually reviewed in the order in which they were generated. (Recall that plans using the shortest paths, most plausible premises, and advised premises and predicates are generated first.)

During review, a user may reject a plan, instantiate it (by requesting data-base search) or suspend further action on it until other plans have been reviewed. In this manner, the user can minimize unnecessary data-base searching by reviewing the derived plan information and reaching conclusions about the likely data-base searching consequences of his original request. Plan review may, for example indicate that additional assumptions, goals, or advice should be associated with the original request, or that the original query should be refined or replaced by a more specific (or general) request. Considerable insight into interpreting complex requests with respect to large data bases can be achieved, short of actually searching the data base, by this process.

Data-Base Search and Answer Generation

An inference plan constitutes a complete proof just in case no search/compute plan is produced (i.e., all subgoals are deduced from premises). More typically, one or more subgoals require data-base and/or procedural (compute) support. Search/compute plans are executed, in general, in three phases: first, all computable functions and predicates having only constants as arguments are evaluated; second, a sequence of relational search requests is executed against the data base; third, remaining computable functions and predicates are applied to the results of data-base search. Answers are extracted from the N-tuples of data values associated with search/compute plan variables. (Each of these N-tuples supplies instantiation values that may be used to convert the original inference plan into a complete proof or "chain of evidence".) An answer may be categorical (for example, "yes" if no variables occur in the original request, and data-base search is satisfied), descriptive (a set of search-derived query-variable values displayed in tabular format), or conditional ("yes if..." the specified predicate-argument conditions can be verified by the user to hold true for the application domain).

Often these categorical, descriptive, or conditional answers will satisfy the user's original information requirement. In other cases, he may wish to proceed to the next (and final) step in the inference plan development-execution-review cycle.

Answer Explanation and Evidence Review

Just as the plan review, plan selection, and query refinement process is designed to aid the user in understanding the full computer-developed implications of his query, the answer explanation and evidence review phase of processing is designed to support him in his evaluation of computer-derived answers. In a later section, several computer examples illustrate current proof displays. Though this form is often sufficient to enable users to determine the validity and/or utility of derived answers, a more interactive and easily comprehended dialog format for evidence display is under development. This new facility will permit a user to selectively interrogate the system concerning particular answers, relations, and domains. By repetitive interrogation, he may delve as deeply as he desires into particular lines of reasoning or evidentary support, without resorting to the current practice of full proof display.

Inference Planning, Data-Base Semantics, and Generalized Navigation

The relational (extensional) data base constitutes a logical model or interpretation for many of the relations used in the premise (intensional) file. Conversely, the intensional information constitutes a partial but precise representation of the semantics of the extensional data base. Inference planning uses this intensional information to develop both the semantic implications of user-request assumptions and the semantic antecedents of user-request goals. Therefore, inference planning may be used to support generalized navigation or browsing operations through the semantics of a data base. Generalized navigation is further supported by allowing users to enter requests containing unrestricted relations (i.e., relations with no arguments). Given queries of this sort, the system can quickly find deductive paths through system restricted concepts supporting goal relations and concepts linking assumptions to goals. This system feature has proved most useful as a tool for exploring the interrelationships between intensional concepts.

DEDUCTIVE PROCESSOR COMPONENTS

Figure 2 shows the components of our DADM system prototype. At present, users communicate directly with the control processor; a language processor will be incorporated at a later date. The control processor accepts premises and queries in primitive conditional form as well as user advice and commands. It accesses and coordinates the use of the several system components briefly described below.

Array Initialization and Maintenance

Information abstracted from the premises is segmented into seven internal arrays. This segmentation contributes to system modularization and increases processing efficiency. The seven arrays are:

(1) Premise Array. Each entry represents a premise and contains a list of the predicate occurrences in the premise, the plausibility of the premise, and the premise itself (both symbolic and English) for purposes of display.

(2) Predicate Array. The predicate array contains the relations known to the system as well as the support indicator associated with each relation, which indicates how to resolve each relation when it occurs as a subgoal (deduce, search data base, compute).

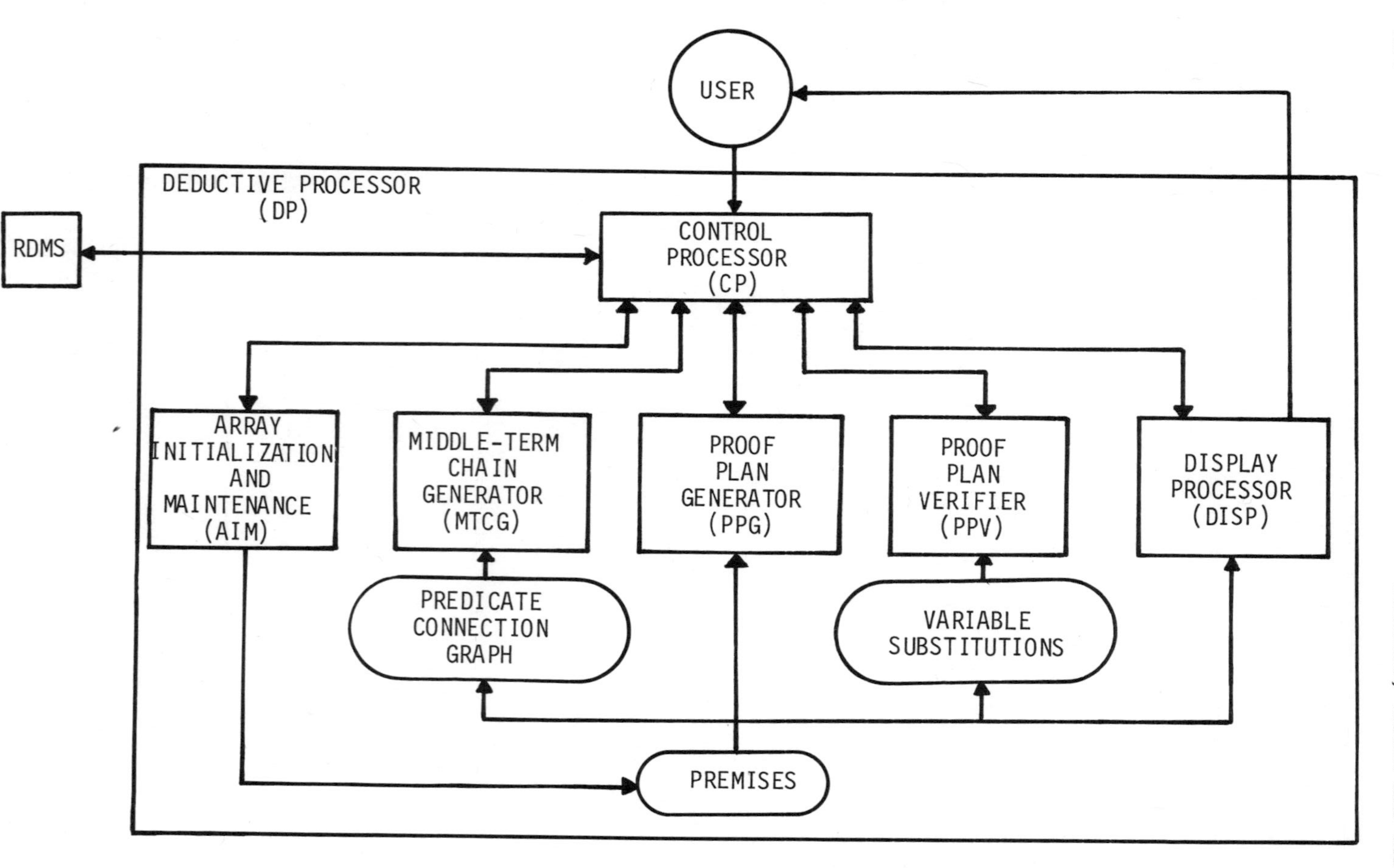

Figure 2. Deductive Processor Components

(3) Predicate Occurrence Array. Each entry represents a predicate occurrence and contains the following information about the occurrence: its predicate name (index into predicate array), the sign of the occurrence (positive or negative), whether the occurrence is in the antecedent or consequent of the implication, the main connective (conjunction or disjunction) governing the occurrence, and the numerical position of the occurence within its premise. The information is compactly stored in a single-word bit vector to save storage space.

(4) Argument Array. The argument strings of the predicate occurrences are stored in the argument array in one-to-one correspondence to the positions of the occurrences in the predicate occurrence array.

(5) Link Array. Truth-functional dependencies within premises are stored in the link array. These dependencies can be implicational, disjunctive, or conjunctive. For each predicate occurrence, a list of the occurrences with which it is truth-functionally connected is entered into the array.

(6) Unifications Array. Each entry contains a list of the unifications (deductive interactions) associated with the given occurrence. The unifications array and the links array comprise the predicate connection graph.

(7) Variable-Substitutions Array. The substitution lists associated with unifications are stored in one-to-one correspondence with the positions of the unifications in the unification array.

Chain Generator, Plan Generator, and Plan Verifier

The Chain Generator, Plan Generator, and Plan Verifier support the deductive pathfinding, plan generation, and verification processes. They communicate with one another by means of the control processor and with the user by means of the display processor.

Display Processor

Plan and proof (evidence) review and query refinement processes are supported by the Display Processor. The user can, for example, examine middle-term chains generated, plans formed, subgoals, verified plans, data-base search requests, data-base values returned, answers, completed proofs, and premises used in proofs.

DEDUCTION EXAMPLES

Figures 3 and 4 illustrate the current operation of the deductive processor (DP) prototype interfaced to a small RDMS. (Both DP and RMS are written in LISP 1.5 and operate on SDC's Amdahl 470/V5 computer.)

The first example illustrates the generation of short inference and search/compute plans for the question, "What ships are closer to the Kittyhawk's home port than the Kittyhawk is?" The query is first shown in English and then in the primitive conditional symbolic form that the prototype currently recognizes. The query is expressed in terms of a conjunctive goal composed of the predicates CLOSER-THAN and HOME-PORT. Constants (such as Kittyhawk) are specified by being enclosed in parentheses, while variables (such as x and y) are not. One of the query goals (HOME-PORT) is to be given data-base support; that is, it has been defined by data base values, while the other goal (CLOSER-THAN) is to be deduced. Since the antecedent in the query is empty, the system back-chains from CLOSER-THAN through premise 29. The plausibility of the plan in this case is simply the plausibility of the single premise used (plausibility measures are assigned by the data-base administrator and range from 1 (very low plausibility) to 99 (always the case)). Two new search requests (in addition to HOME-PORT) result from premise 29, as well as a compute relation containing functional arguments. Computations for the functions and the relation are delayed until values for the variables x and y (the values needed to satisfy the search requests) have been found in the data base.

The system sends the four search requests to the RDMS, which finds two ships, the Forrestal and the Gridley, that are closer to the Kittyhawk's home port (San Diego) than the Kittyhawk is. The system then displays the proof that led to the first answer (the Forrestal). A proof using the other answer would be identical to this one except that Gridley would replace Forrestal in the proof, and the distance between the Gridley and San Diego would replace 310 (the distance between the Forrestal and San Diego). The symbols G2, G3, etc., represent nodes in the proof proposal tree and are used here for reference. G2 and G3 represent the original goals as also shown in the inference plan. G5, G6, and G7 are subgoals that resulted from premise 29, which was used to deduce G2. Thus, these three subgoals are indented below G2.

The middle-term-chaining and planning processes are more evident in the example in Figure 4. The input query contains two assumptions (DAMAGED and DESTINATION) and one goal (TRANSPORT). Taurus and NY are constants; Cargo and x are variables. The query asks the system to find values for x that satisfy the query. The variable x is also restricted to range over ships. This is an example of a type restriction on a variable. In the course of

```
*WHAT SHIPS ARE CLOSER TO THE KITTYHAWK'S HOME PORT
*THAN THE KITTYHAWK IS?

QUERY((()IMP(AND(CLOSER-THAN X (KITTYHAWK) Y)
                (HOME-PORT (KITTYHAWK) Y))))
INFERENCE PLAN:
   DEDUCE   G2 *CLOSER-THAN X KITTYHAWK Y
   SEARCH   G3 *HOME-PORT KITTYHAWK Y
PREMISES USED: (29)     PLAN PLAUSIBILITY:  99
SEARCH/COMPUTE PLAN:
   SEARCH      *SHIPS KITTYHAWK
   SEARCH      *SHIPS X
   SEARCH      *HOME-PORT KITTYHAWK Y
   COMPUTE     *GREATER-THAN (DISTANCE-BETWEEN KITTYHAWK Y) (
                DISTANCE-BETWEEN X Y)
ENTERING DATA BASE
DATA-BASE SEARCH SUCCESSFUL
***************
ANSWER SUMMARY --
VARIABLES:
(X Y)
ANSWERS:
(FORRESTAL SAN-DIEGO)
(GRIDLEY SAN-DIEGO)
***************
PROOF DISPLAY:
   DEDUCED  G2 *CLOSER-THAN FORRESTAL KITTYHAWK SAN-DIEGO
   FACT     G5 **SHIPS KITTYHAWK
   FACT     G6 **SHIPS FORRESTAL
   COMPUTED G7 **GREATER-THAN 378 310
   FACT     G3 *HOME-PORT KITTYHAWK SAN-DIEGO
PREMISES USED: (29)     PROOF PLAUSIBILITY:  99
TYPE PREMISE NUMBER TO DISPLAY, OR 'END':
29
((ALL X79) (ALL X80) (ALL X81)
 (AND (SHIPS X79) (SHIPS X80))
  (GREATER-THAN (DISTANCE-BETWEEN X79 X81)
   (DISTANCE-BETWEEN X80 X81)))
 IMP (CLOSER-THAN X80 X79 X81))
PLAUSIBILITY:  99
TYPE PREMISE NUMBER TO DISPLAY, OR 'END':
END
END DISPLAY
```

Figure 3. Deduction Involving Deduce, Data-Base Search, and Compute Predicates

```
*IF THE TAURUS WERE DAMAGED WHILE DESTINED FOR NEW
*YORK WITH A CARGO, WHAT SHIPS COULD TRANSPORT THE
*CARGO TO NEW YORK?

QUERY(((WHAT (SHIP . X))
      (AND (DAMAGED (TAURUS))
           (DESTINATION (TAURUS) (NY) CARGO))
      IMP (TRANSPORT X CARGO (NY))))
INFERENCE PLAN:
   DEDUCE   G1 *TRANSPORT SHIP#X X75 NY
   ASSUME      *DESTINATION TAURUS NY X75

   DEDUCE   G3 **OFFLOAD TAURUS X75 X72
   ASSUME      **DAMAGED TAURUS
   MID-TERM    **RETURNS TAURUS X72

PREMISES USED: (23 7 15)     PLAN PLAUSIBILITY:  80
SEARCH/COMPUTE PLAN:
   SEARCH      *HOME-PORT TAURUS X72
   SEARCH      *CARRY TAURUS X75
   SEARCH      *AVAILABLE SHIP#X X72
ENTERING DATA BASE
DATA-BASE SEARCH SUCCESSFUL
***************
ANSWER SUMMARY --
VARIABLES:
(X)
ANSWERS:
(PISCES)
(GEMINI)
***************
PROOF DISPLAY:
   DEDUCED  G1 *TRANSPORT PISCES OIL NY
   ASSUME      *DESTINATION TAURUS NY OIL

   DEDUCED  G3 **OFFLOAD TAURUS OIL FREEPORT
   ASSUME      **DAMAGED TAURUS
   MID-TERM    **RETURNS TAURUS FREEPORT

   FACT     G11***HOME-PORT TAURUS FREEPORT
   FACT     G12***CARRY TAURUS OIL
   FACT     G4 ***AVAILABLE PISCES FREEPORT
PREMISES USED: (23 7 15)      PROOF PLAUSIBILITY:  80
END DISPLAY
```

Figure 4. Deduction Using Middle-Term Chaining

developing deductions, the system will not allow values that belong to domain classes other than ships to be substituted for x.

The inference plan shown in Figure 4 has already been verified. To see the planning mechanism more clearly, refer to Figure 5. The first middle-term chain generated connects the DESTINATION assumption to the TRANSPORT goal via premise 23. This is shown by the unifications (deductive interactions) u_1 and u_2 in Figure 5a. The predicate occurrences involving the relations AVAILABLE and OFFLOAD become subproblems. The former is to be given data-base support; the latter is deduced by a middle-term chain from the DAMAGED assumption through premises 7 and 15. This chain is shown in Figure 5b by the unifications u_3, u_4, and u_5. The two new subproblems are to be given data-base support. Thus the plan generated uses three premises and contains three subproblems requiring data-base search. The plausibility of the plan is calculated by a fuzzy intersection (the minimum of the plausibilities of the premises involved--Zadeh [1965]).

The plan is then verified with variable substitutions inserted in the plan and in the search requests (Figure 4). Note the variable constraints in the search requests. The variable x_{72} represents the home port of Taurus; values found for this variable must be the same as those found for x_{72} in the AVAILABLE search request. Thus, those ships that are available in Taurus's home port are the ones we are interested in. The proof display is given for the first answer found (the Pisces).

In Figure 5b, note that the unifications u_4 and u_5 were computed when these premises were first entered into the system and stored in the PCG. Also stored in the PCG were the truth-functional dependencies within the premises (for example, between DAMAGED and RETURNS, between RETURNS and OFFLOAD, and between DESTINATION and TRANSPORT). The unifications u_1, u_3, and u_2 involve query predicates. Hence they were computed after query input to locate possible middle-term-chain end points. Once these were found, only the PCG was used for middle-term chaining.

COMPLETENESS ISSUES

The deductive logic on which our system is based is that of an extensional first-order predicate calculus where the issue of logical completeness often arises. In our discussion, we will distinguish between expressional completeness and derivational completeness.

By expressional completeness is meant the ability to represent, in our primitive-conditional form, equivalents of all the well-formed formulas of a first-order predicate calculus. A worry

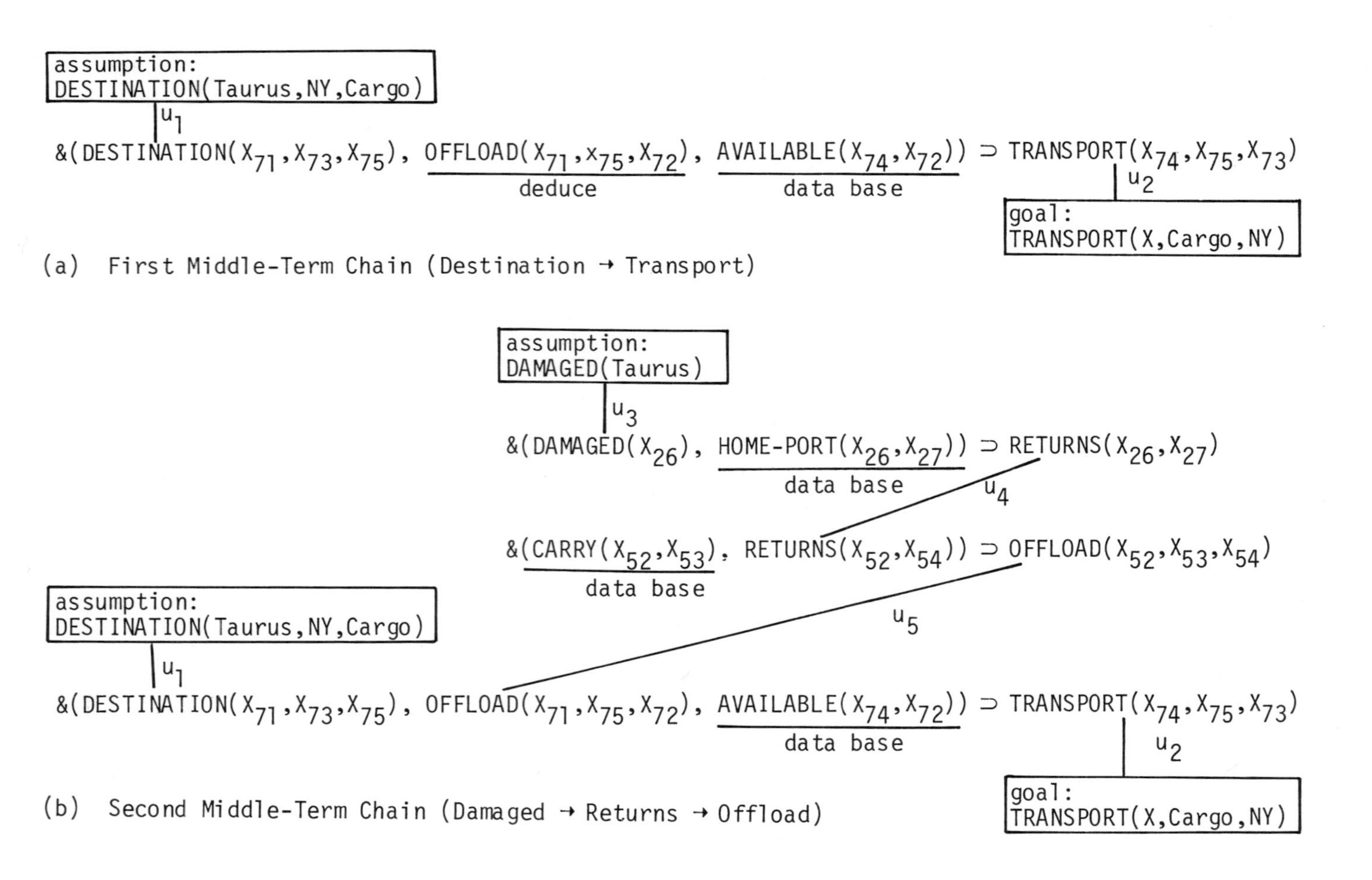

Figure 5. Inference Plan Development for Query in Fig. 4.

might arise because only one level of nesting is allowed in primitive conditionals, i.e., the conjuncts or disjuncts of an antecedent or of a consequent must be composed of literals (negated or unnegated predicate occurrences). The worry can be put to rest, however, when it is recalled that even simpler normal forms are expressionally complete, for example, the conjunctive normal form. A conjunctive normal form (CNF) expression is a conjunction of disjunctions of literals. In our logic, a primitive conditional with no antecedents is interpreted as unconditionally asserting the consequent. Thus a CNF disjunction can always be represented as a primitive conditional with a disjunctive consequent and no antecedent; and any CNF expression as a conjunction of such conditionals. Through the use of the inference rules of simplification (ϕ & $\psi \rightarrow \phi$; ϕ & $\psi \rightarrow \psi$) and of adjunction ($\phi, \psi \rightarrow \phi$ & ψ), primitive conditionals may be combined or separated to provide expressional completeness.

By derivational completeness is meant the ability to generate all valid derivations. Our system is derivationally complete in theory, but the important issue for us has been the system's practical efficiency and effectiveness in an applications-oriented environment. That our system is derivationally complete follows from the fact that it is expressionally complete and handles all of the deductive interactions associated with unification (including Skolem functions) as used in resolution systems, as well as all forms of deductive dependencies that may occur between predicates (see Klahr [1975] for more detail). The derivational completeness problem for our system is analogous to the completeness problem for a resolution system constrained to use a set-of-support strategy which has long been known to be derivationally complete (Wos et al. [1965]). Middle-term chains generated in response to a query initially involve the desired conclusion (query goals). Subsequent chains involve subgoals resulting from premises used in chains to query goals, etc.

In practice, almost any performance-oriented planning strategy including ours will initially apply selection constraints that may preclude certain deductive interactions from being considered and thus lead to possible incompleteness. However, successive relaxation of these selection constraints will enable the system to achieve all possible deductive paths.

SUMMARY AND FUTURE PLANS

We have described a deductive processor specifically designed to augment relational data base systems and user-oriented language processors. The processes of deductive pathfinding, inference planning, verification, user review of plans, answer extraction, and proof display have been outlined and illustrated with several examples.

Several of the more important design features that are integral to this approach are:

- Verification (checking for consistency of variable substitutions) and instantiation (data-base search) are delayed until one or more global inference plans have been con-constructed.
- Precomputed deductive interactions (unifications) among premises are used to avoid their constant recomputation during deductive processing.
- Variable types (domain classes) are used to semantically restrict the range of predicate expressions.
- Shortest assumption-to-goal deductive paths are found first.
- Inference plans and data-base access strategies are created from the premise file without requiring access to data-base values.
- Advice can be given on the use of particular premises and predicates to aid in the discovery of relevant inference plans.

The prototype is currently being expanded along several different dimensions in line with our goal of eventually incorporating the deductive processor into an operational data management system and language processor environment. A number of improvements in man-machine interaction and user displays are being made to support more direct and flexible control of plan-generation and data-base search. Additional semantic constraints on the generation of plans will be introduced by expanded use of the semantic network, and by extension of the semantic-advice formalism. We also plan additional investigations in the use of incomplete and plausible knowledge, and logical properties.

ACKNOWLEDGMENTS

The research reported here has been supported by the Advanced Research Projects Agancy of the Department of Defense and is monitored by the Office of Naval Research under Contract N00014-76-C-0885.

REFERENCES

1. Davis, R. and King, J. [1975] An Overview of Production Systems, AIM-271, Artificial Intelligence Laboratory, Stanford University, 1975.

2. Elliott, R. W. [1965] A Model for a Fact Retrieval System, TNN-42, Computation Center, University of Texas, Austin, 1965.

3. Kellogg, C. H., Burger, J., Diller, T. and Fogt, K. [1971] The CONVERSE Natural Language Data Management System: Current Status and Plans, *Proceedings Symposium on Information Storage and Retrieval,* ACM, New York, 1971, 33-46.

4. Kellogg, C., Klahr, P. and Travis, L. [1976] A Deductive Capability for Data Management, In *Systems for Large Data Bases* (P.C. Lockemann and E. J. Neuhold, Eds.), North Holland, Amsterdam, 1976, 181-196.

5. Kellogg, C., Klahr, P. and Travis, L. [1977] Deductive Methods for Large Data Bases, *Fifth International Joint Conference on Artificial Intelligence,* MIT, Cambridge, Mass., 1977, 203-209.

6. Klahr, P. [1975] "The Deductive Pathfinder: Creating Derivation Plans for Inferential Question-Answering," Ph.D. Dissertation, Computer Science Dept., University of Wisconsin, Madison, Wisconsin, 1975.

7. Klahr, P. [1978] Planning Techniques for Rule Selection in Deductive Question-Answering, In *Pattern-Directed Inference Systems* (D. Waterman and F. Hayes-Roth, Eds.), Adademic Press, New York, 1978.

8. Kowalski, R. [1975] A Proof Procedure Using Connection Graphs, *JACM 22,* 4 (October 1975), 572-595.

9. McSkimin, J. and Minker, J. [1978] A Predicate Calculus Based Semantic Network for Question-Answering Systems, In *Associative Networks - The Representation and Use of Knowledge in Computers* (N. Findler, Ed.), Academic Press, New York, 1978.

10. McSkimin, J. and Minker J. [1977] The Use of a Semantic Network in a Deduction Question-Answering System, *Fifth International Joint Conference on Artificial Intelligence,* MIT, Cambridge, Mass., 1977, 50-58.

11. Reiter, R. [1978] Deductive Question-Answering in Relational Data Bases, In *Logic and Data Bases* (H. Gallaire and J. Minker, Eds.), Plenum Press, New York, New York, 1978, 149-177.

12. Robinson, J. A. [1965] A Machine-Oriented Logic Based on the Resolution Principle, *JACM 12*, 1 (January 1965), 23-41.

13. Sickel, S. [1976] A Search Technique for Clause Interconnectivity Graphs, *IEEE Trans. Computers, C-25*, 8 (August 1976), 823-835.

14. Travis, L., Kellogg, C. and Klahr, P. [1973] Inferential Question-Answering: Extending CONVERSE, SP-3679, System Development Corporation, Santa Monica, Calif., 1973.

15. Wos, L., Robinson, G. A. and Carson, D. A. [1965] Efficiency and Completeness of the Set of Support Strategy in Theorem Proving, *JACM 12*, 4 (October 1965), 536-541.

16. Zadeh, L. A. [1965] Fuzzy Sets, *Information and Control 8*, (1965), 338-353.

DEDUCE 2: FURTHER INVESTIGATIONS OF DEDUCTION IN RELATIONAL DATA BASES

C. L. Chang

IBM Research Laboratory

San Jose, California

ABSTRACT

DEDUCE is a deductive query language proposed for relational data bases. This language allows one to state queries, axioms, integrity constraints, preferences, and heuristics. In this paper, we shall give a new syntax of DEDUCE for uniformly handling queries having existential, universal or numerical quantifiers. Axioms are used to define virtual relations. A user can make a query against virtual relations and original base relations. The query is evaluated in two steps: First, use axioms to transform the query into a query containing only base relations. Second, check if the transformed query can be answered from the front-end intensional information, such as integrity constraints, within a prespecified time limit. If it can, output the answer. Otherwise, evaluate the transformed query by using a data base system such as System R. In this paper, we shall use the rewriting rule approach to transform the query. In addition, an optimization problem about access methods for efficient deductions in a relational data base will be discussed.

INTRODUCTION

The relational model defined by Codd [1970] has been shown to be a convenient and powerful tool for describing a data base. In this model, the data base is viewed as a collection of time-varying relations of assorted degrees. For simplicity, a relation can be viewed as a table consisting of a finite number of columns and rows. Such a table is called a <u>normalized relation</u> (Codd [1970, 1971a, 1971b]). The table name is the relation name. Column names of the table are called attributes. Entries of the table are called values. A row of the table corresponds to a record (fact). The ordering of rows and columns of the table are immaterial. Tables that are explicitly stored in the data base are called base relations. The data base is called the extensional data base by Minker [1975].

It has been shown in Chang [1976], Kellogg et al. [1978], Minker [1975a,1975b,1978], Nicolas and Gallaire [1978], and Reiter [1978b] that inference (deduction) through the use of axioms for a relational data base is needed, because some information may not be stored explicitly, but can be derived from the axioms (intensional data base) and the extensional data base. A classical example is that there may be a base relation, FATHER(x,y), which denotes that x is the father of y. Now, suppose one wants to know who is an ancestor of whom. This type of question can be answered by introducing a new concept ANCESTOR(x,y), which denotes that x is an ancestor of y. The ANCESTOR relation is called a virtual relation because it is not explicitly stored. Given a finite extension of the FATHER relation, one can, of course, explicitly construct an extension of the ANCESTOR relation. However, as discussed in Chang [1976], this approach of building an explicit extension for ANCESTOR introduces storage, updating and consistency problems between the extensions of the FATHER and ANCESTOR relations. In order to circumvent these problems, the ANCESTOR relation could be defined virtually by using the two axioms,

FATHER(x,y) → ANCESTOR(x,y),

FATHER(x,y) & ANCESTOR(y,z) → ANCESTOR(x,z) .

Once virtual relations are defined, a user can make a query against the virtual relations and original base relations.

In Chang [1976], a language called DEDUCE is proposed to allow one to state queries and axioms. In this paper, a new syntax of DEDUCE is given for uniformly handling queries having existential, universal or numerical quantifiers. The main difference between the syntax given in Chang [1976] and the one presented here for DEDUCE is the treatment of numerical quantifiers. Previously, the COUNT function was used to represent numerical quantifiers. Here, numerical quantifiers are used directly because they can be incorporated with unification (or pattern matching) needed in deduction. (Note that other languages for representing queries on relational data bases can be found in Boyce et al. [1975], Chamberlin and Boyce [1974], Codd [1971b], Lacroix and Pirotte [1977], Pirotte [1978], Zloof [1975].) DEDUCE has been used as a target language for an English query system (Codd [1974], Codd et al. [1978]) for relational data bases, because DEDUCE is a relatively flat and symmetric language. Also, in our previous paper (Chang [1976]), it was shown how fuzzy formulas (Lee [1972], Zadeh [1965,1974,1977]) representing preferences can be incorporated into a DEDUCE query. We do not repeat the discussion here.

The approach taken here for deductive relational data base is centered around evaluations of queries. If a query is free of virtual relations, it will be evaluated by a relational data base system such as System R (Astrahan et al. [1976]). If the query contains both base and virtual relations, it will be evaluated in two steps. First, axioms are used to transform the query into one containing only base relations. Second, the transformed query is evaluated by the relational data base system. Before calling upon the relational data base system to evaluate the query, the query could be checked to determine if it is consistent with integrity constraints. If it is inconsistent, the answer to the query will be empty. In this case, there is no need to send the query to the relational data base system for evaluation.

Our evaluational approach is different from the non-evaluational approaches given in Clark [1978], Kellogg et al. [1978], Klahr [1977], McSkimin and Minker [1978] and Minker [1975,1978], where one usually has to show that a question represented by a formula is a logical consequence of facts and axioms. In our evaluational approach, facts are decoupled from axioms. That is, axioms are used to transform queries, while facts are used to evaluate queries. This approach is also used by Reiter [1978]. The evaluational approach can uniformly handle "for all" and "there exist" types of queries, while the non-evaluational approach may have difficulties handling "for all" type queries (see Minker [1975]). Even though the evaluational approach is taken here, most techniques used in theorem proving (Chang and Lee [1973], Chang and Slagle [1977], Kowalski [1975], Sickel [1977]) can be used to transform queries. In this paper, it is shown how the rewriting rule method (Chang and Slagle [1977], Sickel [1977]) for theorem proving can be used to transform a query. We shall also discuss a relational data base model for both base and virtual relations, and an optimization problem about access methods for efficient deduction in a relational data base.

NEW SYNTAX OF THE DEDUCE LANGUAGE

In this section, a new syntax of DEDUCE is given. DEDUCE is based upon symbolic logic (Chang and Lee [1973]). Basically, there are constant (value) symbols, variable symbols, function symbols and predicate (relation) symbols. There are also logical connectives, $\sim$, &, $\vee$, and $\rightarrow$. Also, since the new syntax of DEDUCE is oriented toward uniformly handling many kinds of quantifiers, the following symbols for the quantifiers are provided, where n is a non-negative integer:

Quantifier	Symbol	Read As
universal	$\forall$	for all
existential	$\exists$	there is a
numerical	$\exists < n$	there are less than n
numerical	$\exists \leq n$	there are at most n
numerical	$\exists > n$	there are more than n
numerical	$\exists \geq n$	there are at least n
numerical	$\exists = n$	there are exactly n

Using these symbols, terms and formulas can be constructed as follows:

Definition. A term is defined recursively as:

(1) A variable or a constant is a term;
(2) If f is an n-place function symbol, and $t_1,\ldots,t_n$ are terms, $f(t_1,\ldots,t_n)$ is a term;
(3) Any term can always be constructed by repeated applications of the above two rules.

If P is an n-place predicate symbol, and $t_1,\ldots,t_n$ are terms, $P(t_1,\ldots,t_n)$ is an atomic formula. However, if P is a relation, the atomic formula will be written as $P(a_1=t_1,\ldots,a_n=t_n)$, where $a_1,\ldots,a_n$ are some attributes of P. The reason for this is that the attributes of the relation P in a relational data base may not be ordered, and the atomic formula may contain only some (not all) attributes of the relation.

Definition. Well-formed formulas (formulas) are defined recursively as follows:

(1) An atomic formula is a formula;
(2) If A and B are formulas, then $\sim(A)$, $(A \vee B)$, $(A \& B)$ and $(A \rightarrow B)$ are formulas;
(3) If A is a formula, and x is a free variable in A, and Q is a quantifier, then (Qx)A is a formula, and the scope of x is A;
(4) Formulas are generated by a finite number of applications of (1), (2) and (3).

In DEDUCE, there are the following kinds of queries:

(1) A formula that contains attributes marked by the '*' symbols is called a FIND type DEDUCE query. If there are variables associated with the attributes, they must be free variables. The '*' symbols indicate that each set of values for the attributes which satisfy the formula will be listed. For example, the query "Find the names of employees in the TOY department' can be expressed as:

EMP(*name=x, dept=toy),

where name and dept are the attributes of the EMP relation. The '*' symbols tells the system to output the set of employee names. Since x appears in only one atomic formula, without ambiguity, we may drop x and simply represent the query as

EMP(*name, dept=TOY) .

Mathematically, the DEDUCE query means that one is to find the set:

$\{x \mid \text{EMP(name=x, dept=TOY)}\}$.

In terms of the relational algebra (Codd [1970]), this set can be obtained as follows: First, obtain a restriction of the EMP relation with dept=TOY. That is, obtain all rows of the EMP table whose value in the 'dept' column is TOY. Then, take the projection of the restriction on the 'name'.

(2) A FIND type DEDUCE expression can be preceded by a system-provided function such as COUNT, MAX, MIN, AVG, SUM, TOTAL, EXIST, etc., or a user-defined function. This tells the system that, instead of outputting a set (bag)† S of values, it should output the value obtained from applying the function on the set S. We shall call such a DEDUCE expression a functional expression. A functional expression can be used to represent a DEDUCE query. If a DEDUCE query starts with the function EXIST, the response to the query is a YES/NO or TRUE/FALSE answer. In a functional expression, the symbol '*' is always replaced by the symbol '#'. (If the function is to apply to a bag, another symbol, say '%' could be used in place of the symbol '*'. In this paper, the special symbol for bag is not used because the reader can easily tell whether a set or a bag is meant from the function.) In a DEDUCE query, a functional expression can be used as an argument of a predicate or a function. For example, a query may have a condition that the total salary be greater than 100,000. The total salary will be represented by a functional expression. The BNF grammar of DEDUCE is given in the Appendix.

Examples are used to illustrate DEDUCE. The relational data bases considered and the queries used are taken from Boyce et al. [1975], and Chang [1976]. This data base consists of the following relations:

EMP(NAME, SAL, MGR, DEPT)
SALES(DEPT, ITEM, VOL)

---

† A bag is an unordered collection of elements, where the elements may be duplicated.

```
SUPPLY(COMP, DEPT, ITEM, VOL)
LOC(DEPT, FLOOR)
CLASS(ITEM, TYPE) .
```

The EMP relation has a row for every store employee, giving his name, salary, manager, and department. The SALES relation gives the volume (yearly count) in which each department sells each item. The SUPPLY relation gives the volume (yearly count) in which each department obtained various items from its various supplier companies. The LOC relation gives the floor on which each department is located, and the CLASS relation classifies the items sold into various types. In the following, we declare only x, y, z, u, v, and w are variables. Each query is expressed first in English and then in DEDUCE.

1) Find the volume of guns sold by the toy department.

```
SALES(*vol, dept=toy, item=gun) .
```

2) List the names and managers of employees in the shoe department with salary greater than 10000.

```
EMP(*name, *mgr, sal=x, dept=shoe) & x > 10000.
```

The above query can be abbreviated to

```
EMP(*name, *mgr, sal>10000, dept=shoe),
```

by eliminating the variable x.

3) Find those items sold by departments on the second floor.

```
SALES(*item, dept=x) & LOC(dept=x, floor=2) .
```

This DEDUCE query represents a *join* (Codd [1970]) of relations SALES and LOC, and x is called a *join variable*.

4) Find the salary of Anderson's manager.

```
EMP(name=Anderson, mgr=x) &
EMP(name=x, *sal) .
```

5) Find the names of employees who make more than their managers.

```
EMP(*name, sal=x, mgr=y) &
EMP(name=y, sal<x).
```

6) Find the average salary of employees in the toy or shoe department.

AVG(EMP(#sal, dept=y) & (y=toy V y=shoe)) .

This DEDUCE query is a functional expression, which uses the system-provided function AVG. The interpretation of this query is: First, get the bag of salaries that satisfies EMP(sal, dept=y) & (y=toy V y=shoe), and then apply the AVG function to the bag.

7) How many type A items?

COUNT(CLASS(#item, type=A)).

8) List the name and salary of each manager who manages more than 10 employees.

```
(∃ > 10 y) (EMP(*name=x, *sal) &
            EMP(name=y, mgr=x)) .
```

One way to evaluate this DEDUCE query is given as follows: First, find a temporary join table, TEMP(name-x, sal, name-y, mgr-x) for EMP(name=x, sal) & EMP(name=y, mgr=x). Second, group rows of the TEMP table by mgr-x. Third, count the number of names in the 'name-y' column associated with each distinct manager in the 'mgr-x' column. Then, print those managers and their salaries where the countings are greater than 10.

9) Find the names of those employees who make more than any employee in the shoe department.

(∀y)(EMP(name=y, sal=x, dept=shoe) → EMP(*name, sal > x)) .

10) Find those companies, each of which supplies every item.

(∀y)((y ∈ ITEM) → SUPPLY(*comp, item=y)) ,

where ITEM (in upper case) denotes the domain of all items. (It is assumed that a relational data base schema describes not only relations, but also domains.) In DEDUCE, if a universal variable is used in a query, then a domain or a set must be specified for the universal variable to apply. The formula on the left of → specifies the set.

11) Find the companies, each of which supplies every item of type A to some department on the second floor.

```
(∀ z)(CLASS(item=z, type=A) →
      (∃x)(SUPPLY(*comp, dept=x, item=z) &
           LOC(dept=x, floor=2))) .
```

12) List all companies that supply at least two departments with more than 100 items.

$$(\exists \geq 2y)(\exists > 100z)\ \text{SUPPLY}(\text{*comp, dept=y, item=z})\ .$$

13) Among all departments with total salary greater than 1m, find those departments which sell dresses.

$$\text{SALES}(\text{*dept=x, item=dress})\ \& \\ \text{TOTAL}(\text{EMP}(\text{dept=x, \#sal})) > \text{1m}\ .$$

This query has the predicate > which contains a functional expression, TOTAL(EMP(dept=x, #sal)).

14) Find all items that are sold on more than 2 floors.

$$(\exists y)(\exists > 2z)(\text{SALES}(\text{dept=y, *item})\ \& \\ \text{LOC}(\text{dept=y, floor=z})).$$

15) Among all pairs of departments that sell dresses, find every pair that sells at least 3 items in common.

$$(\exists \geq 3z)(\text{SALES}(\text{*dept=x, item=dress})\ \& \\ \text{SALES}(\text{*dept=y, item=dress})\ \& \\ x \neq y\ \& \\ \text{SALES}(\text{dept=x, item=z})\ \& \\ \text{SALES}(\text{dept=y, item=z}))\ .$$

16) Find all the floors where a department sells all items.

$$(\forall z)((z \in \text{ITEM}) \rightarrow \\ (\exists y)(\text{SALES}(\text{dept=y, item=z})\ \&\ \text{LOC}(\text{*floor, dept=y}))).$$

17) Find every floor where all departments on the floor sell a type A item.

$$(\forall y)(\text{LOC}(\text{*floor, dept=y}) \rightarrow \\ (\exists z)(\text{SALES}(\text{dept=y, item=z})\ \& \\ \text{CLASS}(\text{item=z, type=A})))\ .$$

INTEGRITY CONSTRAINTS IN RELATIONAL DATA BASES

Integrity constraints are properties of relations in a relational data base. The properties that are studied most often are functional dependencies among attributes of relations. Functional dependencies have been used to normalize relations so as to avoid deletion, insertion and updating anomallies (Bernstein [1976], Codd [1970,1971a,1971b], Delobel and Casey [1972], Fagin [1976a, 1976b], Nicolas and Yazdanian [1978], Rissanen [1977]). In this paper, we are interested in the representation of integrity constraints, and their use for checking consistencies of queries. We allow more general integrity constraints than functional dependencies. Formulas defined in the section entitled New Syntax of the DEDUCE Language are used to represent integrity constraints. Therefore, any constraints that can be represented by formulas are allowed. As in the previous section, examples are used to illustrate how DEDUCE can be used to represent integrity constraints.

1) Every department has only one floor.

$$(\forall x)(\mathrm{LOC}(\mathrm{dept}=x) \rightarrow (\exists=1y)\ \mathrm{LOC}(\mathrm{dept}=x,\ \mathrm{floor}=y))\ .$$

The above DEDUCE expression can be read as: For all departments x in the LOC table, there is exactly one floor y where x is located. This constraint is a functional dependency between the attribute 'floor' and the attribute 'dept'.

2) There are no type B items.

$$(\exists=0x)\ \mathrm{CLASS}(\mathrm{item}=x,\ \mathrm{type}=B).$$

3) There are more than 10 type B items.

$$(\exists>10x)\ \mathrm{CLASS}(\mathrm{item}=x,\ \mathrm{type}=B)\ .$$

4) Every manager manages only one department on one floor.

$$(\forall x)(\mathrm{EMP}(\mathrm{mgr}=x) \rightarrow (\exists=1y)(\exists=1z)(\mathrm{EMP}(\mathrm{mgr}=x,\ \mathrm{dept}=y)\ \&\ \mathrm{LOC}(\mathrm{dept}=y,\ \mathrm{floor}=z)))\ .$$

The above DEDUCE constraint requires a join of the EMP and LOC relations on 'dept'. Clearly, using the numerical quantifiers, the constraint can be easily stated in DEDUCE. This constraint is a functional dependency among the attributes of the join.

5) Every company supplies every department with exactly one item.

$$(\forall x)(\forall y)(\mathrm{SUPPLY}(\mathrm{comp}=x,\ \mathrm{dept}=y) \rightarrow (\exists=1z)\ \mathrm{SUPPLY}(\mathrm{comp}=x,\ \mathrm{dept}=y,\ \mathrm{item}=z)).$$

This is a functional dependency.

6) Every manager has two employees with salaries greater than 50000.

$(\forall x)$(EMP(mgr=x) $\rightarrow$
$(\exists = 2y)$ EMP(name=y, mgr=x, sal > 50000)) .

7) There is one type A item that is supplied by all suppliers.

$(\exists = 1x)$(CLASS(item=x, type=A) &
$(\forall y)$(SUPPLY(comp=y) $\rightarrow$ SUPPLY(comp=y, item=x)).

8) Employee names are unique.

UNIQUE(EMP(#name)).

9) Any companies that supply guns also supply bullets.

$(\forall x)$(SUPPLY(comp=x, item=gun) $\rightarrow$
SUPPLY(comp=x, item=bullets)) .

10) Any companies that supply guns do not supply dresses.

$(\forall x)$(SUPPLY(comp=x, item=gun) $\rightarrow$
$\sim$ SUPPLY(comp=x, item=dress)) .

11) Every department cannot have more than 10 employees. (Note that this kind of quota is very common in the real world.)

$(\forall x)$(EMP(dept=x) $\rightarrow$ $(\exists \leq 10y)$ EMP(dept=x, name=y)) .

Declaration in the DEDUCE 2 language are used to distinguish integrity constraints from virtual relation definitions.

DEFINING VIRTUAL RELATIONS BY AXIOMS

New relations are defined through axioms in DEDUCE. A relation that is explicitly stored in a computer is called a base relation, and a relation defined by axioms a virtual relation. Axioms are used which have the following form:

$$(Q_1x_1)\ldots(Q_rx_r)((A_1\&\ldots\&A_n \;\&\; F) \rightarrow B) ,$$

where $Q_1,\ldots,Q_r$ are quantifiers, and each of $A_1,\ldots,A_n$ is an atomic formula containing a base or virtual relation, B is an atomic formula containing a virtual relation, and F is a formula free of base or virtual relations. F may contain user-defined predicates and system-provided predicates such as $=, <, \leq, >, \geq$, etc., that are to be evaluated. (Note that with respect to $A_1,\ldots,A_n$ and B, the axiom is a Horn clause.) We restrict ourselves to this form of axioms because it is more efficient to process them than general ones, and for practical purposes, they can be used to define many useful relations.

Given base and virtual relation symbols, it is necessary to define an interpretation (model) for the symbols. That is, it is necessary to specify an interpretation in which a relation symbol can be interpreted (tested) true or false. In logic (Chang and Lee [1973]) one usually assigns an interpretation arbitrarily. However, in a relational data base, the model is specified as follows:

1) The model of each base relation is its extension represented by a table. Any tuple (row) in the table is interpreted as true. If a tuple does not appear in the table, it is interpreted as false.

2) For each virtual relation defined by an axiom

$$(Q_1x_1)\ldots(Q_rx_r)((A_1 \,\&\ldots\&\, A_n \,\&\, F) \rightarrow B) \;,$$

the model of the virtual relation is obtained as follows: First, a table TEMP1 for the join, $A_1 \,\&\ldots\&\, A_n$, is created. Second, create a table TEMP2 from TEMP1 by using $(Q_1x_1)\ldots(Q_rx_r)$ to select rows of TEMP1 that satisfy the formula F. Then, take a projection of TEMP2 on the columns corresponding to variables specified in B. The projection is the model of the virtual relation. For example, suppose a virtual relation R is defined by

$$(\forall x)(\exists = 2y)((P(A{=}x,\ B{=}y) \,\&\, Q(C{=}x,\ D{=}a)) \rightarrow R(E{=}x)) \;,$$

where P and Q are base relations whose extensions are shown in the following tables:

P

A	B
a	1
a	2
b	3
c	4

Q

C	D
a	a
b	b
c	a

The join TEMP1 for P(A=x, B=y) & Q(C=x, D=a) is given as

TEMP1

A	B	C	D
a	1	a	a
a	2	a	a
c	4	c	a

(Note that TEMP1 contains all attributes A, B, C and D that appear in P(A=x, B=y) & Q(C=x, D=a).) The quantifier $(\forall x)(\exists = 2y)$ means that for every value in column A of TEMP1, if it is associated with exactly two values in column B, then the tuple will be put into table TEMP2. Since value a in column A of TEMP1 is associated with exactly two values 1 and 2 in column B of TEMP1, and value c is associated with one value, TEMP2 consists of the first two rows of TEMP1 as given below:

TEMP2

A	B	C	D
a	1	a	a
a	2	a	a

Since the variable x in R(E=x) corresponds to attribute A, we obtain the projection R of TEMP2 on column A,

R

E
a

This table will be the model of the virtual relation R. If there are two or more axioms defining the virtual relation R, the collection of tables obtained for all the axioms for R is the model of R.

In creating the model for the virtual relations as shown above, since universal variables are to range through all tuples of table TEMP1, any existential or numerical quantifier must be preceded by at least one universal quantifier. That is, in the axiom

$$(Q_1x_1)\dots(Q_rx_r)\ ((A_1\ \&\dots\&\ A_n\ \&\ F) \rightarrow B),$$

there must be an integer p, $1 \leq p \leq r$, such that $(Q_1x_1)\dots(Q_px_p)$ are all universal quantifiers, and $x_1,\dots,x$ must occur in the atomic formula B, and B contains no other variables. Therefore, the axiom

$$(\exists x)(P(A{=}x) \rightarrow R(A{=}x)),$$

where P is a base relation and R is a virtual relation, is not allowed. In addition, since axioms are restricted to a conjunction of atomic formulas for $A_1\ \&\dots\&\ A_n$, the axiom,

$$(\forall x)((SUPPLY(comp{=}x)\ \&\ (\forall y)((y \in ITEM) \rightarrow SUPPLY(comp{=}x,\ item{=}y))) \rightarrow CONGLOMERATE(comp{=}x)),$$

is not allowed. This axiom says that if a company supplies all items, it is called a conglomerate company.

The model for base relations described here has been called a closed world model by Nicolas and Gallaire [1978] and Reiter [1978]. However, they do not consider a model for virtual relations. The difference is that axioms used here are for definitional purposes, while they use axioms strictly in a logical sense.

Examples are presented to illustrate how axioms can be used to define virtual relations.

Example 1. Suppose a new relation, COMMAND(x,y), is desired which denotes that x commands y. Associate x and y with the attributes, superior and name, respectively, and define COMMAND by the following two formulas:

(a) (∀x)(∀y)(EMP(name=y, mgr=x) → COMMAND(superior=x, name=y))

(b) (∀x)(∀z)(∃y)((EMP(name=z, mgr=y) &
COMMAND(superior=x, name=y))
→ COMMAND(superior=x, name=z)) .

The first formula states that if x is the manager of y, then x commands y. The second formula states that if x commands y, and if y is the manager of z, then x commands z. Once the virtual relation is defined, a user can make a query against it and the base relations. For example, the query 'Find all persons who are commanded by Jones, and who sell guns' is represented as:

(∃y)(EMP(*name=x, dept=y) &
SALES(dept=y, item=gun) &
COMMAND(superior=Jones, name=x)) .

Example 2. Suppose the following two base relations are given:

BIRTH(EMPLOYEE, DATE),
HAPPEN(EMPLOYEE, EVENT, DATE-OF-EVENT),

where birth relation gives the birthday of every employee, and the HAPPEN relation gives the date of each event that happened to each employee. Now, besides defining virtual relations, it is possible to define virtual attributes. For example, define the age of an employee when an event occurs by using the following formula:

(a) (∀x)(∀y)(∀z)(∀u)
((BIRTH(employee=x, date=y) &
HAPPEN(employee=x, event=z, date-of-event=u))
→ HAPPEN(employee=x, event=z, date-of-event=u,
age-on-event=u-y)) **

**Note that HAPPEN is used as both a four-place predicate and a three-place predicate. A convention has to exist in the language translator which permits this. The three-place predicate is a projection of the four-place predicate.

Through the above mechanism, new attributes can be added open-endedly to a relation. Once the new attribute, age-on-event, is defined, then the query 'What was Lee's age when he was hired?' can be represented in DEDUCE as follows:

HAPPEN(employee=Lee, Event=HIRE, *age-on-event).

Besides the relations, the following integrity constraint may pertain:

(b) (∀x) HAPPEN(employee=x, event=PRESENT, date-of-event= READCLOCK),

where READCLOCK is a system-provided function that outputs a date at the time a query is evaluated. Now, the query 'What is Lee's present age' can be represented as

HAPPEN(employee=Lee, event=PRESENT, *age-on-event) .

To answer this query, formulas (a) and (b) are used.

PRENEX NORMAL FORMS OF FORMULAS

Like first-order logic, a formula defined in the section entitled New Syntax of the DEDUCE Language, can be transformed into a prenex normal form. A method for doing this is exactly the same as one given in Section 3.3 of Chapter 3 in Chang and Lee [1973], except that the following laws are added to handle numerical quantifiers:

$$\sim((\exists < nx)\ F[x]) = (\exists \geq nx)\ F[x]$$

$$\sim((\exists \leq nx)\ F[x]) = (\exists > nx)\ F[x]$$

$$\sim((\exists > nx)\ F[x]) = (\exists \leq nx)\ F[x]$$

$$\sim((\exists \geq nx)\ F[x]) = (\exists < nx)\ F[x]$$

$$\sim((\exists = nx)\ F[x]) = (\exists \neq nx)\ F[x]$$

$$\sim((\exists \neq nx)\ F[x]) = (\exists = nx)\ F[x],$$

where F[x] is a formula containing variable x. That is, various laws such as De Morgan's laws and the laws given above are used to: (1) eliminate the logical connective →; (2) bring the negation signs immediately before atomic formulas; (3) rename variables if necessary; (4) move quantifiers to the left of the entire formula to obtain a prenex normal form.

Example 3. Let us consider the query (11) of the previous section (New Syntax of the DEDUCE Language), namely,

```
(∀z)(CLASS(item=z, type=A) →
     (∃x)(SUPPLY(*comp, dept=x, item=z) &
          LOC(dept=x, floor=2))) .
```

Since x is not in CLASS(item=z, type=A), the quantifier (∃x) can be moved to the left to obtain

```
(∀z)(∃x)(CLASS(item=z, type=A) →
          (SUPPLY(*comp, dept=x, item=z) &
           LOC(dept=x, floor=2))) .
```

Prenex normal form is convenient for query transformation as is to be discussed in the following sections.

QUERY EVALUATION

As previously stated, a query is evaluated in two steps: First, axioms are used to transform the query into one containing only base relations**. Second, a check is made to determine if the transformed query is consistent with integrity constraints in a prespecified time limit. (Note that integrity constraints are allowed only on base relations.) If it is inconsistent, the answer is empty. Otherwise, the transformed query is evaluated by using a data base system such as System R (Astrahan et al. [1976]). Techniques from theorem proving may be used to check if the transformed query is consistent with the integrity constraints. However, this is outside of the scope of this chapter. (Note that the query can always be evaluated, even when it cannot be proved whether or not the query is consistent with the integrity constraints.) Here, only the first step for transforming a query is discussed. The system block diagram is shown in Figure 1.

The method for transforming a query is based on the idea of replacing virtual relations (if any) in the query by these definitions as specified by the axioms. The substitutions are done repeatedly until a query free of virtual relations is obtained. The transformation method is described for DEDUCE queries that do not contain functional expressions. (If a query contains a functional expression such as shown in query (13) of the section New Syntax of the DEDUCE Language, then the subquery inside the function has to be transformed first.)

** If virtual relations are defined recursively, as explained in the section, Using Rewriting Rules to Transform Queries, a cut-off level can be specified beyond which recursion is terminated.

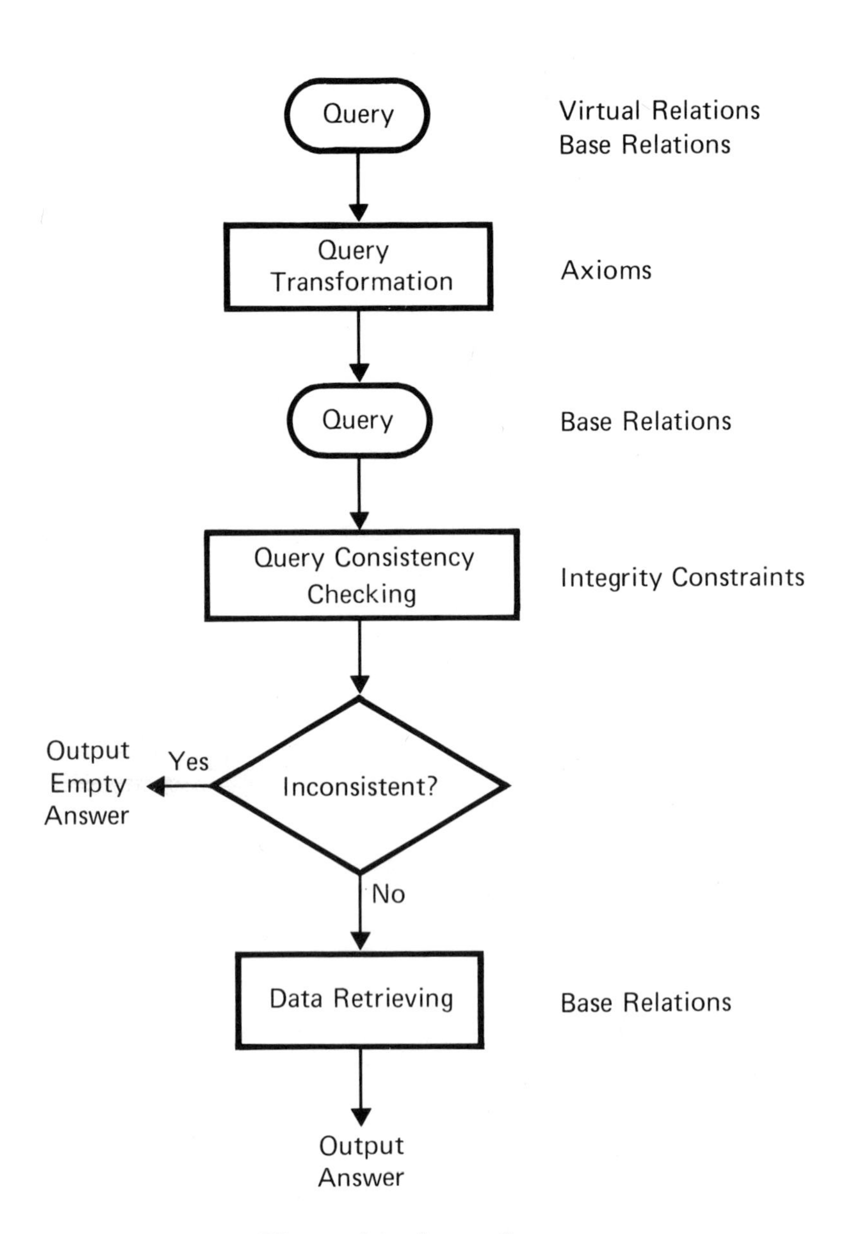

Figure 1. Query Process

Given a DEDUCE query containing virtual relations, its definition is substituted for each virtual relation in the query. For illustration purpose, suppose the query in prenex normal form is given as

$$(1)\quad (Q_1y_1)\ldots(Q_sy_s)(\ldots R(C=t)\ldots),$$

where R is a virtual relation, t is a variable, and ... indicates that the query contains other formulas. Note that no generality is lost by assuming that t is a variable, because if t is a constant or contains a function, R(C=t) can be represented as $(\exists x)$ (R(C=x) & x=t) . Let Q_t be the quantifier that quantifies t. Let an axiom defining R be given as

$$(2)\quad (Q_1x_1)\ldots(Q_rx_r)\ ((A_1\ \&\ldots\&\ A_n\ \&\ F) \rightarrow R(C=u,\ D=v)),$$

where u and v are variables. Let Q_u and Q_v be quantifiers for u and v, respectively. Note that C and D are the attributes of R, and some attribute of R may not appear in the query. (Even though the transformation method is described where R has two attributes, the method can be extended easily to the case where R has more than two attributes or where more than one attribute of R appears in the query.) Assume that (1) and (2) share no variables in common. In order to make a substitution, it is necessary to unify R(C=t) with R(C=u, D=v).

First, consider v in (2). If v is a universal variable, drop (Q_vv) and D=v from (2). If v is an existential or numerical variable, just drop D=v from (2). Therefore, axiom (2) becomes

$$(3)\quad Q((A_1\ \&\ldots\&\ A_n\ \&\ F) \rightarrow R(C=u)),$$

where Q denotes $(Q_1x_1)\ldots[Q_vv]\ldots(Q_rx_r)$, and [] in $[Q_vv]$ means optional.

Now, match R(C=t) with R(C=u). First, substitute t for all u in (3). Thus, (3) becomes

$$(4)\quad Q'(A_1'\ \&\ldots\&\ A_n'\ \&\ F') \rightarrow R(C=t)),$$

where Q', $A_1',\ldots,A_n'$, F' are respectively obtained from Q, $A_1,\ldots,A_n$, F by substituting t for u. Then, substituting the left hand side of $\rightarrow$ in (4) for R(C=t) in (1), a transformed query is obtained as

$$(5)\quad (Q_1y_1)\ldots(Q_sy_s)(\ldots Q'(A_1'\ \&\ldots\&\ A_n'\ \&\ F')\ \ldots)\ .$$

In the transformed query (5), note that variable t is quantified by two quantifiers Q_t and Q_u. In general, to check the compatibility of two quantifiers, associate a quantifier with an interval as shown in Table 1.

Table 1. Interval Quantifier

$\exists$	[1 , n*]
$\forall$	[0 , n*]
$\exists \geq n$	[n , n*]
$\exists > n$	(n , n*]
$\exists < n$	[0 , n)
$\exists \leq n$	[0 , n]
$\exists = n$	[n , n]
$\exists \neq n$	[0 ,n-1] $\cup$ [n+1,n*]

where a bracket indicates a closed interval, and a parenthesis an open interval, and n* is the total number of all possible values for the attribute that a variable quantified by the quantifier is associated with. The meaning of an interval is: If x is associated with a quantifier Q, whose corresponding interval is I, then (Qx) means that the number of values for x has to be a number in the interval I. Two quantifiers Q_1 and Q_2 are said to be <u>compatible</u> if and only if their corresponding intervals of the quantifiers are not disjoint. For example, ($\exists \geq$ 2t) and ($\exists <$ 2t) are not compatible. However, ($\exists \leq$ 5t) and ($\exists$ = it) are compatible. In (5), if (Q_tt) and (Q_ut) are not compatible, then (5) should be deleted. That is, R(C=t) and R(C=u) cannot be unified. Otherwise, (5) will be transformed again if it contains virtual relations.

<u>Example 4.</u> Assume that two distinct departments are similar if they sell more than 3 items in common. In DEDUCE, this is stated by the following axiom

```
(∀x)(∀y)(∃ > 3z)((SALES(dept=x, item=z) &
                  SALES(dept=y, item=z) &
                  x ≠ y ) →
                  SIMILAR(dept1=x, dept2=y)) .
```

Now, given the query 'Find all departments which are similar to exactly 2 departments', the query is represented in DEDUCE as:

```
(∃ = 2y) SIMILAR(*dept1=x, dept2=y) .
```

Since the query contains the virtual relation SIMILAR, it needs to be transformed. To do this, first rename variables x and y in the query, and obtain

$(\exists = 2v)$ SIMILAR(*dept1=u, dept2=v) .

Note that before unification, variables have to be renamed so that variables in a query are different from variables in any axiom. Unifying SIMILAR(*dept1=u, dept2=v) in the query and SIMILAR(dept1=x, dept2=y), the axiom is transformed into

$(\exists = 2v)(\exists > 3z)$((SALES(*dept=u, item=z) &
SALES(dept=v, item=z) &
$u \neq v$) $\rightarrow$
SIMILAR(*dept1=u, dept2=v)) .

Replacing the query by the left hand side of $\rightarrow$ in the axiom, the transformed query becomes:

$(\exists = 2v)(\exists > 3z)$(SALES(*dept=u, item=z) &
SALES(dept=v, item=z) &
$u \neq v$).

Since the final transformed query does not contain virtual relations, it can be evaluated by a relational data base management system such as System R.

The transformation method described here can be applied to any DEDUCE query. However, for conjunctive queries, i.e., queries having the following form,

$$(Q_1 x_1) \ldots (Q_m x_m)(A_1 \,\&\ldots\&\, A_n \,\&F) ,$$

where $Q_1, \ldots, Q_m$ are existential or numerical quantifiers, and each of $A_1, \ldots, A_n$ is an atomic formula containing a base or virtual relation, and F is a formula free of base or virtual relations, a technique developed in theorem proving can be used to transform the queries. This is discussed in the subsequent sections. (Note that the majority of queries encountered in practice probably fall within this type of query. With respect to $A_1, \ldots, A_n$, each of this type of query is a Horn clause. In Codd et al. [1978], conjunctive queries without numerical quantifiers are considered.)

USING REWRITING RULES TO TRANSFORM QUERIES

As discussed in the last section, to evaluate a query, it is necessary to transform it into one that is free of virtual relations. Since, in general, there are many axioms for many virtual relations, an efficient method is needed for selecting which axioms to apply. In this section, a method based on rewriting rules (Chang and Slagle [1977], Sickel [1977]) is described. The rewriting rule method has been proposed for proving theorems in first-order logic. In particular, it is shown that this method can be used easily for query transformation. Essentially, the rewriting rule method consists of the following steps:

(a) Find a directed connection graph for a set of axioms and a query; (For efficiency, a connection graph may be prestored for a set of axioms, and every time a new query is presented, the connection graph is expanded to include the query.)

(b) From the connection graph, obtain a set of rewriting rules;

(c) Use the rewriting rules to generate a plan;

(d) Check whether or not the plan is acceptable for transforming the query. If it is acceptable, obtain a transformed query. Otherwise, use the rewriting rules again to generate another plan.

The method is now described in detail.

Connection Graph

A connection graph for a set of axioms and a query is constructed as follows:

(a) Every axiom

$$(Q_1x_1)\ldots(Q_rx_r)((A_1 \;\&\ldots\&\; A_n \;\&\; F) \rightarrow B) \;,$$

is represented in the graph by

$(Q_1x_1) \cdots (Q_rx_r)$	A_1	$\cdots$	A_n	F	‖	B

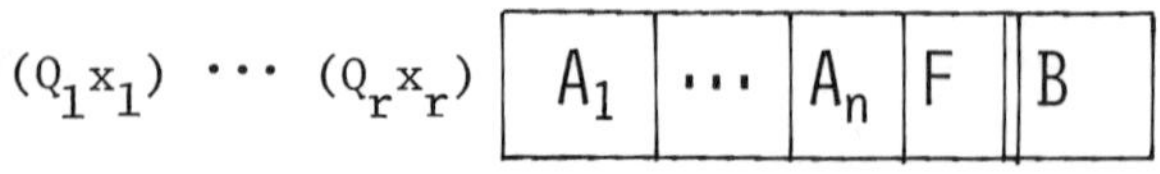

$A_1,\ldots,A_n$ are called left literals, F is a left formula, and B is a right literal.

A query

$$(Q_1y_1)\ldots(Q_sy_s)(C_1 \;\&\ldots\&\; C_m \;\&\; G) \;,$$

is represented in the graph by

$(Q_1y_1)\ldots(Q_sy_s)$	C_1	$\cdots$	C_m	G	‖	

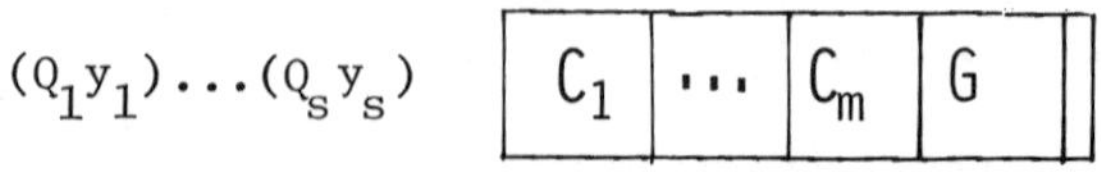

Note that in the above, $A_1,\ldots,A_n$, $C_1,\ldots,C_m$ are atomic formulas

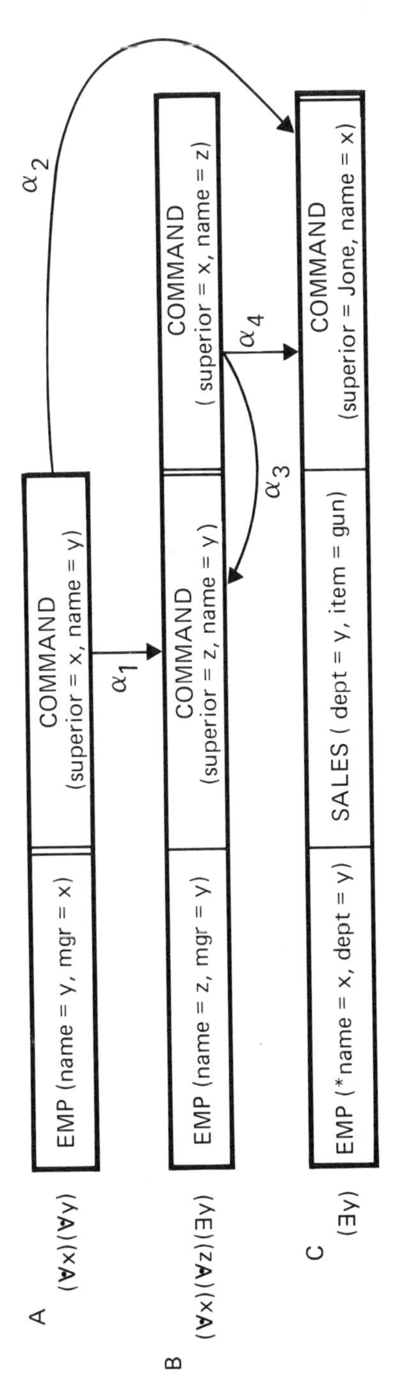

Figure 2. Connection Graph

containing relations, and F and G are formulas free of base or virtual relations.

(b) For every pair of literals L1 and L2 in the graph, if both L1 and L2 contain a virtual relation and are unifiable, and if L1 is a right literal and L2 is a left literal, draw a directed edge from L1 to L2 and label the edge.

Example 5. Figure 2 is a connection graph for the axioms and query given in Example 1.

Obtaining Rewriting Rules

Rewriting rules are obtained as follows:

(a) For each left literal n, if $m_1,\ldots,m_r$ are all the right literals having edges pointing to n as shown in Figure 3, the rewriting rules obtained is:

$$W(n) = \alpha_1 W(m_1) \cup \ldots \cup \alpha_r W(m_r)$$

(b) For each axiom, if there is an edge leaving the right literal n as shown in Figure 4, the rewriting rule obtained is:

$$W(n) = P_1 \ldots P_r ,$$

where $P_i = W(m_i)$ if m_i is a literal containing a virtual relation;

$= m_i$ otherwise.

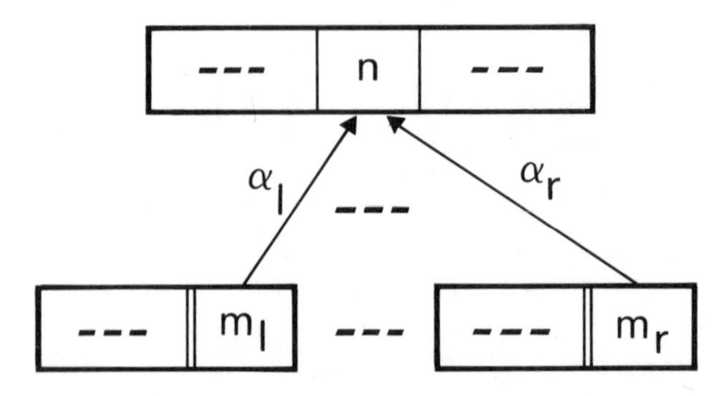

Figure 3. Rewriting Rule Diagram for Left Literals

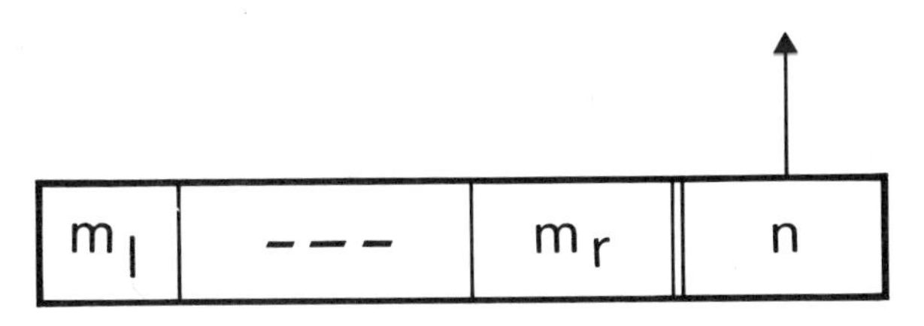

Figure 4. Rewriting Rule Diagram for Right Literals

(c) For the query shown in Figure 5, the rewriting rule obtained is:

$$T = Q_1 \cdots Q_m$$

where $Q_i = W(C_i)$ if C_i is a literal containing a virtual relation;

$= C_i$ otherwise.

In the above rules, T or W(L) are treated as non-terminal symbols, where L is a literal, and the other symbols are treated as terminal symbols in a context-free grammar. Before presenting an example, a naming scheme is used for literals. That is, label a clause (i.e., an axiom or a query) by a distinct name and then refer to a literal in the clause by its position in the clause. More formally, if c names a clause, then c_n names the n-th literal (counting from the left) of clause C, where n is an integer.

Example 6. For the connection graph shown in Figure 2, using the above naming scheme for literals, the following rewriting rules are obtained:

(1) $W(b_2) = \alpha_1 W(a_2) \cup \alpha_3 W(b_3)$ by (a) this section

(2) $W(c_3) = \alpha_2 W(a_2) \cup \alpha_4 W(b_3)$ by (a) this section

Figure 5. Query Clause

(3) $W(a_2) = a_1$ by (b) this section

(4) $W(b_3) = b_1W(b_2)$ by (b) this section

(5) $T = c_1c_2W(c_3)$ by (c) this section

In the above rules, T, $W(c_3)$, $W(b_2)$, $W(b_3)$ and $W(a_2)$ are non-terminal symbols, and a_1, b_1, c_1, c_2, α_1, α_2, α_3 and α_4 are treated as terminal symbols in a context-free grammar.

Using these rules, plans can be generated by rewriting T into sentences, or strings of terminal symbols. (Note that to use sentences as plans, the order of symbols in the sentences is immaterial.) To do this, rules (1) through (5) are first simplified as follows:

$$W(b_2) = \alpha_1W(a_2) \cup \alpha_3W(b_3) \quad \text{from (1)}$$

$$= \alpha_1a_1 \cup \alpha_3b_1W(b_2) \quad \text{from (3) and (4)}$$

$$T = c_1c_2W(c_3) \quad \text{from (5)}$$

$$= c_1c_2[\alpha_2W(a_2) \cup \alpha_4W(b_3)] \quad \text{from (2)}$$

$$= c_1c_2\alpha_2W(a_2) \cup c_1c_2\alpha_4W(b_3)$$

$$= c_1c_2\alpha_2a_1 \cup c_1c_2\alpha_4b_1W(b_2) \quad \text{from (3) and (4)}$$

$$= a_1c_1c_2\alpha_2 \cup b_1c_1c_2\alpha_4W(b_2)$$

Therefore, it is clear that T can be rewritten as following sentences: $a_1c_1c_2\alpha_2$, $b_1c_1c_2\alpha_4\alpha_1a_1, \ldots$ Each of these sentences is called a <u>plan</u>. Next, we describe how plans are used to transform a query.

Renaming Variables

To use plans to transform a query, variables in clauses have to be renamed properly. (For a detailed discussion, see Chang and Slagle [1977].) This is done as follows: First, build a table for edges and literals linked by them. For example, for Figure 2, Table 2 is built for the edges in the graph.

In Table 2, the first row (α_1, a_2, b_2) indicates that α_1 is an edge linking from the 2-nd literal of clause A (i.e., a_2) to the 2-nd literal of clause B (i.e., b_2), and so on. Using Table 2, $\alpha_1, \ldots, \alpha_4$ in a plan can be replaced by their corresponding pairs of literals. That is, replace α_1 by (a_2, b_2), α_2 by (a_2,c_3) and so on. For example, since $a_1c_1c_2\alpha_2$ is a plan in Example 6, it

Table 2. Edge-Literals

α_1	a_2	b_2
α_2	a_2	c_3
α_3	b_3	b_2
α_4	b_3	c_3

can be expressed as $a_1c_1c_2(a_2,c_3)$ by replacing α_2 by (a_2, c_3). Now, in order to rename variables in a plan so that copies of clauses share no variables in common, literals are grouped in a plan P. To do this, the method given in Chang and Slagle [1977] is used. That is, obtain a linked plan from the plan P as follows: for each pair of literals within a pair of parentheses, draw an edge, and for all literals that belong to a copy of a clause, draw edges from the literals to a common dot attached by the prefix of the clause. Since Horn clauses are used with respect to atomic formulas containing relations in axioms and the query, a linked plan must not have any cycle. For details, see Chang and Slagle [1977].

Example 7. In Example 6 the plan obtained was:

$$a_1c_1c_2(a_2, c_3) \ .$$

From this plan, the following linked plan is obtained:

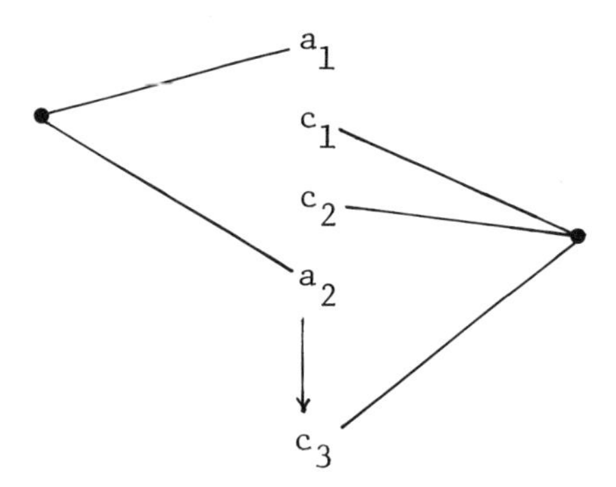

This linked plan does not have a cycle. Now, substituting actual literals for a_1, a_2, c_1, c_2, and c_3 in the linked plan, one obtains:

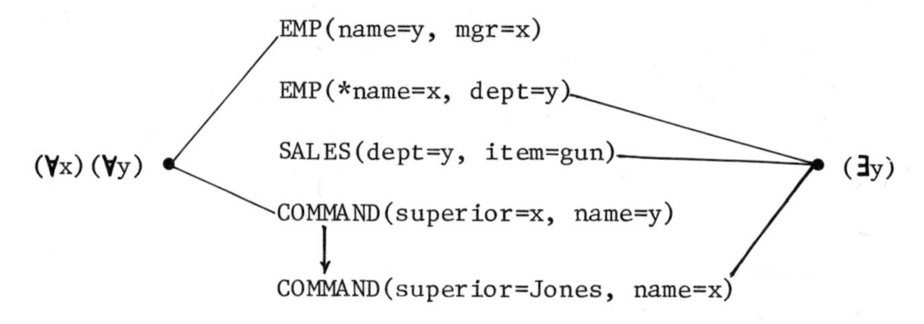

Renaming the variables so that the different clauses share no variables in common, the following linked plan is obtained.

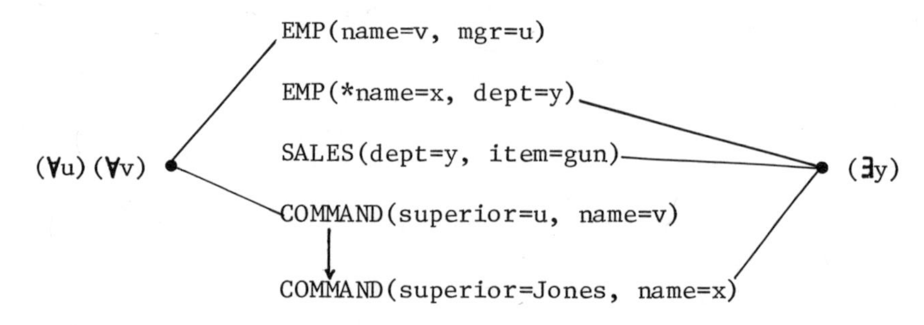

From the above linked plan, unifying COMMAND(superior=u, name=v) and COMMAND(superior=Jones, name=x) the following query is obtained:

(∃y) EMP(name=x, mgr=Jones) &
EMP(*name=x, dept=y) &
SALES(dept=y, item=gun) .

Since the above transformed query does not contain any virtual relations, it can be evaluated by a relational data base management system.

In Example 6, it was shown that a sequence of plans can be generated. For example, $b_1 c_1 c_2 \alpha_4 \alpha_1 a_1$ is another plan. Replacing

α_4 and α_1 by (b_3, c_3) and (a_2, b_2) ,

respectively from Table 2, the following plan is obtained:

$b_1 c_1 c_2 (b_3, c_3)(a_2, b_2) a_1$.

The linked plan for this plan is:

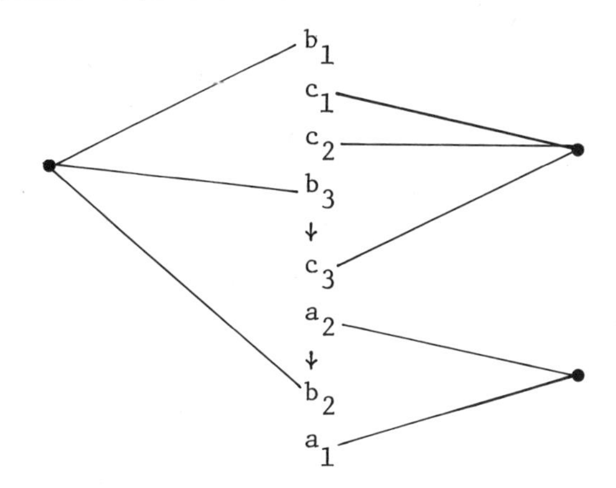

Substitution the actual literals for a_1, a_2, b_1, b_2, b_3, c_1, c_2, c_3, and renaming the variables, one obtains:

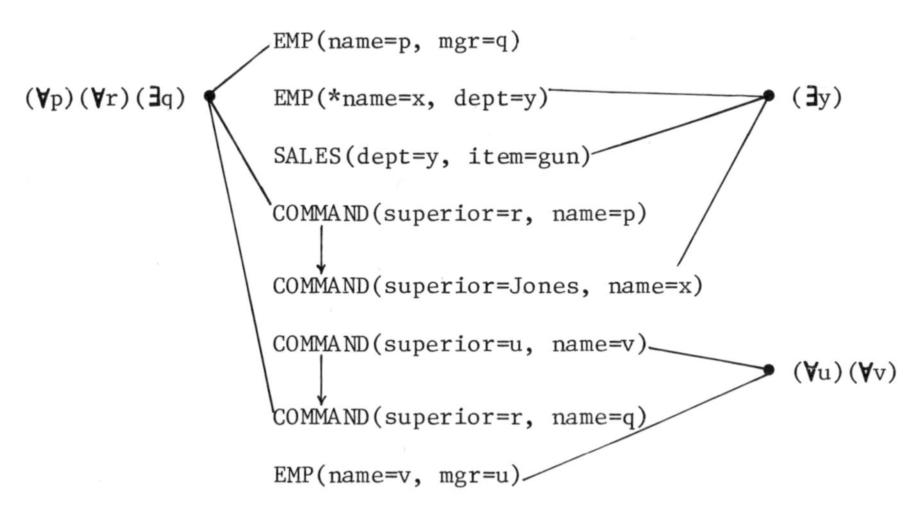

From the above linked plan, unifying COMMAND(superior=r, name=p) and COMMAND(superior=Jones, name=x), one obtains:

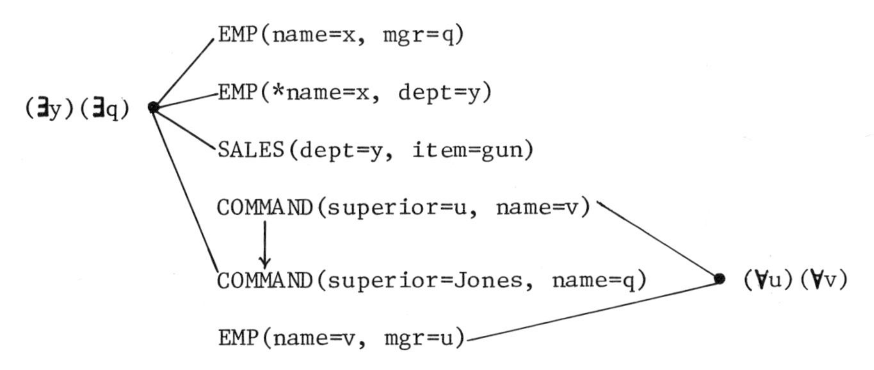

Unifying COMMAND(superior=u, name=v) and COMMAND(superior=Jones, name=q) again, one obtains:

$$(\exists y)(\exists q)\ \text{EMP(name=x, mgr=q)}\ \&$$
$$\text{EMP(*name=x, dept=y)}\ \&$$
$$\text{SALES(dept=y, item=gun)}\ \&$$
$$\text{EMP(name=q, mgr=Jones)}\ .$$

Again, the above transformed query can be evaluated by a data base management system.

As has been shown, rewriting rules can be used to generate a sequence of plans. Each of these plans can be used to transform the query. Therefore, one obtains a sequence of transformed queries that do not contain virtual relations. This sequence is terminated when a transformed query Q* is encountered which contains a subcondition contained by all the subsequent transformed queries generated beyond Q* in the sequence such that the subcondition is not satisfied by any values. In general, the termination problem is still an open problem. The problem may be formulated as follows: Given a set of axioms for virtual relations and a query, the problem is to synthesize a program to evaluate the query. The program will certainly contain a loop for generating and evaluating a sequence of transformed queries. We believe that this problem is simpler than the general program-synthesizing problem. Using the rewriting rule method discussed above for transforming queries, it may be possible to determine a terminating condition for the sequence of the transformed queries.

AN OPTIMIZATION PROBLEM

In relational data bases, three basic operations are projection, restriction and join. Among these, only the join operation is discussed in this section because it is usually the most expensive to compute. There are many methods (Astrahan et al. [1976], Gotlieb [1975]) for computing joins. For example, one can first sort values on a column of a table which is to join with another column of the same or another table, or one can index the values, or one can explicitly create linking pointers between the join columns. Each method creates its access paths and has its own cost in terms of speed, space, deletion, insertion and updating complexities. If queries that the users will ask are known in advance, we can precompute (support) the necessary access paths to aid in computing joins. Thus, when the user enters a query, it can be evaluated speedily.

Given a set Q of user queries, a set J of joins used in the queries of Q can be obtained. Now, the question is whether or not it is necessary to support all the joins in J. Since a query may be evaluated through many different access paths, it is not necessary to support all joins. For example, suppose a query has the condition

P(x,y) & Q(x,y,z) & R(x,z) ,

where P, Q, and R are base relations, and x, y and z are join variables qualified by some quantifiers. (For simplicity, the attributes of x, y and z are omitted.) For our convention, if v is a join variable, use the upper case of v to denote the join of v. In the above query condition, there are three joins X, Y, and Z as described below:

Join	Attributes Joined
X	P1, Q1, R1
Y	P2, Q2
Z	Q3, R2

where P1 and P2 respectively denote the first and second attributes of the relation P, and so on. Clearly, to evaluate the query condition efficiently, it is not necessary to support all three joins X, Y and Z. Either join X can be supported, or both joins Y and Z. This can be represented by a Boolean function F as

F = X + YZ ,

where addition and multiplication denote a disjunction and conjunction, respectively, and the upper case of a join variable denotes the proposition that its join is supported. An algorithm describing how one obtains the Boolean function is given in Chang [1978]. Usually, there is a cost for supporting a join. The cost may take into consideration the complexity of the join, its frequency of use, the access method used for the join, etc. Then, the problem is to find a set of joins such that the sum of costs of all the joins is minimum. For instance, assume the costs for supporting X, Y and Z are 3, 2 and 2, respectively. Then, in the Boolean function, the cost of X is 3, and the cost of YZ is 4. Therefore, support of X for evaluating the query condition leads to the least cost. Thus, the problem of finding an optimal set of joins to support has been formulated as a minimization problem for a Boolean function. An efficient algorithm for solving this problem is given in Slagle, Chang and Lee [1970]. If there are more than one query, then the Boolean function is the conjunction of Boolean functions of all queries. For example, suppose there is another query given by the condition

P(u,v) & Q(w,u,z) & R(v,z) ,

whose joins are described below:

Join	Attributes Joined
U	P1, Q2
V	P2, R1
Z	Q3, R3

The Boolean function representing joins needed to be supported for this query is

$$UZ + VZ .$$

Then, for the above two queries, the Boolean function F to minimize is

$$F = (X + YZ)\ (UZ + VZ) .$$

In the above discussion, it was assumed that every query in the set Q was free of virtual relations. In the event that a set queries, Q, are not free of virtual relations, first obtain a set Q' of transformed queries for all queries in Q. Then, from a set J' of joins used in queries in Q', the above Boolean function method can be used to find an optimal set of joins to support.

If virtual relations exist, and the set of user queries, Q, are not known, let Q be a set of queries each of which is represented by a single virtual relation, $R(x_1,\ldots,x_n)$. This set is the most general set in the following sense: Every $R(x_1,\ldots,x_n)$ in set Q corresponds to printing all tuples in the table for the virtual relation R. Since other queries usually involve subtables of table R, $R(x_1,\ldots,x_n)$ is the most general one. Therefore, if we can find an optimal set of joins in Q to support, then we have optimal access paths to compute all virtual relations.

CONCLUDING REMARKS

We have described the DEDUCE language for representing queries and axioms, and discussed an optimization problem. In addition, we have given a method based upon rewriting rules to transform conjunctive queries containing virtual relations into queries free of virtual relations. We believe that our evaluational approach to deductive relational data bases is natural, because it matches nicely with non-deductive relational data bases. The concept of virtual relations is similar to the concept of views (Astrahan et al. [1976]). However, using axioms to define virtual relations is more general, because a virtual relation can be defined recursively. Besides, if virtual relations are defined by axioms, techniques developed for theorem proving can be used for transforming queries.

As noted in the section Using Rewriting Rules to Transform Queries, an open problem is the termination problem. That is, if a virtual relation is defined recursively, then a query containing the virtual relation is transformed into a sequence of queries. Since the models for base and virtual relations are finite, the sequence must terminate. The problem is how to find a termination condition. This problem may be related to program-synthesizing. However, the termination problem described in this paper must be solvable because it is assumed that models for base and virtual relations are finite. The rewriting rule method given here may lead to a solution of the problem, because one may find repeated patterns in the rewriting rules. In any case, this is an interesting problem for researchers in the field to attempt to solve. As stated by Reiter [1978b] in the workshop from which these chapters were drawn, this may be the last hurdle for putting deductive relational data bases into practical use.

ACKNOWLEDGMENTS

The author would like to thank members of the RENDEZVOUS project, E. F. Codd, J. R. Rhyne and L. G. Hemphill for their comments and conversations. Also, comments by Professor L. A. Zadeh of the University of California at Berkeley, Dr. J. R. Slagle of the Naval Research Laboratory, Professor J. Minker of the University of Maryland, and the referees are greatly appreciated.

APPENDIX

New DEDUCE Syntax

```
 1. <char> ::= A|B|C|D|E|F|G|H|I|J|K|L|M|N
             | O|P|Q|R|S|T|U|V|W|X|Y|Z
             | a|b|c|d|e|f|g|h|i|j|k|l|m|n|o|p|q|r|s|t|u|v|w|x|y|z
 2. <digit> ::= 0|1|2|3|4|5|6|7|8|9
 3. <string> ::=  <char>
               |  <digit>
               |  <string><string>
 4. <constant> ::= <string>
 5. <variable> ::= <string>
 6. <relation> ::= <char><string>
 7. <attribute> ::= <char><string>
 8. <predicate> ::= <char><string>
 9. <function> ::= <char><string>
10. <comparator> ::= <
                   | ≤
                   | >
                   | ≥
                   | =
                   | ≠
```

```
11. <quantifier>  ::= ∀
                    | ∃
                    | ∃<num
                    | ∃≤num
                    | ∃>num
                    | ∃≥num
                    | ∃=num
                    | ∃≠num
12. <tuple1>   ::=  <constant>
                 |  <variable>
                 |  <function>(<tuple1>)
                 |  <functional-expression>
                 |  <tuple1>,<tuple1>
13. <term>  ::=  <constant>
             |  <variable>
             |  <function>(<tuple1>)
14. <tuple2>  ::=  <attribute><comparator><term>
               |  <tuple2>,<tuple2>
15. <*tuple2>  ::=  *<attribute>
                 |  *<attribute><comparator><term>
                 |  <*tuple2>,<#tuple2>
                 |  <*tuple2>,<tuple2>
                 |  <tuple2>,<*tuple2>
16. <#tuple2>  ::=  #<attribute>
                 |  #<attribute><comparator><term>
                 |  <#tuple2>,<*tuple2>
                 |  <#tuple2>,<tuple2>
                 |  <tuple2>,<#tuple2>
17. <atom>  ::=  <predicate>(<tuple1>)
18. <clause>  ::=  <relation>(<tuple2>)
19. <*clause>  ::=  <relation>(<*tuple2>)
20. <#clause>  ::=  <relation>(<#tuple2>)
21.<connective>  ::=  &| ∨| →
22. <formula>  ::=  <atom>
                |  <clause>
                |  ( <quantifier><variable>)<formula>
                |  ~( <formula>)
                |  ( <formula><connective><formula>)
23. <*formula>  ::=  <*clause>
                  |  ( <quantifier><variable>)<*formula>
                  |  ~( <*formula>)
                  |  ( <*formula><connective><*formula>)
                  |  ( <*formula><connective><formula>)
                  |  ( <formula><connective><*formula>)
24. <#formula>  ::=  <#clause>
                  |  (<quantifier><variable>)<#formula>
                  |  ~(<#formula>)
                  |  (<#formula> <connective><#formula>)
                  |  (<#formula><connective><formula>)
                  |  (<formula><connective><#formula>)
```

25. <functional-expression> ::= <function>(<#formula>)
26. <query> ::= <*formula>
| <functional-expression>

REFERENCES

1. Astrahan, M. M., Blasgen, M. W., Chamberlin, D. C., Eswaran, K. P., Gray, J. N., Griffiths, P. P., King, W. F., Lorie, R. A., McJones, P. R., Mehl, J. W., Putzolu, G. R., Traiger, I. L., Wade, B. W., and Watson, V. [1976] System R: Relational Approach to Database Management, *ACM Transactions on Database Systems 1*, 2 (June 1976), 97-137.

2. Bernstein, P. A. [1976] Synthesizing Third Normal Form Relations from Functional Dependencies, *ACM Transactions on Database Systems 1*, 4 (Dec. 1976), 277-298.

3. Boyce, R. F., Chamberlin, D. D., King, W. F., III, and Hammer, M. M. [1975] Specifying Queries as Relational Expressions: SQUARE, *CACM 18*, 11 (November 1975), 621-628.

4. Chamberlin, D. D., and Boyce, R. F. [1974] SEQUEL: A Structured English Query Language, *Proceedings of the 1974 ACM-SIGFIDET Workshop on Data Description, Access and Control*, ACM, New York, 1974.

5. Chang, C. L. [1976] DEDUCE --- A Deductive Query Language for Relational Data Bases, In *Pattern Recognition and Artificial Intelligence* (C. H. Chen, Ed.), Academic Press, Inc., New York, 1976, 108-134.

6. Chang, C. L. [1978] An Opitmization Problem in Relational Data Bases, *IBM Research Report RJ2287*, San Jose, Calif., 1978.

7. Chang, C. L. and Lee, R. C. T. [1973] *Symbolic Logic and Mechanical Theorem Proving*, Academic Press, New York, N. Y., 1973.

8. Chang, C. L. and Slagle, J. R. [1977] Using Rewriting Rules for Connection Graphs to Prove Theorems, *IBM Research Report RJ 2117*, San Jose, Calif., 1977.

9. Clark, K. L. [1978] Negation as Failure, In *Logic and Data Bases* (H. Gallaire and J. Minker, Eds.), Plenum Press, New York, 1978, 293-322.

10. Codd, E. F. [1970] A Relational Model for Large Shared Data Banks, *CACM 13*, 6 (June 1970), 377-387.

11. Codd, E. F. [1971a] Further Normalization of the Data Base Relational Model, In *Data Base Systems, Courant Computer Science Symposia Series, Vol. 6* (R. Rustin, Ed.), Prentice-Hall, 1971, 33-64.

12. Codd, E. F. [1971b] A Data Base Sublanguage founded on the Relational Calculus, *Proceedings of 1971 ACM-SIGFIDET Workshop on Data Description, Access, and Control*, ACM, New York, 1971.

13. Codd, E. F. [1974] Seven Steps to RENDEZVOUS with the Casual User, *Proceedings IFIP Working Conference on Data Base Management*, North-Holland Publishing Co., Amsterdam, 1974, 179-200.

14. Codd, E. F., Arnold, R. S., Cadiou, J-M., Chang, C. L. and Roussopoulos, N. [1978] RENDEZVOUS Version 1: An Experimental English Language Query Formulation System for Relational Data Bases, *IBM Research Report RJ2144*, San Jose, Calif., 1978.

15. Delobel, C., and Casey, R. G. [1972] Decomposition of a Data Base and the Theory of Boolean Switching Functions, *IBM J. of Research and Development 17*, 5 (Sept. 1972), 370-386.

16. Fagin, R. [1976a] Relational Data Base Decomposition and Propositional Logic, *IBM Research Report RJ1776*, San Jose, Calif., 1976.

17. Fagin, R. [1976b] Multivalued Dependencies and a New Normal Form for Relational Databases, *IBM Research Report RJ1812*, San Jose, Calif., 1976.

18. Gotlieb, L. R. [1975] Computing Joins of Relations, *Proc. of the ACM International Conference on Management of Data*, San Jose, Calif., 1975, 55-63.

19. Kellogg, C., Klahr, P. and Travis, L. [1978] Deductive Planning and Pathfinding for Relational Data Bases, In *Logic and Data Bases* (H. Gallaire and J. Minker, Eds.), Plenum Press, New York, 1978, 179-200.

20. Klahr, P. [1977] Planning Techniques for Rule Selection in Deductive Question-Answering, In *Pattern-Directed Inference Systems* (D. Waterman and F. Hayes-Roth, Eds.), Academic Press, New York, 1977.

21. Kowalski, R. [1975] A Proof Procedure Using Connection Graphs, *JACM 22*, 4 (October 1975), 572-595.

22. Lacroix, M., and Pirotte, A. [1977] Domain-Oriented Relational Languages, *Proceedings of Third International Conference on Very Large Data Bases*, Tokyo, Japan, Oct. 6-8, 1977, 370-378.

23. Lee, R. C. T. [1972] Fuzzy Logic and the Resolution Principle, *JACM 19*, (1972), 109-119.

24. McSkimin, J. R. and Minker, J. [1978] A Predicate Calculus Based Semantic Network for Question-Answering Systems, In *Associative Networks - The Representation and Use of Knowledge* (N. Findler, Ed.), Academic Press, New York, 1978.

25. Minker, J. [1975a] Performing Inferences over Relational Data Bases, *Proc. of 1975 ACM-SIGMOD International Conference on Management of Data*, 1975, 79-91.

26. Minker, J. [1975b] Set Operations and Inferences Over Relational Data Bases, Invited Paper, *Proc. 4th Texas Conf. on Computing Systems*, Nov. 1975. Also Univ. of Md. Technical Report TR-427, December 1975.

27. Minker, J. [1978] An Experimental Relational Data Base System Based on Logic, In *Logic and Data Bases* (H. Gallaire and J. Minker, Eds.), Plenum Press, New York, 1978, 107-147.

28. Nicolas, J. M., and Demolombe, R. [1977] A Short Note on the Use of First Order Logic in the Formalization of Functional and Multivalued Dependencies, ONERA-CERT, Toulouse, France, 1977.

29. Nicolas, J. M. and Gallaire, H. [1978] Data Bases: Theory vs. Interpretation, In *Logic and Data Bases* (H. Gallaire and J. Minker, Eds.), Plenum Press, New York, 1978, 33-54.

30. Nicolas, J. M. and Yazdanian, K. [1978] Integrity Checking in Deductive Data Bases, In *Logic and Data Bases* (H. Gallaire and J. Minker, Eds.), Plenum Press, New York, 1978, 325-344.

31. Pirotte, A. [1978] High Level Data Base Query Languages, In *Logic and Data Bases* (H. Gallaire and J. Minker, Eds.), Plenum Press, New York, 1978, 409-436.

32. Reiter, R. [1978a] On Closed World Data Bases, In *Logic and Data Bases* (H. Gallaire and J. Minker, Eds.), Plenum Press, New York, 1978, 55-76.

33. Reiter, R. [1978b] Deductive Question-Answering on Relational Data Bases, In *Logic and Data Bases* (H. Gallaire and J. Minker, Eds.), Plenum Press, New York, 1978, 149-177.

34. Rissanen, J. [1977] Independent Components of Relations, *IBM Research Report RJ1899*, IBM, San Jose, Calif. 1977.

35. Sickel, S. [1977] Formal Grammars as Models of Logic Derivations, *Proceedings of IJCAI-77*, 1977, 544-551.

36. Slagle, J. R., Chang, C. L., and Lee, R.C.T. [1970] A New Algorithm for Generating Prime Implicants, *IEEE Trans. Computers C-19*, 4 (April 1970), 304-310.

37. Zadeh, L. A. [1965] Fuzzy Sets, *Information and Control 8*, 1965, 338-353.

38. Zadeh, L. A. [1974] Fuzzy Logic and Approximate Reasoning, *Memo No. ERL-M479*, Electronics Research Laboratory, Univ. of Calif., Berkeley, November 1974.

39. Zadeh, L. A. [1977] PRUF -- A Meaning Representation Language for Natural Language, Electronics Research Laboratory, Univ. of Calif., Berkeley, 1977.

40. Zloof, M. M. [1975] Query by Example, *Proceedings of the National Computer Conference*, Vol. 45, Anaheim, Calif., May, 1975, 431-438.

NONDETERMINISTIC LANGUAGES USED FOR THE DEFINITION OF DATA MODELS

Marco Colombetti*, Paolo Paolini**, Giuseppe Pelagatti**

Milan Polytechnic Artificial Intelligence Project,
Politecnico di Milano*

Istituto di Elettrotecnica ed Elettronica, Politecnico
di Milano**

ABSTRACT

Data models have played an important role in the Data Base field. In recent years discussion has focused on the comparison between several data models which have been proposed (relational, hierarchical, networks, etc.). Yet, very little attention has been devoted to the problem of defining a data model formally.

A data model can be considered to be a collection of Abstract Data Types. Following the albegraic approach to the definition of Abstract Data Types, a data model can be described by its signature (set of typed operations) and its presentation (set of algebraic equations). It is possible to write such equations in such a way that they can be viewed as recursive definitions of the operations on terms. It is then straightforward to derive an implementation of the data model described by the equations using a predicate logic based language such as PROLOG.

Examples of this technique applied to a data model based on binary relations will be shown.

INTRODUCTION

Many different data models have been proposed as general tools for the description of data in Data Base Management Systems. Among the most widely known are: the network model (Codasyl [1971]), the hierarchical model (IMS360), the relational model (Codd [1970]), the entity-relationship model (Chen [1976]), the binary model

(Abrial [1974], Bracchi, Fedeli and Paolini [1974], Pelagatti, Paolini and Bracchi [1977]), and the irreducible model (Hall, Owlett and Todd [1976]). There is still considerable discussion as to which data model is best. However, this discussion suffers because of the lack of a precise and formal definition of a data model. In fact, despite the relevance of the subject, very little effort has been devoted to the definition of the concept of a data model itself, and very often no distinction is made between data models and languages. Even less effort has been paid to the development of techniques that can be used in the definition of a specific data model.

In this paper we define the concept of a data model. We then introduce a technique for the formal definition of the data model and show the use of this technique by an example. Finally, we show that, starting from the formal definition consisting of algebraic equations, it is possible to derive a straightforward implementation of the data model itself using a predicate logic language such as PROLOG (Roussel [1975]).

THE CONCEPT OF A DATA MODEL

Before defining our concept of data model, we should like to show that the two most used interpretations of this concept - that a data model is a language and that it is a data structure - are not satisfactory.

A Data Model is Not a Language

Sometimes a specific language is taken as the definition of a data model. In this way elements which do not really belong to the data model itself are introduced into it. Let us consider for example the network model. Very often the language proposed by the Codasyl Data Base Task Group [1971] is taken as the definition of the data model. Therefore, criticisms are raised against the low level of many concepts - like AREA, Data Base KEY, Location Mode, etc. - and against the low procedural level of the control statements of the Data Manipulation Language and its currency indicators. It is conceivable, instead, to have high level languages for the network data model, as suggested by Held and Stonebraker [1975], and to remove from such languages low level implementation oriented features. This "make-up" does not affect at all the fundamental idea of the data model, i.e. to consider a data base to consist of records connected by network structures. We believe that the common assumption of the relational model as being more "logical" or "abstract" than the network model is based upon the confusion between the concept of the network model and the specific language used for its first definition.

A Data Model is Not a Data Structure

Sometimes data structures are taken as data models. This is unsatisfactory because a data model should describe not only the organization of data, but also the operations to be made upon the data. For example, consider the definition of the relational model. The fact that the data are organized in relations does not characterize the model completely. To do so, one also requires a precise description of the meaning of the possible operations to be performed on the data ; otherwise ambiguities in the interpretation can (and do) arise. In particular, consider any Data Base Management System supporting table-like data structures. One might enquire if this is a relational system. If only the data structure is considered, the answer could be in the affirmative. However, unless the system also provides a set of operations appropriate for relational manipulation, as usually intended, we believe that the answer should be in the negative. In fact, a data model is characterized more by the set of operations than by the data structure. Moreover these operations must have a precise semantic definition in order to avoid ambiguities. For example, in the original definition of the relational model (Codd [1970]), relations are defined as sets of *n*-tuples. Each relation has a key, and it is illegal to have two *n*-tuples with the same key value in the same relation. The union between two relations is defined as the set union of the two sets of *n*-tuples. But, what happens if one desires to perform the union of two relations containing two *n*-tuples - one for each relation - with the same key value? Is the operation illegal? If it is legal, how is the resulting relation defined? Thus, it can be seen that ambiguities may arise from informal specifications.

We believe that an appropriate data model definition should include, as a minimum, the following:

1. A formal specification of all the operations allowable on objects belonging to the data model; and

2. A formal specification of the semantics of the operations.

A definition which contains such specifications is then analogous to an Abstract Data Type specification (Hoare [1972], Goguen et al. [1976]). In fact, an Abstract Data Type is a "high level" data type defined through a syntactic definition of allowable operations and a semantic specification of the meaning of such operations.

Two basically different techniques have been devised for Abstract Data Type specification: the axiomatic approach, due to Hoare [1972], and the algebraic approach, whose most complete mathematical treatment is due to Goguen et al. [1975]. In the axiomatic approach, the semantics of an operation is given by two predicates, respectively called "precondition" and "postcondition". The truth of the precondition before the application of an operation implies the truth of the postcondition after such application, provided it terminates. Paolini and Pelagatti [1978] use such a technique to define the semantics of multiple views in a Data Base.

It is not the purpose of this paper to discuss properties and tradeoffs of the two techniques. We have chosen to specify a data model using the algebraic approach. We do so because it allows definitions which can be implemented in a very straightforward manner in a predicate calculus programming language such as PROLOG, and can be tested and used readily. In the next section we shall present the mathematical background of the albegraic techniques.

THE DATA MODEL DEFINITION

In the last section we explained why we consider a data model to be an Abstract Data Type. We shall now present the algebraic methodology for the definition of Abstract Data Types (Goguen et al. [1976]). Following such a methodology, a data model will be described as a many sorted algebra. The idea is that the data items belonging to the data model constitute an "algebra" under the operations allowed by the model. The algebra is "many sorted " because we shall think of the data items as instances of different data structures (sorts); it will be possible to apply operations only to arguments of allowed sorts.

To specify the semantics of the data model, it is sufficient to describe the mutual interactions of the operations, and this will be done using algebraic equations. Data items will not appear explicitly in the model definition, and will be reduced to the operations by which they are built.

More formally, a _many sorted algebra_ is a family of sets (the _carriers_) with some operations among them. The carriers are indexed by elements of the _sort set_, which specifies the "types" used for the data model definition. For example, for the definition of a data model based on binary relations, the sort set could be the following:

S = {KEY, DOMAIN, PAIR, BINARY, BOOLEAN}

where KEY is the sort for the domain that represents the key for the relation; DOMAIN is the sort for the second argument of the relation; PAIR is the sort for the 2-tuples of the relation; BINARY is the sort for binary relations; and BOOLEAN is the sort for truth values.

The operations of the algebra are indexed by pairs $\underline{w},\underline{s}$ where $\underline{w} \in S^*$ and $\underline{s} \in S$ (S^* is, as usual, the set of all strings which can be obtained by concatenation of elements of S, including the empty string); $\underline{w}$ determines the sorts of the operands and $\underline{s}$ the sort of the result. For example, the operation RETRIEVE has the following index

KEY BINARY, DOMAIN

where $\underline{w}$ is KEY BINARY, and $\underline{s}$ is DOMAIN. This specifies that the operation RETRIEVE has a binary relation and a key as operands, and yields an element of the domain as a result.

The symbol $\Sigma_{\underline{w},\underline{s}}$ will be used for the set of all operations with index $\underline{w},\underline{s}$. The symbol Σ is used for the union of all sets $\Sigma_{\underline{w},\underline{s}}$. Σ is also called the signature of the algebra.

The symbol T_Σ is used to denote the Σ-word algebra. Intuitively T_Σ can be described as the set of all valid terms which can be constructed using the operation of the algebra. Valid terms have the form

$$\sigma(\tau_1,\tau_2,\ldots,\tau_n)$$

where σ is an operation with $\underline{n}$ operands, and the τ_i's are valid terms of the appropriate sorts for σ.

A Σ-equation is an order pair $<\tau_1,\tau_2>$ of terms (usually written $\tau_1 = \tau_2$) in which free variable names are allowed to appear. The meaning of a Σ-equation is that whatever terms (of the appropriate sorts) we substitute for the free variable names, the resulting terms must be considered equivalent.

We use the symbol ε for a set of Σ-equations. The set of equations ε generates an equivalence relation among members of T_Σ. Two elements of T_Σ (i.e. two terms) are equivalent if they can be derived as the left side and the right side of an equation (through appropriate substitutions of terms for free variables) or if they are equivalent to equivalent elements of T_Σ (transitivity). The equivalence relation defined in such a way is not in general a congruence relation, i.e. it is not necessarily true that the terms

$$\sigma(\tau_1,\ldots,\tau_n) \quad \text{and} \quad \sigma(\hat{\tau}_1,\ldots,\hat{\tau}_n)$$

are equivalent if the τ_i's are pairwise equivalent to the $\hat{\tau}_i$'s and σ is an operation. Let us call Σ-congruence relation the least congruence relation containing the above defined equivalence relation, and let us denote it by $\equiv_\varepsilon$ (actually we should speak of a family of congruence relations, one for each sort). If we group together all the elements of T_Σ belonging to the same congruence class (in algebraic terms, if we build the quotient of T_Σ modulo $\equiv_\varepsilon$), we obtain the algebra $T_{\Sigma,\varepsilon}$ where the carriers are no longer the original ones, but the partitions determined on them by $\equiv_\varepsilon$, and the operations are defined canonically (if $C_1,\ldots,C_n$ are classes of $T_{\Sigma,\varepsilon}$ the operation σ_ε is unambiguously defined by

$$\sigma_\varepsilon(C_1,\ldots,C_n) = \sigma(\tau_1,\ldots,\tau_n)$$

where τ_i is any term belonging to C_i; for simplicity we shall denote σ_ε by σ).

As an example, suppose we define a set by the equation

INSERT(i,INSERT(j,s)) = INSERT(j,INSERT(i,s))

The equation states that the order of insertion of elements in a set is irrelevant; its effect is to make all expressions which differ by the order of insertion equivalent. If we substitute 5 for i, 6 for j and ∅ (the empty set) for s, we get

INSERT(5,INSERT(6,∅)) = INSERT(6,INSERT(5,∅)).

We do not analyse further the mathematical properties of this algebraic machinery. In the following section we show an application of it, defining binary relations.

THE DEFINITION OF BINARY RELATIONS

We shall now give an intuitive description and a formal definition of a binary relation, intended as a collection of pairs built from key values and elements of a domain.

The basic operations for manipulating binary relations are INSERT (to insert a new pair into a relation), UPDATE (to update a pair of a relation), DELETE (to remove a pair from a relation), RETRIEVE (to find the domain element associated with a key value in a relation), HAS (to check whether a given key value appears in a pair of a relation), K-RESTRICTION (to restrict the relation to those pairs - at most one - having a given key value) and D-RESTRICTION (to restrict the relation to those pairs having a given domain element as second co-ordinate). Moreover we need the auxiliary operation _._ to make a pair out of a KEY value and an element of a DOMAIN.

The above operations are not the most typical ones for binary relations. We have selected these operations for the following reasons:

- the technique we describe can be comprehended better using an easy example, whereas a more complicated set of operations would require a more extensive explanation;

- even a more comprehensive set of operations might not define a binary relation model as some would like to define it; as stated in the section entitled, The Concept of a Data Model, data models are defined presently in a fuzzy manner, so that different authors use different sets of operations for nominally identical data models (which, in our opinion, is bad);

- the set of operations we use is powerful enough to perform most of the operations upon binary relations that one may desire;

- two operations, K-RESTRICTION and D-RESTRICTION, will show that there is no problem in defining typical relational operations;

- a complete specification of the relational model as presented by Codd [1970] would be too large for this paper, but raises no conceptual problem (Paolini [1976]); different data models - such as hierarchies or networks - can be defined as well, but require consideration of many details (we are presently working on such definitions).

We now give the formal specification of the data model as a many sorted algebra, following the steps described in the previous section. We first define the sort set. We then give the signature for the algebra. For each operation we provide its informal definition and an algebraic equation which provides its formal semantics. We freely use the if-then-else operation in the usual sense; this could have been defined within our algebra.

Definition of the Sort Set

S = {KEY, DOMAIN, PAIR, BINARY, BOOLEAN}

Definition of Syntax and Semantics for the Operations

1. $\Sigma_{\text{KEY DOMAIN, PAIR}} = \{\_.\_\}$

   The operation _._ takes a given key and a domain element and constructs a pair consisting of the two items. In the following, the notation k.d is used as a short-hand expression for _._(k,d). No equation is needed to describe the semantics of the operation:

2. $\Sigma_{\_,\text{ BINARY}} = \{\_\wedge\_\}$

The operation Λ generates the empty binary relation; it has no arguments. No equation is needed to describe the semantics of the operation.

3. $\Sigma_{\text{PAIR BINARY, BINARY}} = \{\text{INSERT, UPDATE}\}$

The operation INSERT inserts a pair into a binary relation. If the binary relation already contains a pair with a key equal to the one to be inserted, the operation has no effect.

The semantics for INSERT is described by:

(1) INSERT(k.d,INSERT(k'.d',b)) =

<u>if</u> k=k' <u>then</u> INSERT(k'.d',b)

<u>else</u> INSERT(k'.d',INSERT(k.d.b))

The operation UPDATE updates the domain value of a pair in a binary relation. If the binary relation does not contain a pair with the same key as the argument pair, the operation has no effect.

The semantics for UPDATE is described by:

(2.1) UPDATE(k.d, Λ) = Λ

(2.2) UPDATE(k.d,INSERT(k'.d',b)) =

<u>if</u> k=k' <u>then</u> INSERT(k.d,UPDATE(k.d,b))

<u>else</u> INSERT(k'.d',UPDATE(k.d,b))

4. $\Sigma_{\text{KEY BINARY, BINARY}} = \{\text{DELETE, K-RESTRICTION}\}$

The operation DELETE deletes a pair having a given key from a given binary relation. If no such pair is found, the operation has no effect.

The semantics for DELETE is described by:

(3.1) DELETE(k, Λ) = Λ

(3.2) DELETE(k,INSERT(k'.d,b)) =

<u>if</u> k=k' <u>then</u> DELETE(k,b)

<u>else</u> INSERT(k'.d,DELETE(k,b))

The operation K-RESTRICTION returns the binary relation made of all pairs (at most one) that have a given key in a specified binary relation.

The semantics for K-RESTRICTION is described by:

(4.1) $\text{K-RESTRICTION}(k, \Lambda) = \Lambda$

(4.2) $\text{K-RESTRICTION}(k, \text{INSERT}(k'.d, b)) =$

$$\underline{\text{if}}\ \text{HAS}(k,b)\ \underline{\text{then}}\ \text{K-RESTRICTION}(k,b)\ \underline{\text{else}}\ \underline{\text{if}}\ k=k'\ \underline{\text{then}}\ \text{INSERT}(k.d, \Lambda)\ \underline{\text{else}}\ \Lambda$$

5. $\Sigma_{\text{KEY BINARY, DOMAIN}} = \{\text{RETRIEVE}\}$

The operation RETRIEVE returns the corresponding domain value from a given key and a binary relation. If the key is not found in the binary relation, the value $\perp$ (*bottom* or *undefined*) is returned.

The semantics for RETRIEVE is described by:

(5.1) $\text{RETRIEVE}(k, \Lambda) = \perp$

(5.2) $\text{RETRIEVE}(k, \text{INSERT}(k'.d, b)) =$

$$\underline{\text{if}}\ k=k' \wedge \neg \text{HAS}(k',b)\ \underline{\text{then}}\ d\ \underline{\text{else}}\ \text{RETRIEVE}(k,b)$$

6. $\Sigma_{\text{DOMAIN BINARY, BINARY}} = \{\text{D-RESTRICTION}\}$

The operation D-RESTRICTION returns the binary relation made of all pairs having a given domain value in a specified binary relation.

The semantics for D-RESTRICTION is described by:

(6.1) $\text{D-RESTRICTION}(d, \Lambda) = \Lambda$

(6.2) $\text{D-RESTRICTION}(d, \text{INSERT}(k.d', b)) =$

$$\underline{\text{if}}\ \text{HAS}(k,b)\ \underline{\text{then}}\ \text{D-RESTRICTION}(d,b)\ \underline{\text{else}}\ \underline{\text{if}}\ d=d'\ \underline{\text{then}}\ \text{INSERT}(k.d', \text{D-RESTRICTION}(d,b))\ \underline{\text{else}}\ \text{D-RESTRICTION}(d,b)$$

7. $\Sigma_{\text{KEY BINARY, BOOLEAN}} = \{\text{HAS}\}$

The operation HAS returns T if a given key is in a specified binary relation, F otherwise.

The semantics for HAS is described by:

(7.1) HAS(k, Λ) = F

(7.2) HAS(k,INSERT(k'.d,b)) = <u>if</u> k=k' <u>then</u> T
<u>else</u> HAS(k,b)

8. $\Sigma_{\_, \text{BOOLEAN}} = \{T, F\}$

The operations T and F generates the two boolean values. They take no arguments.

No equation is needed to describe the semantics of the operations.

The signature of the algebra is represented graphically in Figure 1.

In the next section the rationale behind the equations will be explained.

THE STRUCTURE OF THE EQUATIONS

Our purpose now is to illustrate the methodology used in writing the algebraic equations presented in the previous section. Such a methodology is not necessarily implied by the algebraic framework for the definition of Abstract Data Types. However we believe it is a useful tool for the achievement of the following points:

- <u>correctness of the equations</u>: when writing large sets of equations it is very easy to make mistakes, the most common of which are the following:

    - the equations written are <u>redundant</u>, in the sense that some (or parts) of them may be removed without affecting the congruence relation being defined

    - the equations are <u>inadequate</u>, in the sense that they do not define the intended congruence relation, but a weaker or a stronger one

- <u>clarity of the equations</u>: large sets of equations are not easily readable unless they are structured in a well defined manner

- <u>straightforward implementability</u>: in order to achieve a straightforward implementation of the data model possible and practical, it is necessary to give an appropriate structure to the equations.

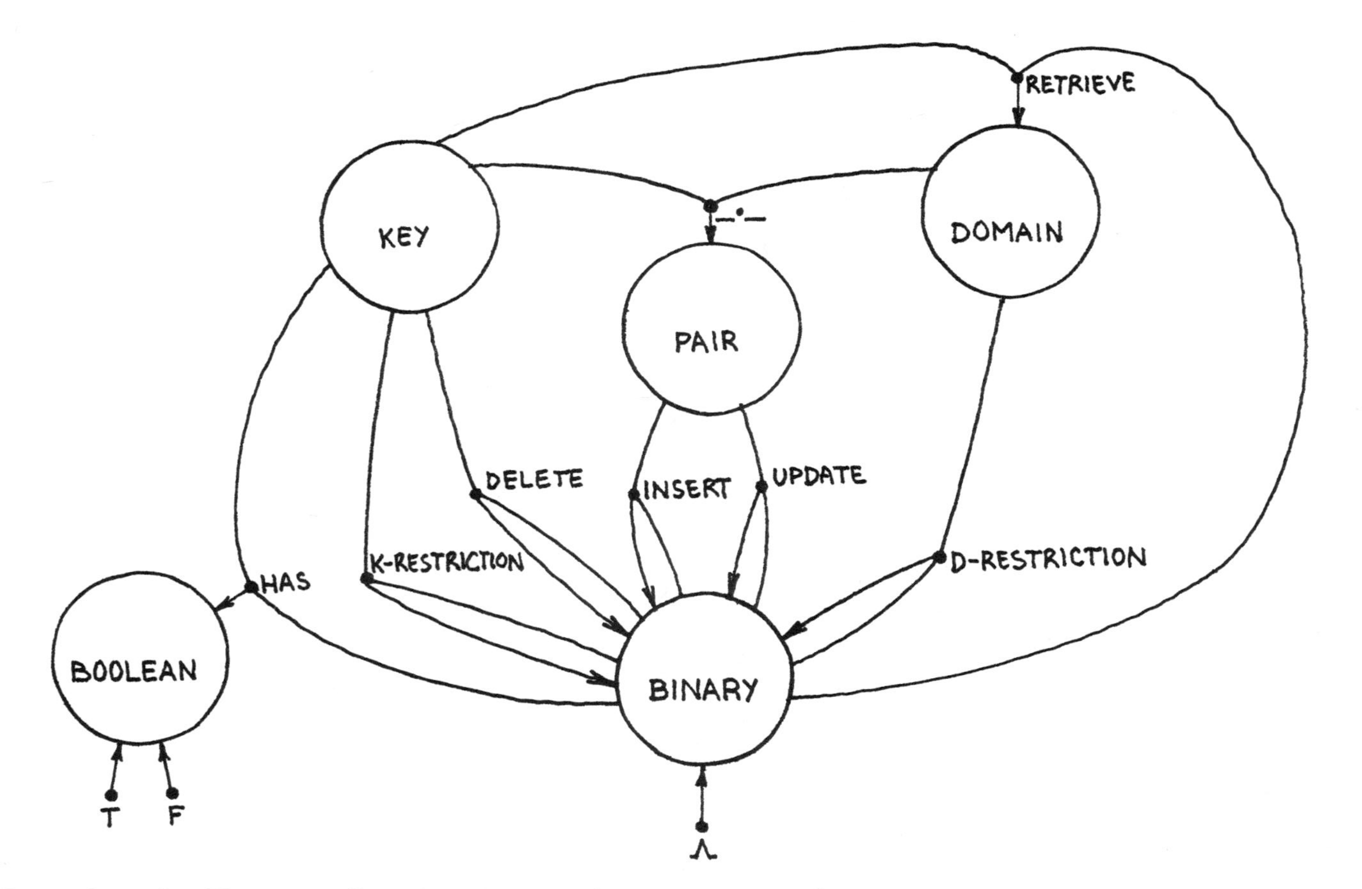

Figure 1. The Signature for the Binary Relation Model. (Circles correspond to sorts and multi-arcs to operations. Operations with no operands define constant values.)

The last point deserves some explanation. What we desire from an implementation is the ability to define an instance of the data model and to execute on it the operations according to their meaning (as given by the algebraic equations). As regards our example, we want to build particular objects of sort PAIR, BINARY etc. and operate on them with INSERT, DELETE etc. In our approach an object naturally corresponds to a congruence class of terms of the same sort; intuitively, this class is constituted by all terms that, when executed as chains of operations, produce the corresponding object. For each congruence class we can choose some canonical terms as their representations. Such canonical terms will then play the role of objects of the various sorts. For our example we made the following choice:

can[BOOLEAN] : {T, F}

can[PAIR] : $\{\underline{k}.\underline{d} \mid \underline{k} \in$ can[KEY] $\wedge\ \underline{d} \in$ can[DOMAIN]$\}$

can[KEY] : any set of symbols

can[DOMAIN] : any set of symbols

can[BINARY] : $\{\Lambda\} \cup \{$INSERT$(\underline{k}.\underline{b},\underline{d}) \mid \underline{k}.\underline{d} \in$ can[PAIR] $\wedge$
$\wedge\ \underline{b} \in$ can[BINARY]$\}$

The main point here is the representation of congruence classes of sort BINARY as chains of INSERT operations.

The use of canonical terms makes the equations more intuitive, since they can now be written to define <u>the effect of operations on objects</u> in terms of the other operations. Thus, we regard the equations as recursive and possibly nondeterministic definitions of the operations. The methodology we propose consists of two steps:

(i) For each sort define the set of <u>canonical terms</u>, i.e. terms $\in T_\Sigma$ such that at least one canonical term belongs to each congruence class into which we intend to partition T_Σ. At this step it is not necessary that the canonical terms be unique for each intended congruence class.

(ii) For each operation write a set of equations that allows the <u>reduction of the operation applied to canonical terms</u> (of the appropriate sorts) <u>to a canonical term</u> (of the appropriate sort). In other words, let σ be an operation and $\tau_1,\ldots,\tau_n$ be canonical terms of the appropriate number and sorts for σ. An equation for σ will be of the form

$$\sigma(\tau_1,\ldots,\tau_n) = \tau$$

where τ is either a canonical term of the appropriate sort, or is reducible to such a canonical term by iterative use of the equations.

As an example, let us consider the equations for UPDATE. Equation (2.1) is:

$$\text{UPDATE}(k.d,\Lambda) = \Lambda$$

It clearly satisfies our methodology (k and d are considered to vary on canonical terms of sort KEY and DOMAIN). As regards Equation (2.2),

UPDATE(k.d,INSERT(k'd',b)) = <u>if</u> k=k'
<u>then</u> INSERT(k.d,UPDATE(k.d,b))
<u>else</u> INSERT(k'.d',UPDATE(k.d,b)),

the left member clearly has the required form (with similar assumptions as above on k, k', d, d', b). By induction it is then possible to show that the right side of the equation reduces to a canonical term of sort BINARY by the iterative application of (2.1) and (2.2).

PROLOG IMPLEMENTATION OF THE DATA MODEL

As already suggested, the equations defining the data model can be viewed as programs, i.e. they can be run directly. This allows one to test the data model definition looking for possible errors, redundancies or inadequacies. What is done here is close to symbolic execution; proving properties of the model would in general require a much wider use of theorem proving techniques - mainly induction - but we shall ignore this problem here.

To test a data model one needs an implementation of it. We shall show that it is possible to derive a very high level implementation directly from the equations. The implementation will consist of objects of sort BINARY, PAIR etc. and of programs corresponding to the operations INSERT, DELETE etc. that will transform the objects according to the equations.

As we did in the last section, we shall use canonical terms as objects. However, to compare objects among them it is desirable to associate a unique canonical term to each congruence class. This is already true for all sorts different from BINARY. On the contrary, to each equivalence class of sort BINARY belongs an infinity of different canonical terms. For instance, the following terms are equivalent (by (1)), and are all canonical:

INSERT(K1.BOB,INSERT(K2.PAUL, Λ))

INSERT(K2.PAUL,INSERT(K1.BOB, Λ))

INSERT(K2.JANE,INSERT(K2.PAUL,INSERT(K1.BOB, Λ)))

To eliminate this, we shall represent KEYs by integers, and consider as canonical terms of sort BINARY only those terms built solely by INSERT and Λ operations with KEYs appearing uniquely and in descending order (with respect to term construction, i.e., from right to left). For example

Λ

INSERT(5.$\underline{d}$,INSERT(8.$\underline{d}'$, Λ))

where $\underline{d}$ and $\underline{d}'$ are canonical terms of sort DOMAIN, are canonical terms of sort BINARY; while

INSERT(8.$\underline{d}$,INSERT(5.d', Λ))

INSERT(5.$\underline{d}$,INSERT(5.$\underline{d}'$, Λ))

are not canonical terms. To prove existence and uniqueness of such a representation for each congruence class one must prove that:

- no two different canonical terms are equivalent
- each term is equivalent to at least one canonical term.

This can be shown by structural induction. Note that if INSERT($\underline{k}$.$\underline{d}$,$\underline{b}$) is the canonical term of a class $\in T_{\Sigma,\varepsilon}$, then $\underline{b}$ is the canonical term of a (different) class $\in T_{\Sigma,\varepsilon}$.

All canonical terms of the various sorts will constitute the input and output data for the programs implementing the operations. As an example consider:

τ_1 : 5 (canonical term of sort KEY)

τ_2 : INSERT(3.SHEILA,INSERT(5.PAUL, Λ)) (canonical term of sort BINARY)

The term

τ : DELETE(τ_1,τ_2)

is of sort BINARY, but is not canonical. The task of the program P_{DELETE} implementing DELETE is to map the couple τ_1,τ_2 onto the canonical term $\overline{\tau}$ representing τ, i.e. belonging to the same congruence class as τ. In this case we have:

$$\bar{\tau} : \quad P_{DELETE}(\tau_1, \tau_2) = \text{INSERT}(5.\text{SHEILA}, \Lambda)$$

This amounts exactly to computing DELETE according to the equations.

In general, to each operation σ we associate a program P_σ such that: if $\tau_1, \ldots, \tau_n \in T_\Sigma$ are the canonical terms representing classes $C_1, \ldots, C_n \in T_{\Sigma,\varepsilon}$ of appropriate number and sorts for σ, then the application of P_σ to $\tau_1, \ldots, \tau_n$ yields the canonical term $\bar{\tau}$ representing the class $\bar{C} \in T_{\Sigma,\varepsilon}$ to which the term $\sigma(\tau_1, \ldots, \tau_n)$ belongs. The 1-argument case is depicted in Figure 2.

Our term manipulation bears a strong similarity to λ-conversion as developed in λ-calculus. We regard the equations as stating allowable term reductions (i.e. we only read them "from left to right"). The congruence on T_Σ corresponds to the equivalence relation on term induced by the reductions in the usual way. The term τ representing C can be viewed as the normal form of all terms belonging to C. Again one has to guarantee existence and uniqueness of the normal form. Although the KEY ordering we have adopted may seem unpleasant, some restriction on the KEYs appearing in terms is necessary, if uniqueness of the representation is to be obtained. This is the nasty but inevitable effect of the commutative property of insertion in sets.

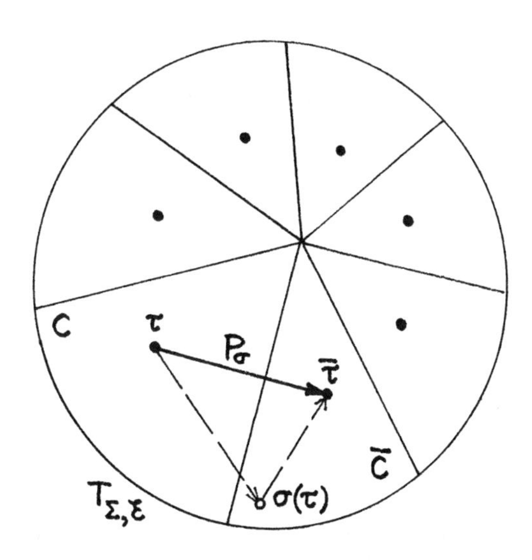

Figure 2. Effect of the Application of Program P_σ to the Canonical Term τ.

The problem we face now is to write the programs for the operations in our example. If the equations are put in an adequate form (as described in the last section) this can be done in a straightforward manner. Our implementation is written in PROLOG (Roussel [1975]), a very general programming system based on a top-down Horn-clause resolution theorem prover, using an exhaustive depth first search strategy with backtracking. At present we are developing an equation oriented system based on the specification language CLEAR by Brustall and Goguen [1977], which is being implemented at the Politecnico di Milano. PROLOG is a convenient language for similar applications because of its tree manipulation and pattern matching capabilities.

To translate our equations into PROLOG, we have followed the usual representation of recursive functional definitions in clausal form. The result is given in the Appendix together with some sample applications. Canonical terms are represented by PROLOG terms, which are constructed from constant, variable and function symbols as ordinary terms of first order predicate logic. An $\underline{n}$-ary operation σ is represented by an $\underline{n}$+1-ary predicate (which we shall also denote by σ) whose $\underline{n}$+1-th argument represents the result of the operation applied to the first $\underline{n}$ arguments. The clauses are written in such a way that a single-operation goal statement

$$\leftarrow \sigma(\tau_1,\ldots,\tau_n,u)$$

where the τ_i's are canonical terms and u is a variable, starts a resolution refutation which ends reaching the empty clause with the substitution

$$u \ : \ P_\sigma(\tau_1,\ldots,\tau_n) \ ,$$

and similarly for goal statements built by chains of operations. The PROLOG program can then be used as an implementation of the data model, in the sense that it allows the computation of any chain of operations applied to arbitrary objects (represented by canonical terms). For example, the chain of operations

RETRIEVE(10,UPDATE(8.SHEILA,INSERT(10.JANE,$\underline{b}$)))

where $\underline{b}$ is any canonical term of sort BINARY representing a binary relation, will be computed by the PROLOG program submitting the goal statement

← INSERT(10.JANE,$\underline{b}$,x), UPDATE(8.SHEILA,x,y), RETRIEVE(10,y,z).

The result of the computation can then be output using the PROLOG system predicate PRINT (see Appendix).

We shall end this section with a few comments on our PROLOG program.

Clauses 1 and 2 (see Appendix) are the only two clauses which are not obtained by translating equations. The reason is that the operation symbol INSERT is used in two distinct ways, as a canonical term constructor and as a program acting on canonical terms. In the former case INSERT is used as a PROLOG function symbol (written in lower case in the Appendix), in the latter as a predicate symbol (like DELETE, UPDATE etc.). Clauses 1 and 2 implement the necessary connection between the two uses of INSERT, in such a way that only terms which are canonical can be built. Thus, these clauses realize a part of the implementation which did not appear in the original definition.

To prove termination of all refutations of goals which have canonical terms $\tau_1,\ldots,\tau_n$ as input, note that the right side of all clauses (except clause 4) are either empty or constituted by a conjunction of predicates applied to canonical terms which are structurally simpler than $\tau_1,\ldots,\tau_n$. Clause 4 must instead be considered in connection with clauses 1 to 3: it will permute KEYs until a canonical term can be built.

We shall finally remark that type checking is done implicitly (via unification) for the objects of sort PAIR and BINARY. For the remaining sorts it could be introduced easily.

CONCLUSIONS

The main purpose of this paper was to show the practical possibility of using algebraic equations for the definition of data models for data bases. After an introduction to the algebraic methods, we have presented the definition of a model based on binary relations.

We have then shown the possibility of translating the algebraic equations defining the data model into PROLOG clauses. The implementation obtained in such a way makes it possible to test the equations through automatic execution. In fact, such a technique allowed the authors to correct a previous version of the data model, whose algebraic definition turned out to be unsatisfactory.

Besides testing the equations, we believe that PROLOG implementations could be practically useful (i) to compare different data models from the end-user viewpoint, and (ii) to define and test mappings between different views in a data base. The last point is presently under investigation (Paolini and Pelagatti [1978]).

APPENDIX

We list here the PROLOG clauses implementing equations (1) to (7), together with a few examples of testing. A clause of the form

$$\underline{A} \leftarrow \underline{B}_1,\ldots,\underline{B}_n \qquad (n \geq 0)$$

can be read

$$\underline{A} \text{ if } \underline{B}_1 \text{ and } \ldots \text{ and } \underline{B}_n .$$

A clause of the form $\underline{A}\leftarrow$ is an assertion. A clause of the form

$$\leftarrow \underline{B}_1,\ldots,\underline{B}_n \qquad (n \geq 1)$$

is a goal statement. The system will try to refute the goal statement top-down, taking care of subgoals in the order from left to right. In case more than one clause can be applied to a subgoal, the system will select the first one listed, and will backup to try the other ones both in case of success or failure, unless this is explicitly forbidden by a "slash" (/). For further details, refer to Roussel [1975].

```
1.  INSERT(k.d, Λ ,insert(k.d, Λ )) ←

2.  INSERT(k.d,insert(k'.d',b),insert(k.d,insert(k'.d',b)))
                 ← LESS(k.k'),/

3.  INSERT(k.d,insert(k.d',b),v) ← INSERT(k.d',b,v),/

4.  INSERT(k.d,insert(k'.d',b),v)←INSERT(k.d,b,u),INSERT(k'.d',u,v)

5.  UPDATE(k.d, Λ , Λ ) ←

6.  UPDATE(k.d,insert(k.d',b),v)←UPDATE(k.d,b,u),INSERT(k.d,u,v),/

7.  UPDATE(k.d,insert(k'.d',b),v)←UPDATE(k.d,b,u),INSERT(k'.d',u,v)

8.  DELETE(k, Λ , Λ ) ←

9.  DELETE(k,insert(k.d,b),v) ← DELETE(k,b,v),/

10. DELETE(k,insert(k'.d,b),v) ← DELETE(k,b,u), INSERT(k'.d,u,v)

11. RETRIEVE(k, Λ , ⊥) ← PRINT(failure message),/, FAIL

12. RETRIEVE(k,insert(k.d,b),d) ← HAS(k,b,F),/

13. RETRIEVE(k,insert(k'.d,b),v) ← RETRIEVE(k,b,v)
```

```
14.  HAS(k, Λ, F) ←

15.  HAS(k,insert(k.d,b),T) ← /

16.  HAS(k,insert(k'.d,b),v) ← HAS(k,b,v)

17.  K-RESTRICTION(k, Λ, Λ) ←

18.  K-RESTRICTION(k,insert(k'.d,b),v)
                       ← HAS(k,b,T),K-RESTRICTION(k,b,v), /

19.  K-RESTRICTION(k,insert(k.d,b),v) ← INSERT(k.d, Λ ,v), /

20.  K-RESTRICTION(k,insert(k'.d,b), Λ) ←

21.  D-RESTRICTION(d, Λ, Λ) ←

22.  D-RESTRICTION(d,insert(k.d',b),v)
                       ← HAS(k,b,T), D-RESTRICTION(d,b,v), /

23.  D-RESTRICTION(d,insert(k.d,b),v)
                       ← D-RESTRICTION(d,b,u), INSERT(k,d,u,v), /

24.  D-RESTRICTION(d,insert(k.d',b),v) ← D-RESTRICTION(d,b,v)
```

Notes: LESS(x,y) (see clause 2) is a system predicate which succeeds if $x < y$ and fails otherwise; PRINT(x) is a system predicate that always succeeds, and prints x on the output device as side-effect (see clause 11 and examples below); FAIL (see clause 11) is a generic predicate symbol not appearing in the left side of any clause, and causes a failure when activated. The slash allows the implementation of *if*-*then*-*else* operations by exploiting the depth-first search strategy; it is also used to guarantee termination.

Definition of an object of sort BINARY to be used in the examples:

```
BINARYOB(insert(3.PAUL,insert(8.BOB,insert(14.DAVE, Λ))))←
```

Object manipulation:

```
← BINARYOB(x), INSERT(10.JANE,x,y),UPDATE(8.SHEILA,y,w),
  RETRIEVE(10,w,z), PRINT(w), PRINT(z)

  output: insert(3.PAUL,insert(8.SHEILA,insert(10,JANE,
                    insert(14.DAVE, Λ))))

          JANE

← BINARYOB(x), INSERT(5.DAVE,x,y), D-RESTRICTION(DAVE,y,z),
  PRINT(y), PRINT(z)
```

output: insert(3.PAUL,insert(5.DAVE,insert(8.BOB,insert(14.DAVE, ∧))))
insert(5.DAVE,insert(14.DAVE, ∧))

Equivalence of operation chains:

← BINARYOB(x), DELETE(8,x,y), INSERT(8.VALERIE,y,z), UPDATE(8.VALERIE,x,z), PRINT(z)

output: insert(3.PAUL,insert(8.VALERIE,insert(14.DAVE, ∧)))

REFERENCES

1. Abrial, J.R. [1974] Data Semantics, In *Data Base Management* (J. W. Klimbie and K. L. Koffeman, Eds.), North-Holland/ American Elsevier, 1-60.

2. Bracchi, G., Fedeli, A., Paolini, P. [1974] A Multilevel Relational Model for Data Base Management Systems, In *Data Base Management* (J. W. Klimbie and K. L. Koffeman, Eds.), North-Holland/American Elsevier, 211-226.

3. Burstall, R. M., Goguen, J. A. [1977] Putting Theories Together to Make Specifications, *Proceedings 5th International Joint Conference on Artificial Intelligence*, Cambridge, Mass., August 1977, 1045-1058.

4. Chen, P. [1976] The Entity-Relationship Model: Toward a Unified View of Data, *TODS 1*, 1 (March 1976), 9-36.

5. Codasyl Data Base Task Group [1971] Codasyl Data Base Task Group Report, ACM, New York, 1971.

6. Codd, E. [1970] A Relational Model of Data for Large Shared Data Banks, *CACM 13*, 6 (June 1970), 377-387.

7. Goguen, J. A., Thatcher, J. W., Wagner, E. G. [1976] An Initial Algebra Approach to the Specification, Correctness, and Implementation of Abstract Data Types, In *Current Trends in Programming Methodology, Vol. 3, Data Structuring* (R. Yeh, Ed.) Prentice-Hall, Englewood Cliffs, N.J., 1976.

8. Hall, P., Owlett, J., and Todd, S. [1976] Relations and Entities, In *Modelling in Data Base Management Systems* (G. M. Nijssen, Ed.), North Holland/American Elsevier, 201-220.

9. Held, G., Stonebraker, M. [1975] Networks, Hierarchies and Relations in Data Bases Management Systems, *Pacific-75 Regional Conference of ACM*, San Francisco, Calif., April 1975, 1-9.

10. Hoare, C.A.R. [1972] Proof of Correctness of Data Representations, *Acta Informatica 1*, 1972, 271-281.

11. IMS/360 - Application Description Manual, IBM White Plains, New York, GH-20-0765.

12. Paolini, P. [1976] Formal Description of the Relational Model, unpublished paper, Istituto di Elettronica, Politecnico di Milano, 1976.

13. Paolini, P., Pelagatti, G. [1978] Specifications of Views and Mappings in Multilevel Data Bases, *Internal Report 78-2*, Istituto di Elettronica, Politecnico di Milano, February 1978.

14. Pelagatti, G., Paolini, P. and Bracchi, G. [1977] Mappings in Data Bases Systems, *Information Processing 77* (B. Gilchrist, Ed.), North Holland, 447-452.

15. Roussel, P. [1975] PROLOG: Manuel de reference et d'utilization, U.E.R. de Marseille, Group d'Intelligence Artificielle, 1975.

AN AXIOMATIC DATA BASE THEORY

Sten-Åke Tärnlund

The Royal Institute of Technology and

The University of Stockholm, Sweden

ABSTRACT

A deductive data base theory is developed in first order predicate logic with identity. This development follows the usual method of setting up a deductive theory. Axioms and definitions are written down and theorems are derived. Some of these theorems can be understood as computer programs. A data base is a model of the theory. A model, supposed to characterize a world, can be interrogated by queries which are theorems of the theory. A main result of the paper is the formalization of good programming methods so that derivations can be used as efficient computations when answering queries.

INTRODUCTION

The great advantages of deductive theories are their clarity and certainty. We shall not enter into a discussion of these advantages but merely make some preliminary remarks about their advantages for data bases. One problem of a data base is to maintain its consistency; that is, a data base should not give contradictory answers, i.e., it should not specify both yes and no for the same question. Another problem of a data base is its completeness; that is,the data base should give all possible answers provided they are not in conflict.

It is interesting to notice that the concepts of consistency and completeness are related to the idea of a correct program. In particular, a data base proved consistent and complete necessarily consists of correct and halting programs for providing the answers.

Not only is it desirable to know that there would eventually be an answer to a question but it is also preferable to know the computational cost involved in posing the question.

It is a successful development of deductive theories that these problems can be studied; moreover, they are solvable since data bases usually have finite domains.

There are several ideas that can be exploited in developing a deductive data base theory. Take, for instance, an axiomatization of the idea of a Turing machine, which would not be too narrow in the sense of leaving out any data base computation. But this treatment has, in spite of its theoretical simplicity, the disadvantage of not characterizing practice. For example, there is very little correspondence between a computation by a Turing machine and a computation by a modern computer. In contrast, a less limited theory would have to take information structures and operations on them into account in order to characterize practice.

Our formal system is intended as a formalization of practice in the sense that good information structures and programs are formalized. In particular, the behaviour of a program in the theory should correspond to the behaviour of a program in practice.

To pursue this line of thought we shall need a symbolic language, some kind of natural language is too ambiguous and cumbersome. As we shall see, predicate logic is a suitable language for our purposes.

Now the first stage in the development is to write down axioms and definitions of the primitive concepts. Nothing is used in the theory which cannot be deduced from these axioms and definitions, and so we shall need a deductive apparatus. In fact, we shall make use of a system which is a first order theory with identity.

There are a few points of methodological interest. The concept of a logic program, as understood from the PROLOG programming system by Colmerauer's group (Colmerauer et al. [1972]) and Kowalski's IFIP-paper (Kowalski [1974]), is a theorem deduced from the axioms and definitions in the theory. The set of inference rules runs a logic program by establishing a derivation. The characteristics of the length of this derivation show whether or not the logic program is good. For a rational choice between programs we are led to an intensive study of derivations which is unusual even in mathematics, although the idea of a derivation is central and very old. Similarily, a query to the data base is also a theorem and a study of its derivation shows how expensive it is to pose a query (cf., Bibel [1976]). A natural idea is to classify the queries according to their derivations. We shall not focus on this subject but at least make a distinction between primary and secondary key search queries (see Knuth [1973]).

In our section on data base models we shall show a miniature data base which is a model of the theory. The important point about the model is the method by which it is constructed and its application to large amounts of data. The purpose of the method is to carry out efficient computations in the theory, even in comparison to other computational methods; in this way computations become derivations (cf., Hayes [1973]). Needless to say, nearly any method will suffice for small amounts of data.

This view raises a point of wider interest. For this reason let us for a moment consider ordinary computer programs for simulation of dynamical phenomena. In comparison to computer programs formal mathematical models have displayed difficulties to characterize dynamical phenomena. But with derivations as efficient computations a new situation arises.

We shall take up the methodology used by Clark and Tärnlund [1977] for developing a theory of data and programs in order to show correctness of programs. There is some overlap to make this paper self-contained.

BASIC INFORMATION STRUCTURES AND OPERATIONS

In this section we shall set up an axiomatic system for information retrieval. Briefly, we can think of information retrieval in terms of searching out and inserting data. There are some suitable information structures and operations for this purpose (see Knuth [1968,1973]). The intention of our theory is to characterize good practice, therefore, we shall have to formalize several of these structures and operations. In our development we shall follow the usual method of setting up a deductive theory. We write down the axioms and definitions and derive theorems. Some of these theorems can be understood as computer programs. We shall explain this idea in more detail.

It has been suggested for a long time that it is useful to specify the important properties of information structures and their operations (cf., Guttag [1977], Hoare [1973], McCarthy [1963], Liskov and Zilles [1974]). We shall take up this idea and build a first order theory on a formalization of these properties by axioms and definitions.

A program is a representation of an algorithm, which thus is a more abstract object. We understand an algorithm from the behavior of the program when it is running provided we presuppose that we understand the treatment of the program by a compiler or an interpreter down to a machine. This idea is an informal instance of the general notion of proof theory. The programming system PROLOG is an example of this idea (see Roussel [1975]). Thus, we can make use of the same underlying idea to understand an algorithm written in logic as well as in any other programming language. But formal inference rules and proof procedures offer an advantage in clarity comparied with ordinary programming systems.

It is important to notice that the first order theory has a truth-functional semantics, which offers a different view of an algorithm in terms of what is true between the input and output objects of the algorithm, without considering interpreters or compilers.

This simple and abstract semantic approach reduces the complexity of an algorithm and, thus, makes it easier to understand and write a program.

Simple Lists

The simple list which is displayed in fig. 1. has four nodes and each of them has a label. The list starts at the head and ends with $\emptyset$, which is a symbol for the empty list.

In predicate logic lists are readily written as terms, for example, the following term represents the list in fig. 1:

$$1(a,1(b,1(c,1(d,\emptyset)))) \tag{1}$$

where 1 is a function symbol in the language and a, b, c and d are individual constants representing the labels of the list.

We can now formalize the notion of a list.

Axiom 1

$$\forall w\{list(w) \leftrightarrow \exists x\exists y[w = \emptyset \vee (w = 1(x,y) \wedge element(x) \wedge list(y))]\}$$

where $\emptyset$ is a primitive term denoting the empty list. Moreover, we assume that the element predicate is primitive.

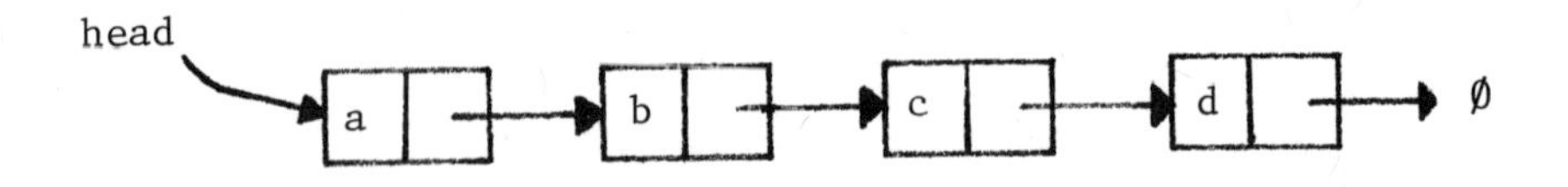

Figure 1. A simple list

Unfortunately, this symbolism for a list is cumbersome in practical programming. We would prefer an infix representation, x.y , of a list where the first element and the remaining part of the list are separated by a dot. The dot is added as a constant to the theory by a definition, thereby the meaning of the new symbolism will be clear.

Definition 1

$$\forall x \forall y \{x.y = 1(x,y)\}$$

For didactical or practical reasons we are always free to introduce a new symbolism to the theory by definitions in this way.

It is important, for several operations on lists, to recognize whether or not two lists are identical. Generally, there is no non-empty list identical to the empty list; moreover, two non-empty lists are identical if and only if they have identical labels and identical remaining lists. We shall have to axiomatize these notions.

Axiom 2

$$\forall x \forall y \{x.y \neq \emptyset\}$$

Axiom 3

$$\forall x \forall x' \forall y \forall y' \{x.y = x'.y' \leftrightarrow x = x' \wedge y = y'\}$$

We shall now turn our attention to stack and queue operations on lists. Surprisingly enough, the latter raises difficulties.

Stacks. Presumably, stack operations are the simplest operations on lists. They consist either of adding a new element to the front of the list or of deleting an element from the front. We can now define a stack relationship.

Definition 2

$$\forall x \forall y \forall w \{stack(x,y,w) \leftrightarrow w = x.y\}$$

A trivial derivation in logic gives us the following theorem which is also a logic program for stack operations.

Theorem 1

stack(x,y,x.y)

We follow a normal practice in mathematics and omit, in the formulation of theorems which also are programs, any universal quantifier whose scope is the entire formula.

A simple example shows theorem 1 as a logic program for stack operations.

Example 1

First, suppose that we have a stack b.c.∅ of two elements b and c. We want to push a new element a on top of it and get the stack a.b.c.∅ . To accomplish this result by an indirect proof procedure we simply deny that there is a stack relationship between the element a and the list b.c.∅ :

$$\sim \text{stack}(a,b.c.\emptyset,x.y) \tag{2}$$

This statement contradicts theorem 1 for x.y = a.b.c.∅ .

A proof procedure like PROLOG would discover this fact in a derivation of length one (one inference step). It is easily seen that the length of the derivation of a proof procedure never has to be longer than one step for this stack operation.

Secondly, suppose that we have the stack a.b.c.∅ and want to pop-up the first element. Similarily, we get the result by denying that there is an element x and a stack y in a stack relationship a.b.c.∅ :

$$\sim \text{stack}(x,y,a.b.c.\emptyset) \tag{3}$$

This statement contradicts theorem 1 for x = a and y = b.c.∅ .

Again it is easily seen that the length of a derivation is one step for this stack operation.

Combining this remark with our earlier observation about length of derivations it is clear that this logic program characterizes stack operations in practical programming with respect to the number of computational steps.

Finally, the definition of the stack relationship is framed to guarantee the relation to be defined when popping-up an empty stack; in fact, the relationship is false. This case is useful in programming for controlling a program.

The first theorem in the development of the thoery gives a simple instance of a point of methodological interest, namely, logic programs are mathematical objects and are used to derive objects that satisfy the theorems. This raises a question of great interest, namely, how long are the derivations? As we have seen for stack operations, the derivations characterize the situations in practice. We shall see that this observation about logic programs is an instance of a principle.

d-lists

Suppose that we have the problem of adding a new element at the end of the list in fig. 1. Unfortunately, we shall have to traverse the entire list before we can insert the new element. This solution does not characterize the situation in practical programming where a new element normally can be inserted at the end of a list in one computational step.

We pause only a moment over what a solution of this problem looks like in pure LISP (see McCarthy et al. [1962]) in order to find that there is no solution where we do not have to traverse a whole list.

It is undesirable that we should restrict the generality of our treatment to consequences like traversing a whole list for inserting an element at its rear, since the formal system is intended as a formalization of praxis.

These preliminary remarks bring us to a new representation of a list which is called d-list, short for difference list, in Clark and Tärnlund [1977]. We introduce them by an example.

Example 2

A simple list a.b.c.d.∅ can be represented by the following d-list <a.b.c.d.x,x>, which consists of a pair separated by a comma. Briefly described, the idea of a d-list is that the second part of the pair always occurs at the end of the first part and the d-list denotes the remaining list of the first part when the second part is deleted from it. It is to be emphasized that the variable is implicitly universally quantified and, as a consequence, any instantiation also denotes the same list.

We finish the example by fig. 2, which displays the list a.b.c.d.∅ as a d-list.

Unfortunately, the angled brackets do not belong to the language and a representation by a function symbol like d(a.b.c.d.x,x)

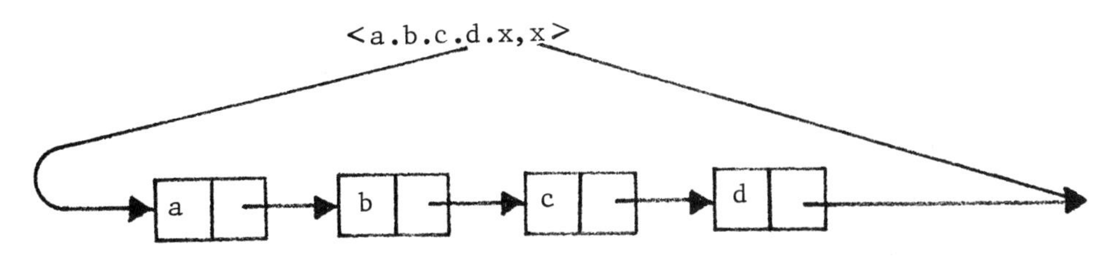

Figure 2. A d-list.

becomes too cumbersome in practice. So, for the same purpose as for the dot representation, we introduce angled brackets as constants in the theory.

Definition 3

$$\forall u \forall w \{ \langle u,w \rangle = d(u,w) \}$$

We shall now axiomatize d-lists. We distinguish between three cases depending on the number of elements in a d-list: an empty list written $\langle w,w \rangle$, a single element list written $\langle v.w,w \rangle$ and for longer lists a recursive part which splits a d-list $\langle u,w \rangle$ into two d-lists $\langle u,v \rangle$ and $\langle v,w \rangle$.

Axiom 4

$$\forall z \{ \text{d-list}(z) \leftrightarrow \forall w \exists u \exists v [z = \langle u,w \rangle \land . \ u = w \lor u = v.w \lor . \ \text{d-list}(\langle u,v \rangle) \land \text{d-list}(\langle v,w \rangle)] \}$$

To reduce the number of parentheses we shall adopt a notation which indicates the priority of connectives. For example, we write $p \land q \ .\lor\ r$ for $(p \land q) \lor r$ and $p \lor q \ .\land.\ r \lor s$ for $(p \lor q) \land (r \lor s)$. This notation goes back to Peano but it is also used by modern logicians, see Quine [1974]. We shall have to define the empty list $\emptyset$ written as a d-list.

Definition 4

$$\forall w \{ \langle w,w \rangle = \emptyset \}$$

As for simple lists we occasionally need to distinguish between identical and different d-lists.

Axiom 5

$$\forall u \forall w \forall u' \forall w' \{ \langle u,w \rangle = \langle u',w' \rangle \leftrightarrow \exists x \exists x' \exists v \exists v' [u = w \land u' = w' \ .\lor. \ u = x.v \land u' = x'.v' \land x = x' \land \langle v,w \rangle = \langle v',w' \rangle] \}$$

Queue. Now, in view of these axioms and definitions of d-lists we shall introduce a queue relationship. It is particularly to be noticed that this relationship will solve the problem at the beginning of this section (d-lists) which, as we recall, was used to introduce d-lists.

A queue is an operation on lists under the restriction that a new element is inserted at the rear of the list and a deleted element is taken from the front.

Definition 5

$$\forall x \forall y \forall z \{ queue(x,y,z) \leftrightarrow \forall w \exists u \exists v [x = < u,v > \wedge y = < v,w > \wedge z = < u,w >]\}$$

One interpretation of this definition is that x is the original queue, y a new element to be inserted and z the resulting queue.

A simple proof, which makes use of the "if-part" of the definition and of identity in the first order theory, gives the following theorem which also is a program for queue operations.

Theorem 2

$$queue(< u,v > , < v,w > , < u,w >)$$

An insert operation on a queue is illustrated in the next example. It shows an instance of a solution to the problem of inserting an element at the rear of a list in one computational step.

Example 3

We wish to insert an element e into the list a.b.c.d.$\emptyset$ in example 2. Now suppose that we represent both these objects as d-lists and deny that there is a queue relationship between them:

$$\sim queue(< a.b.c.d.x,x >, < e.z,z >, < u,w >) \qquad (4)$$

This statement contradicts theorem 2 for

$$u = a.b.c.d.e.z \quad \text{and} \quad w = z$$

hence,

$$< u,w > = < a.b.c.d.e.z,z >$$

is the resulting queue "a.b.c.d.e" .

It is easily seen that the length of this derivation is one computational step.

We notive that the queue relationship is false when an element is deleted from an empty list. In addition, we have defined more than a queue relationship, since definition 5 also can be interpreted as a concatenation relationship between three lists. In particular, we have a double ended queue called deque (see Knuth [1968]).

Reverse. While we will not focus on an analysis of proof procedures in this paper, we should comment on PROLOG here. This subject is not used in later sections so this section (Reverse) can be omitted at a first reading without disadvantage.

The proof procedure of PROLOG is an instance of the resolution principle. Its main procedure is the unification algorithm, which does the computational work during a derivation (see Robinson [1965]). For this reason, it is important to find a most efficient unification algorithm. The approach in PROLOG is to simplify the unification algorithm so that there is no check whether or not a variable substituted by a term occurs in this term. On the one hand this procedure, called occur check, of course leads to computational reductions, although without restriction it is known to contain a contradiction. On the other hand it is to be noticed that logic programs seem to follow this restriction. This raises a question of some interest; is this a principle of logic programs? Unfortunately, the answer is "no", as we see in the next example.

Example 4

Suppose that we want to reverse a list, for example "a.b.c.d". We need a logic program for this problem. The first step is to set up a definition of a reverse relationship between two lists. We distinguish between two cases: first, the reverse of the empty list is the empty list and second, if the reverse of a list l is l' then the reverse of a one element larger list l.x is x.l'. We now make this idea precise with the help of d-lists.

Definition 6

$$\forall u \forall w \forall u' \forall w' \{ reverse(\langle u,w \rangle, \langle u',w' \rangle) \leftrightarrow \exists x \exists v \exists v' [u = w \wedge u' = w' \ .\vee. \ u' = x.v' \wedge v = x.w \wedge reverse(\langle u,v \rangle, \langle v',w' \rangle)] \}$$

There is a simpler explicit definition of a reverse relationship but this one is more adequate for our purpose, which is to derive a reverse program from the definition. Again, a trivial derivation making use of the "if-part" and of identity gives the logic program.

Theorem 3

$$reverse(\langle u,u \rangle, \langle u',u' \rangle)$$

$$reverse(\langle u,w \rangle, \langle x.v',w' \rangle) \leftarrow reverse(\langle u,x.w \rangle, \langle v',w' \rangle)$$

We notice a point of programming interest, both arguments of this program can be used for input or output to solve the same problem. This observation is, of course, true of all symmetric relationships.

Now, a reversed list of any input is afforded by this program. For example, we deny that there is a list in a reverse relationship to the list "a.b.c.d" :

$$\sim \text{reverse}(< a.b.c.d.z_1, z_1 >, < u_1, w_1 >) \tag{5}$$

From this statement and theorem 3 we get the following derivation which is displayed in Kowalski's notation (Kowalski [1974]):

$u = a.b.c.d.z_1 \quad w = z_1 \quad u_1 = x_1.v_1' \quad w = w_1'$

1. $\leftarrow$ reverse($< a.b.c.d.z_1, x_1.z_1 >, < v_1', w_1' >$) Th. 3&(5)

$u_2 = a.b.c.d.z_1 \quad w_2 = x_1.z_1 \quad v_1' = x_2.v_2' \quad w_1' = w_2'$

2. $\leftarrow$ reverse($< a.b.c.d.z_1, x_2.x_1.z_1 >, < v_2', w_2' >$) Th. 3&1

$u_3 = a.b.c.d.z_1 \quad w_3 = x_2.x_1.z_1 \quad v_2' = x_3.v_3' \quad w_2' = w_3'$

3. $\leftarrow$ reverse($< a.b.c.d.z_1, x_3.x_2.x_1.z_1 >, < v_3', w_3' >$) Th. 3&2

$u_4 = a.b.c.d.z_1 \quad w_4 = x_3.x_2.x_1.z_1 \quad v_3' = x_4.v_4' \quad w_3' = w_4'$

4. $\leftarrow$ reverse($< a.b.c.d.z_1, x_4.x_3.x_2.x_1.z_1 >, < v_4', w_4' >$) Th. 3&3

$u_5 = a.b.c.d.z_1 \quad u_5' = v_4' = w_4'$

$x_1 = d \quad x_2 = c \quad x_3 = b \quad x_4 = a$

$< u_1, w_1 > = < d.c.b.a.w_1, w_1 >$

5. □ Th. 3&4

From the character of this derivation the following observations are clear. First, the derivation cannot terminate earlier due to an occur check. However, this is perfectly possible without an occur check but the results do not satisfy the reverse relationship. Secondly, the length of this derivation is linear to the number of elements in the input list. Thus, by d-lists the problem of reversing a list in logic is not only solved, the solution also characterizes practical programming.

Trees

We have been considering hitherto a few elementary data structures and operations on them. In relation to the problem of information retrieval it must be admitted that these data structures and operations are inadequate. It is therefore necessary to study the process by which we make information retrieval. It turns out that the best retrieval methods using comparison are tree operations in character. Moreover, it has been shown that binary search is the best comparison search method (see Knuth [1973]). Hence, not only can we focus our theory on trees but also on binary trees to reduce the number of axioms in the theory, which is a point of methodological interest. The idea of a binary tree is not only important in itself, variations of the idea can be extended to other useful data structures, for example, balanced trees and multiway trees. We shall specifically set up axioms for a generalization of binary trees called k-dimensional trees, which are adequate for secondary key search - also called associative search.

Binary Trees. Our understanding of a binary tree is recursive in nature. We shall distinguish between two cases: the empty tree and a tree of a root, a left subtree and a right subtree which are trees themselves. (When we can write tree for binary tree without ambiguity we shall do so for convenience.)

We shall now formalize the notion of a binary tree of which an example is displayed in fig. 3.

Axiom 6

$$\forall w\{\text{tree}(w) \leftrightarrow \exists x \exists y \exists z[w = \emptyset \lor . \ w = t(x,y,z) \land \text{root}(y) \land \text{tree}(x) \land \text{tree}(z)]\}$$

For the purpose of searching we are only interested in the part of a root upon which comparison is made. We shall call this part label or key and the remaining part data. Now, we formalize this idea.

Axiom 7

$$\forall y\{\text{root}(y) \leftrightarrow \exists y' \exists y''[y = r(y',y'') \land \text{label}(y') \land \text{data}(y'')]\}$$

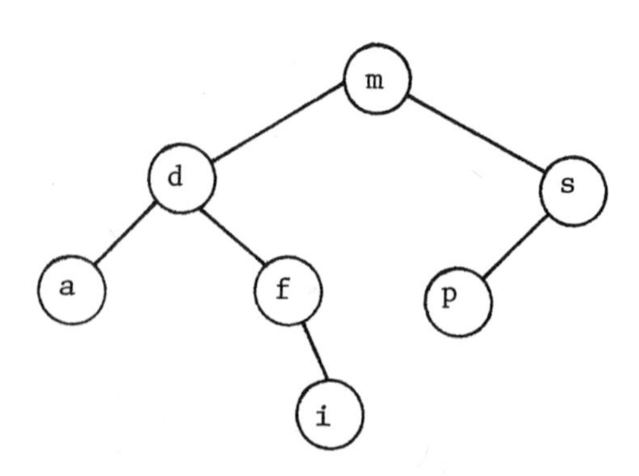

Figure 3. A binary tree with labels

We shall assume that the labels and the data are defined elsewhere.

As we recall, we distinguish between identical and different lists and d-lists, and we have also to do the same for trees.

Axiom 8

$$\forall x \forall y \forall z\{t(x,y,z) \neq \emptyset\}$$

Axiom 9

$$\forall x \forall x' \forall y \forall y' \forall z \forall z'\{t(x,y,z) = t(x',y',z') \leftrightarrow y = y' \wedge x = x' \wedge z = z'\}$$

For the purpose of information retrieval the concept of ordering is important. Therefore, we shall usually be more interested in ordered binary trees than in binary trees. In order to formalize the notion of a binary tree we shall need an axiom of weak trichotomy for labels and an axiom for a membership relation between a label and a tree.

Axiom 10

$$\forall x \forall y[\text{label}(x) \wedge \text{label}(y) \rightarrow x < y \vee x = y \vee y < x]$$

Axiom 11

$$\forall u \forall w\{u \in w \leftrightarrow \exists x \exists y \exists z \exists y' \exists y''[w = t(x,y,z) \wedge y = r(y',y'') \wedge. \; u = y' \vee u \in x \vee u \in z]\}$$

An immediate consequence of axiom 8 and axiom 11 is that there is no label on the empty tree:

$$\sim \exists x\{x \in \emptyset\} \tag{6}$$

Now intuitively, the idea of an ordered binary tree (ob-tree) is: an empty tree or an ordered binary tree that has two subtrees which are ordered binary trees themselves. Moreover, all labels on the left subtree are less than the label of the ob-tree and all labels on the right subtree are greater than the label of the ob-tree.

In view of axioms 10 and 11 we shall now formalize the idea of an ordered binary tree.

Axiom 12

$$\forall w\{\text{ob-tree}(w) \leftrightarrow \exists x \exists y \exists z \exists y' \exists y''[w = \emptyset \lor .\ w = t(x,y,z) \land y = r(y',y'') \land \text{ob-tree}(x) \land \text{ob-tree}(z) \land \forall u[u \in x \rightarrow u < y'] \land \forall u[u \in z \rightarrow y' < u]]\}$$

The operations on a tree that arise in practical information retrieval are essentially to search an item, insert a new item or to delete an item. Our next step is to set up a formal system for these operations.

Ordered Binary Tree Search. We think of an ob-tree search relationship as a relation between an ob-tree and a key. There are four cases:

(i) the relation is false for the empty tree
(ii) the result is the root of an ob-tree if the label of the root is identical to the key
(iii) the result is the relationship between the key and the left subtree of an ob-tree if the key is less than the label of the ob-tree
(iv) the result is the relationship between the key and the right subtree of an ob-tree if the key is greater than the label of the ob-tree.

This idea is formalized in the following definition.

Definition 7

$$\forall u \forall v \forall w\{\text{search}(u,v,w) \leftrightarrow \exists x \exists y \exists z \exists y' \exists y''[u = t(x,y,z) \land y = r(y',y'') \land .\ v = y' \land w = y\ .\lor.\ v < y' \land \text{search}(x,v,w)\ .\lor.\ v > y' \land \text{search}(z,v,w)]\}$$

A simple derivation gives a theorem, which is a logic program for ob-tree searching.

Theorem 4

$$\text{search}(t(x,r(y',y''),z),y',r(y',y''))$$
$$\text{search}(t(x,r(y',y''),z),v,w) \leftarrow v < y' \land \text{search}(x,v,w)$$
$$\text{search}(t(x,r(y',y''),z),v,w) \leftarrow y' < v \land \text{search}(z,v,w)$$

Ordered Binary Tree Search and Insert. Occasionally, we are not only interested in making an ob-tree search but also in inserting a new root if its corresponding label is not already in the tree. The definition of an insert relationship has, naturally, a close resemblance to the search relationship and a small modification of definition 7 gives this new relationship.

Definition 8

$$\forall u \forall v \forall w \{ insert(u,v,w) \leftrightarrow \exists x \exists y \exists z \exists y' \exists y'' \exists v' \exists v'' [u = \emptyset \wedge w = t(\emptyset,v,\emptyset) \;.\vee.\; u = t(x,y,z) \wedge y = r(y',y'') \wedge v = r(v',v'') \wedge (y' = v' \wedge w = t(x,v,z) \;.\vee.\; v' < y' \wedge insert(x,v,x') \wedge w = t(x',y,z) \;.\vee.\; y' < v' \wedge insert(z,v,z') \wedge w = t(x,y,z'))] \}$$

Another short derivation gives a theorem which is a logic program for computing objects in the insert relationship.

Theorem 5

$insert(\emptyset,v,t(\emptyset,v,\emptyset))$

$insert(t(x,r(y',y''),z),r(y',v''),t(x,r(y',v''),z))$

$insert(t(x,r(y',y''),z),r(v',v''),t(x',r(y',y''),z) \leftarrow v' < y' \wedge insert(x,r(v',v''),x')$

$insert(t(x,r(y',y''),z),r(v',v''),t(x,r(y',y''),z') \leftarrow y' < v' \wedge insert(z,r(v',v''),z')$

Before proceeding to other relations, let us get a firmer idea of the insert relationship.

Example 5

Suppose that we want to insert a new label h into the tree in fig. 3. In relation to this problem we can, for simplicity, ignore the data of a root. This brings us also to a simplification of theorem 5; we can simply substitute all occurrences of the terms $r(y',y'')$ and $r(v',v'')$ by y and v respectively.

We still have to represent the tree in fig. 3 in logic, but unfortunately, this representation is not convenient as a name. We shall therefore also, by definition, give the tree a shorter name. We say that

$$t_0 = t(t(t(\emptyset,a,\emptyset),d,t(\emptyset,f,t(\emptyset,i,\emptyset))),m,t(t(\emptyset,p,\emptyset),s,\emptyset)) \quad (7)$$

Now, a simplified theorem 5 affords a solution to the problem if we deny that there is an insert relationship between the tree t_0, the label h and any tree w :

$$\sim insert(t_0,h,w) \quad (8)$$

We have made a point of the fact that the derivations characterize practical programming, and so this derivation and its assignments of variables are also of interest. We have

$$w = t(x',m,t(t(\emptyset,p,\emptyset),s,\emptyset))$$

1. $\leftarrow h<m \wedge insert(t(t(t(t(\emptyset,a,\emptyset),d,t(\emptyset,f,t(\emptyset,i,\emptyset))),h,x')$

$$x' = t(t(\emptyset,a,\emptyset),d,z')$$

2. $\leftarrow d<h \wedge insert(t(\emptyset,f,t(\emptyset,i,\emptyset)),h,z')$

$$z' = t(\emptyset,f,z'')$$

3. $\leftarrow f<h \wedge insert(t(\emptyset,i,\emptyset),h,z'')$

$$z'' = t(x'',i,\emptyset)$$

4. $\leftarrow h<i \wedge insert(\emptyset,h,x'')$

$$x'' = t(\emptyset,h,\emptyset)$$

5. $\square$

Hence, w now denotes the intended ordered binary tree with a label h inserted at its unique position in the left subtree of label i of the tree displayed in fig. 3.

It is evident that the exhibited derivation can be understood as a computation in accordance with the binary tree search and insert algorithm. We may think of an algorithm as an abstract object represented by programming languages analogously to the representation of numbers by numerals. In this way theorem 5 is a program representing the binary tree search and insert algorithm in first order logic, but only with respect to a proof procedure like PROLOG that actually would characterize the behaviour of the search and insert algorithm.

This brings us to a few points of methodological interest. It is, of course, important that an algorithm of an effectively calculable function can be written in the form we have used for logic programs (theorems). It has been shown that this form, usually called a Horn clause, is not too narrow for any of the computable functions (see Tärnlund [1977]). For this result we do not need all the axioms and definitions of this theory. But we remember that a central purpose of the theory is to characterize practical programming and we need them for this purpose.

In principle, the theory is successful when an algorithm is represented naturally by a logic program and the derivation of this program characterizes the behaviour of the algorithm. While the first point is aesthetic the second is mathematical. This subject usually called analysis of algorithms has, for example, given the result that binary search is the best comparison based search algorithm (see Knuth [1973]).

This result carries over to a binary tree search algorithm for a balanced tree and to our derivation of the logic program for search and insert.

Analysis of algorithms has thus brought us to an intensive study of derivations which is exceptional in mathematics, although the concept of derivation is not only central in mathematics but the general idea of proof is also very old indeed. It is even to be found in the works of Pythagoras (sixth century B.C.).

For reasons of space we have to omit the subject of proof procedure implementations which, of course, is relevant for running programms efficiently (see Bruynooghe [1976], Roussel [1975] and Warren [1977]).

Ordered Binary Tree Search and Deletion. The operation to delete a node from an ordered binary tree while preserving the ordering of the tree is slightly more complicated than the former operations.

Before turning to the general problem we observe that the special case of deleting a leaf node has a simple solution by the logic program in theorem 5. For example, suppose that we wish to delete node i from the tree depicted in fig. 3. We arrive at a solution by denying that there exists a tree in the search and insert relationship with the label i and the tree in expression (7):

$$\sim \text{insert}(w,i,t_0) \tag{9}$$

We shall now present a more complicated definition of a search and delete relationship. It is useful in relation to our purpose to derive a logic program from this definition, though there exists a simpler one.

We shall make use of an auxiliary relation in the binary tree search and delete relationship. This "reorder" relationship specifies a relation between three objects: an ordered binary tree, the first root of the tree with respect to the ordering on the labels and the new tree after deleting the first root. The definition consists of two cases:

(i) the first root of a tree with an empty left subtree is the root itself. The new tree is the right subtree.

(ii) the first root of a tree with a non-empty left subtree is the first root of the left subtree. The new tree is the original tree after deleting the first root.

Let us now write an exact definition.

Definition 9

$$\forall u \forall w' \forall w\{\text{reorder}(u,w',w) \leftrightarrow \exists x \exists y \exists z \exists x'[u = t(x,y,z) \land (x = \emptyset \land w' = y \land w = z \ .\lor.\ x \neq \emptyset \land \text{reorder}(x,w',x') \land w = t(x',y,z))]\}$$

We notice that the relation is false for the empty tree, there is no first root of the empty tree.

A short derivation gives a theorem which is a logic program for computing the first root in the ordering on the labels and a reordered tree.

Theorem 6

$$\text{reorder}(t(\emptyset,y,z),y,z)$$

$$\text{reorder}(t(x,y,z),w',t(x',y,z)) \leftarrow x \neq \emptyset \land \text{reorder}(x,w',x')$$

The answer to the exercise of applying theorem 6 to the binary tree in fig. 3 is label a and the original tree with label a removed.

Let us now return to the search and delete algorithm. There are two main cases compounded of the already defined binary tree search relationship and the reorder relationship:

(i) find the root to delete according to a label
(ii) delete a root and reorder the tree of this root:
 a) one of the subtrees is empty, substitute the tree by the other subtree
 b) none of the subtrees are empty, the reorder relationship specifies the reordering of the tree.

Definition 10

$$\forall u \forall k \forall w\{\text{delete}(u,k,w) \leftrightarrow \exists x \exists y \exists z \exists x' \exists z' \exists y' \exists y'' \exists w'[u = t(x,y,z) \land y = r(y',y'') \land [k < y' \land \text{delete}(x,k,x') \land w = t(x',y,z) \ .\lor.\ k > y' \land \text{delete}(z,k,z') \land w = t(x,y,z') \ .\lor.\ k = y' \land (x = \emptyset \land w = z \ .\lor.\ z = \emptyset \land w = x \ .\lor.\ \text{reorder}(z,w',z') \land w = t(x,w',z'))]]\}$$

We notice that this relationship is false for an empty tree; we cannot delete a root from the empty tree.

Another simple derivation gives a theorem which is a logic program for binary tree search and deletion.

Theorem 7

delete(t(x,y,z),k,t(x',y,z)) ← y = r(y',y") ∧ k<y' ∧ delete(x,k,x')

delete(t(x,y,z),k,t(x,y,z')) ← y = r(y',y") ∧ y'<k ∧ delete(z,k,z')

delete(t(∅,y,z),k,z) ← y = r(y',y") ∧ y' = k

delete(t(x,y,∅),k,x) ← y = r(y',y") ∧ y' = k

delete(t(x,y,z),k,t(x,w',w)) ← y = r(y',y") ∧ y' = k ∧ reorder(z,w',w)

Notice that neither the third nor the fourth statement is a consequence of statement five since the reorder relationship is false for the empty tree. This formulation improves the efficiency of the program.

As an exercise the reader may verify that the binary tree search and delete program works for deleting label m from the binary tree displayed in fig. 3. (We can simplify the delete program for this problem by substituting labels for roots i.e., eliminating all occurrences of y = r(y',y") and substituting all occurrences of y' by y because the roots simply are labels (see Tärnlund [1975].)

So far we have been considering a few good methods for information retrieval which are usually called primary key search methods. We shall now focus on secondary key search methods.

k-Dimensional Trees. We shall now take up a data structure which is a generalization of the binary tree idea for searching. It was discovered by Bentley [1975] and he called it a k-dimensional tree. According to this terminology a binary tree is a 1-dimensional tree. In this way a binary tree has one discriminator for the entire tree, while in contrast, the k-dimensional tree has k discriminators which are used cyclically down the tree. Apart from the elegant idea of a k-dimensional tree, Bentley's analysis also seems to indicate that this data structure is one of the best for secondary key search.

Let us first display a 3-dimensional tree in fig. 4 and then write down the concept of a k-dimensional tree precisely.

It is worthwhile understanding the intuitive idea of an ordered k-dimensional tree (ok-tree). For example, in fig. 4 all nodes to the left of the root contain a name preceding Lee and all nodes in the right subtree of the discriminator CS (computer science) contain a subject succeeding CS e.g., Math (mathematics). The discriminator counter is an integer function n mod m , where n is the level of the tree and m the number of discriminators.

In order to formalize the concept of an ok-tree we need a mapping from a number to a discriminator of a list of labels.

Definition 11

$$\forall u \forall k \forall w\{disc(w,k,u) \leftrightarrow \exists x \exists y \exists u'[w = x.y \wedge (u = 0 \wedge k = x \ .\vee. \ u = u'+1 \wedge disc(y,k,u'))]\}$$

A short derivation gives a theorem which is a logic program for computing the u:th discriminator of a list.

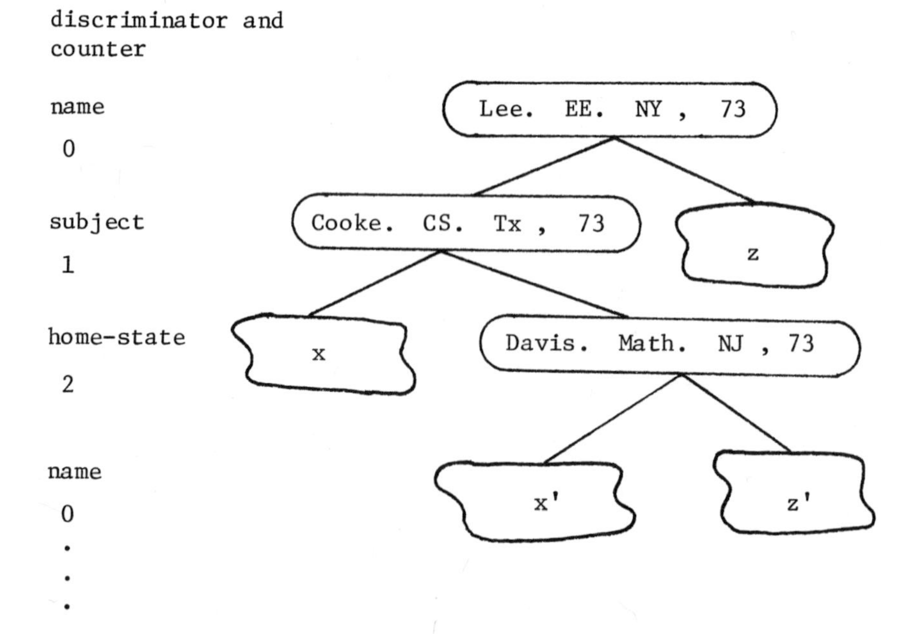

Figure 4. A 3-dimensional tree with three keys and data. A counter keeps track of the discriminators.

Theorem 8

disc(x.y,x,0)

disc(x.y,k,u'+1) ← disc(y,k,u')

For example, the second discriminator of the list Davis.Math.NJ in fig. 4 is Math. We get this answer from theorem 8 by writing

$$\sim \mathrm{disc}(\mathrm{Davis.Math.NJ}.\emptyset,x,1) \quad (10)$$

We might view all the labels of a tree which have the same discriminating number as a class. It is on these classes that we shall define an ordering relation on ok-trees. We shall need the extension of this class, but before we write down this specification exactly we shall comment on the idea of a root in an ok-tree. In comparison with axiom 7 we shall now accept that a root has not only a label but also a list of labels.

We can now formalize the extension of a class of discriminators.

Definition 12

$$\forall w \forall k \forall u\{\mathrm{disco}(w,k,u) \leftrightarrow \exists x \exists y \exists z \exists y' \exists y''[w = t(x,y,z) \wedge (y = r(y',y'') \wedge \mathrm{disc}(y',k,u) \;.\!\vee\; \mathrm{disco}(x,k,u) \vee \mathrm{disco}(z,k,u))]\}$$

A short derivation gives a theorem which is a program for computing the extension of a class of discriminators.

Theorem 9

disco(t(x,y,z),k,u) ← y = r(y',y") ∧ disc(y',k,u)

disco(t(x,y,z),k,u) ← disco(x,k,u)

disco(t(x,y,z),k,u) ← disco(z,k,u)

For example, the class of visible first discriminators of the tree in fig. 4 is {Lee, Cooke, Davis} .

We can now think of an ordered k-dimensional tree (ok-tree) in these terms. A discriminator belongs to exactly one class. A discriminator of a root is greater or equal to all discriminators of the left subtree in the class and less than the discriminators of the right subtree in the class.

Let us now write down the notion of an ok-tree precisely.

Definition 13

$$\forall w\{\text{ok-tree}(w) \leftrightarrow \exists x\exists y\exists z\exists y'\exists y''\exists u\forall k[w = t(x,y,z) \wedge y = r(y',y'') \wedge \text{disc}(y',k,u) \wedge \forall k'[\text{disco}(x,k',u) \rightarrow k' \leq k] \wedge \forall k'[\text{disco}(z,k',u) \rightarrow k < k'] \wedge \text{ok-tree}(x) \wedge \text{ok-tree}(z)]\}$$

We have made use of the "less or equal" relation $x \leq y$, which is equivalent to $x < y \vee x = y$.

Ordered k-Dimensional Tree Search and Insert. As in the treatment of operations on binary trees we shall now focus on operations on ok-trees. In the process of making information retrieval there are a few operations of special interest, for example, search, search and insert, and search and deletion. A search relation follows conveniently after introducing a search and insert relation for ok-trees. Moreover, the search and delete relation for ok-trees is analogous to the one of binary trees, so we leave to the reader the pleasure of writing down the two latter relations.

As appears from the definitions and theorems set out above, the step from one to several discriminators raises the problem of keeping track of discriminators. For this purpose we shall make use of the disc relation which picks out a discriminator for a natural number and the integer function $n \bmod m$, which we may think of as the remainder when n is divided by m. It is to be noticed that we do not need this integer function to define the search and insert relationship, but it is convenient to have it. Again we ask the reader to write down a definition and to derive a theorem which is a program to compute the mod function.

Before proceeding to the search and insert relation for ok-trees let us recall the corresponding relation for ordered binary trees. In comparison with the former relation we shall add another argument, namely, a discriminator counter. In this way we arrive at a relation between: an ok-tree which we may think of as an input tree, a node containing a list of labels and data which might be inserted into the input tree, a discriminator counter and an output ok-tree. We can now write down this idea precisely.

Definition 14

$$\forall w \forall k \forall n \forall w' \forall m\{insert(w,k,n,m,w') \leftrightarrow \exists x \exists y \exists z \exists u \exists u' \exists l \exists l' \exists k' \exists k''[w = \emptyset \wedge w' = t(\emptyset,k,\emptyset) \;.\vee.\; w = t(x,y,z) \wedge y = r(u,u') \wedge k = r(l,l') \wedge (u = l \wedge w' = t(x,k,z) \;.\vee.\; u \neq l \wedge disc(u,k',n) \wedge disc(l,k'',n) \wedge (k'' \leq k' \wedge insert(x,k,n',m,x') \wedge w' = t(x',y,z) \wedge n' = (n+1 \bmod m) \;.\vee.\; k' < k'' \wedge insert(z,k,n',m,z'') \wedge w' = t(x,y,z') \wedge n' = (n+1 \bmod m)))]\}$$

Let us suppose that the integer function n mod m is defined elsewhere.

We notice that we conveniently get a search relation after deleting the first alternative in the definiens.

We readily derive the following theorem which is a logic program for ok-tree search and insert.

Theorem 10

$$insert(\emptyset,k,n,m,t(\emptyset,k,\emptyset))$$

$$insert(t(x,y,z),k,n,m,t(x,k,z)) \leftarrow y = r(u,u') \wedge k = r(l,l') \wedge u = l$$

$$insert(t(x,y,z),k,n,m,t(x',y,z)) \leftarrow y = r(u,u') \wedge k = r(l,l') \wedge u \neq l \wedge disc(u,k',n) \wedge disc(l,k'',n) \wedge k'' \leq k' \wedge insert(x,k,n',m,x') \wedge n' = (n+1) \bmod m$$

$$insert(t(x,y,z),k,n,m,t(x,y,z')) \leftarrow y = r(u,u') \wedge k = r(l,l') \wedge u \neq l \wedge disc(u,k',n) \wedge disc(l,k'',n) \wedge k' < k'' \wedge insert(z,k,n',m,z') \wedge n' = (n+1) \bmod m$$

Evidently we get a search program if we delete the first statement.

If we take the view that the theory should contain a minimum of redundant concepts it may be interesting to notice that the discriminator counter, the disc relation and the mod function could be eliminated from definition 14 and theorem 10. In pursuing this line of thought the main problem is to write down a proper organization of the discriminators and the labels of the ok-tree. (For an instance of a solution see Tärnlund [1976].)

Before proceeding to the next section on interrogative statements, it is particularly to be noticed that we have built up a system intended as a formalization of practical programming for information retrieval. The system has been used in practice by M. Janning and A-L Johansson to implement an experimental data base in PROLOG.

DATA BASE MODELS

We shall display a miniature data base in this section. For this purpose we shall set up a model of the theory. At this point two problems demand solutions simultaneously. On the one hand the purpose of the model is to characterize a "world" so that we can pose questions to the model and get answers from it about the "world". Data bases usually have finite domains so there is no problem of logic involved in answering these questions.

On the other hand there arises a computational problem of finding efficient computations for answering the questions. A main result of this paper is the formalization of good programming methods so that derivations can be used as efficient computations. This point is even more important where larger data bases are involved.

Not only is the notion of derivation useful for computations but it will, of course, also apply to the general idea of making inferences. This is an important subject of data bases, which ordinary data base systems have difficulties with since they are missing a formal logic calculus (cf., Codd [1970]). In fact, several authors treat the subject of making inferences in a logic data base, for example, Chang [1978], van Emden [1978], Kellogg et al. [1978], Kowalski [1978], McSkimin and Minker [1978], Minker [1978] and Nicolas and Gallaire [1978].

Queries

In our data base theory we may think of queries as statements in first order logic. Taking this view, an answer to a query is found by solving the problem whether or not a query is a logical consequence of our theory. To solve this problem efficiently we shall make use of the formalized theory in the Basic Information Structures and Operations section.

Most data bases have a finite domain, and so we are in principle in a position to answer the queries. In practice, though, this fact is, unfortunately, of little use. By contrast, however, the length of a derivation of a query is very important and we shall indicate the length of a derivation for answering a query. Generally speaking, it is known that primary key search queries have shorter derivations than secondary key search queries (see Knuth [1973]).

Now let us suppose that we have a university data base which, among other things, contains the names of students, their subjects, home states and years of enrollment. An efficient organization of this information is depicted in fig. 4. First, let us view the tree as an ordered binary tree i.e., only the first label is used as a discriminator. We call this tree t_2 and specify it as a stud-tree.

$$t_2 = t(t(x,r(Cooke.CS.Tx,73),t_2'),r(Lee.EE.NY,73),z) \quad (11)$$

where

$$t_2' = t(x',r(Davis.Math.NJ,73),z') \quad (12)$$

Definition 15

$$\forall w\{\text{stud-tree}(w) \leftrightarrow w = t_2\}$$

We can now say that an individual is a student if and only if this individual belongs to the student tree. This idea is written more precisely as follows.

Definition 16

$$\forall w\{\text{student}(w) \leftrightarrow \exists u[\text{stud-tree}(t_2) \wedge \text{search}(t_2,r(w,u),u)]\}$$

The "search" predicate is specified in definition 7.

After these preliminary comments we can now turn to some classes of queries.

Unquantified Queries. We shall not treat statements with free variables. So, any query without a variable belongs to this class. A simple example is the question whether or not there is a student Davis. We write formally:

$$\text{student(Davis)} \quad (13)$$

As can be seen from fig. 4 the answer is yes. The interesting point about this example is of course the derivation that proves that this query is a logical consequence of the data base.

Now, a proof procedure evidently has to make use of definition 16. Statement 13 is true if and only if the following statement is true:

$$\exists u[\text{stud-tree}(t_2) \wedge \text{search}(t_2,\text{Davis},u)] \quad (14)$$

which is true if and only if

$$\text{search}(t_2,\text{Davis},u) \quad (15)$$

is true.

After these few steps we have thus arrived at a problem that we can solve with the help of theorem 4, which is a binary search program. To go a little further we recall that binary search is the best possible comparison search method, so, we cannot find a solution of the latter problem which has a shorter length of the derivation.

We want to call attention to the fact that our theory provides an answer to a query with a negative answer as well. For example, suppose that Mills is not a student i.e., Mills does not belong to the tree t_2 in definition 15. Now in view of this information the query:

student(Mills) (16)

has the expected answer no. We notice that this problem is solved similarily to the first query. However, to be able to say no we now also need definition 7, which is a definition of a binary search relationship.

We should mention that PROLOG cannot answer this query in logic since it does not furnish definitions. The solution method of PROLOG is analogous to the method of PLANNER (see Hewitt [1972]). In fact, Clark [1978], Nicolas and Gallaire [1978] and Reiter [1978] have studied this method.

We now turn to the important notion of secondary search. The tree in fig. 4 is conveniently viewed as an ordered 3-dimensional tree.

$$t_1 = t(t(x,r(Cooke.CS.Tx,73),t_3),r(Lee.EE.NY,73),z) \quad (17)$$

where

$$t_3 = t(x',r(Davis.Math.NJ,73),z') \quad (18)$$

Obviously, the trees t_1 and t_2 in (11) denote the same tree, so we write

$$t_1 = t_2 \quad (19)$$

An example of a secondary key search query without quantifiers is to ask whether or not there is a student Davis who studies mathematics and is from New Jersey:

student(Davis.Math.NJ) (20)

If we now suppose that we have a logic program for 3-dimensional search (an exercise in the section on Basic Information Structures and Operations), then after an efficient search derivation the answer is yes.

It is evident that we also can answer negative secondary key search queries.

Existentially Quantified Queries. An existential query is a query of the form $\exists x A(x)$, where $A(x)$ is a formula in first order logic. A simple example of this class of queries is whether or not there exists a student:

$$\exists w \; student(w) \tag{21}$$

Almost all the steps in the derivations which arise in practice when answering a query come from running a logic program such as the binary search program. In relation to this observation this class of queries has very short derivations. For example, the binary search program halts already at its first step for $w = Lee$, which is an answer to the query.

Universally Quantified Queries. A universally quantified query is of the form $\forall x A(x)$. In contrast to the existentially quantified queries the universally quantified queries have derivations of maximal length. For example, suppose that we want to know the names of all the students:

$$\forall w \; student(w) \tag{22}$$

To answer this query we have to traverse the entire tree in fig. 4. Cooke, Davis and Lee are among the individuals in the tree that belongs to the answer of the latter query.

Numerically Quantified Queries. Phrases such as "Exactly two students" and "Exactly three students of which at least one is a computer scientist and one is a mathematician" are examples of queries in this class. In these phrases we single out the special mathematical objects "two" and "three". With the help of quantifiers and the notion of identity we can express these numerals in logic.

For example, we write the first phrase

$$\exists x \exists y \{student(x) \wedge student(y) \wedge x \neq y \wedge \forall z(student(z) \rightarrow z = x \vee z = y)\} \tag{23}$$

It is to be noticed that the left part of the main conjunction is an existentially quantified query expressing the phrase "at least two students". The right part of the main conjunction expresses the phrase "at most two students".

Now in view of the derivation for answering this query it is worthwhile noticing that the left part of the query uses all the derivation steps. Thus the right part is computationally free. Combining this observation with the situation in PROLOG we notice that this phrase can be implemented with the help of a special sign for control called "slash".

Obviously, Lee and Cooke is an answer to this primary key search query which is solved by the help of the binary search program in theorem 4.

Let us now take up the second phrase.

$$\exists x \exists x' \exists y \exists y' \exists z \exists z' \exists z'' \{student(x.CS.x') \land student(y.Math.y') \land student(z.z'.z'') \land x \neq y \land x \neq z \land y \neq z \land \forall u \exists u' \exists u'' [student(u.u'.u'') \rightarrow u = x \lor u = y \lor u = z]\} \quad (24)$$

This statement is a simple example of a secondary key search query. It is solved efficiently with a 3-dimensional search program. An answer is: Cooke is a computer scientists, Davis is a mathematician and Lee a third student.

FINAL REMARKS

We have set up a deductive theory for information retrieval. A data base is a model of the theory. Programs are theorems. Efficient computations are derivations in first order predicate calculus by means of some familiar rules of inference.

Green's work [1969] seems to be the first application of predicate calculus to information retrieval. It is to be noticed that he viewed derivations as simulations of computations. In contrast, we have focused on programming methods to make derivations efficient computations. More generally, the theory applies to abstract specifications of algorithms and information structures, derivations of programs and verifications of programs (cf., Clark and Tärnlund [1977]). These broad outlines derive from the research program set out by McCarthy [1963].

Finally, our theory is formalized in first order predicate calculus which is a point of methodological interest for metatheoretical studies of the system.

ACKNOWLEDGMENTS

I wish to thank Åke Hansson for stimulating discussions. The Swedish Natural Science Research Council has supported this work.

REFERENCES

1. Bentley, J. L. [1975] Multidimensional Binary Search Trees Used for Associative Searching, *CACM 18*, 9 (September 1975), 509-516.

2. Bibel, W. [1976] A Uniform Approach to Programming, *Report 7633*, Technische Universität München, 1976.

3. Bruynooghe, M. [1976] An Interpreter for Predicate Logic Programs, Part 1. *Report CW 10*, Applied Maths & Programming Division, Katholieke Univ Leuven, Belgium, Oct 1976.

4. Chang, C. L. [1978] DEDUCE 2: Further Investigations of Deduction in Relational Data Bases, In *Logic and Data Bases* (H. Gallaire and J. Minker, Eds.), Plenum Press, New York, New York, 1978, 201-236.

5. Clark, K. [1978] Negation as Failure, In *Logic and Data Bases* (H. Gallaire and J. Minker, Eds.), Plenum Press, New York, New York, 1978, 293-322.

6. Clark, K. and Tärnlund, S-Å. [1977] A First Order Theory of Data and Programs, *Proc. IFIP Congress 1977*, North-Holland Publishing Company, Amsterdam, 1977, 939-944.

7. Codd, E. F. [1970] A Relational Model for Large Shared Data Banks, *CACM 13*, 6 (June 1970), 377-387.

8. Colmerauer, A., Kanoui, H., Pasero, R. and Roussel, P. [1972] Un Système de Communication Homme-Machine en Francais, Groupe d'Intelligence Artificielle, U.E.R. de Luminy, Université d'Aix-Marseille, Luminy, 1972.

9. Green, C. [1969] "The Application of Theorem Proving to Question-Answering Systems," Ph.D. Thesis, Computer Science Department, Stanford University, 1969.

10. Guttag, J. [1977] Abstract Data Types and the Development of Data Structures, *CACM 20*, 6 (June 1977), 396-404.

11. Hayes, P. [1973] Computation and Deduction, *Proc. MFCS Conf., Czechoslovakian Academy of Sciences*, 1973.

12. Hewitt, C. [1972] Description and Theoretical Analysis (Using Schemata) of PLANNER: A Language for Proving Theorems and Manipulating Models in a Robot, *A. I. Memo No. 251*, MIT Project MAC, 1972.

13. Hoare, C.A.R. [1973] Recursive Data Structures, Computer Science Dept., Stanford University, STAN-CS-73-400, Oct. 1973.

14. Kellogg, C., Klahr, P. and Travis, L. [1978] Deductive Planning and Pathfinding for Relational Data Bases, In *Logic and Data Bases* (H. Gallaire and J. Minker, Eds.), Plenum Press, New York, New York, 1978, 179-200.

15. Knuth, D. [1968] *The Art of Computer Programming, Vol. 1, Fundamental Algorithms,* Addison-Wesley, Reading, Massachusetts, 1968.

16. Knuth, D. [1973] *The Art of Computer Programming, Vol. 3, Sorting and Searching,* Addison-Wesley, Reading, Massachusetts, 1973.

17. Kowalski, R. [1974] Predicate Logic as Programming Language, *Proc. IFIP Congress 1974,* North-Holland Publishing Company, Amsterdam, 1974, 569-574.

18. Kowalski, R. [1978] Logic for Data Description, In *Logic and Data Bases* (H. Gallaire and J. Minker, Eds.), Plenum Press, New York, New York, 1978, 77-103.

19. Liskov, B. H. and Zilles, S. [1974] Programming with Abstract Data Types, *ACM SIGPLAN Notices 9,* 4 (April 1974), 50-59.

20. McCarthy, J., et al. [1962] *LISP 1.5 Programmer's Manual,* MIT Press, Cambridge, Massachusetts, 1962, 33-70.

21. McCarthy, J. [1963] A Basis for a Mathematical Theory of Computation, In *Computer Programming and Formal Systems* (P. Braffort and D. Hirschberg, Eds.), North-Holland Publishing Company, Amsterdam, 1963.

22. McSkimin, J. R. and Minker, J. [1978] A Predicate Calculus Based Semantic Network for Question-Answering Systems, In *Associative Networks - The Representation and Use of Knowledge* (N. Findler, Ed.), Academic Press, New York, New York, 1978.

23. Minker, J. [1978] An Experimental Data Base System Based on Logic, In *Logic and Data Bases* (H. Gallaire and J. Minker, Eds.), Plenum Press, New York, New York, 1978, 107-147.

24. Nicolas, J. M. and Gallaire, H. [1978] Data Bases: Theory vs. Interpretation, In *Logic and Data Bases* (H. Gallaire and J. Minker, Eds.), Plenum Press, New York, New York, 1978, 33-54.

25. Quine, W. V. [1974] *Methods of Logic, Third Edition*, Routledge & Kegan Paul, London, 1974.

26. Reiter, R. [1978] On Closed World Data Bases, In *Logic and Data Bases* (H. Gallaire and J. Minker, Eds.), Plenum Press, New York, New York, 1978, 55-76.

27. Robinson, J. A. [1965] A Machine-Oriented Logic Based on the Resolution Principle, *JACM 12*, 1 (January 1965), 23-41.

28. Roussel, P. [1975] PROLOG: Manuel de Reference et d'utilisation, Groupe d'Intelligence Artificielle, U.E.R. de Luminy, Marseille, September 1975.

29. Tärnlund, S-Å. [1975] Logic Information Processing, Dept. of Inofrmation Processing Computer Science, TRITA-IBADB 1034, The Royal Institute of Technology and The University of Stockholm, Sweden, 1975.

30. Tärnlund, S-Å. [1976] A Logical Basis for Data Bases, Department of Information Processing Computer Science, TRITA-IBADB-1029, The Royal Institute of Technology and The University of Stockholm, Sweden, 1976.

31 Tärnlund, S-Å. [1977] Horn Clause Computability, *BIT 17*, 2 (1977), 215-226.

32. van Emden, M. [1978] Computation and Deductive Information Retrieval, In *Formal Description of Programming Concepts* (E. Neuhold, Ed.), North-Holland Publishing Company, (to appear).

33. Warren, D. [1977] Implementing Prolog - Compiling Predicate Logic Programs, Dept. of AI, No. 39, Edinburgh, 1977.

NEGATIVE INFORMATION AND DATA BASES

NEGATION AS FAILURE

Keith L. Clark

Department of Computer Science & Statistics

Queen Mary College, London, England

ABSTRACT

A query evaluation process for a logic data base comprising a set of clauses is described. It is essentially a Horn clause theorem prover augmented with a special inference rule for dealing with negation. This is the negation as failure inference rule whereby ~ P can be inferred if every possible proof of P fails. The chief advantage of the query evaluator described is the effeciency with which it can be implemented. Moreover, we show that the negation as failure rule only allows us to conclude negated facts that could be inferred from the axioms of the completed data base, a data base of relation definitions and equality schemas that we consider is implicitly given by the data base of clauses. We also show that when the clause data base and the queries satisfy certain constraints, which still leaves us with a data base more general than a conventional relational data base, the query evaluation process will find every answer that is a logical consequence of the completed data base.

INTRODUCTION

Following Kowalski [1978] and van Emden [1978] we consider a logic data base to comprise a set of clauses. The ground unit clauses are the extensional component of the data base. They provide us with a set of instances of the data base relations. The remaining clauses constitute the intensional component, they are the general rules of the data base. The general rules as well as the explicit 'data' are to be used in the deductive retrieval of information.

The shortcoming of such a data base is that, like a more conventional relational data base (Codd [1970]), it only contains information about true instances of relations. Even so, quite straightforward queries make use of negation, and can be answered only by showing that certain relation instances are false. Thus, to answer a request for the name of a student not taking a particular course, C, we need to find a student, S, such that Takes(S,C) is false. For his relational calculus (Codd [1972]), Codd's solution to the problem is to assume that a tuple is in the complement of the relation if it is not a given instance of the relation. For a logic data base, where a relation instance which is not explicitly given may still be implied by a general rule, the analogous assumption is that a relation instance is false if we fail to prove that it is true. The great advantage of such a 'solution to negation' is the ease with which it can be implemented. To show that P is false we do an exhaustive search for a proof of P. If every possible proof fails, $\sim$ P is 'inferred'. This is the way that both PLANNER (Hewitt [1972]) and PROLOG (Roussel [1975], Warren et al. [1977]) handle negation.

What we have here is a proof rule:

$$\vdash \sim \vdash P \quad \text{infer} \quad \vdash \sim P$$

where the proof that P is not provable is always the exhaustive but unsuccessful search for a proof of P. Let us call it the negation as failure inference rule. For pragmatic reasons this is adopted as the sole inference rule for negated formulae. Is the consequence that we have given "$\sim$" a new meaning as "fail to prove", or can we perhaps reconcile negation, operationally understood as "fail to prove", with its truth functional semantics? In other words, can we interpret a failure proof of $\sim$ P as a valid first order inference that P is false.

Note that to assume that a relation instance is false if it is not implied, is to assume that the data base gives complete information about the true instances of its relations. This is the closed world assumption referred to by Reiter [1978] and Nicolas and Gallaire [1978]. More precisely, it is the assumption that a relation instance is true only if it is given explicitly or else is implied by one of the general rules for the relation. Thus, let us suppose that the data base contains just two instances of the unary relation, Maths-course:

$$\begin{array}{l} \text{Maths-course(C101)} \leftarrow \\ \text{Maths-course(C301)} \leftarrow \end{array} \qquad (1)$$

and no general rules about this relation. For any course name C, different from C101 and C301, Maths-course(C) is not provable. But to conclude, in consequence, that Maths-course(C) is false, is to assume that C101 and C301 are the only Maths-courses, and that C is not an alternative name for either course. If we were to make these assumptions explicit we would need to add to our data base the completion law:

$$(\forall x)[\text{Maths-course}(x) \rightarrow x=C101 \lor x=C301] \quad (2)$$

and the inequality schemas:

$C101 \neq C$ for all names C different from C101
$C301 \neq C$ for all names C different from C301

Note that (1) and (2) are together equivalent to a definition

$$(\forall x)[\text{Maths-course}(x) \leftrightarrow x=C101 \lor x=C301]$$

of the Maths-course relation.

As we might expect, every negated fact $\sim$ Maths-course(C) that we can 'infer' by showing that Maths-course(C) is not given, can now be proved by a first order deduction using the completion law and inequality schemas. More than that, the failure proof of Maths-course(C) and the first order deduction are structurally almost identical (see Figure 1). The alternatives of the failed proof space become explicit disjunctions in the first order deduction, match failures of the former become false equalities of the latter. Thus the failure proof is essentially a structural representation of a natural deduction style proof:

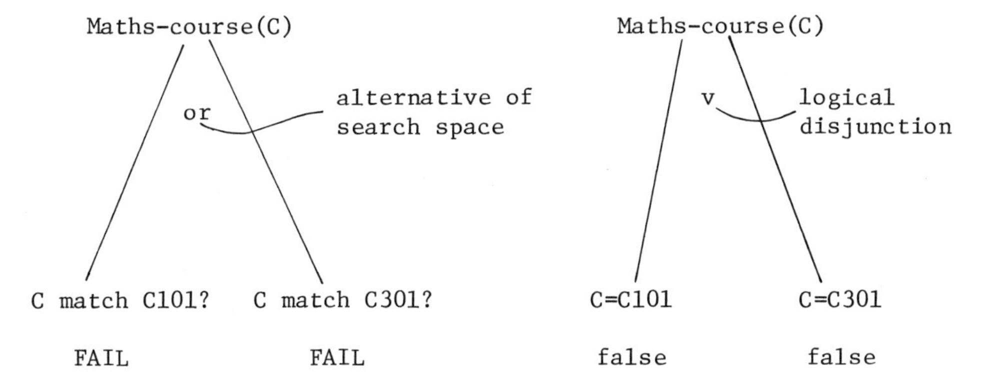

Figure 1. First Order Deduction

$$\text{Maths-course(C)} \leftrightarrow C{=}C101 \vee C{=}C301$$

$$\leftrightarrow \text{false} \vee \text{false}$$

$$\leftrightarrow \text{false}$$

$$\therefore \sim \text{Maths-course(C)}$$

This suggests a way of reconciling negation as failure with its truth functional semantics. We can assume that the clauses that appear in a logic data base B comprise just the if-halves of a set of if-and-only-if definitions of the data base relations, the only-if half of each definition being a completion law for the relation. The completed data base C(B) , implicitly given by the clauses of B, comprises this set of definitions together with a set of equality schemas which make explicit the convention that different object names denote different objects. If we can show that every failed attempt to prove P using just the data base of clauses B, is in effect a proof of ~ P using the completed data base C(B), then 'negation as failure' is just a derived inference rule for deductions from C(B).

In this paper we present just such a validation of the negation as failure inference rule. The structure of the paper is as follows. In the next section, Query Evaluation for a Data Base of Clauses, we make precise what constitutes a data base of clauses, a data base query, and the deduction process of query evaluation. As we describe it, query evaluation is a non-deterministic process for which every evaluation path either succeeds, or fails, or does not terminate. A negated literal ~ P is evaluated by recursively entering the query evaluator with the query P. If every possible evaluation path for P ends in failure, we return with ~ P evaluated as true. These recursively constructed failure proofs can be nested to any depth.

In the section, Data Base Completion, we define the completion of a data base of clauses. Then in the section, Correctness of Query Evaluation, we give the formal results validating the use of the negation as failure inference rule. We prove that a query evaluation will only produce results that are implied by the completed data base. The proof is constructive. It gives us a method for reformulating a query evaluation from the data base of clauses as a deduction from the completed data base. In the last section, Completeness of Query Evaluation, we address the issue of the deductive completeness of the query evaluation process. That is, we deal with the issue of whether or not there are answers to a query implied by the completed data base which are not the answer of any evaluation of the query.

As a final word of introduction we should say something about the relationship between the negation as failure inference rule treated here and the deduction rules considered by Kramosil [1975]. Kramosil shows that the adoption of sound deduction rules of the form

$$\text{from} \quad \vdash A, \ \sim\vdash B \quad \text{infer} \quad \vdash C$$

which contain preconditions such as $\sim\vdash B$ about unprovability of certain formula, cannot extend the class of theorems that are derivable in a first order theory. There are two differences between the negation as failure rule

$$\text{from} \ \vdash \sim\vdash P \quad \text{infer} \quad \vdash \sim P$$

and the rules to which Kramosil's result applies.

The first difference, which is not the major difference, is that the single rule that we consider has a definite and proscribed method for proving unprovability. It is, in fact, a relatively weak rule, for the unprovability condition is so strong. Kramosil leaves unspecified the means by which the unprovability of a formula would be determined.

The second, and crucial difference, is that his formal result applies only to inference rules that sit on top of a complete inference system for first order logic. However, the negation as failure inference rule sits on top of a resolution inference procedure which, without the rule, can only cope with Horn clause refutations. In other words, it is used to extend the deduction power of inference system that is <u>not</u> a complete deductive system for first order logic. We show that the enrichment of a Horn clause theorem prover with this inference rule is, at least when seeking answers to a query logically implied by the axioms of a completed data base, somewhat of an alternative to using a more conventional deductive system which is not restricted to Horn clauses.

QUERY EVALUATION FOR A DATA BASE OF CLAUSES

We assume a familiarity with the terminology of resolution logic (but see Chang and Lee [1973] for an introduction). The statements of the data base are a set of clauses each of which contains a distinguished positive literal. The relation of this literal is the relation that the clause is <u>about</u>. Using the notation of Kowalski [1978], the clauses are written as implications of the form

$$R(t_1,..,t_n) \leftarrow L_1 \& L_2 \& ... \& L_m \ , \ m \geq 0 \qquad (3)$$

Here, $R(t_1,\ldots,t_n)$ is the distinguished positive literal (so the clause is <u>about</u> the relation R), the $L_1,\ldots,L_m$ are all literals, and each free variable is implicitly universally quantified over the entire implication. In more conventional clause notation this would be written as the disjunction

$$R(t_1,\ldots,t_n) \vee \sim L_1 \vee \sim L_2 \vee .. \vee \sim L_m \tag{4}$$

Note that any other positive literal of the disjunctive form (4) will appear as a negated precondition of the implication (3). When m=0, we have a unit clause.

Example Data Base

Table 1 gives the clauses of a micro logic data base. The unit clauses, which are all ground, are the explicitly given relation instances. The single non-unit clause is a general rule for the relation Non-maths-major. Since the variable y appears only in the antecedent of this clause we can read it as

> Anything x is a Non-maths-major if there is a Maths-course y which x does not take.

The functor "." is simply a data constructor, constructing a compound name "J.Brown" from the initial "J" and the surname "Brown". Every functor of a logic data base has this data constructor role. In logic parlance, the functors implicitly have their free or Herbrand interpretation. In our example data base, if we required to refer to the surname or initial of a name separately, we would include the general rules:

Initial(x.y,x)←
Surname(x.y,y)←

Table 1. Micro Data Base

Student(J.Brown)←	
	Takes(J.Brown,C101)←
Student(D.Smith)←	
	Takes(D.Smith,C101)←
	Takes(D.Smith,C301)←
Maths-course(C101)←	
Maths-course(C301)←	
Non-maths-major(x) ← Maths-course(y) & ~ Takes(x,y)	

Queries

A query is a conjunction of literals written as

$$\leftarrow L_1 \& \ldots \& L_n$$

If $x_1,\ldots,x_k$ are the variables appearing in the query we interpret this as a request for a constructive proof that

$$(\exists x_1,\ldots,x_k)\ L_1 \& \ldots \& L_n \ ;$$

constructive in the sense that the proof should find a substitution

$$\theta = \{x_1/e_1, x_2/e_2, \ldots, x_k/e_k\}$$

such that

$$(L_1 \& \ldots \& L_n)\theta$$

is a logical consequence of the completed data base. θ is an answer to the query. For the time being we ignore the more general query which asks for the set of all answers.

Example Queries

The following are queries for the logic data base of Table 1.

(i) ←Student(x) & Takes(x,C101)

(ii) ←Student(x) & Non-maths-major(x)

(iii) ←Student(x) & ~ Non-maths-major(x)

The first is a request for the name of a student who takes course C101; the second is a request for a student who is a non-maths-major, for a student who does not take all the maths courses; in contrast the third is a request for a student who is <u>not</u> a non-maths-major, for a student who <u>does</u> take all the maths courses. In the relational calculus, or a more elaborate query notation, such a condition on the data to be retrieved would be expressed by the formula

(iv) ←Student(x) & ∀y[Maths-course(y) → Takes(x,y)]

in which the free variable x refers to the data to be retrieved. There is no reason why the user query language should not allow such general form queries. For, by the simple expedient of introducing clauses about auxiliary relations, we can translate such a query into our standard form of a conjunction of literals. Thus, the expression of query (iv) is equivalent to

$\leftarrow$Student(x) & $\sim\exists$y [Maths-course(y) & $\sim$ Takes(x,y)]

which is equivalent to

$\leftarrow$Student(x) & $\sim$ Non-maths-major(x)

where

Non-maths-major(x) $\leftrightarrow$ $\exists$y[Maths-course(y) & $\sim$ Takes(x,y)]

The if-halve of the definition of Non-maths-major is the clause about the relation that we included in the micro data base of Table 1. It was because of this that we were able to express query (iv) directly as the standard form query (iii). As we shall see, the presence of this single clause about Non-maths-major is tantamount to giving it to the above definition in the completed data base.

The Query Evaluation Process

The query evaluation process is essentially a linear resolution proof procedure with negated literals 'evaluated' by a failure proof. However we shall view the alternate derivations of the search space as different paths of a non-deterministic evaluation which can SUCCEED, FAIL or not terminate. A path terminates with SUCCESS if its terminal query is the empty query. The binding of the variables of the initial query induced by a successful evaluation is an answer to the query. A path terminates with FAILURE if the selected literal of its terminal query does not unify with the consequent literal of the selected data base clause. The literal is selected using a prescribed selection rule, but the subsequent selection of a data base clause, and the attempted unification, is a non-deterministic step of the evaluation. Finally, a non-terminating evaluation path comprises an infinite sequence of queries each of which is derived from the initial query as described below.

Evaluation Algorithm

Until an empty query is derived, and the evaluation succeeds, proceed as follows:

Using the selection rule, select a literal L_i from the current query $\leftarrow L_1\&\ldots\&L_n$. The selection rule is constrained so that a negative literal is only selected if it contains no variables.

Case 1

L_i is a positive literal $R(t_1,\ldots,t_n)$

Non-deterministically choose a database clause

$$R(t_1',\ldots,t_n') \leftarrow L_1'\&\ldots\&L_m'$$

about R and try to unify L_i, with $R(t_1',\ldots,t_n')$. If there are several data base clauses about R, the selection of a clause together with the attempted unification is a non-deterministic step in the evaluation. Each of the other clauses offer an alternative evaluation path. If L_i does not unify with $R(t_1',\ldots,t_n')$, FAIL (this path). If L_i does unify, with most general unifier θ, replace the current query with the derived query

$$\leftarrow\{L_1\&\ldots\&L_{i-1}\ \&\ L_1'\&\ldots\&L_m'\ \&\ L_{i+1}\&\ldots\&L_n\}\theta$$

Should there be no data base clauses about the relation of the selected literal, we consider that there is just one next step to the evaluation of the query

$$\leftarrow L_1\&\ldots\&L_n$$

which immediately FAILS.

Case 2

L_i is a negative ground literal $\sim P$. There is just one next step for the evaluation. This is the attempt to discover whether $\sim P$ can be assumed as a lemma. To do this we recursively enter the query evaluation process with $\leftarrow P$ as a query.

If the evaluation of $\leftarrow P$ SUCCEEDS, FAIL.

If the evaluation of $\leftarrow P$ FAILS for every path of its nondeterministic evaluation, assume $\sim P$ as a lemma. Hence replace the current query by

$$L_1\&\ldots\&L_{i-1}\ \&L_{i+1}\&\ldots\&L_n\ .$$

Remarks

(1) Note that in the special case that no negative literals appear in the query evaluation what we have described is essentially LUSH resolution (Hill [1974]), a linear resolution inference procedure for Horn clauses.

(2) Only the distinguished positive literal of each clause of the data base is a candidate for unification with a query literal. Other positive literals of the clause (that appear as negated preconditions of the implication) are never resolved upon; they can only be deleted after a failure proof.

(3) The different possible selections of a literal in a query do not provide alternatives for the evaluation process. However any

rule for selecting the literal can be used. The PROLOG selection rule is - always choose the leftmost literal in a query.

(4) The constraint that a negative literal should only be selected if it is ground is not a significant restriction. It just means that every variable appearing in a negated condition should have its 'range' specified by some unnegated condition. This is just the constraint that Codd imposes on the use of negation in his relational calculus.

(5) Let $\theta_1,\ldots,\theta_n$ be the sequence of unifying substitutions of a successful evaluation of some query Q. Let θ be the composition

$$\theta_1 \circ \theta_2 \circ \ldots \circ \theta_n$$

of these unifying substitutions. The subset of θ which gives the substitutions for variables of the query Q, augmented with the identity substitution for any variables of Q not bound by θ , is the answer given by the evaluation. If Q has no variables, the answer is <u>true</u>. On the other hand, if every evaluation path of the query Q ends with FAIL, the answer is <u>false</u>.

(6) Suppose that for some selection rule every branch of the evaluation tree rooted at a query Q terminates with a SUCCESS or FAIL. By König's Lemma (see Knuth [1968]), the evaluation tree contains a finite number of queries. Hence, by back-tracking when the non-deterministic evaluation succeeds or fails, we can find every answer of the evaluation tree. In the section, Completeness of Query Evaluation, we shall consider constraints which guarantee finite evaluation trees.

(7) Using Boyer and Moore [1972] structure sharing methods a back-tracking search for a successful evaluation can be achieved by manipulating a stack of activation records as in a more conventional computation. Broadly speaking, the currently derived query is represented by the entire stack. The i'th activation record on the stack records the subset of literals that were introduced at the i'th resolution step but which have not yet been deleted by a subsequent resolution. These literals are represented implicitly by a pointer to the data base clause that was used and a tuple of substitutions - the binding environment for this activation of the data base clause. The activation record also contains information about the data base clauses that have not yet been used to resolve on its literals. This information is used for back-tracking. Should one of these literals have a relation R that is extensionally characterised by a large set of unit clauses, the back-tracking information might be a pointer into a file of R-records. In which case a back-tracking search for a clause that matches the literal is just a search through the file. We can of course index the file to speed up the search. This is a very brief and slightly simpli-

fied description of the implementation possibilities. For more details the reader can consult Warren et al. [1977]. However, with the query evaluation process implemented using such techniques we can justly claim that its execution is a computational retrieval of information.

DATA BASE COMPLETION

Remember we are going to validate the query evaluation process as an inference not from the data base of clauses, but from the completed data base, the data base of definitions and equality schemas implicitly given by the set of clauses.

Suppose that

$$R(t_1,\ldots,t_n) \leftarrow L_1 \& \ldots \& L_m \tag{5}$$

is a data base clause about relation R. Where = is the equality relation, and $x_1,\ldots,x_n$ are variables not appearing in the clause, it is equivalent to the clause

$$R(x_1,\ldots,x_n) \leftarrow x_1=t_1 \& \ldots \& x_n=t_n \& L_1 \& \ldots \& L_m$$

Finally, if $y_1,\ldots,y_p$ are the variables of (5), this is itself equivalent to

$$R(x_1,\ldots,x_n) \leftarrow (\exists y_1,\ldots,y_p)[x_1=t_1 \& x_2=t_2 \& \ldots \& x_n=t_n \& L_1 \& \ldots \& L_m] \tag{6}$$

We call this the <u>general form of the clause</u>.

Suppose there are exactly k clauses, $k > 0$, in the data base about the relation R. Let

$$\begin{array}{l} R(x_1,\ldots,x_n) \leftarrow E_1 \\ \quad\vdots \\ R(x_1,\ldots,x_n) \leftarrow E_k \end{array} \tag{7}$$

be the k general forms of these clauses. Each of the E_i will be an existentially quantified conjunction of literals as in (6). The <u>definition of R</u>, implicitly given by the data base, is

$$(\forall x_1,\ldots,x_n)[R(x_1,\ldots,x_n) \leftrightarrow E_1 \vee E_2 \vee \ldots \vee E_k]$$

The if-half of this definition is just the k general form clauses (7) grouped as a single implication. The only-if half is the completion law for R.

Should there be no data base clauses for R, the definition implicitly given by the data base, is

$$(\forall x_1,\ldots,x_n)[R(x_1,\ldots,x_n) \leftrightarrow \text{false}]$$

Example

Suppose

$P(a)\leftarrow$

$P(b)\leftarrow$

$P(f(y)) \leftarrow P(y)$

are all the clauses about a unary relation P. Its disjunctive definition is

$$(\forall x)[P(x) \leftrightarrow x=a \lor x=b \lor \exists y[x=f(y)\&P(y)]]$$ ■

In moving to the disjunctive definitions from the original clauses we have been forced to introduce equalities. Thus the onus is upon us to say something about the equality relation for the objects of the data base. That is we need to state explicitly that the constants and functors have their free interpretation. The following schemas suffice. Each schema is implicitly universally quantified with respect to its variables.

$c \neq c'$ c,c' any pair of distinct constants (8)

$f(x_1,\ldots,x_n) \neq g(y_1,\ldots,y_m)$ f,g any pair of distinct functors (9)

$f(x_1,\ldots,x_n) = f(y_1,\ldots,y_n) \rightarrow x_1=y_1\&\ldots\&x_n=y_n$ f any functor (10)

$f(x_1,\ldots,x_n) \neq c$ f any functor, c any constant (11)

$\tau(x) \neq x$ $\tau(x)$ any term structure in which x is free (12)

Schema (8) tells us that different constants denote different objects. Schema (9) tells us that different functors are different data constructors, and (10) tells us that constructed objects are equal only if they are constructed from equal components. Axioms (11) and (12) together tell us that the data constructors always generate new objects.

The above axioms, together with the following general axioms for equality:

$$x = x$$

$$x = y \rightarrow y = x$$

$$x = y \,\&\, y = z \rightarrow x = z$$

Substitution schema:

$$x = y \rightarrow [W(x) \leftrightarrow W(y)], \text{ W any wff}$$

we call the identity theory for a completed data base.

The identity theory, together with the set of relation definitions implicitly given by a logic data base, constitute the completed data base.

Example

The definitions and axioms of Table 2 are the completed data base of Table 1. In the definitions each free variable is implicitly universally quantified.

CORRECTNESS OF QUERY EVALUATION

In this section we give the formal results that validate query evaluation from a data base of clauses as a first order inference from the completed form of the data base. The main results are Theorems 2 and 3. Theorem 2 is the validation of negation as failure. It is the proof that whenever for some selection rule every branch of the query evaluation tree ends in a failure, then the

Table 2. Completed Data Base of Table 1

Student(x) ↔ x=J.Brown ∨ x=D.Smith
Maths-course(x) ↔ x=C101 ∨ x=X301
Takes(x,y) ↔ x=J.Brown & y=C101 ∨ x=D.Smith & y=C101 ∨ x=D.Smith & y=C301
Non-maths-major(x) ↔ (∃y)[Maths-course(y) & ~ Takes(x,y)]
For any other relation, a definition that it is always false.
The identity theory

construction of the tree is in effect a proof that there are no answers to the query. Theorem 3 is a generalisation of this result for an evaluation tree every branch of which terminates with a failure or a success. It tells us that the set of answers given by the success branches are provably the only answers to the query. Each of these theorems relies on Theorem 1. Roughly speaking, this tells us that a query Q is equivalent to the disjunction of the queries derivable from Q by resolving on any positive literal. This, in turn, relies on the fact that by using the identity theory we can emulate unification by inference about equalities:

Lemma

(1) If $R(t_1,\ldots,t_n)$ unifies with $R(t'_1,\ldots,t'_n)$ with m.g.u.

$$\theta = \{x_1/e_1,\ldots,x_k/e_k\}$$

then, using the identity theory of the completed data base, the conjunction of equalities

$$t_1=t'_1 \;\&\ldots\&\; t_n=t'_n$$

is provably equivalent to

$$x_1=e_k \;\&\ldots\&\; x_k=e_k$$

(2) If $R(t_1,\ldots,t_n)$ does not unify with $R(t'_1,\ldots,t'_n)$ then, using the identity theory,

$$t_1=t'_1 \;\&\ldots\&\; t_n=t'_n$$

is provably equivalent to false.

Proof

For brevity we simply sketch the proof. What is needed is an induction on the number of steps of an attempt to unify the two literals. Schema (10) of the identity theory is used to infer e=e' where e and e' are corresponding sub-terms which differ. If e is a variable and e' a term in which the variable does not appear, we use the substitution schema for equality to 'apply' the substitution {e/e'}. Otherwise, one of the inequalities (8), (9), (11) or (12) gives us the contradiction. ■

Our first theorem is a direct application of this lemma and the fact that the completed data base defines a relation as the disjunction of antecedents of its general form clauses. To state it we need the concept of the general form of a derived query.

Definition

Let Q' be the query derived from some query Q by selecting a positive literal $R(t_1,...,t_n)$ and resolving with a data base clause C. The general form of the resolvent Q' is

$$(\exists y_1,...,y_p)[z_1=e_1 \& ... \& z_k=e_k \ \& \ Q']$$

Where $\{z_1/e_1,...,z_k/e_k\}$ is the subset of the m.g.u. θ which applies to variables of Q, and $y_1,...,y_p$ are the variables of data base clause C that remain in $e_1,...,e_k$ or Q'. ■

Theorem 1

Let Q be a query which contains the positive literal $R(t_1,...,t_n)$. Suppose $Q_1,...,Q_j$ are all the alternative queries that are derivable from Q by resolving on $R(t_1,...,t_n)$ with some data base clause about R. If $G_1,...,G_j$ are the general forms of these derived queries

$$Q \leftrightarrow G_1 \vee G_2 \vee .. \vee G_j$$

is a theorem of the completed data base. If j=0, i.e., there are no queries derivable from Q by resolving on $R(t_1,...,t_n)$, then

$$Q \leftrightarrow \text{false}$$

is a theorem of the completed data base. ■

The proof of this theorem is quite straightforward. We are now in a position to establish our first main result. We want to show that the construction of a failure evaluation tree - an evaluation tree every branch of which terminates with a failure - is tantamount to a first order proof that the root query has no solutions.

Figure 2 gives the structure of such a failure evaluation tree. Every branch of the tree, every evaluation path, ends at a terminal query Q' whose off-springs are all failure nodes. We want to prove that whenever some query Q is the root of a failed evaluation tree

$$Q \leftrightarrow \text{false}$$

or, equivalently

$$\sim (\exists z_1,...,z_n)Q$$

where $z_1,...,z_n$ are the free variables of Q, is a theorem of the completed data base.

As a special case let us consider a failure tree T which records the top-level structure of a failure proof that does not depend on any subsidiary failure proofs. For such a failure tree the selected literal of the root query Q must be a positive literal $R(t_1,\ldots,t_n)$, with $Q_1,\ldots,Q_j$ the set of resolvents with the data base clauses about R. But Theorem 1 tells us that

$$Q \leftrightarrow G_1 \vee .. \vee G_j$$

where $G_1,\ldots,G_j$ are the general forms of $Q_1,\ldots,Q_j$. Clearly, if each of the Q_i is provably equivalent to false so is its general form. What we need therefore is an induction of the structure of T.

The above use of Theorem 1 is our induction step. The base case of the induction is established by considering the two single query failure trees of Figure 3 and Figure 4.

Theorem 1 again covers the case of Figure 3. When T is as depicted in Figure 4 it records a failure proof of the root query because the recursively entered evaluation of $\leftarrow P$ has succeeded. But in this case the successful evaluation of $\leftarrow P$ will be a resolution proof of P. It would be other than a straightforward resolution proof only if it involved the failure proof of some negated literal. However we have discounted this possibility by our assumption that the failure tree records a failure proof that does not

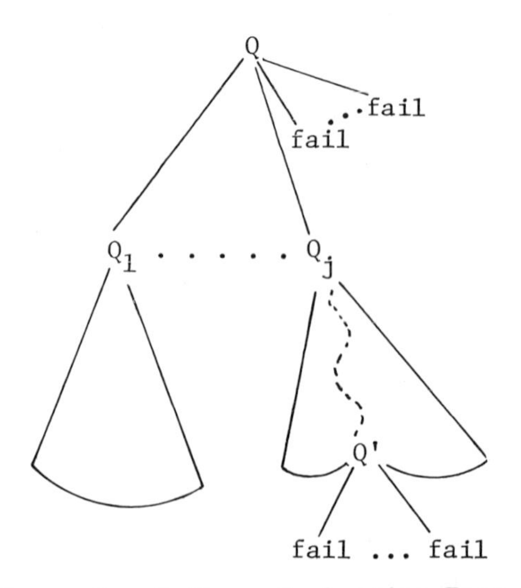

Figure 2. Failure Evaluation Tree

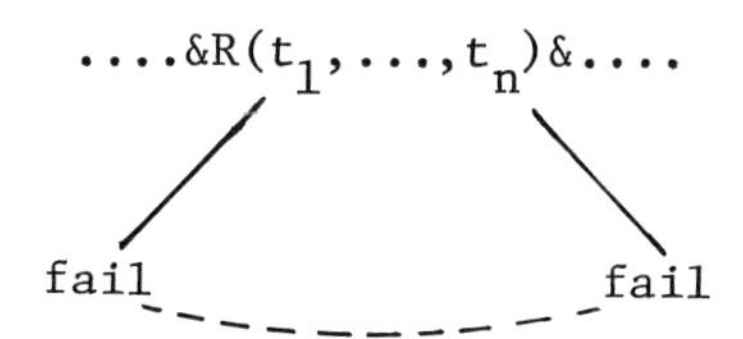

$R(t_1,\ldots,t_n)$ fails to unify with any data base clause about R.

Figure 3. Single Failure Tree

depend on any subsidiary failure proofs. Moreover, a resolution proof of P from the data base of clauses is also a proof that

$$\sim P \leftrightarrow \text{false}$$

from the completed data base. Hence the root query is again provable equivalent to false.

We now need to establish the result for a failure tree T whose construction may depend on auxiliary failure proofs. Since the number of such auxiliary proofs must be finite, we do this by an induction on the number, n, of these auxiliary failure proofs.

The above argument establishes the base case, n=0, of this induction. Let us now assume that the root query of a failure tree whose construction depends on less than n subsidiary failure proofs is provably equivalent to false. Let T be a failure tree whose construction depends on at most n failure proofs $n > 0$.

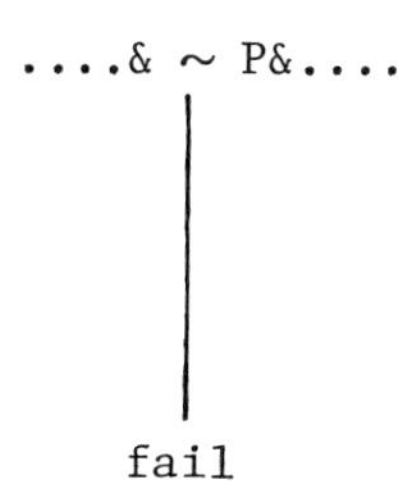

A query evaluation for $\leftarrow P$ succeeds.

P is a ground literal

Figure 4. Single Failure Tree

As above, we show that the root query of T is provably equivalent to false by a secondary induction of the structure of T. Again the base cases of this structural induction are as depicted in Figures 3 and 4. As before, Theorem 1 covers the case of Figure 3. However, this time the single query tree of Figure 4 records a successful evaluation of $\leftarrow P$ which may depend on a failure proof of some negated literal $\sim L$, this failure proof being the construction of a failure tree rooted at L. But such a failure proof can itself make use of at most n-1 subsidiary failure proofs. By the induction hypothesis

$$L \leftrightarrow \text{false}$$

and hence

$$\sim L$$

is a theorem of the completed data base. This applies to any failure proved negated literal selected in the evaluation of $\leftarrow P$. The deletion of such a negated literal can therefore be regarded as a resolution step which uses a lemma $\sim L$ of the completed data base. Since every other step in the evaluation of $\leftarrow P$ is just a resolution with a data base clause, we have again that

$$\sim P \leftrightarrow \text{false}.$$

is a thoerem of the completed data base.

The induction step of our structural induction on T is just a slight elaboration of the argument for the special case failure tree that required no subsidiary failure proofs. This time we must also consider the failure tree structure depicted in Figure 5. Here the root query has a single off-spring derived by deleting a negated literal $\sim L$, which has been failure proved. But again the failure proof of $\sim L$

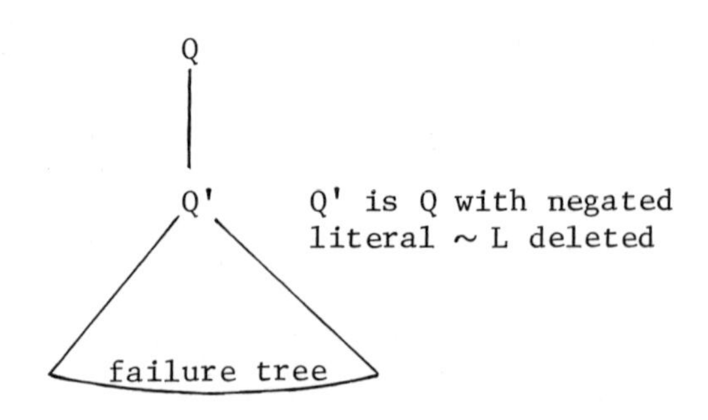

Figure 5. Failure Trees

can itself depend on at most n-1 failure proofs, so $\sim L$ is a theorem of the completed data base. Therefore

$$Q \leftrightarrow Q'$$

is also a theorem. But Q' is the root of a sub-tree which is a failure tree, so

$$Q' \leftrightarrow \text{false}$$

and hence

$$Q \leftrightarrow \text{false}$$

as required. We have proved:

Theorem 2

If for some literal selection rule every branch of the evaluation tree of a query $\leftarrow Q$ terminates with failure, then

$$\sim(\exists x_1,\ldots,x_k)Q$$

where $x_1,\ldots,x_k$ are the free variables of Q, is a theorem of the completed data base. ■

Let us now look at the case of a successful query evaluation. By the above theorem, any failure evaluation of a negated literal $\sim L$ that it might use can be viewed as the derivation from the completed data base of a lemma $\sim L$. Thus the whole evaluation can be viewed as a linear resolution proof using the data base clauses (the if-halves of the relation definitions) and a set of negated ground literal lemmas. Suppose that the answer given by the successful evaluation is

$$\theta = \{x_1/e_1,\ldots,x_i/e_i,x_{i+1}/x_{i+1},\ldots,x_k/x_k\}$$

$x_1,\ldots,x_i$ being the subset of the free variables $x_1,\ldots,x_k$ of the query Q that are bound by the evaluation. By the soundness of resolution

$$(\forall x_{i+1},\ldots,x_k)(\forall y_1,\ldots,y_n)Q\theta\ ,$$

where $y_1,\ldots,y_n$ are the extra free variables of $Q\theta$ introduced by the substitution θ , is a theorem of the completed data base.

It follows that

$$(\forall x_1,\ldots,x_i,x_{i+1},..,x_k)(\forall y_1,\ldots,y_n)[x_1=e_1\&\ldots\&x_i=e_i \rightarrow Q]$$

is also a theorem. Finally, since $y_1,..,y_n$ were introduced by θ and do not appear in Q, this is equivalent to

$$(\forall x_1,\ldots,x_k)[(\exists y_1,\ldots,y_n)(x_1=e_1\&\ldots\&x_i=e_i) \rightarrow Q]$$

Let us call the antecedent of this conditional the general form of the answer θ, and denote it by $\hat{\theta}$.

Suppose now that there are exactly j successful evaluations of the query $\leftarrow$Q with answer substitutions $\theta_1,\ldots,\theta_j$. Then we know that

$$(\forall x_1,\ldots,x_k)\ [\hat{\theta}_1 \rightarrow Q]$$
$$\vdots$$
$$(\forall x_1,\ldots,x_k)\ [\hat{\theta}_j \rightarrow Q]$$

are all theorems of the completed data base. Suppose further that every other branch of the evaluation tree (constructed using some particular selection rule) ends in a failure node. By an exhaustive search we can discover that there are no other solutions given by this evaluation tree. We should like to know no other evaluation tree would provide us with an extra solution. Assuming that the completed data base is consistent, this is guaranteed by:

Theorem 3

If for some literal selection rule every branch of the evaluation tree of a query $\leftarrow$Q ends with a success or failure, and $\theta_1,\ldots,\theta_j$ are all the answers given by the evaluation paths that end in success, then

$$(\forall x_1,\ldots,x_k)[Q \leftrightarrow \hat{\theta}_1 \vee \hat{\theta}_2 \vee .. \vee \hat{\theta}_j]$$

is a theorem of the completed data base. Here, $x_1,\ldots,x_k$ are the free variables of Q and $\hat{\theta}_1,\ldots,\hat{\theta}_j$ are the general forms of the answers. ■

The proof is a straightforward induction on the structure of the evaluation tree.

Example Application of Theorem 2

Figure 6 is the failure tree generated by the PROLOG selection rule for the query $\leftarrow$Non-maths-major(D.Smith). The proof of Theorem 2 gives us a method for lifting this failure tree into a first order proof of

$\sim$ Non-maths-major(D.Smith).

We simply climb down the tree substituting for each query the disjunction of general forms of its immediate descendents. By Theorem 2 each substitution preserves equivalence. For FAIL we substitute false. This deduction, with some intermediary steps inserted, is :-

$$\text{Non-maths-major(D.Smith)}$$

$$\leftrightarrow \exists y[\text{Maths-course}(y) \,\&\, \sim\text{Takes(D.Smith},y)] \quad \text{by definition of Non-maths-major}$$

$$\leftrightarrow \exists y[(y=\text{C101} \vee y=\text{C301}) \,\&\, \sim\text{Takes(D.Smith},y)] \quad \text{by definition of Maths-course}$$

$$\leftrightarrow \exists y[y=\text{C101} \,\&\, \sim\text{Takes(D.Smith},y) \vee y=\text{C301} \,\&\, \sim\text{Takes(D.Smith},y)]$$

$$\leftrightarrow \sim\text{Takes(D.Smith,C101)} \vee \sim\text{Takes(D.Smith,C301)}$$

$$\leftrightarrow \sim\text{true} \vee \sim\text{true}$$

$$\leftrightarrow \text{false}$$

$$\therefore \sim\text{Non-maths-major(D.Smith)} \blacksquare$$

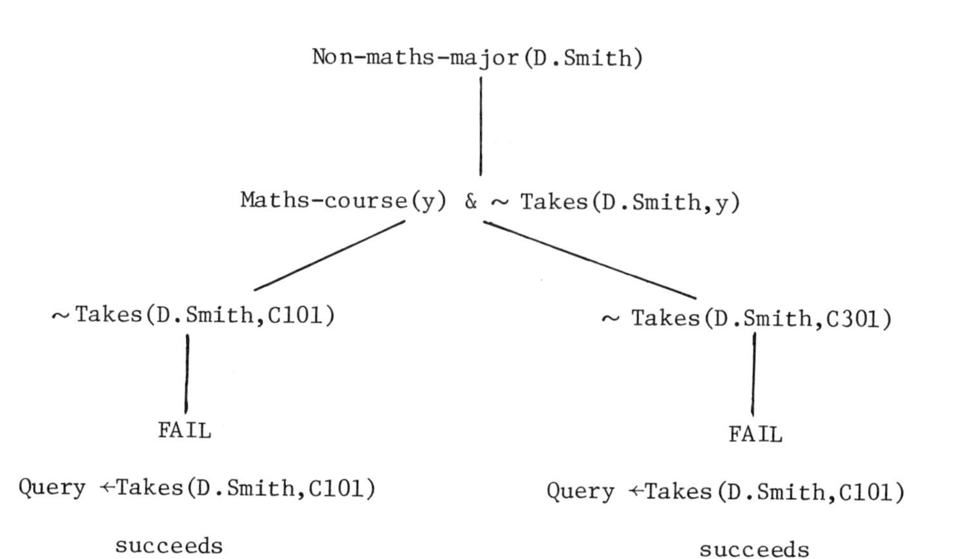

Figure 6. Failure Tree Generated by PROLOG Selection Rule

COMPLETENESS OF QUERY EVALUATION

We have argued that the evaluation of a query can and should be viewed as a deduction from the completed data base. However, when we evaluate a query, that is try to discover whether or not some instance is implied by the completed data base, we ignore the completion laws and inequality schemas. As a substitute we augment a Horn clause theorem prover for the remaining if-halves of the relation definitions - the data base clauses - with our negation as failure inference rule. Is this an adequate substitute? Will we still be able to infer every answer to the query implied by the completed data base? With certain restrictions on the data base and its queries, yes. In general, no.

Let us look at the ways in which query evaluation falls short of a complete inference system. To begin with there is the restriction that our failure inference rule should only be applied to a ground literal. With this restriction we cannot even begin to answer a query

$$\leftarrow \sim R(x,a)$$

which is a request for any x not related to a by R. We could relax this restriction on failure proofs. Let us suppose that the recursively entered evaluation of $\leftarrow R(x,a)$ constructs a failure tree rooted at $R(x,a)$. By Theorem 2 we can infer $(x)\sim R(x,a)$, giving as an answer to the query the identity substitution x/x. We can also give an answer when the evaluation of $\leftarrow R(x,a)$ succeeds, providing the answer is the identity substitution x/x. For in this case the evaluation is a proof of $(x)R(x,a)$, i.e. $\sim \exists x \sim R(x,a)$. So false is the answer to the query $\leftarrow \sim R(x,a)$. However, should we have a successful evaluation of $\leftarrow R(x,a)$ with an answer other than the identity substitution we cannot conclude anything about the query $\leftarrow \sim R(x,a)$. To patch our query evaluation process in this circumstance, we would need to resort to a systematic search for a ground instance of $\sim R(x,a)$ that can be failure proved. But of course, just such a systematic search will be invoked by the modified query,

$$\leftarrow Q(x) \& \sim R(x,a)$$

providing $Q(x)$ only has ground solutions. Our insistence that queries must have this form is a requirement that the querier must implicitly constrain the search.

The second limitation associated with failure proofs is much more serious. It is the fact that we search for a failure proof by constructing just one evaluation tree.

For a query that has a successful evaluation we do not have to search alternative evaluation trees, at least not for the top-level deduction. This is because at the top-level we can view each deletion of a negated literal as a resolution step. Thus, the evaluation is in essential respects a Horn clause refutation. In the search for such a refutation we know we need only consider one selection rule (Hill [1974]). In other words, if a successful evaluation of a query Q with answer substitution θ appears on one evaluation tree rooted at Q, then it appears on every evaluation tree rooted at Q. The problem arises when we recursively enter the query evaluation process to check that some negated literal $\sim P$ is indeed a lemma of the completed data base. When we do this, to grow just one evaluation tree is to risk 'missing' a failure proof.

Suppose we have the following clauses in the data base,

P(x) ← Q(y) & R(y)
Q(h(y)) ← Q(y)
R(g(y))←

and we want to failure prove ~ P(a). If we use the PROLOG selection rule, and always select the leftmost literal, we get an evaluation tree with a single infinite branch (see Figure 7a). Using another selection rule, in fact any other rule in this instance, we get a finite failure tree (see Figure 7b).

A complete search for a failure proof should therefore search over the space of alternative evaluation trees. That is the different selections of a literal in a query should be treated as alternatives when we search for a failure proof. Interestingly, the different ways of resolving on the selected literal are not alternatives for a failure proof. Every one of them must eventually be investigated and shown to FAIL. This gives us a nice duality between search for a successful evaluation, and search for a failure proof.

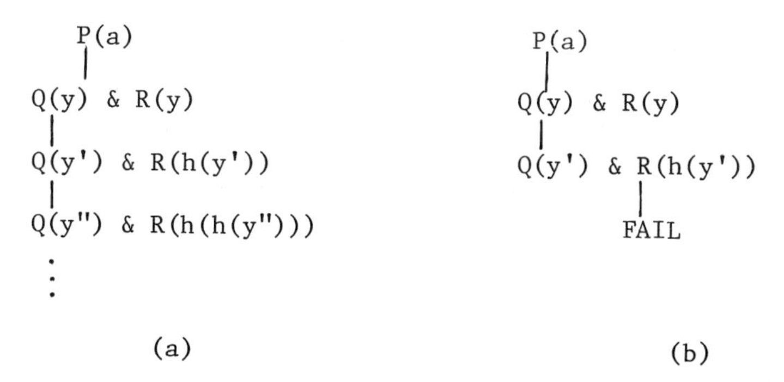

Figure 7. Incompleteness of PROLOG Selection Rule

We have seen that we might miss the failure proof of some negated literal $\sim P$ by restricting ourselves to the construction of just one evaluation tree rooted at P. In consequence, we may not be able to successfully complete a query evaluation that depends on the lemma $\sim P$. However, this very insistence that all negated literals should be inferred as lemmas; and the consequent neglect of a case analysis proof - check if the same answer is given on the assumption that P is true, and on the assumption that P is false - is another hole in the query evaluation process.

The following clauses give an example of this:

$$
\begin{aligned}
&R(x,y) \leftarrow P(x) \;\&\; Q(x,y)\\
&R(x,y) \leftarrow \sim P(x) \;\&\; T(x,y)\\
&P(x) \leftarrow P(f(x))\\
&Q(a,b) \leftarrow\\
&T(a,b) \leftarrow
\end{aligned}
\qquad (13)
$$

R(a,b) is implied by these clauses. This is because

$$R(x,y) \leftarrow Q(x,y) \;\&\; T(x,y) \qquad (14)$$

is a consequence of the two clauses for R. If we resolve these two clauses on the 'test' literal P(x) we get

$$R(x,y) \vee R(x,y') \leftarrow Q(x,y) \;\&\; T(x,y'),$$

which we can factor to give (14). Clause (14) tells us that no matter whether P(x) is true or false we can conclude R(x,y) if only Q and T can 'agree' on y. R(a,b) is now an immediate consequence of (14) and the ground clauses for Q and T. However, no evaluation of the query

$$\leftarrow R(a,b)$$

which uses only the given clauses (13) can terminate. This is because the single clause for P, which amounts to a definition

$$\forall x[P(x) \leftrightarrow P(f(x))]$$

in the completed data base, does not allow us to prove or disprove P(a), and the query evaluator insists on the proven truth or falsity of every literal encountered in the evaluation. Like intuistionist logic, the query evaluator does not countenance the law of the excluded middle

$P \vee \sim P$.

Put another way, it treats

$P \vee Q$

as a statement that is true only when $\vdash P$ or $\vdash Q$.

There is also an interesting analogy with the two different interpretations that can be given to the conditional expression

if P(x) then q(x) else t(x)

in a more conventional programming formalism. For any x, the value is g(x) if P(x) is true, and t(x) if P(x) is false. But what if P(x) is undefined, i.e., its evaluation for some argument x does not terminate, just as our evaluation of $\leftarrow$P(a) does not terminate. The 'sequential' semantics for the conditional says that the conditional is undefined. The 'parallel' semantics says that it is undefined except in the special case that g(x) and t(x) agree, i.e. return the same value. In this case the value of the conditional is this common value. This is precisely what derived clause (15) asserts. First order logic, then, insists on the 'parallel' semantics. Our query evaluation gives us the 'sequential'.

Finally, let us note that an SL refutation (Kowalski and Kuehner [1971]) used to evaluate the query would cope with the case analysis allowed by classical logic by an ancestor resolution.

Where does that leave us? In the light of the above shortcomings is query evaluation as we have described it worth considering? It is, because as we have already remarked, coupled with a back-tracking search strategy it can be most efficiently implemented. Can we perhaps side-step its inadequacies?

Firstly, the constraint that every variable in a negated literal should have its range specified by an unnegated literal that will generate a candidate set of ground substitutions is perfectly acceptable. Let us call this an allowed query. For an allowed query no evaluation can flounder because it encounters a query with only unground negative literals. (Remember the literal selection rule is constrained so that it can only select a negative literal if it is ground.) Now suppose that for some given data base we can define a literal selection rule such that the evaluation tree for every allowed query is finite. Providing the completed data base is consistent (and I think that the finiteness of every evaluation tree guarantees this, although I have not checked it out) query evaluation is complete. This is because the back-tracking traversal of the finite evaluation tree will find each and every answer given by a successful evaluation path, and Theorem 3 tells us that these are the only answers. Note that a proof that a data base + selection rule has a finite evaluation tree for each and every query is a termination proof for the data base viewed as a non-deterministic program, each posed query being a 'call' of the program.

With regards providing such a termination proof for a data base I have no ready suggestions, although I think it is an interesting area to explore. Typically we might have to modify the selection rule and perhaps further restrict the legitimate queries as a data base evolves. We can however lay down a strong but quite general condition for a logic data base which ensures termination of every allowed query evaluation for <u>any</u> selection rule. It is that each relation R of the data base, whether it be explicitly or implicitly defined, should have finite extension that can be computed by constructing any evaluation tree for the query

$$\leftarrow R(x_1, \ldots, x_k)$$

Let us call this the condition of <u>computable finite extensions</u>.

It is quite easy to show that for a data base which only has computable finite extensions the evaluation tree for an allowed query

$$\leftarrow L_1 \;\&\; L_2 \;\&\ldots\&\; L_n$$

is finite no matter what selection rule is used. Remember that any variable in a negative literal appears in some positive literal for which there are only computable ground solutions. So negative literals present no problem, all selection rules being constrained to select a negative literal only after it has become ground. We leave the reader to provide the termination proof for a query comprising only positive literals. There is a slight complication due to the fact that we can, in effect, coroutine between the evaluations of

$$\leftarrow L_1, \leftarrow L_2, \ldots, \leftarrow L_n$$

We can now come back on ourselves and use this result to specify a hierarchical data base in which each relation does have a computable finite extent, hence a data base with the termination property for any selection rule. The clauses of the data base must be such that they can be grouped into disjoint sequence of sets

$$S_0, S_1, \ldots, S_n$$

which satisfy the following condition.

Let us call a relation R of the data base in i-level relation if it is completely specified by the clauses in

$S_0 \cup S_1 \cup \ldots \cup S_i$

That is, there are no clauses about R, or any relation referred to directly or indirectly by the clauses for R, that are outside this set. The data base of clauses satisfies the hierarchical constraint if:

(i) S_0 is the set of all unit clauses which all ground

(ii) S_{i+1} only contains clauses of the form

$L \leftarrow L_1 \ \& \ .. \ \& \ L_n$

where the antecedent $L_1 \& .. \& L_n$ is an allowed query using only j-level relations, $j \leq i$.

Note that this rules out recursive or mutually recursive definitions of relations. It is, unfortunately, a very strong constraint. It derives from the data base structuring proposals of Reiter [1977].

By an induction on i, it is easy to show that each i-level relation has a computable finite extent. Each 0-level relation is a relation completely defined by a set of ground instances. The induction step makes use of the fact that each i+1 level relation that is not also an i-level relation is defined by a set of clause each of which has a precondition

$\leftarrow L_1 \ \& \ .. \ \& \ L_n$

which is an allowed query about j-level relations, $j \leq i$, i.e. relations with computable finite extents. The details are quite straightforward. Another induction on i can be used to prove the consistency of the completed data base. The induction step is a proof that we can extend the model for the completion of $S_0 \cup .. \cup S_i$ to a model for the completion of $S_0 \cup \ldots \cup S_i \cup S_{i+1}$. We can conclude:

Theorem 4

For a data base satisfying the hierarchical constraint the evaluation process for allowed queries is complete. ■

The hierarchical constraint guarantees that our query evaluation process will be find each and every answer to a query. Is it too restrictive? Perhaps, but it still characterizes a data base which generalizes a conventional relational data base in the following respects:

(1) We can define the computable finite extensions of the relations by a set of instances, or by general rules, or by a mixture

of both.

(2) The components of a relation are not restricted to strings and numbers. They can be quite general data structures (terms of the logic program).

(3) The clausal notation fills the role of data description language, query language and host programming language. Indeed, a data base is just a logic program with a large number of ground clauses. This multi-role aspect of logic programs is more fully explored by van Emden [1978] and Kowalski [1978].

(4) Finally, the retrieval of information is not just a search over a set of files. It genuinely involves a computational deduction.

FINAL REMARKS

We have shown that the negation as failure inference rule applied to a data base of clauses is a sound rule for deductions from the completed data base. As a generalization of this, we have shown that an exhaustive search for solutions to a query, if it returns a finite set of solutions, is a proof that these are exactly the set of solutions. We have described a query evaluation process for a data base of clauses which uses negation as failure as its sole proof rule for negated literals. Although it is in general not complete, its chief advantage is the efficiency of its implementation. Using it the deductive retrieval of information can be regarded as a computation. However, by imposing constraints on the logic data base and its queries, which generalise the constraints of a relational data base, the query evaluation process is guaranteed to find each and every solution to a query.

ACKNOWLEDGMENTS

I have benefited much from discussions with Bob Kowalski and Maarten van Emden. The research was supported by the Science Research Council.

REFERENCES

1. Boyer, R.S. and Moore, J.S. [1972] The Sharing of Structure in Theorem Proving Programs. In *Machine Intelligence 7* (B. Meltzer and D. Michie, Eds.), Edinburgh University Press, 101-116.

2. Chang, C. L. and Lee, R.C.T. [1973] *Symbolic Logic and Mechanical Theorem Proving*, Academic Press, New York, 1973.

3. Codd, E. F. [1970] A Relational Model for Large Shared Data Banks, *CACM 13*, 6 (June, 1970), 377-387.

4. Codd, E. F. [1972] Relational Completeness of Data Base Sub-languages, In *Data Base Systems* (R. Rustin, Ed.), Prentice-Hall, 65-98.

5. Hewitt, C. [1972] Description and Theoretical Analysis (Using Schemata) of PLANNER: A Language for Proving Theorems and Manipulating Models in a Robot, *A. I. Memo No. 251*, MIT Project MAC, 1972.

6. Hill, R. [1974] Lush-Resolution and Its Completeness, *DCL Memo No. 78*, Department of Artificial Intelligence, Edinburgh University, 1974.

7. Knuth, D. [1968] *Fundamental Algorithms, The Art of Computer Programming, Vol. 1*, Addison-Wesley, Reading, Mass, 1968.

8. Kowalski, R. and Kuehner, D. [1971] Linear Resolution with Selection Function, *Artificial Intelligence 2*, 3/4 (1971), 221-260.

9. Kowalski, R. [1978] Logic for Data Description, In *Logic and Data Bases* (H. Gallaire and J. Minker, Eds.), Plenum Press, New York, N.Y., 77-103.

10. Kramosil, I. [1975] A Note on Deduction Rules with Negative Premises, *Proceedings IJCAI 4*, Tbilisi, USSR, 1975, 53-56.

11. Nicolas, J. M. and Gallaire, H. [1978] Data Bases: Theory vs. Interpretation, In *Logic and Data Bases* (H. Gallaire and J. Minker, Eds.), Plenum Press, New York, N.Y., 1978, 33-54.

12. Reiter, R. [1978] On Closed World Data Bases, In *Logic and Data Bases* (H. Gallaire and J. Minker, Eds.), Plenum Press, New York, N.Y., 1978, 55-76.

13. Reiter, R. [1977] An Approach to Deductive Question-Answering, *BBN Report No. 3649*, Bolt, Beranek and Newman, Cambridge, Mass., 1977.

14. Roussel, P. [1975] PROLOG: Manual d'Utilisation, *Rapport Interne, G.I.A., UER de LUMINY*, Universite d'Aix-Marseille, 1975.

15. van Emden, M. [1978] Computation and Deductive Information Retrieval, In *Formal Description of Programming Concepts*, (E. Neuhold, Ed.), North-Holland, 1978.

16. Warren, D., Pereira, L. and Pereira, F. [1977] PROLOG - The Language and Its Implementation Compared with LISP, *Proceedings of SIGART/SIGPLAN Conference on Programming Languages*, Rochester, New York, 1977.

LOGIC
AND
DATA BASE INTEGRITY

INTEGRITY CHECKING IN DEDUCTIVE DATA BASES

J. M. Nicolas and K. Yazdanian

ONERA-CERT

Toulouse, France

ABSTRACT

This paper is concerned with the use of general laws in data bases. It consists of two main parts respectively devoted to state laws and to transition laws. Some of the state laws are used as derivation rules while others are used as integrity rules. Integrity rules as well as derivation rules can be treated in many ways which are presented. For each such method, the actions to be undertaken when querying, adding, suppressing and updating information in the data base are studied. For transition laws, a formalism is proposed which enables them to be handled in the same way as integrity rules stemming from state laws. The self-consistency of transition laws is also discussed.

INTRODUCTION

A data base defined on a world can be seen as an interpretation of a first order theory, where the non logical axioms are general laws perceived on the world. There are two types of laws: (1) transition laws dealing with world evolution, and (2) state laws dealing with informations in a single state of the world. In the first section we discuss the different types of laws, and we also make some remarks on the origin of laws relevant to data bases and on the nature of operations on data bases.

Notwithstanding their partition between integrity rules and derivation rules (see Nicolas and Gallaire [1978]), state laws can be used in many ways which are presented in the section Handling State Laws. For each such method we study actions to be undertaken in each utilization phase of a data base. Integrity has also been discussed by other authors such as Abrial [1976] in a procedural context, Hammer and McLeod [1975] from a general specification viewpoint, Stonebraker [1974,1975] for a specific implementation.

Transition laws are studied in the section Formalization and Exploitation of Transition Laws. A formalism is given which allows them to be handled in the same way as integrity rules stemming from state laws. Their self-consistency problem is also touched upon in this last section.

VARIOUS TYPES OF LAWS

State Laws and Transitions Laws

A data base state is a snapshot of the world with which it is dealing. Worlds to be considered in data base applications are evolving and this evolution is accounted for through three out of the four standard operations on data, i.e. the operations of adding, of suppressing, and of updating. Each such operation triggers a change in the state of the data base. However, all data base states are not valid ones and integrity rules are precisely used to characterize valid states.

General laws which are considered by Nicolas and Gallaire [1978], are laws referring only to one state of the world: the current state independent of previous or future states. Such laws are generally called state laws. They are interpreted as integrity rules by restricting valid states of the data base to models of a first order theory (T) which has these laws, expressed by logical formulas (wffs), as proper axioms. However, characterizing valid states only through state laws is not sufficient. One must take into account laws relative to world evoluation, i.e. laws constraining consecutive states of the data base. Such laws are usually called transition laws. Their net effect is to restrict valid states to a subset of models of theory T defined above. Because they link together informations on different interpretations, transition laws cannot be treated directly as proper axioms of T; we shall see in the section Formalization and Exploitation of Transition Laws how to handle them.

A Few Remarks on the Nature of Operations and on the Origin of Laws Relevant to a Data Base

For a given application, laws stem from the modelled world and are to be used as rules (integrity and derivation) on the data base. But one should notice that another family of rules have to be expressed in a data base. These rules are introduced by the data base administrator depending on the choice of relations he makes to represent informations. An example will help in characterizing this second family of rules. The following example is borrowed from Date [1975] and reproduced by Cadiou [1976].

Let us consider a world constituted of students, teachers and courses, in which teachers teach courses and students take courses. Two laws* are observed on this world: "A teacher only teaches one course" and "A student does not take the same course from several teachers". Informations perceived on this world can be represented either through the two binary relations T1 (TEACHER, COURSE) and T2 (STUDENT, TEACHER) or with the ternary relation TE (STUDENT, COURSE, TEACHER). For reasons out of the scope covered here, Cadiou considers the second choice. But in this case, as quoted by Cadiou, there is no way to keep the information that a teacher is assigned to a course before there are students registered in it. A solution consists in supplementing TE with another relation TE' (TEACHER, COURSE) which will be used to hold the information that a teacher teaches a course when no information is available on students taking the course. Thus a new rule, which does not stem from the considered world, has to be introduced: "A teacher shall never be in TE and TE' at the same time". This last rule, expressed as

$$\forall x\ (\neg \exists y\ \exists z\ TE\ (z,y,x) \vee \neg \exists u\ TE'\ (x,u)) ,$$

precisely belongs to our second family of rules.

Although they come from different sources, these two families of rules are expressed in a similar way, and will be used similarly too. But we wanted to emphasize that it would be useless to wish to check the validity of all operations on a data base only through laws stemming from the world.

Similarly, among all operations on a data base, two classes have to be distinguished. Some update operations are a direct translation of an evolution of the world, while others are modifications of incorrectly registered data (e.g.: error handling). If the former operations have to be such that all the rules are satisfied, it would be quite incorrect to make it compulsory for each of the latter operations to be controlled by all these rules. Thus some laws must be inhibited during certain operations.

HANDLING STATE LAWS

In the following we will consider that a data base is viewed as described in the third approach by Nicolas and Gallaire [1978]. Briefly, in this approach, the data base constituted by the set of

---

* These two laws are of a particular kind of general law usually called functional dependencies (see Date [1975]).

elementary informations, is viewed as an interpretation of a first order theory whose proper axioms are the general laws (only state laws were considered). But, instead of using all these laws as integrity rules, some of them are proposed to be used as derivation rules. Thus the extensions of relations are both defined explicitly and implicitly.

We discuss below how each type of rule can be handled and we also consider some aspects of integrity recovery. As far as integrity recovery is concerned, we assume that all of the general laws are accepted* and whenever a conflict between general laws and elementary informations is detected, the elementary informations are to be suspected first.

Integrity Rules (I-rules)

I-rules have to be used essentially when one of the three operations of adding, suppressing or updating the data base takes place. When such an operation deals with elementary informations - i.e. a tuple of a given relation - two questions arise. First, which rules have to be activated? That is, which rules might be falsified by this operation, and thus shall be evaluated on the interpretation in order to determine whether they are effectively falsified. Second, if a rule is falsified, which actions are to be taken?

Activating I-rules. In order to determine which rules to activate, we will consider the corresponding wffs to be in a special form, called the Skolem standard form (see Chang and Lee [1973]). Briefly, this standard form is the conjunct of the clauses corresponding to the wff, all variables being universally quantified. For example the Skolem standard form of the wff "$\forall x(\neg \exists y\ P(x,y) \vee (Q(x) \wedge R(x)))$" is

$$\forall x\ \forall y\ ((\neg P(x,y) \vee Q(x)) \wedge (\neg P(x,y) \vee R(x)) .$$

Let SW be the Skolem standard form of a wff W. In all interpretations in which SW is true, W is true, therefore starting from an interpretation in which SW and W are both true, if SW remains true in the new interpretation obtained by an operation on the data base, then so does W. Furthermore, as SW is a conjunct of clauses, it will remain true if and only if each of the clauses remains true. Consequently, we can now reason on these clauses.

We shall find it convenient to rewrite a clause into an equivalent form. A clause is a disjunction of literals where a literal is either a positive atom or a negative atom. Let the clause be

---

* The self-consistency of state laws is addressed in Nicolas and Gallaire [1978].

$\neg P \vee \cdots \vee \neg P_n \vee Q_1 \vee \cdots \vee Q_m$, where the atoms P_i, $i=1,\ldots,n$ are negated in the clause, and the atoms Q_j, $j=1,\ldots,m$ are not negated. Then, the clause may be written as an implication clause, as,

$$P_1 \wedge \cdots \wedge P_n \rightarrow Q_1 \vee \cdots \vee Q_m .$$

An I-rule clause is such that m and n are both not null, because if they were, we would have the empty clause, and the corresponding I-rule would be always invalid.

When I-rules are in the form of implication clauses, we may reason about them as follows. Let us call P the left hand part and Q the right hand part of the implication. Suppose $P \rightarrow Q$ is true, then, according to the semantics of the connector "imply", either P and Q are both true, or P is false, Q being true or false. So, when information is suppressed in one P_i or is added in one Q_j, $P \rightarrow Q$ will remain true. The following results can then be stated:

- when adding* (respectively, suppressing) a tuple in a relation R, activate (i.e. undertake the test of) only those I-rules where R appears in the left hand (respectively, right hand) part (of one of its clauses).

- when updating a tuple in a relation R, all rules where R appears have to be activated, no matter where R appears.

These results will be examplified in the following section.

Integrity recovery. Two types of actions can be though of when rules are falsified.

(i) The first action consists of denying the operation which yielded an invalidation of this rule, and in giving this rule to the user. At this point the user can do one of two things. Either he accepts this denial, or he does an extra operation on the data base, prior to retrying the original one, until it does not falsify this rule (nor any other).

Example: Let us consider the relations TE and TE' from the section entitled "A Few Remarks...", and the rules dealing with them:

I1 : $\forall x \ldots \forall z \quad (TE(x,y,z) \wedge TE(x',y',z) \rightarrow (y=y'))$

---

* Adding or suppressing information can be implicit. We shall detail this point in the section d-rules and their Coexistence with I-rules. Also, an update can be logically seen as an indivisible sequence "suppress, add", at least as far as state laws are concerned.

I1' : $\forall x \forall y \forall y'$ $(TE'(x,y) \wedge TE'(x,y') \rightarrow (y=y'))$

I2 : $\forall x \ldots \forall z'$ $(TE(x,y,z) \wedge TE(x,y,z') \rightarrow (z=z'))$

I3 : $\forall x\ (\neg \exists y\ \exists z\ TE(z,y,x) \vee \neg \exists u\ TE'(x,u))$

The rules I1, I1' and I2 are already in Skolem standard form with clauses written as in the preceding section. The standard form of rule I3 is: $\forall x \ldots \forall u\ (TE(z,y,x) \wedge TE'(x,u) \rightarrow\ )$.

Let us now suppose that TE and TE' extensions are in the following state:

TE (STUDENT, COURSE, TEACHER)

STUDENT	COURSE	TEACHER
s1	c1	t1
s2	c1	t1
s1	c2	t2

TE' (TEACHER, COURSE)

TEACHER	COURSE
t3	c3

The reader can easily verify that I1, I1', I2 and I3 are true in this interpretation.

Consider now the following operation: add < t2,c2 > in TE'. According to the results of the preceding section (Activating I-rules), only I1' and I3 have to be evaluated on the new interpretation (the extension of TE' being augmented with the tuple < t2,c2 >). It happens that while I1' remains true, I3 is falsified by the adding operation because a teacher cannot be in TE and TE' at the same time. Consequently, this operation is rejected. Now, due to the semantics of TE and TE', the user will certainly conform to the first attitude presented in point i) above, i.e.: simply accept this denial.

Let us consider another operation: add < s3,c3,t3 > in TE. This time, I1, I2 and I3 have to be activated. It happens that only I3 is falsified by the adding operation which then will be rejected. Again, the rejection is because a teacher cannot be in TE and TE' at the same time. But this time, after being notified of the refusal, the user will certainly conform to the second attitude presented in point i) because a teacher is in TE' when no students have been specified for the course. However, now a student has been specified for the course. Hence, according to the semantics of TE and TE', he should suppress < t3,c3 > in TE'. Following this operation, the request to add < s3,c3,t3 > in TE would then be obeyed.

ii) The second action which could be undertaken when a rule is made invalid, amounts to automating the process just described as the second user's behaviour. That is, instead of rejecting the operation, accept it and generate another operation such that the rule would be satisfied. In the example above the operation "add < s3,c3,t3 > in TE" would then be accepted and the operation "suppress < t3,c3 > in TE' " would be generated.

But the problem is now to determine what operation must be generated. For a given rule, $A_1 \wedge \ldots \wedge A_n \rightarrow B_1 \vee \ldots \vee B_m$, when an addition on A_i invalidates the law, any operation which would either falsify the left part, or validate the right part, can be used to make the law valid again. Hence, suppress on A_j* and add on B_k are candidates for re-validating this law. Two solutions can easily be thought of. Either limit the automation to specific rules (syntactic restrictions), or give the user a way to indicate which operations he wants to privilege (i.e. which operation to do between all those possible: suppression on A_j or addition on B_k).

We shall notice, however, that it is possible that, for certain kinds of laws, operations to be privileged not only depend on this law, but also on the type of operation which first made it invalid. This is precisely so in the example presented in case i) above.

In SEQUEL2 (Chamberlin et al. [1976]), the so-called "triggers" enables the system to provide some automatic integrity recovery. But in a "trigger" the rule (even if implicitly expressed) and the way it is used are merged (Eswaran and Chamberlin [1975]). If there are several ways to use a rule, depending on the operation that invalidates it, they are defined in different "triggers", and then the rule is "duplicated". Our belief is that describing how to use a law is a separate issue from stating a law. See for example Demolombe and Nicolas [1976] where we argue for the need of expressing how to manipulate informations in a language different (co-language or meta-language) from the language in which informations is stated. This yields two advantages. First, we only have one statement of the law, thus avoiding potential incompatibility between different occurrences of the law. Second, we keep an assertional (or declarative) representation of the law, which allows for a possible checking of its consistency with respect to the laws.

Derivation Rules (d-rules) and their Coexistence with I-rules

For reasons explained in Nicolas and Gallaire [1978], d-rules are restricted to be Horn clauses with exactly one positive literal. D-rules are used to deduce informations. However it is possible to exploit them during two separate phases of data base manipulation: either during a query phase when looking for deducible yet implicit informations, or during the information entry phase to generate (and thus make explicit) informations deducible from the informa-

---

* For j=i we get back to case i) which appears as a particular case of ii).

tion entered. In the first (respectively second) case we say that d-rules are used in query (respectively generation) mode and we shall talk about query-d-rules (respectively generation-d-rules). Note that the difference between query-d-rules and generation-d-rules is about the same as the difference between antecedent theorems and consequent theorems in Planner (see Hewitt [1971]).

For a given law there is a similarity between its use as a generation-d-rule and as an I-rule with automatic integrity recovery. In order to make clear this similarity, let us consider a very simple example. Let $P(x) \rightarrow Q(x)$ be a law and suppose the extensions of P and Q only contain the element a. When an operation such as "add b in P" occurs then:

- if the above law is used as a generation-d-rule then Q(b) will be inferred and b added to the extension of Q.

- if the law is used as an I-rule, it is falsified by the operation and one way to revalidate it consists in generating the operation "add b to Q".

The coexistence of d-rules and I-rules will make it necessary to use a deduction process in several phases of data base manipulation. We are to study this problem for each of the possible usages of d-rules.

<u>Coexistence of I-rules and Query-d-rules</u>.

i) <u>querying</u> - Because deducible informations are implicit, a deduction process is obviously needed in the query phase. And, each time a given relation will appear in different queries, its implicit extension will have to be derived again. These derivations can be run either with a top-down or a bottom-up search, depending on the search strategy used. Either it tries to decompose the query into subqueries until it yields only subqueries evaluable on the extensional data base, or it tries to build instances of the query from the extensional relations of the data base (see Minker and VanderBrug [1975] or Kowalski [1974, 1976], or the Gallaire, Minker, and Nicolas paper in this book). But a top-down search appears to be more natural with query-d-rules.

ii) <u>adding information</u> - Introducing information will clearly modify the explicit extension on a relation, and sometimes the implicit extension of other relations which can be subject to I-rules. In order to determine whether these I-rules are falsified or not, the implicit informations have to be derived. Thus, the deduction process has to run during the add operation phase.

Adding information can yield a redundancy between implicit

information and explicit information; however, this redundancy shall not be eliminated because it comes from different perceptions of the world. Consider a query-d-rule $P(x) \rightarrow Q(x)$ and the explicit information Q(a). When adding the explicit information P(a) we are in a redundant state, where the information Q(a) comes from a direct observation of Q(a), while the redundant (implicit) information comes from the knowledge of P(a). Suppose that in order to eliminate this redundancy the explicit information Q(a) is suppressed. Now, if P(a) is suppressed the information Q(a) is completely lost. But, due to world evoluation, P(a) may become false at some time, while Q(a) remains true. Then an explicit information shall not be suppressed in order to eliminate a redundancy with an implicit one.

iii) suppressing information - When suppressing explicit information, it is possible to modify implicit extensions of other relations. It must then be determined which relations are so modified, so as to activate the corresponding I-rules.

Furthermore it must be verified whether the information to be suppressed cannot be obtained implicitly too. Were this the case, it would then be necessary to act as follows: when the information to be suppressed is implicit, one must find the explicit informations and laws which allow for its deduction. The user is supplied with the explicit informations and he can then request again his information manipulation in terms of the explicit informations.

Coexistence of I-rules and Generation-d-rules

i) adding informations - When adding information, one must find through a deduction process all informations that can be deduced from the added information and make them explicit. This deduction process now runs bottom-up. For reasons linked to suppression of information (see below), it will be useful to memorize redundancies when they exist.

ii) suppressing informations - Due to the fact that deduced informations have been made explicit in the add operation phase, the information to be suppressed can be:

- a deduced information obtained from other informations called antecedent informations,

- the antecedent itself of informations called derived informations.

Suppressing information necessitates a particular treatment with respect to its antecedent, or to its derived informations when they exist.

Derived informations. When suppressing information, it is necessary to suppress its derived informations in as much as they are not deducible from other informations, nor given explicitly. For instance consider laws $P(x) \to Q(x)$ and $R(x) \to Q(x)$ and information P(a), which produces Q(a). When suppressing P(a), then Q(a) must be suppressed too, unless R(a) is known to be true, or Q(a) has been explicitly entered.

Two cases can be considered, depending on whether redundancies are memorized, in order to handle the hypothetical suppression of derived informations. If they are not memorized, then, when information is explicitly suppressed, each of its derived informations have to be found; and for each of them it must be determined whether they can be obtained through another way. Thus, this leads to the necessity to run two nested deduction processes. In order to avoid this, one can consider memorizing redundancies. This should not be done by actually representing each occurrence of the redundant information, but by associating to a unique occurrence, a counter which holds the occurrences number for it. This counter shall be incremented (or set to one) during the adding process when derived informations are generated. It will be decremented during the suppressing process, a derived information being suppressed when its counter takes the null value.

In order to make more precise the management of such a counter let us define what we will call a one step derivation. It corresponds to applying a d-rule once rather than applying an inference rule once (as in resolution). For example, given P(a), Q(a) and the two d-rules $P(x) \wedge Q(x) \to R(x)$ and $R(x) \to S(x)$, we will say that R(a) is derived in one step from P(a), as well as from Q(a) whereas S(a) is derived in two steps from them.

Adding information will now imply that the following process is to be run:

> If the added information is already in the data base, the only action to execute, is to increment by one the counter associated with it. Otherwise, introduce the information in the data base, set its counter to one, generate all informations derivable from it in one step, and repeat the whole process for each entry generated.

Example:

Consider the three following d-rules: $P(x,y) \wedge Q(y,z) \to R(x,z)$, $P(x,y) \wedge T(y,z) \to R(x,z)$, $R(x,y) \wedge S(x) \to U(x,y)$ and suppose that the data base is in the following state :

$Q(b,c)^{[1]}$, $T(b,c)^{[1]}$, $S(a)^{[1]}$. Now what happens when the operation "add < a,b > in P" occurs? First, $P(a,b)^{[1]}$ is added to the data base, then R(a,c) is generated twice. Adding its first occurrence to the data base will lead to $R(a,c)^{[1]}$ and in the same way to $U(a,c)^{[1]}$. Adding its second occurrence will simply lead to $R(a,c)^{[2]}$. Now, the data base is in the following state: $P(a,b)^{[1]}$, $Q(b,c)^{[1]}$ $T(b,c)^{[1]}$, $R(a,c)^{[2]}$, $S(a)^{[1]}$, $U(a,c)^{[1]}$.

Before describing the suppresion process, two remarks can be make. First, because generation-d-rules are applied on finite set of elements they will lead to a finite number of derivations. Second, according to the addition process, when inforamtion is entered explicitly several times, the counter associated with it is incremented by one each time. This does not matter, because when entered explicitly, information must only be suppressed explicitly; and in this case the counter is set to zero as described in the suppression process.

The suppression process is as follows:

The counter associated with the information to be suppressed is set to zero, i.e. the information is actually suppressed. Then, the counters associated with each information which was derivable in one step from the suppressed one, are decremented by one (as many times as there are different ways to get them). The process is iterated, for all informations the counter of which has taken the value zero. It stops when no such counter is found.

Let us consider the data base (in the last state) of the preceding example. If the operation "suppress < b,c > in Q" occurs, then Q(b,c) will be suppressed and the counter associated with R(a,c) will be decremented by one. If, instead of the prededing one the following operation occurs "suppress < a,b > in P", then P(a,b) will be suppressed, and because its counter will have been decremented twice, R(a,c) will be suppressed too and finally so is U(a,c).

Antecedent information. Here, the problem is analogous to what we discussed in the suppression phase for query-d-rules. One must find all information and all laws from which the information to be suppressed was derivable. This time, however, because deduced informations have been made explicit, this search can only be carried out step by step. Having suppressed the informations, one has to find generation-d-rules which are falsified by this new suppression, and repeat this treatment until a suppression does not falsify any rule. All of this yields a quite complex process.

iii) querying - Having made the deduced informations explicit when adding informations, query evaluation is done on extensions of relations that are purely explicit. Thus, no deduction is necessary in this phase.

FORMALIZATION AND EXPLOITATION OF TRANSITION LAWS

As opposed to state laws, transition laws link together information on different states of the world. Then, a priori, then cannot be expressed in the same way as the latter ones and be considered as the proper axioms of a first order theory which admits the data base as a model. But, we will see that, with an ad-hoc extension of the data base, that can in fact be done.

As far as one wants to express a transition law by means of a wff, the wff should take the FALSE value when an operation on the data base is not compatible with the law it represents, and the TRUE value otherwise. To do so, we must extend the data base by introducing new relations. These relations will be defined from both the other relations in the data base and actions which are achievable on them.

We shall call these new relations "<u>action relations</u>". With each relation R in the data base, three action relations will be associated, one for each of the three operations: update, deletion and enter. In the following, these action relations are noted as follows: UPD-R, DEL-R, and ENT-R.

Transition laws which are considered in the following are only concerned with two states, referred to as the old state and the new state. We note that transition laws dealing with more than two states can, by suitable transformation, be reduced to an equivalent transition law dealing with two states.

UPD-R Type Relations

If R is an n-ary ($n \geq 2$) relation, then UPD-R is a 2n-ary relation. The meaning of a 2n-tuple $< a_1,\ldots,a_n,\ a_1',\ldots,a_n' >$ in the extension of UPD-R is: the tuple $< a_1,\ldots,a_n >$ of R is being updated and the corresponding new values are $< a_1',\ldots,a_n' >$ *. The UPD-R extension is always empty, except when an update operation is attempted on R. In order to define how a transition law can be expressed in terms of such an action relation, let us make precise the connection between a transition law and an update operation.

Let us call $X = \{x_1,\ldots,x_n\}$ the set of arguments of the relation R. An update operation on a tuple of R may modify simultaneously several of its elements. Thus any update operation defines a partition of the arguments of R into two sets (one of them pos-

---

* In this section, primed symbols refer to the new state, while unprimed symbols refer to the old state.

sibly empty): those modified (say M) and those unmodified (say UM).

Also, a transition law on R expresses a constraint on the variation of some arguments while some others may stay invariant, the remaining ones (if any) being irrelevant to the law. Let us call respectively V and I the first two sets of arguments. It follows that the properties below are obviously verified: $I \subset X$, $V \subset X$, $I \cap V = \emptyset$, $I \neq \emptyset$ and $V \neq \emptyset$.

As an example, let us consider the relation $PAS(x_1,x_2,x_3)$. The meaning of a tuple < p,a,s > in this relation is that person p has age a and salary s. The law that "for any person, his age can only increase" defines the following partition on X: $I = \{x_1\}$, $V = \{x_2\}$, $X - \{I \cup V\} = \{x_3\}$. Clearly, the constraint on x_2 must be enforced only for updatings modifying x_2 while keeping x_1 constant.

More generally, the constraint expressed by a law must be enforced only for those actions keeping the invariant arguments constant and modifying at least one variant argument, i.e.: $UM \supseteq I$, $M \cap V \neq \emptyset$.

This implies that the wff which corresponds to a law be:

- true, whether the constraint is satisfied or not, for update operations which do not satisfy the conditions above;

- true or false depending on whether the constraint is satisfied or not, for other update operations.

Such a wff could be* of the following form:

$$\forall x_1 \ldots \forall x'_n \; [(\text{UPD-R}\;(x_1,\ldots,x_n,x'_1,\ldots,x'_n) \wedge [(x_{i_1} = x'_{i_1}) \wedge \ldots \wedge (x_{i_p} = x'_{i_p})] \wedge [(x_{v_1} \neq x'_{v_1}) \vee \ldots \vee (x_{v_q} \neq x'_{v_q})]) \rightarrow \text{CONSTRAINT}(x_{v_1},x'_{v_1},\ldots, x_{v_q},x'_{x_q})]$$

where $I = \{x_{i_k}\}$ $k = 1,\ldots,p$.

$V = \{x_{v_j}\}$ $j = 1,\ldots,q$ and $p + q \leq n$.

For the preceding example, the wff corresponding to the law will be:

---

* Of course, other wffs than the proposed one, which also satisfy the preceding conditions can be found.

$$\forall x_1 \ldots \forall x_3' [(\text{UPD-PAS}(x_1,x_2,x_3,x_1',x_2',x_3') \wedge (x_1=x_1') \wedge (x_2 \neq x_2')) \rightarrow (x_2' > x_2)]$$

Assuming that there exists another law enforcing the increase of salary for a given person, the corresponding wff would be:

$$\forall x_1 \ldots \forall x_3' [(\text{UPD-PAS}(x_1,x_2,x_3,x_1',x_2',x_3') \wedge (x_1=x_1') \wedge (x_3=x_3')) \rightarrow (x_3' > x_3)]$$

We shall notice that on an update operation which affects both x_2 and x_3, and keeps x_1 unmodified, both wffs will have their left side true and then both constraints will have to be satisfied. However, when an updating concerns only either x_2 or x_3, this will be true only for the corresponding wff.

The constraints of the preceding example use only the ">" connective which is a predefined relation in any data base system. But, of course, relations in constraints are not restricted to be only predefined relations.

As an example, let us consider a relation FS(x,y), where y is the family situation of some person x; y may take the value: single, married, divorced, etc... For a given person, all transitions are abviously not possible, for a person may go into the state "divorced" only when he is in the state "married". A single expression may define some transition rules concerning the updatings of the relation FS:

$$\forall x \ldots \forall y' [(\text{UPD-FS}(x,y,x',y') \wedge (x=x') \wedge (y \neq y')) \rightarrow \text{VALT}(y,y')]$$

Here VALT is a relation which defines the valid transitions. Its extension could be:

VALT (x	, y)
single	married
married	divorced
married	widowed
widowed	married
divorced	married

DEL-R (delete) and ENT-R (enter) Relations

Given a relation R, DEL-R (respectively ENT-R) is the action relation associated with the operation DELETE (respectively ENTER). The semantics of its arguments are identical to those of R. The extension of DEL-R (respectively ENT-R) is made of the tuple to be deleted (respectively entered) whenever a delete (respectively enter) operation takes place on relation R, and empty otherwise. Let us give an example, using a relation INCOME(x,y) the extension of which corresponds to couples (employee, income). Let us suppose that lay-off of employees whose income is less than a given minimum Sl should be prevented. The constraint is expressed as follows:

$\forall x \; \forall y \; (\text{DEL - INCOME}\ (x,y) \rightarrow (y \geq \text{Sl}))$

One should note that this transition law has no equivalent state law.

Since an ENTER operation preserves information of the previous state in the next state, one could think that ENTER constraints might be expressed by state laws. In fact, this is not possible, for there is a fundamental difference between a state law and a transition law. The constraint associated with a transition law has to be satisfied only at the time the operation occurs, while a state law must be always valid and thereby a state law is more constraining.

Let us make this point more precise through the following example. Let LOAD(x,y,z) and STATUS(x,y) be two relations, their intended meaning being defined as follows:

- a tuple < p,t,r > satisfies the relation LOAN iff person p gets a loan of type t whose reference is r.

- a pair < p,s > satisfies the relation STATUS iff the status of person p is s, where s is either: state, private, military,...

Consider the following law: In order to qualify for an ACEF type loan a person must be state employed. But it is a fact that if a person changes status after getting the loan he (or she) is still awarded the loan.

It is this last point that makes the preceding law a transition law and not a state law. Thus, it will be expressed as:

$\forall x \; \forall y \; [\text{ENT-LOAN}\ (x,\text{ACEF},y) \rightarrow \text{STATUS}\ (x,\text{State})]$

whereas a state law would have been expressed as

$\forall x \; \forall y \; [\text{LOAN}\ (x,\text{ACEF},y) \rightarrow \text{STATUS}\ (x,\text{State})]$

requiring that a person keeps his status in order to preserve his loan.

Laws for Multiple Actions

So far we have been concerned only with laws associated with one operation or simultaneous operations on the same tuple. We shall now consider transition laws imposing relationships between different actions.

In a world composed of employees (with grade and income) let us consider the law: "a change in grade must be accompanied by a change in income". We assume that there is no known function which given a grade determines an income: if such a function existed, it would be expressed by a state law.

Let INC(x,y) and GRADE(x,z) be the relations; the transition law is expressed as follows:

$$\forall x \forall y \forall z \forall y' \forall z' [(\text{UPD-GRADE}(x,z,x,z') \wedge (z \neq z')) \rightarrow (\text{UPD-INC}(x,y,x,y') \wedge (y \neq y'))]$$

It seems clear that, if both updatings are not performed concurrently (though both actions may lead to a valid state), the wff will not be verified during the transient state. Therefore it is necessary to define composite actions considered as indivisible with respect to the verification of integrity.

<u>Note</u>: If, instead of the two relations INC(x,y) and GRADE(x,z), only one relation, say INGR(x,y,z), had been used to represent the same informations, then the same transition law would have been expressed by:

$$\forall x \ldots \forall z' [(\text{UPD-INGR}(x,y,z,x',y',z') \wedge (x=x') \wedge [y=y') \vee (z=z')] \rightarrow (y \neq y')]$$

or equivalently by:

$$\forall x \ldots \forall z' [\text{UPD-INGR}(x,y,z,x',y',z') \wedge (x=x') \wedge (z=z') \rightarrow (y \neq y')]$$

Consistency of Transition Rules

In the preceding paragraphs of this section we made no difference between transition laws and transition rules. Here we will "restrict" transition rules to transition laws which are verified when no action occurs. Obviously, only transition rules are relevant to a data base, because the other transition laws would imply continuous operations*. An example will make this point clearer; but first we show that any set of transition rules is consistent.

By means of action relations, transition rules are expressed as wffs. Thus the consistency of a set of transition rules is the same problem as the consistency of a set of wffs. By "construction", such a wff is true in the data base extended with action relations, when there is no operation on the data base. Thus,

* As far as time is not explicitly represented in the data base.

every interpretation in which all action relations have an empty extension, satisfies any set of such wffs. Because a set of wffs is consistent iff there exists an interpretation that satisfies it (i.e.: a model), any set of transition rules is consistent.

How will this result be interpreted?

This result is precisely due to the fact that transition laws which are not verified when no action occurs, are not transition rules.

Example:

INC(x,y) is a relation, L1 and L2 a couple of rules for it and W1 and W2 the corresponding wffs:

L1 : "When varying, an income shall increase."

W1 : $\forall x\ \forall y\ \forall y'\ ((\text{UPD-INC}(x,y,x,y') \wedge (y \neq y')) \rightarrow (y' > y))$

L2 : "When varying, an income shall decrease."

W2 : $\forall x\ \forall y\ \forall y'\ ((\text{UPD-INC}(x,y,x,y') \wedge (y \neq y')) \rightarrow (y' < y))$

Both rules are not contradictory as they are verified altogether in a world where incomes are not subject to change. However, L1, L2 and the following law L3: "an income must vary"

W3 : $\forall x\ \forall y\ \forall y'\ (\text{UPD-INC}(x,y,x,y') \wedge (y \neq y'))$

are not consistent.

Although there is no consistency problem for a set of transition rules, situations in which such a set prevents all operations of a given type on a relation have to be determined. In order to do that, it is sufficient to prove that the wff expressing the forbidding of any action of that type for this relation, is a logical consequence of the set of rules.

It should be noted that such a situation is not unacceptable per se. One may actually wish to forbid any operation of a given type for a given relation. This can easily be done with a single rule. For example:

$\forall x\ \forall x'\ \forall y\ \forall y'\ (\text{UPD-INC}(x,y,x',y') \rightarrow (x=x') \wedge y=y'))$

would prevent all updating operations on the relation INC.

CONCLUSION

In Nicolas and Gallaire [1978], a formalization of data bases is proposed in which the set of elementary informations is seen as an interpretation of a first order theory whose proper axioms are the general laws. However, if an "interpretation" is only defined in the usual way, only laws referring to informations in a given state (state laws) can be taken into account. In order to deal in a similar way with laws referring to informations in several states (transition laws), it has been necessary to extend these "interpretations" by introducing particular relations called action relations.

The above classification of laws is syntactic. Considering their use, a different partition has been achieved, distinguishing laws used as integrity rules (I-rules), and on the other hand, laws used as derivation rules (d-rules) which must satisfy syntactic constraints (see Nicolas and Gallaire [1978]). Then, for each kind of rule, the handling of these rules in the different phases of data base manipulation has been considered. We brought to light that d-rules could be used either during update (so as to generate and make explicit deducible informations), or during the query phase (so as to determine those deducible yet implicit informations). We showed that, due to coexistence of these rules with integrity rules, the choice made is responsible for the activation frequency of the deduction process.

This study is to be followed by an implementation of these results in a specific conceptual model. We believe that a model based on atomic relations (see Demolombe and Nicolas [1977]) is the most appropriate.

ACKNOWLEDGMENTS

The authors would like to thank the referees for their helpful comments on this paper.

This work was supported by the DRET with a contribution from the CNRS.

REFERENCES

1. Abrial, J. R. [1974] Data Semantics, *Proceedings of Working Conference on Management of Data*, Cargese, France, April 1974, 1-59.

2. Cadiou, J. M. [1976] On Semantic Issues in the Relational Model of Data, In *Mathematical Foundations of Computer Science* (A. Mazurkiewiz, Ed.), Vol. 45, Springer-Verlag, 1976, 23-38.

3. Chamberlin, D.D. et al.[1976] SEQUEL2: A Unified Approach to Data Definition, Manipulation, and Control, *IBM Journal of Research and Development 20*, 6 (Nov. 1976), 560-575.

4. Chang, C. L. and Lee, R.C.T. [1973] *Symbolic Logic and Mechanical Theorem Proving*, Computer Science and Applied Mathematics, Academic Press, Inc., New York (1973).

5. Date, C. J. [1975] *An Introduction to Data Base Systems*, Addison-Wesley, Reading, Mass., 1975.

6. Demolombe, R. and Nicolas, J. M. [1976] Knowledge Representation and Evolutivity in Data Base Management Systems, *T-Report CERT-LBD-76/5*, Toulouse, France (Nov. 1976).

7. Demolombe, R. and Nicolas, J. M. [1977] Normal Form and Irreducible Relations. Atomic Relations: A New Proposal, *T-Report CERT-LBD-77/2*, Toulouse, France (Oct. 1977).

8. Eswaran, K. P. anc Chamberlin, D. D. [1975] Functional Specifications of a Subsystem for Data Base Integrity, *Proceedings of the Int. Conference on VLDB*, Framington, Mass., Sept. 1975, 48-68.

9. Hammer, M. M. and McLeod, D. J. [1975] Semantic Integrity in a Relational Data Base System, *Proceedings of the Int. Conference on VLDB*, Framington, Mass., Sept. 1975, 25-47.

10. Hewitt, C. [1971] "PLANNER: A Language for Providing Theorem and Manipulating Models in Robots," Ph.D. Thesis, M.I.T., Cambridge, Mass., Feb. 1971.

11. Kowalski, R. A. [1974] Logic for Problem Solving, *Memo. 75*, Department of Computational Logic, University of Edinburgh, (March 1974).

12. Kowalski, R. A. [1976] Algorithm = Logic + Control, Imperial College, London, (Nov. 1976).

13. Minker, J. and VanderBrug, G. [1975] State Space Problem Resolution and Theorem Proving - Some Relationships, *CACM* (Feb. 1975), 107-115.

14. Nicolas, J. M. and Gallaire, H. [1978] Data Base: Theory vs. Interpretation, In *Logic and Data Bases* (H. Gallaire and J. Minker, Eds.), Plenum Press, New York, 1978, 33-54.

15. Stonebraker, M. [1974] High Level Integrity Assurance in Relational Data Base Management Systems, *Mem. ERL-M473*, University of California, Berkeley, California, August 1974.

16. Stonebraker, M. [1975] Implementation of Integrity Constraints and Views by Query Modification, *Proceedings of the 1975 SIGMOD Conference*, San Jose, California, May 1975, 65-78.

QUERY LANGUAGES AND APPLICATIONS

THE APPLICATION OF PROLOG TO THE DEVELOPMENT OF QA AND DBM SYSTEMS

I. Futó, F. Darvas, and P. Szeredi

NIM IGÜSZI

Budapest, Hungary

ABSTRACT

Experience gained in the development of Question-Answering (QA) and Data Base Management (DBM) systems using a logic-based, very high level language, PROLOG, is summarized. The PROLOG language is introduced first. Those modifications to the language that were necessitated by the above applications are described. Subsequently, an experimental QA system dealing with drug data and drug interactions, and two operative DBM systems are described. Finally, some advantages obtained in using PROLOG for QA and DBM system implementations are discussed, and continued developments of PROLOG are presented.

INTRODUCTION

PROLOG (PROgramming language based on LOGic) is a programming language based on a restriction of the first-order predicate calculus that permits only Horn clauses. It has a built-in mechanical theorem-prover which operates in a top-down, depth-first manner. A brief introduction to PROLOG is presented below. The PROLOG language was developed at Marseille (Battani and Meloni [1973]), and is based on work by Kowalski [1974].

A Clause Form of Propositions

A proposition in clause form is a set

$\{C_1,........,C_n\}$

of the clauses C_i. A <u>clause</u> is a set of literals

$$\{+B_1, \ldots\ldots, +B_m, -A_1, \ldots\ldots, -A_n\}.$$

The subset of literals of form $+B_i$ is the <u>conclusion</u> (consequent) of the clause while the subset of literals of form $-A_j$ is the <u>hypothesis</u> (antecedent) of the clause. The <u>empty</u> (null) clause, for which n=0, m=0, is denoted by □ .

A literal is an atomic formula prefixed with + or - . An <u>atomic formula</u> (or atom) is an expression of the form

$$P(t_1, t_2, \ldots, t_n) ,$$

where P is an n-ary predicate symbol and $t_1, \ldots, t_n$ are terms. A <u>term</u> is a variable symbol, a constant symbol, or an expression of the form

$$f(t_1, \ldots, t_r) ,$$

where f is an r-ary function symbol and $t_1, \ldots, t_r$ are terms.

The Interpretation of Clause Form

Clause form in PROLOG may be interpreted in the following manner. The set of clauses $\{C_1, \ldots, C_N\}$ is interpreted as the conjunction of the clauses C_i;

C_1 <u>and</u> C_2 <u>and</u> ... <u>and</u> C_N .

The clause $\{+B_1, \ldots, +B_m, -A_1, \ldots, -A_n\}$ which contains the variables $X_1, \ldots, X_k$ is interpreted as follows:

<u>forall</u> $X_1, \ldots, X_k$

B_1 <u>or</u> ... <u>or</u> B_m <u>if</u> A_1 <u>and</u> ... <u>and</u> A_n .

The empty clause, □, resulting from m=0, n=0 is interpreted as a contradiction.

Horn Clauses (Horn Formulas)

Those clauses, $+B_1, \ldots, +B_m, -A_1, \ldots, -A_n$, where $m \leq 1$ are called <u>Horn clauses</u>.

The various Horn clauses are named as follows:

(1) m=0 n=0 , □,

the <u>empty</u> clause ;

(2) m=1 n=0 , {+B} ,

the assertion or unit clause;

(3) m=0 n≠0 , $\{ -A_1, \ldots, -A_n \}$,

the goal or goal-sequence ;

(4) m=1 n≠0 , $\{+B, -A_1, \ldots, -A_k\}$,

the rule of inference .

The Procedural Interpretation of Horn Clauses

In the remainder of this paper, we will omit the braces from the notation for clauses, the commas appearing between literals, and place a period at the end of clauses; this gives the current syntax of PROLOG. A clause representing a goal sequence ,

$-A_1 \ldots -A_n .$,

can be interpreted as a sequence of procedure calls. That is, each literal $-A_i, i=1,\cdots,n$ is interpreted as a procedure call. A Horn clause,

$+B \; -A_1 \; \ldots - A_n .$

may be viewed as a procedure declaration, where B is the head of the procedure and the procedure calls A_i , form the body of the procedure. Assertions of form +B, may be looked upon as procedures with empty bodies, while the empty clause, □ , is the STOP instruction. The arguments of the literals correspond to the parameters of procedures (procedure calls).

The Very High Level Language PROLOG

The PROLOG language may be introduced in the simplest form through the procedural interpretation of Horn clauses. In the language, procedures are declared with Horn clauses, whose calls are controlled using, pattern matching, by a theorem-prover with top-down, depth-first strategy. The pattern matcher executes the unification algorithm (Robinson [1965]). Using the procedural view of clauses, it is possible to step outside of the frame of the first order predicate calculus to introduce other procedures. There are two types of procedures in PROLOG.

(1) Procedures defined by the user in the PROLOG language.

(2) Procedures provided by the interpreter; that is, built-in

procedures.

A user defined procedure means that it is the responsibility of the user to provide for each procedure call (a literal of the form $-A$), a procedure definition with an applicable head, $(+A)$. If this is not the case, backtracking results according to the strategy of the theorem-prover contained in PROLOG.

Built-in procedures may be called in the same way as user defined procedures, however, the user does not have to provide their corresponding definitions as these are contained in the interpreter.

Such built-in procedures are used to perform arithmetic functions (addition, multiplication, etc.), comparisons, input-output, and file handling operations. An important role is played by the program modification procedures which can be used by a running program (during the theorem-proving process) to change the set of clauses which comprise the program.

The built-in control procedures deserve special mention, as they can be used to modify the strategy of the theorem-prover and thus the order of procedure calls (in case of backtracking). Figure 1 gives a small example of a PROLOG program and its execution.

THE HUNGARIAN VERSION OF PROLOG

The interpreter used by us was developed in 1975 and programmed in CDL (Compiler Definition Language)*. The interpreter currently runs on the following machines: ICL 1903/A, 1905/E, ICL SYSTEM 4/70 (interactive version), HWB 66/20, 66/60, IBM/370, SIEMENS 7·755 (interactive), ODRA 1305, EMG 840 and RIAD R22.

Enhancements to PROLOG

The various applications for which we wished to use PROLOG required certain extensions with respect to the original Marseille (Battani and Meloni [1973]) and Edinburgh (Warren [1974]) versions. These changes were important primarily for Question Answering and Data-Base Management programs and may be grouped as follows:

(1) Secondary storage handling.

(2) Fast lookup within a given partition.

---

* The implementation and application of PROLOG was carried out based on a commission of KSH OSZI and the Research Institute for Chemical Heavy Industry at NIM IGÜSZI.

The program is

```
[1]  +FATHER(A,B).                      "A is the father of B"
[2]  +FATHER(C,D).                      "C is the father of D"
[3]  +FATHER(A,C).                      "A is the father of C"
[4]  +GRANDFATHER(*X)                   "X is the grandfather if
                -FATHER(*X,*Z)          "X is father of Z and if
                -FATHER(*Z,*Y).          Z is father of Y"
```

The goal statement is

```
    - GRANDFATHER(*X)  - OUTPUT(*X)     "find and print out a
                                          grandfather"
```

The execution diagram of the program is

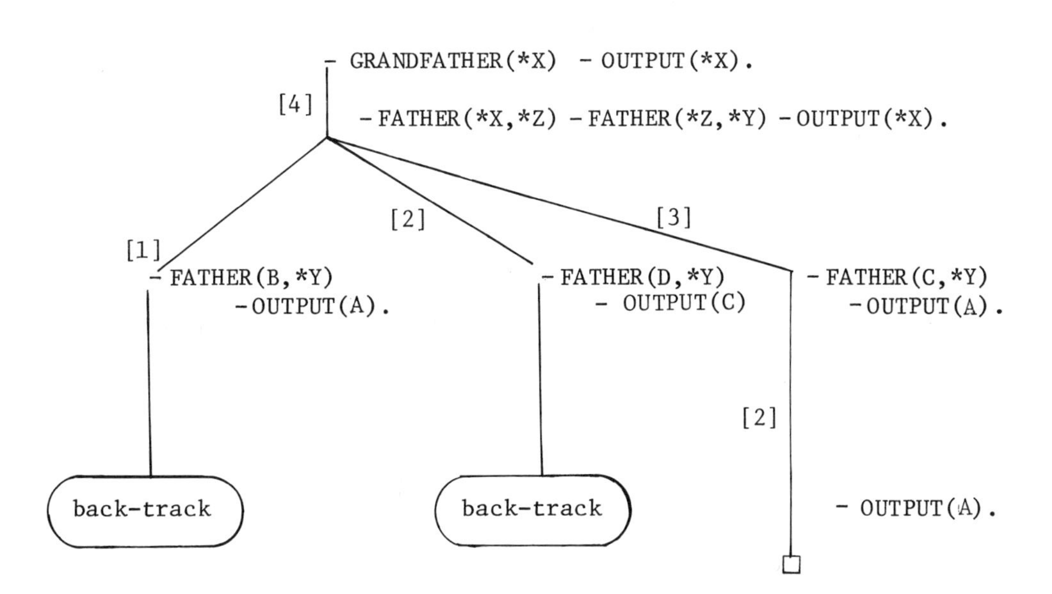

Note: (1) -OUTPUT is a built in procedure.

(2) Identifiers preceded by an asterisk are variables.

(3) Symbolic input operations.

Figure 1. PROLOG Program and Execution

File Handling

Since an "unlimited' memory area was not available to our programs (in fact PROLOG has only lately been implemented on machines with a large virtual memory), it was necessary to store several program modules on secondary storage to be called into memory by the program when required. This was especially important for our data-base handling system where the data were stored in the form of assertions in character form (more details are provided below). Although our system, in contrast to other DBM systems, is not large, the data-bases we have to work with have to be separated into files of non-core resident modules to achieve efficient search and to economize primary memory.

In the current implementation it is possible to open files named during run-time for input or output. This is provided by the built-in procedures named:

INOPEN(filename), and

OUTOPEN(filename) .

The effect of the procedure call INOPEN(A) is to open the file A for input; reading may be done with the input built-in procedures. The procedure call OUTOPEN(A) works in the same way, however it opens the file for output; writing may be done with the output built-in procedures.

Fast Search Within a Given Partition

The data bases from which data are to be retrieved, consist of relations expressed by unit clauses in PROLOG. The PROLOG interpreter places unit clauses with identical relation names in the same partition. For retrieval efficiency it is necessary to provide a procedure which can find a required clause quickly. The traditional unification procedure (Robinson [1965]) is too slow for this purpose. To achieve fast search within a given partition, a bit mask based on the first few arguments of the clause is used as a preselection technique. This is applied for those partitions which are large enough.

In particular, for every clause in these large partitions, a (one word) code is stored consisting of two parts. In the first part there is a bit-mask describing which arguments are variables and which are not. In the second part, for each argument some portion of its value is stored. A similar code is calculated for a literal which is to be unified with the clause-heads of the given partition.

The preselection technique now works as follows: one compares the two codes using a mask that cuts out the argument-positions containing a variable (i.e., compares the corresponding arguments in all non-variable positions). If any difference is found, it means that unification cannot succeed.

In our implementation (24 bit words on the ICL 1900), all this is done for the first four arguments with the last five bits stored for each. The resulting speed-up is quite good: doubling the partition increases the search time only by a factor of 1.25 times (rather than a factor of 2).

Symbolic Input

The symbolic input facility provides a convenient tool for writing user oriented question answering systems in PROLOG. Symbolic input provides for backtracking as well, and is, therefore, very useful for parsing the input stream. The following built-in procedures may be used to manipulate symbolic input:

INSYMB(A)

INATOM(A)

INTERM(A)

INPROG .

Of the above procedures INSYMB(A), INATOM(A), INTERM(A) are capable of, respectively, reading a symbol, an atomic formula, or a term, while the interpreter attempts to unify the argument A with the symbol, atomic formula, or term just read. If unification is unsuccessful, backtrack occurs in the input stream, and the call of the input procedure fails.

The procedure INPROG is used to read PROLOG programs. It successively reads clauses until the clause +FIN. is encountered; by definition this is the last clause of the program. A simple program is shown in Figure 2 to illustrate the above-mentioned built-in procedures.

A SURVEY OF QA AND DBMS SYSTEMS WRITTEN IN PROLOG

General Remarks

PROLOG can be used to implement many problems in the area of information retrieval and data base manipulation. Some of these are as follows:

The program is

```
[5]  +FIND
        - INOPEN(FATHERS)
        - INPROG
        - GRANDFATHER(*X)
        - OUTPUT(*X) .
[4]  +GRANDFATHER(*X)
        - FATHER(*X,*Z)
        - FATHER(*Z,*Y).
```

Contents of file FATHERS

```
[1]  +FATHER(A,B).
[2]  +FATHER(C,D).
[3]  +FATHER(A,C).
[6]  +FIN.
```

The goal statement is

```
        - FIND.
```

The diagram of execution

```
[5]     - FIND.
          |
        - INOPEN(FATHERS) - INPROG - GRANDFATHER(*X) - OUTPUT(*X).
          |
          |     INOPEN opens the file FATHERS for reading.
          |
        - INPROG - GRANDFATHER(*X) - OUTPUT(*X).
          |
          |     INPROG reads the contents of the file.
          |
        - GRANDFATHER(*X) - OUTPUT(*X)

                from this point execution follows as in Figure 1.
```

Figure 2. PROLOG PROGRAM AND BUILT-IN PROCEDURES

(1) constructing question answering systems that require the deduction mechanism of PROLOG;

(2) constructing working models of information retrieval and data base manipulation systems that utilize the ease with which PROLOG programs can be modified;

(3) constructing information retrieval and data base manipulation systems that utilize the facilities of high level programming languages.

The main characteristic of our programs is that the data to be stored are placed in well-structured files containing at most 50-100 unit clauses without variable arguments. This ensures efficient retrieval. The complete data base can, in general, contain about 3000-5000 unit clauses (records in the traditional sense).

Since we did not wish to develop a natural language query system, questions are obtained from the users with the aid of menues. These menues list the alternatives available to the user at each phase of the retrieval process.

This means that while we are searching for a concrete datum in the data-base we descend to ever lower levels in the hierarchy of the data-base. Meanwhile at every level of the hierarchy we have a choice of directions in which to pursue the search. It is this choice where we aid the user by listing the alternatives and giving their codes.

For instance, in the data-base containing the data of drugs (to be described later), the user has to choose between four alternatives at the top level when he wants to ask a question:

1) He is interested in the drug data.

2) He is interested in the active ingredients of data.

3) He is interested in drug interactions.

4) He wants to modify the data-base.

When the appropriate response is supplied, the search proceeds according to the corresponding alternative, and only the program modules required for the search reside in the central memory.

We store two types of relations (unit clauses) in our systems; normalized and unnormalized in the sense of Codd [1970]. Normalized relations are represented by assertions with constant arguments. Certain arguments of unnormalized relations are used as references and in our system denote file names. Figure 3 shows the notation we have used to denote files and their contents.

Currently we have two working systems and one system under construction in PROLOG which are of an information retrieval or data-base manipulation character. The working systems are applications in the areas of air pollution control and insecticides, while the system under construction is for analysis of drug interactions. The first version of the drug interaction system (which is the deduction module of the new system) has actually been working for two years.

SPECIFIC SYSTEMS

Program System for Prediction and Retrieval of Drug Interactions

The aim of the program system - one of the earliest written in PROLOG in Hungary - was to investigate the efficiency of PROLOG in making a relatively large number of deductions of low logical depth (2-4 steps). The system comprises the data of 57 drug preparations available in Hungary (see Appendix 1). For each preparation the following pieces of information have been stored:

(1) Name of preparation.

(2) Active principles of preparation.

(3) Chemical groups and sub-groups of active principles.

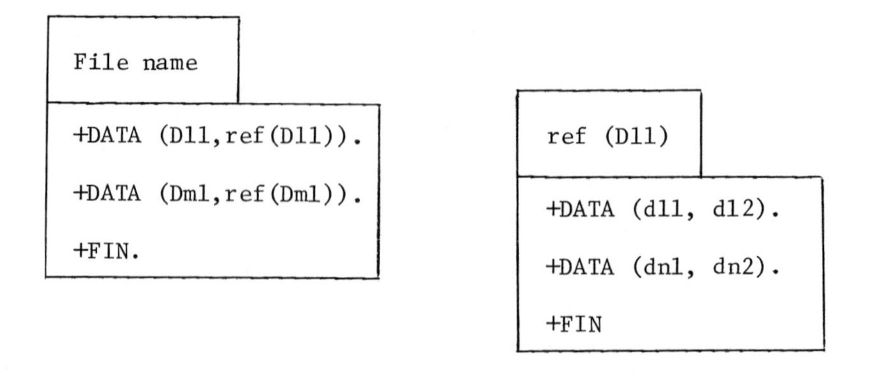

Figure 3. Notation for Files and File Content

(4) Activity groups, activity sub-groups and particular activities of active principles.

(5) Manner of administration of drug preparation.

On the basis of literature data, 135 general rules have been given for deduction. Of the deduction rules, 70 pertain to particular active principles, while 65 define general pharmacokinetic, pharmacodynamic and other biochemical observations (see Appendix 2).

These latter rules permit the prediction of new drug interactions by logic, whereas the former 70 enable the program to retrieve already published interactions (i.e., also known by us).

This deductive system implies that our knowledge about the interactions between particular drug preparations can be given in concise form, since it is not necessary to list all the known interactions between particular pairs of preparations for their retrieval.

The system retrieved and printed all possible and deducible interactions of any pair of preparations within 2-3 seconds (on the ICL 1903A).

During the test runs, 131 interactions were predicted by the program system on the basis of the 65 general rules, and about 560 further interactions were retrieved from the 70 rules pertaining to particular active principles.

Two of the interactions have later been discovered in the literature, and some of them are under experimental testing. It is obvious, however, that most of the interactions, although logically correct, are trivial or immaterial.

We were interested in the question as to the extent to which the inferred interactions correspond to the really existing ones. Unfortunately, the papers on interactions are rather poorly mentioned in reference journals, and thus the deduced interactions could be compared with reported observations only in a few cases. A first example was the interaction between Warfarin and Phenylbutazone. The program derived, via deduction rule (4), that the haemostatic activity of Warfarin is potentiated by Phenylbutazone. Deduction rule (4) occurs in the data base as a rule generalized from at most 10 cases observed on humans. The interaction has been observed and published several times, e.g., by O'Reilly (O'Reilly [1970], and Aggeler (Aggeler [1967]).

Concerning the parallel administration of Dicoumarol and Tolbutamide, the program has found, via deduction rule (19), that the haemostatic activity of Dicoumarol is potentiated by Tolbutamide. The possibility of interaction occurs in the data base as a generalization on humans. Chaplin et al. [1958] found that the parallel administration of Tolbutamide and Dicoumarol synergetically extends the plasma prothrombine time of the patients.

After modifying PROLOG to include file handling and fast search within a given partition, we have further altered the program. The new version of the program makes possible a larger data base and allows retrieval of the characteristics of drugs and active principles.

The flow chart of the present system is shown in Figure 4.

The operating cycle of the system is as follows. The search and the operation of the various modules are controlled by the supervisor. First it calls in the Input Module which the user will use to pose his questions. The question is passed through an appropriately coded interface to the Manipulation Control Module. (The interfaces between the modules are also controlled and called in by the Supervisor since these, too, are PROLOG programs.) The Manipulation Control Module calls the Manipulation Submodule appropriate to the question, or the Error Handling Module. (The Input Module does no checking. If a question is in error, or cannot be answered, this is discovered by the Manipulation Control Module and answered with the Error Handling Module.) After the appropriate data manipulation, control is returned either to the Supervisor (if the question concerned interaction), or the Manipulation Control Module calls Output Module 2 through the appropriate interface and, as a result of the actions of the Output Module, the answer to the question appears on the user's terminal.

If a question concerns interactions, the Supervisor also calls the Deduction Module and this will answer the question using Output Module 1.

Several cycles can be executed in one session. The general structural model (Raver and Hubbard [1977]) of the data base is given in Figure 5.

Since we could not perform a preliminary survey of user requirements, the temporary segment structure of the experimental data base was determined as shown in Figure 6. We did not provide connections between the various segments in the figure (there is no parent-child graph).

The PROLOG implementation of segments is shown in Figure 7.

The following notation (Figure 8) corresponds to binary relations.

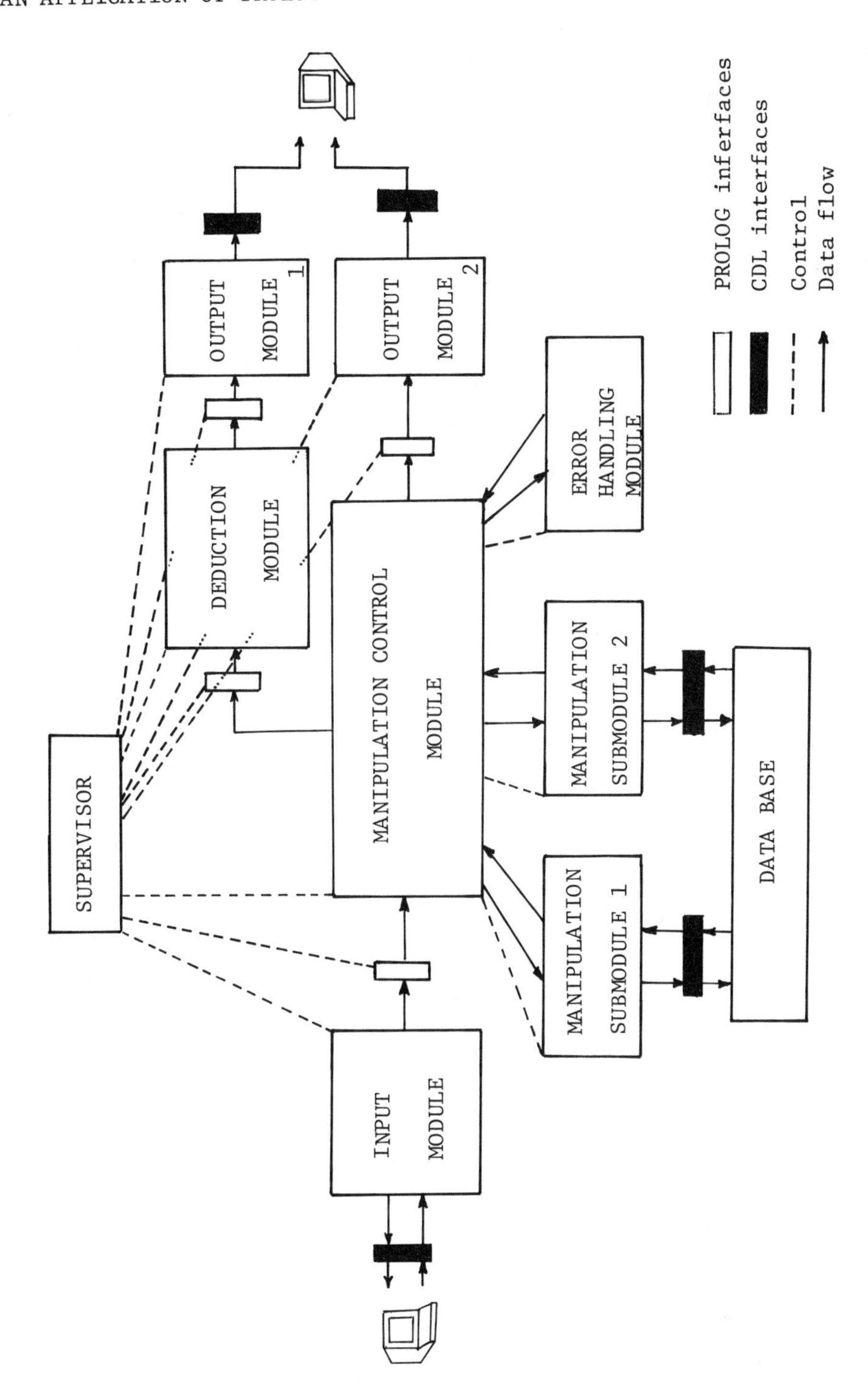

Figure 4. System Flow Chart

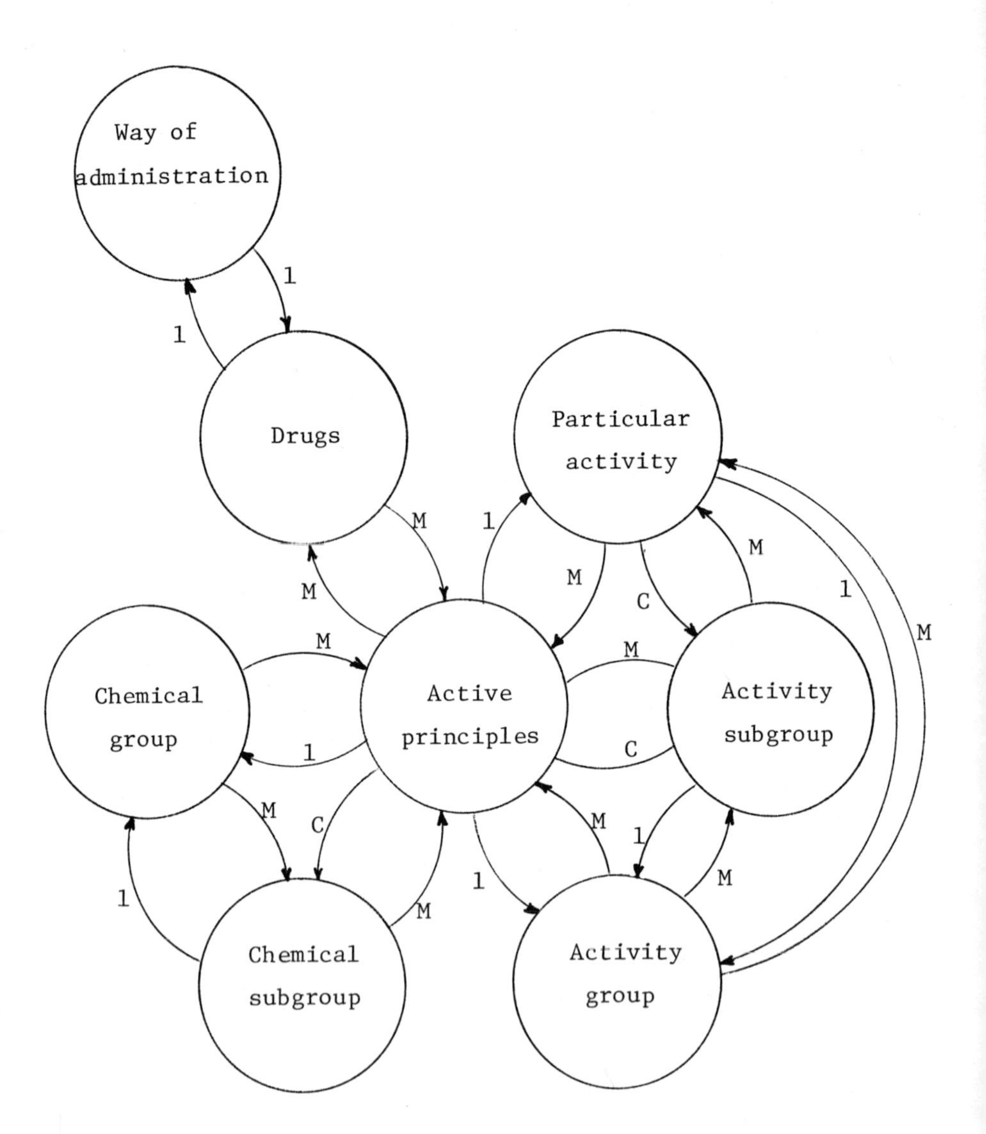

M: complex association /type M/

C: conditional association /type C/

1: simple association /type 1/

Figure 5. Composite Network of the Data Base

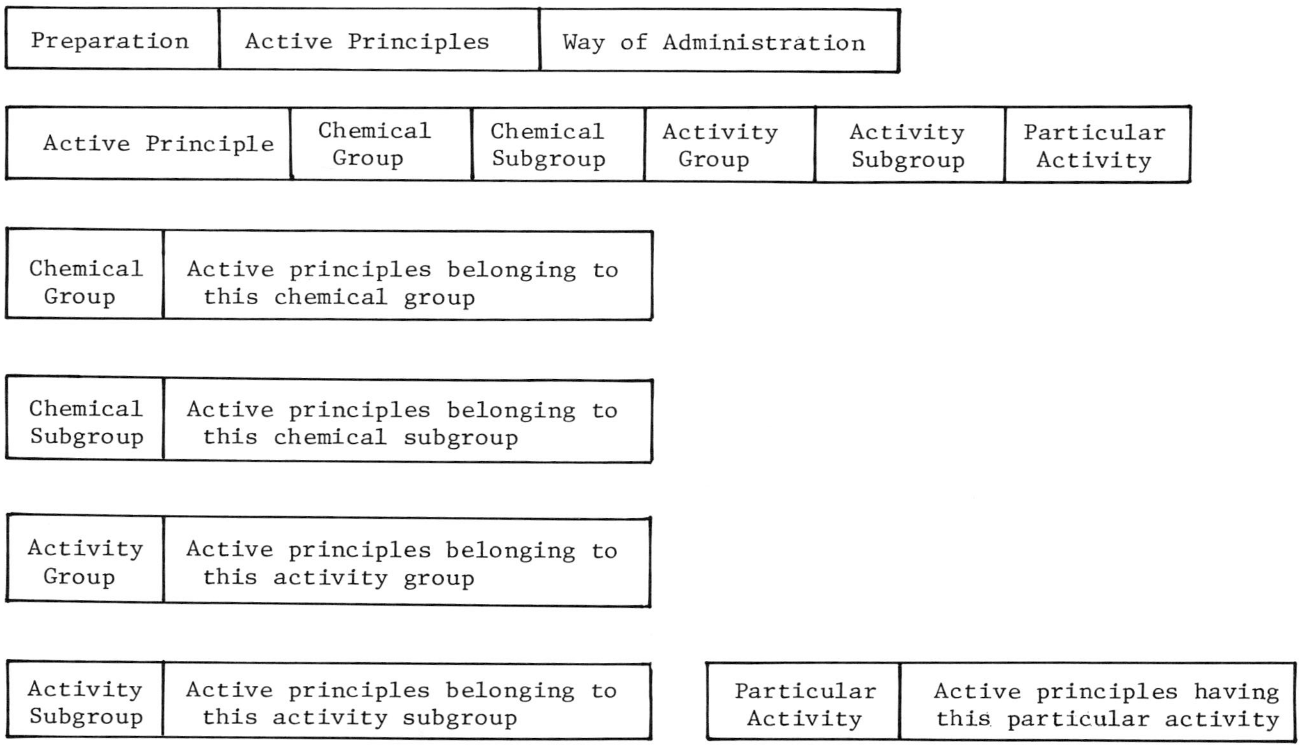

Preparation	Active Principles	Way of Administration

Active Principle	Chemical Group	Chemical Subgroup	Activity Group	Activity Subgroup	Particular Activity

Chemical Group	Active principles belonging to this chemical group

Chemical Subgroup	Active principles belonging to this chemical subgroup

Activity Group	Active principles belonging to this activity group

Activity Subgroup	Active principles belonging to this activity subgroup

Particular Activity	Active principles having this particular activity

Figure 6. Segment Contents

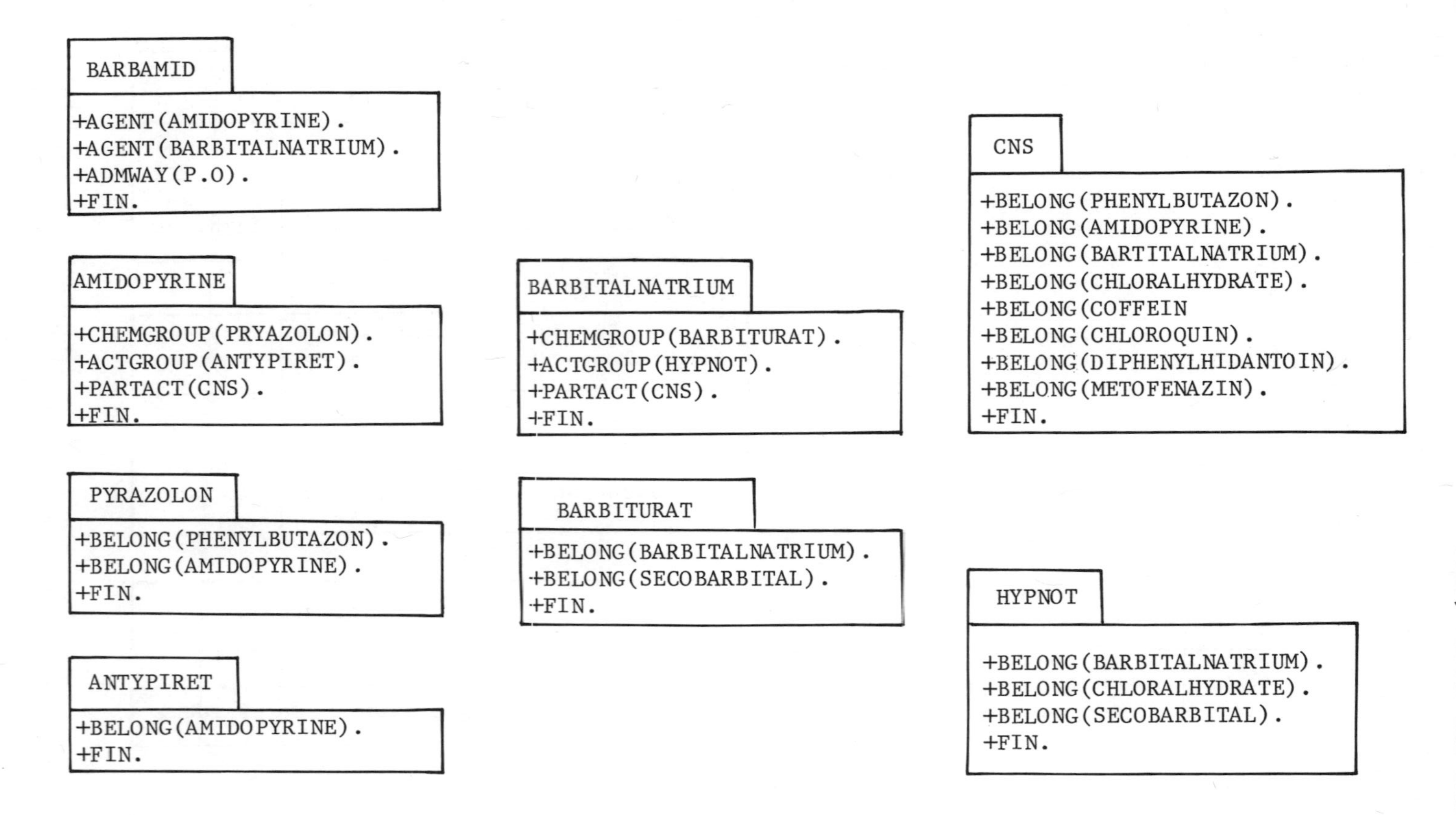

Figure 7. PROLOG Implementation of Segments

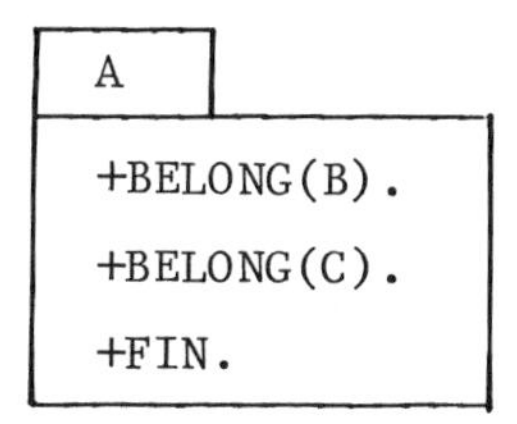

Figure 8. Relation Entries

As we did not require all data concerning all drugs, we preferred to use binary rather than n-ary relations (Deliyanni and Kowalski [1977]). The relation means, that B and C belong to the set A. Nevertheless, we do not store them in a single big file like +BELONG(B,A)., +BELONG(C,A)., etc., because of the problem of program efficiency.

CHEMGROUP, ACTYGROUP, PARTACT denote respectively, the chemical group, the activity group and the specific activity.

In its present version, according to the user's demands, the program system is able to answer the following types of questions:

1) retrieve all data pertaining to given preparations;

2) list the preparations which contain given agents;

3) retrieve all data pertaining to given agents;

4) list all agents belonging to a given chemical group or sub-group;

5) list all agents belonging to a given activity group or sub-group;

6) find the preparations or agents with a given particular activity;

7) check if there is a given interaction between given preparations;

8) list all expectable interactions between given preparations;

9) modify data;

or any combination of the above mentioned questions.

Questions are posed with the help of menues, or directly using a simple query language (for users familiar with the system). Menues give the syntax of the query language for the wanted alternatives. A question is a formula of logic in infix notation. An example of a question is:

LIST PREPARATIONS CONTAINING METHOTREXAT OR ALUMINIUM-HYDROXYDE MOREOVER INTERACTIONS BETWEEN ALUCOL AND AMETHOPTERIN.

The words, LIST, CONTAINING, OR, BETWEEN, MOREOVER, and AND are infix or prefix function symbols with different priority levels. The words, PREPARATIONS, and INTERACTIONS, are key words which refer to question types (2) and (8) above. The simple query language is very easy to process in PROLOG and satisfies the users' requirements. The query language is written in Hungarian, though an equivalent English version is given. The Hungarian version is more complicated, because we have three different and convenient synonyms for 'AND'. This permits the users to ask complex questions without using parentheses, by giving them different priority levels.

A typical example of the internal representation of consequence rules and a possible chain of consequences is now provided. We specify several axioms in the system and a typical query.

```
+ACTIVITY(AMOD, *K1, *X1)

          - CHARACT(ABIL, *K1, *X1, *Q1)

          - CHARACT(RGAE, *K2, *X2, *Q2)

          - NOT(EQUAL(*K1, *K2))

          - WRI(AMOD,*K1,*X1,*K2,*X2)

          - WRI(ABIL,*K1,*X1,*Q1)

          - WRI(RGAE,*K2,*X2,*Q2).
```

The above axiom specifies that the activity of the active principle X1 in the preparation K1 is modified by the active principle X2 in the drug K2 if the active principle X1 in K1 is absorbed from the ileum and the active principle X2 in K2 is to influence the rate of gastric emptying. (Identifiers preceeded by asterisks are variables.)

The last three lines of the above axiom:

WRI(AMOD,*K1,*K2,*X1,*X2)

WRI(ABIL,*K1,*X1,*Q1)

WRI(RGAE,*K2,*X2,*Q2)

are procedures for the printing of certain sentence schemata. The schemata contain some variables which get concrete values when the procedure is called, e.g.,

*K1,*K2 may be instantiated with product names;

*X1,*X2 may be instantiated with active ingredient names;

*Q1,*Q2 may be instantiated with a list containing book titles and page numbers.

Output Module 1 contains as many such sentence schema definitions as there are inference rule types leading to interactions in the Deduction Module. The five parameter version of the WRI procedure does not have the referenced book as an input parameter. The explanation of this is that the first version of the Deduction Module was written in 1975, and at that time each sentence scheme directly contained the publication that was the basis of the deduction rule.

A second axiom is given by:

+CHARACT(ABIL,*K1,*X1,*Q1)

- CHEMGROUPS(*K1,*X1,BARBITURAT,*V)

- CIT(ABIL,*Q1)

It signifies that the X1 active principle in the preparation K1 is absorbed from the ileum if X1 in K1 belongs to the chemical group BARBITURAT and the sub-group V.

A third axiom is given by:

+CHARACT(RGAE,*K2,*X2,*Q2)

- ACTYGROUPS(*K2,*X2,ANTIPARKINSON,*U,*V)

- CIT(RGAE,*Q2)

It signifies that the active principle X1 in the preparation X1 influences the rate of gastric emptying if the active principle X1 belongs to the activity group ANITPARKINSON, and further it belongs to the activity sub-group U and has a specific activity V.

CIT(A,*B) gives the source where the axiom was published.

Finally, a characteristic answer provided by the system for the required interaction of Seconal and L-Dopa is shown in Figure 9.

The output of the system is in Hungarian, the output examples given in the paper are translations. The underlined parts are the actual values of the parameters of the sentence scheme.

THE ACTIVITY OF THE ACTIVE PRINCIPLE SECOBARBITAL IN THE PREPARATION SECONAL IS MODIFIED BY THE MODIFICATION OF ABSORPTION THE ACTIVE PRINCIPLE L-DOPA IN THE PREPARATION L-DOPA:

THE STATEMENT LEADING TO THE CONSEQUENCE IS PUBLISHED BY P. L. MORSELLI, N. S. COHEN, S. GARATTINI IN "DRUG INTERACTIONS", RAVEN PRESS, NEW YORK, 1974, P. 13.

ONE OF THE PREMISSA OF THE CONSEQUENCE IS ITSELF A CONSEQUENCE MEANING THAT THE ACTIVE PRINCIPLE SECOBARBITAL IN SECONAL IS ABSORBED MAINLY FROM THE ILEUM.

THE STATEMENT LEADING TO THE CONSEQUENCE IS PUBLISHED BY P. L. MORSELLI, N. S. COHEN, S. GARATTINI IN "DRUG INTERACTIONS", RAVEN PRESS, NEW YORK, 1974, P. 14.

ONE OF THE PREMISSA OF THE CONSEQUENCE IS ITSELF A CONSEQUENCE MEANING THAT ACTIVE PRINCIPLE
L-DOPA IN L-DOPA INFLUENCES THE RATE OF GASTRIC
EMPTYING.

THE STATEMENT LEADING TO THE CONSEQUENCE IS PUBLISHED BY P. L. MORSELLI, N. S. COHEN, S. GARATTINI IN "DURG INTERACTIONS", RAVEN PRESS, NEW YORK, 1974, P. 14.

Figure 9. System Answer to Deduction Problem

In defining the control mechanism of the deduction module we faced the fundamental problem that PROLOG has a top-down, depth-first theorem prover. Finding all possible interactions of two or more drugs, nevertheless, requires a bottom-up, breadth-first strategy; as the number of the pharmacons involved in an interaction query is significantly smaller than the number of deduction rules, a bottom-up inferential strategy which starts from the pharmacons would be rational.

However, we decided to use the built-in control mechanism of PROLOG to simulate a bottom-up search. To do this, we call all the inference rules relating to interactions one after the other using the procedure call -ACTIVITY(*X,*Y,*Z) and, if it succeeds, the built-in procedure FAIL (always unsuccessful) is used to force the theorem-prover to backtrack. This is done until the complete search space has been traversed. (It should be noted that the heads of all inference rules relating to interaction are of the form +ACTIVITY(a,*X,*Y)). Our decision regarding the problem solution strategy was justified by the short running times.

A Simple Data Base Manipulation System for Pesticides*

The second application of PROLOG was that of developing a system to handle pesticides. The data base of the system contains three types of basic data.

(1) The diseases, pests, etc. detrimental to a culture (listed in a separate file for each culture).

(2) The insecticides, pesticides, etc. effecting a given disease, pest, etc. (listed by pests).

(3) The application areas of given insecticides, pesticides, etc. (that is, the cultures for which they can be utilized), given by agents.

The task of the system is to answer the questions of the users in an interactive mode. The questions can be the following.

(1) List the insecticides, etc. applicable to a given culture or pest.

List the cultures affected by a given agent or pest.

List the pests belonging to a given culture or agent.

(2) Determine the applicable insecticides for a given culture-pest pair. (That is the selection of those agents which can be used against the given pest in the given culture.)

---

* L. Naszvadi participated in the implementation.

Determine the cultures belonging to a given pest-agent pair. (That is the selection of those cultures in which the given agent can be used against the given pest.)

Determine the pests belonging to a given agent-culture pair. (That is the selection of those pests against which the given agent can be used in the given culture.)

(3) The analysis of a given culture-agent-pest triple, i.e., the determination of the feasibility of applying the given pesticide against the pest in the culture.

A further task of the system is to carry out required modifications of the data base.

An Information Retrieval System for Air Pollution Control*

The third application of PROLOG was to develop a system for air pollution control. The goal of the system is to aid in the solution of the air pollution problems of chemical factories, further to be in compliance with the air pollution law, and in general to reduce air pollution.

After the retrieval of required information, the system verifies whether the factory complies with the appropriate law; that is, the concentration of a given pollutant that the factory emits must be under the lawfully allowed concentration.

If this is not the case, the system will try to determine whether increasing the height of the smoke stacks of the factory will reduce the concentration below the required limit (a height increase results in the same quantity of pollutant being dispersed into a larger space). The system will also try to select an appropriate industrial filter from those stored in its data base, and notify the user of its characteristics.

The system treats Hungary in a twenty county division. A county is usually further subdivided into 15 districts. The districts can fall into three distinct categories each with a different allowable pollutant concentration, which is at the same time a function of the type of pollutant.

The system is currently capable of handling 7 pollutants; the analysis can be performed for 9 branches of heavy industry. The selection of the appropriate industrial filter takes place on the basis of 6 parameters, while 12 further parameters are supplied by the system to provide extra information.

---

* Zs. Márkusz and Gy. Lugosi participated in the implementation.

SUMMARY

PROLOG is a language with a very simple syntax and an understandable, not necessarily algorithmic semantics. This simplicity of the language makes it possible to achieve fast implementations and easy portability.

The semantics of PROLOG can be learned easily even by the non-programmer user. Because of this, even at the definition level, the problem can be specified in PROLOG-like conditional sentences. Rewriting these into the required formalism then is a relatively easy task.

To illustrate this, the PROLOG-like specification of the 10th statement relating to interactions in Appendix 2, as given in English is:

The absorption of preparation A is increased by

preparation B if

A is sulfonamid

and B is antacid.

In general, the coded form of the statements are also easily understandable to the expert, which is very important in applications requiring frequent modifications or extensions.

This aspect was proved in practice where, during the development of the drug planning system, the solution method frequently had to be modified depending on the partial results.

During the construction of the system described in this paper, it become evident that PROLOG is suitable for the design of simple data base management systems. This is facilitated by the property of the language that it is very easy to modify programs written in PROLOG. Thus, various ways of structuring of the data base can be tried and verified by actually running them. It is therefore possible, during the system design phase, to construct a data base management system using PROLOG; run test problems against various data storage structure and retrieval strategies (not too efficiently since PROLOG is implemented in an interpretive manner); and finally after the selection of the appropriate representation, construct the final and efficient version of the system in another programming language. The advantage of the method is that even during the design phase one has a working system.

The work is made very convenient by the high level programming facilities of PROLOG (pattern matching, character handling facilities, operator declaration possibilities), and in our experience in the case of smaller data bases (5000-10,000 records) these programs prove to be efficient enough to make the recoding phase redundant. For example, the implementation of the system for pesticides and diseases occurring in Hungary required 6 man-months. The system satisfied the demands of the customers and users, as well. The latter found it very convenient to pose questions using the menues for selecting alternative action, because they didn't need any previous knowledge about the structure of the system. The response times were good compared with other similar interactive programs written in traditional languages.

With the implementation of file-handling it became possible to implement data base manipulation systems in PROLOG even for machines that were available to us that had small memories.

This partially solves the "space problem", however, a severe problem still remains in that records of the data base are represented by unit-clauses, and linear-search and the unification algorithm is used for retrieval.

In our system we solved the speed-up problem without significantly modifying the interpreter, by using the bit mask method described earlier. Although this way we do not avoid the necessity of linear search within a partition, the search becomes fast by eliminating unusable alternatives with a few simple bit operations instead of requiring the more complex, but general unification algorithm. For us it is also important that this speed-up applies not only to the first argument, but to the first four arguments of a predicate since, in our programs which had to handle chemical structures, the same data base is used for several purposes and several argument positions might be important during the look-up stage (Darvas et al. [1976], Futo et al. [1977]). This also explains why the solution suggested by Warren [1977] which enables the omission of the search of the complete partition but applies only to the first argument of a predicate is unsatisfactory for our purposes. The approach described by Minker [1978] in this book also permits indexing on many arguments.

PROLOG requires further developments to enhance its use for large data base problems. In our current view an existing, traditional file-handling system should be combined with PROLOG in such a way as to allow query, reply and control to be performed by PROLOG programs while data retrieval would be handled by the traditional file-handling system, similar to the system described by Bruynooghe [1977]. The implementation of this concept arose first in early 1977, however, at that time the bit masking technique described was satisfactory for user requirements at that time.

ACKNOWLEDGMENT

We wish to thank all our colleagues, without whose help PROLOG and its applications could not have been realized; L. Jarabek of KSH OSZI, Bálint Dömölki and Peter Köves of SZKI, György Lugosi of the Research Institute for Chemical Heavy Industry, Judit Bendl of NIM IGÜSZI and Kati Nagy for the fast organization and typing of the manuscript.

APPENDIX 1

Drugs in the Data Base Applied in the Mechanical Deduction of New Drug Interactions

Alucol
Ametophterin
Barbamid
Bucarban
Butazolin
Clacimusc
Clorarum-hydratum
Coffenium
Coumadin
Delagil
Debenal
Diabenese
Dicoumarolum
Digoxin
Dimelor
Diphedan
Dopegyt
Fercupar
Frenolon
Istopyrin
Klorocid
L-Dopa
Lidocain
Magnesiumoxide
Melipramin
Miscleron
Natrium-nitrosium
Natrium-Citricum
Neopepulsan
Nevigramon
Nidrazid
Nirvanol
Novocain
Oterben
Peritol
Pertofran
PGE1
Pipolphen
Procainamide
Rifamycin
Sacerho
Sapilent
Teperin
Seduxen
Sodabikarbona
Syncumar
Tabletta-Antropini-Sulf
Tebaminál
Tetran
Thriptasin
Tonogen
Trisulfil
Tromexan
Valeriana
Verospiron
Vitamin-B12

APPENDIX 2

The Logical Relationship of the Data Base Applied in the Mechanical Deduction of New Drug Interactions

General Rules

(1) The activity of pharmacons absorbed from the small intestine is influenced via a modification in absorption, by pharmacons influencing the rate of gastric emptying.

(2) The metabolism of tricyclic antidepressants is inhibited by neuroleptics. The metabolism of Salazo-sulfapyridin is modified by antibiotics.

(3) The simultaneous administration of sulfixosazole and penicilline causes lethal kernicterus on premature infants.

(4) The activity of haemostatics is potentiated by phenylbutazone.

(5) Antibiotics modify the activity of agents metabolised by the intestinal microflora.

(6) The activity of haemostatics is potentiated by oxyphenylbutazone.

(7) Bases decrease the absorption rate of bases.

(8) The absorption of quaternary ammonium salt antiarrhythmic agents is increased by salicyclates.

(9) The absorption of pentobarbital is decreased by antacids.

(10) The absorption of sulfonamides is increased by antacids.

(11) The tubular secretion of organic acids is decreased by organic acids.

(12) The tubular secretion of bases is decreased by bases.

(13) The serum level of tolbutamide is increased by sulfonamides.

(14) The absorption of weak acids is decreased by bases.

(15) The absorption of weak bases is decreased by acids.

(16) The simultaneous administration of amphetamines and monoamine oxidase inhibitors causes hypertension and circulation troubles.

(17) The respiration depressing activity of analgetics is potentiated by tranquillants.

(18) The activity of haemostatics is potentiated by antibiotics.

(19) The activity of haemostatics is potentiated by sulfonamides.

(20) The activity of haemostatics is potentiated by barbiturates.

(21) The activity of haemostatics is decreased by oral contraceptives.

(22) The simultaneous administration of tricyclic antidepressants and monoamine oxidase inhibitors may cause severe reactions and and even fatalities.

(23) The activity of atropine is potentiated by tricyclic antidepressants.

(24) The depressant activity of barbiturates is potentiated by antihistamines.

(25) The sedative activity of barbiturates is potentiated by benzodiazephines.

(26) The activity of phenothiazines is potentiated by benzodiazephines.

(27) The activity of tricyclic antidepressants is potentiated by benzodiazephines.

(28) The activity of penicillins is decreased by bacteriostatic agents.

(29) The activity of barbiturates is potentiated by cholinesterase inhibitors.

(30) The activity of L-Dopa is influenced by hypotensive agents.

(31) The activity of L-Dopa is influenced by monoamine axidase inhibitors, they cannot be administered simultaneously.

(32) Tricyclic antidepressants affect the rate of gastric emptying.

(33) Phenothiazines affect the rate of gastric emptying.

(34) Nitrites affect the rate of gastric emptying.

(35) Prostaglandines affect the rate of gastric emptying.

(36) Symphatomimetic agents affect the rate of gastric emptying.

(37) Anti-parkinsonian agents affect the rate of gastric emptying.

(38) Hypotensive agents affect the rate of gastric emptying.

(39) Anticholinerg agents affect the rate of gastric emptying.

(40) Antihistamines affect the rate of gastric emptying.

(41) Bases are absorbed from the ileum.

(42) Barbiturates are absorbed mainly from the small intestine.

(43) Antacids are bases.

(44) Drugs causing gastro-intestinal lesions may decrease the absorption of other drugs.

(45) Pyrazolones may cause gastro-intestinal lesions.

(46) Salycilates may cause gastro-intestinal lesions.

(47) Drug metabolism can be accelerated by administration of compounds which cause induction of liver microsomal enzymes.

(48) Patients receiving chronic therapy with p-aminosalicyclic acid may develop a malabsorption syndrome leading to impairing the absorption of other drugs.

(49) Broad-spectrum antibiotics are said to potentiate oral anticoagulants by reducing vitamin K synthesis by gut flora.

(50) Barbiturates are enzyme inducing agents.

(51) Hydantoins are enzyme inducing agents.

(52) Pyrazolons are enzyme inducing agents.

(53) Meprobamate is an enzyme inducing agents.

(54) Drugs present in the plasma in high concentration will tend to displace those present in low concentration.

(55) Many acidic drugs are bound to plasma albumin in high concentration.

(56) Phenylbutazone is bound to plasma albumin in high concentration.

(57) Coumarin anticoagulants are highly protein-bound acidic drugs.

(58) Salicylates are highly protein-bound acidic drugs.

(59) Hydantoins are highly protein-bound acidic drugs.

(60) Sulphonamides are highly protein-bound acidic drugs.

(61) Nalidixic acid is a highly protein-bound acidic drug.

(62) Sulphonamides share a common proximal tubular active transport system with other drugs in the data base.

(63) Thiazide diuretics share a common proximal tubular active transport system with other drugs in the data base.

(64) Salycilates share a common proximal tubular active transport system with other drugs in the data base.

(65) Phenylbutazone shares a common proximal tubular active transport system with other drugs in the data base.

REFERENCES

1. Battani, G. and Meloni, H. [1973] Interpreteur dur language de programation PROLOG, Groupe de l'Intelligence Artificielle, U.E.R. de Luminy, Marseille, 1973.

2. Bruynooghe, M. [1977] An Interface between PROLOG and CYBER-EDMS, *Proceedings of Workshop on Logic and Data Bases*, Toulouse, 1977, VII/1-VII/7.

3. Codd, E. F. [1970] A Relational Model of Data for Large Shared Data Banks, *CACM 13*, 6 (June 1970), 377-387.

4. Deliyanni, A. and Kowalski, R. [1977] Logic and Semantic Networks, *Proceedings of Workshop on Logic and Data Bases*, Toulouse, 1977, XII/1-XII/7.

5. Darvas, F. and Futó, I. and Szeredi, P. [1976] Some Applications of Theorem-Proving Based Machine Intelligence in QSAR, *Proceedings of the International Symphosium on QSAR Suhl*, GDR, in press.

6. Futó, I., Darvas, F. and Cholnoky, E. [1977] Practical Application of an AI Language, II, *Proceedings of the Hungarian Conference on Computing*, Budapest, 1977, 385-400.

7. Kowalski, R. [1974] Predicate Logic as a Programming Language, *DCL Memo No. 70*, Edinburgh University, Edingurgh, 1974.

8. Minker, J. [1978] An Experimental Data Base System Based on Logic, in *Logic and Data Bases* (H. Gallaire and J. Minker, Eds.), Plenum Press, New York, 1978, 107-147.

9. Raver, N. and Hubbard, G. U. [1977] Automated Logical Data Base Design: Concepts and Applications, *IBM Systems Journal 16*, 3 (1977), 287-312.

10. Robinson, J. A. [1965] Machine Oriented Logic Based on Resolution Principle, *JACM 12*, (1965), 23-44.

11. Warren, D. [1974] "What is PROLOG", Manuscript, University of Edinburgh, Edinburgh, 1974.

12. Warren, D. [1977] How Should Clauses in a Logic Data Base be Indexed, *Proceedings of the Workshop on Logic and Data Bases*, Toulouse, 1977, XX/1.

THE PREDICATE CALCULUS-LANGUAGE KS AS A QUERY LANGUAGE

Werner Dilger and Gisela Zifonun

Institut fuer deutsche Sprache

Mannheim, F.R.G.

ABSTRACT

An extended first order predicate calculus language 'KS' is defined as the internal representation language for the deductive question-answering system PLIDIS. It serves the functions of a semantic representation language for German, of a knowledge representation language, and of a data base query language. KS incorporates the following extensions: equality, recursively constructed argument terms, 'list terms' for representing sets of individuals, and many-sorted domains of individuals. The PLIDIS data base contains ground atomic formulas and axioms. The evaluation of KS-queries proceeds in two steps: first, queries are normalized, i.e., made quantifier-free by means of term-embedding; next, an evaluation graph for the normalised query is constructed. The evaluation of the graph is described.

INTRODUCTION

Within the framework of the deductive question-answering system PLIDIS (cf. Berry-Rogghe and Wulz [1978])*, the predicate calculus oriented language KS** was defined. This language is suita-

---

* PLIDIS is being developed in the context of a project in automated language processing at the Institut fuer deutsche Sprache, Mannheim. The field of experimental application of the system will be the control of water pollution. Examples are taken in part from this domain.

** KS is an abbreviation for the German word "Konstruktsprache". A more detailed description of KS is given in Zifonun [1977].

ble as a semantic representation language for German, for the representation of knowledge, and as a data base query language with deductive capacity. Research projects with similar aims are, among others, presented by Reiter [1977], Landsbergen and Scha [1978], Woods et al. [1970], Chang [1978], Kellogg [1978], and McSkimin and Minker [1978].

In the first part of this paper motivation is given for the definition of KS, and the syntax of the language is described. In the second part an outline is provided of the use of KS as a query language. Some remarks are given concerning the data base used in the system; and a detailed specification is provided as to what is meant by the answering process and the answer to a query.

THE LANGUAGE KS

General Principles in Constructing KS

KS has been designed to represent knowledge about the world in an information system, to have a problem solving capability, and to provide natural language interaction. Thus, two main principles of design had to be considered:

[1] the representation language should be a suitable base for problem solving operations, i.e., in the case of PLIDIS for the derivation of implicit knowledge by means of a theorem proving mechanism;

[2] the representation language should be a suitable means for expressing natural language interaction between the user and the system in a possibly nonrestrictive way, i.e., the language should come close enough to the expressive power and structural principles of a natural language, here German. This naturally only holds in so far as interaction types of natural language are dealt with which are relevant in the context of an information system. It is not intended that the artificial language KS should simulate natural language by incorporating its redundancies, ambiguities or vagueness.

With respect to the first principle, the representation language might be the first-order predicate calculus. It has the well known advantages of a truth-functional semantics that allows deduction and therefore permits the application of an automatic theorem prover. On these grounds the representation language KS is based on predicate calulus.

However, pure predicate calculus does not satisfy the second principle. Many natural language formulations can be constructed in predicate calculus only in a very complicated and clumsy manner, and some formulations can only be rendered in predicate calculus with a high loss of information.

The communicative quality of natural language expressions cannot be expressed adequately in every case by predicate calculus counterparts. This is, for example, the case for natural language individual descriptions as in the phrase,

the sample (of sewage) taken from the firm G+L on 15.7.77.

Predicate calculus with descriptions could render this by the iota-operator-expression as,

(ιx (SAMPLE G+L 77/07/15 x)) ,

'the unique x such that x is a sample taken from G+L on 15.7.77' ,

where 'SAMPLE' is a three-place relation symbol and 'G+L' and '77/07/15' are individual constants.

Iota-operator expressions of the form

(ιx *p*) ,

where *p* is a formula containing one or more free occurrences of x and no other free variable, have a contextual definition as given for instance in Quine [1972]. According to this definition, the formula

(*G* (ιx *p*)) ,

containing the unary predicate *G* is defined as:

(∃y (∀x (*p* <=> (x = y)) ∧ (*G* y))) .

That is, 'one and only one thing has the properties described by *p*, and *G* is true of this thing'. This definition can be used to delete the iota-operator from formulas. Such removal would be necessary in ordinary theorem provers.

Thus a sentence like

(1) *"The sampler of the sample taken from the firm G+L on 15.7.77 was Brecht.",*

could be formulated in the predicate calculus with descriptions as

(SAMPLER (ιx (SAMPLE G+L 77/07/15 x))BRECHT).

The result of removing the iota-operator is

$$(\exists y\ (\forall x\ ((\text{SAMPLE G+L } 77/07/15\ x) \Leftrightarrow (x=y)) \wedge (\text{SAMPLER } y \text{ BRECHT})))\ .$$

One problem here is that the characteristic term embedding is deleted so that natural language and predicate calculus formulation structurally diverge in a high degree. But there are stronger arguments against this reduction. Suppose we want to use sentence (1) as a data base query:

(1) *"Was the sample taken from the firm G+L on 15.07.77 taken by Brecht?"*

We indicate the use as a query by a question mark:

$$(?(\text{SAMPLER } (\iota x\ (\text{SAMPLE G+L } 77/07/15\ x))\ \text{BRECHT}))$$

$$\equiv$$

$$(?(\exists y (\forall x\ ((\text{SAMPLE G+L } 77/07/15\ x) \Leftrightarrow (x=y)) \wedge (\text{SAMPLER } y \text{ BRECHT}))))\ .$$

In this question no distinction is made between the conjuncts. If one conjunct is false, the whole conjunction becomes false. If the 'closed world assumption' (Reiter [1977])* is adopted, then in the event there is no sample taken from G+L on 15.07.77, the conjunction becomes false and the system will reply "no".

But, this answer does not correspond to the sense of the question. In asking the question we presuppose that there is a sample taken on 15.07.77 from the firm G+L and do not query nor assert this. The user of the system will therefore always interpret a negative answer as a negation of the SAMPLER-statement and not as a negation of the presupposed existential commitment regarding the individual 'sample taken from G+L on 15.07.77'. If this existential commitment is not verified by the data base, the system should react by explicitly refusing the presupposition, not by pure negation of the whole sentence. An adequate response could be:

But there is no sample taken from G+L on 15.07.77.

In predicate calculus, it is not possible, as we have seen, to make a distinction between a presupposed existential commitment and an existential statement. In natural language this distinction is

---

* The closed world assumption states that, if we assume that all information concerning the micro-world is contained in the data base, the lack of information about a particular fact is equivalent to its not being the case.

made by the use of denotative terms, syntactically having the form of definite noun phrases.

Term constructing mechanisms therefore seem to be suitable tools for expressing individual descriptions in a presupposition preserving manner. The representation language KS adapts natural language term construction possibilities.

Individual descriptions in the form of singular noun phrases are not the only important kind of natural language descriptions. As important are plural noun phrases describing various types of sets or exactly members of various types of sets. As the example,

> *"The samplers of the samples taken from G+L on 15.07.77 and on 29.08.77 were Brecht and Meier."* ,

shows, in the normal case natural language "set" descriptions do not imply any higher type entities. Exceptions are noun phrases in contexts of natural language, "count"-predicates as *diminish* or *grow* or in the contexts of a noun like *number:*

> *"The number of samples taken from the firm G+L in 1976 was five."*

where the plural descriptions do not refer to members of sets but to the set as a whole. Both kinds of plural descriptions should be accounted for in the representation language. As these examples indicate, the requirement to incorporate natural language term constructing possibilities meets the postulates of data base query languages for expressing descriptions of objects, sets, and set theoretic operations. Such set theoretic operations as union, intersection, and complement are initiated in a natural language information system by the natural language query expressions. That is, certain natural language formulations are indicators of set theoretic operations. The translation mechanisms from natural language to KS have to recognize that fact; KS itself has to contain the corresponding tools for expressing natural language set theoretic indicators and in the evaluation process for a query these KS-indicators must be interpreted as triggers for carrying out the corresponding operations.

Description of KS

In the following, the structure and syntax of KS are described: the concept of sorts, and well-formedness conditions for formulas and terms of KS are given. An informal explanation is given of the semantics of certain syntactically well-formed expressions.

Sorts

KS imitates the natural language ability to impose certain "semantic" co-occurrence restrictions on its expressions. Particularly the co-occurrence of a predicate (verb) and the noun phrases governed by it is guided by semantic selection restrictions of the verbs. The sentence,

"Colourless green ideas sleep furiously." ,

violates these semantic selection restrictions. They are semantic restrictions because they reflect the structure of the domain of individuals underlying the corresponding world model.

In the same way, KS-assertions presuppose a structured domain: The domain of individuals is sorted. The sorts constitute a directed set with respect to the set-inclusion relation, i.e., for any two sorts s_i and s_j there exists a sort s_h such that

$$s_i \subseteq s_h \wedge s_j \subseteq s_h .$$

This kind of structure is suggested by micro-world analysis and differs only notationally from the 'semantic graph' structure in McSkimin and Minker [1978], where the introduction of the equality relation allows a more concise representation of the set of sorts. When the equality relation is omitted, the semantic graph has the form of a tree, called sort tree.

The definition of concrete sorts depends on the respective world model and therefore is not a matter for the KS-language itself.

As a consequence of the many-sortedness of the individual domain, the individual symbols of KS have to be sorted symbols, and for every n-place predicate symbol it is necessary to define the sort of every element of the n-tuple of arguments.*

As it is shown by McSkimin and Minker [1978], Minker [1978], Reiter [1978], Chang [1978], Kellogg [1978], and Lacroix et al.[1977] sort structures or semantic graphs can be used for 'narrowing down the search space in a deductive search' and for a set theoretic handling of negation.

---

*The concept of sorts within the context of representation languages is also discussed by Hayes [1971], McCarthy and Hayes [1969], Pople [1972] and Sandewall [1970]. For a linguistic and philosophical study refer to Thomason [1972].

<u>Well-Formedness Conditions for Formulas</u>

[1] If *P* is an n-ary predicate symbol of KS,

$< s_{i_1},\ldots,s_{i_n} >$

is the argument-sort-tuple of *P* and

$t_1^{s_{i_1}},\ldots,t_n^{s_{i_n}}$

are terms of the sorts $s_{i_1},\ldots,s_{i_n}$ respectively, then

$(P\ t_i^{s_{i_1}} \ldots\ t_n^{s_{i_n}})$

is an atomic formula of KS.

Symbols for computable functions like PLUS, COUNT or MAX are also represented as predicate symbols with the appropriate number of arguments.

<u>Example:</u>

P = SAMPLE , argument-sort-tuple = < firm,int,stuffcoll > *

Let 'G+L', '77/07/15' and 'STUFFCOLLØ1' be terms of the sorts firm, int and stuffcoll respectively, then

(SAMPLE G+L 77/07/15 STUFFCOLLØ1)

is an atomic formula of KS.

Non-atomic formulas are constructed by the usual junctors and quantifiers of predicate calculus. Thus, the set of formulas of KS can be defined recursively by:

[2] Atomic formulas are formulas of KS.

[3] Let NOT (unary), AND, OR, IMPLY, EQUIV (binary) be the propositional junctors, let *p* and *q* be formulas, then

(NOT *p*)

(AND *p q*)

(OR *p q*)

---

* 'firm', 'int', and 'stuffcoll' are to be understood as mnemotechnics for Natural Language *firm, interval,* and *collection of matter.*

(IMPLY *p q*)

(EQUIV *p q*) ,

are formulas of KS.

[4] Let FORALL and EXIST be the quantifiers, let x^{s_i} be a variable of sort s_i and *p* a formula of KS, then

(EXIST x^{s_i} *p*)

(FORALL x^{s_i} *p*)

are formulas of KS.

Well-Formedness-Conditions for Terms

[5] Sorted variables and constants are terms of KS.

[6] Let *p* be a formula of KS, let x^{s_i} be a variable of sort s_i, then

(LAMBDA x^{s_i} *p*)

is a term of KS. The sort of the term is s_i. It is not necessary that x^{s_i} occurs in *p* nor that it occurs uniquely.

Examples:

(2) (LAMBDA x^{per} (FATHER x^{per} JOHN))

'that person/those persons whose father is John'

(3) (LAMBDA $x^{stuffcoll}$ (SAMPLE G+L 77/07/15 $x^{stuffcoll}$))

'the collection of matter constituting the sample taken from G+L on 15.07.77'

(4) (LAMBDA $x^{stuffcoll}$ (AND(SAMPLE G+L 77/07/15 $x^{stuffcoll}$)
(SAMPLER $x^{stuffcoll}$ BRECHT)))

'the collection of matter constituting the sample taken from G+L on 15.07.77 and the sampler of which is Brecht'

Informal semantic explanation: By a LAMBDA-term we intend to denote the mumbers of the set of individuals satisfying the formula with respect to the abstracted position, i.e., the extension of the unary predicate (LAMBDA x^{s_i} *p*). In the case of (2) the members of the set

$\{x \mid \text{(FATHER x JOHN)}\}$

are denoted. If the abstracted variable x^{s_i} does not occur in *p* the denotation of the LAMBDA-term is the empty set.

Comment: We interpret LAMBDA-terms in a way slightly different from the way syntactic entities of this form are defined in LAMBDA-calculus: According to this definition the expression

$(\lambda\ x^{s_i}\ p)$

denotes a function from the sort s_i to the set of truth-values, i.e., a one-place predicate. In the framework of our extensional approach this one-place predicate can now be identified with its extension, that is the set of elements for which the predicate yields the value 'true'.

[7] Sorted variables and constants are individual terms of KS. If in a term

$$(\text{LAMBDA}\ x^{s_i}(P\ t_1^{s_{i_1}}\ \ldots\ t_{j-1}^{s_{i_{j-1}}}\ x^{s_i}\ t_{j+1}^{s_{i_{j+1}}}\ \ldots\ t_n^{s_{i_n}}))\ ,$$

the predicate symbol *P* is unique in the j-th position, and the terms

$t_1^{s_{i_1}},\ldots,t_n^{s_{i_n}}$

are individual terms, the whole term is an individual term.

All other terms are called "list terms".

Examples:

(7) (LAMBDA x^{per} (FATHER JOHN x^{per}))

'the father of John'

is an individual term.

(8) (LAMBDA x^{per} (BROTHER JOHN x^{per}))

'the brothers of John'

is a list term.

(9) (LAMBDA x^{per} (FATHER (LAMBDA y^{per} (FRIEND JOHN y^{per}))x^{per}))

'the fathers of the friends of John'

is a list term.

Comment: From examples (4) and (9), the term-embedding capability of KS becomes apparent. This is another feature which makes KS appear to be close to natural language.

Natural language questions asking for objects in the data base and satisfying certain properties refer to these objects by complex noun phrases, usually augmented by attributes, relative sentences or participial constructions. KS uses nested constructions for representing such complex noun phrases. A similar approach is proposed by Lacroix [1978] for the language ILL.

It should be noted that the sort symbols of KS can be regarded as unary relation symbols. Thus, if s_i is a sort symbol of KS, we write,

$$(\text{LAMBDA } x^{s_i} \ (s_i \ x^{s_i})) \quad \text{or for short:} \quad (s_i)$$

for a list term, denoting the members of the sort denoted by the sort symbol s_i.

In the case of term-embedding, the semantic explanation corresponds to the simple case as follows.

Assume we denote by

$$(\text{LAMBDA } x^{per} \ (\text{FRIEND JOHN } x^{per}))$$

the members of a set

$$N = \{x \mid (\text{FRIEND JOHN } x)\} \ .$$

Then we denote by

$$(\text{LAMBDA } x^{per} \ (\text{FATHER } (\text{LAMBDA } y^{per} \ (\text{FRIEND JOHN } y^{per})) \ x^{per}))$$

the members of the set,

$$M = \{y \mid \exists x(\text{FRIEND JOHN } x) \wedge \forall x((\text{FRIEND JOHN } x) \rightarrow (\text{FATHER } x \ y))\} \ ,$$

where it is not presupposed that there is only one friend of John and therefore there may be more than one father of the friends of John assuming John's friends are not brothers.

In general we denote by a term of the form (the sorts are omitted)

$$(\text{LAMBDA } x \ (P \ t_1 \ldots t_{i-1} (\text{LAMBDA } y \ (Q \ s_1 \ldots s_{i-1} \ y \ s_{i+1} \ldots s_m)) \ t_{i+1} \ldots t_{j-1} \ x \ t_{j+1} \ldots t_n))$$

the set

$$\{x \mid \exists y(Q\, s_1 \ldots s_{i-1}\; y\; s_{i+1} \ldots s_m) \wedge \forall y((Q\, s_1 \ldots s_{i-1}\; y\; s_{i+1} \ldots s_m) \rightarrow (P\, t_1 \ldots t_{i-1}\; y\; t_{i+1} \ldots t_{j-1}\; x\; t_{j+1} \ldots t_n))\}$$

[8] If $t_1^{s_1}, \ldots, t_n^{s_n}$ are terms of the sorts $s_1, \ldots, s_n$ respectively, then

$$(\text{LIST } t_1^{s_1} \ldots t_n^{s_n})$$

is a list term (enumerated list term) of the sort s_h if for all

$$i \in \{1, \ldots, n\}: \quad s_i \subseteq s_h \; .$$

As the sorts constitute a directed set, such an s_h always exists.

Example:

(10) (LIST JOHN JAMES)

'John and James'

(11) (LIST JAMES (LAMBDA x^{per} (FRIEND JOHN x^{per})))

'James and the friends of John'.

The semantic explanation of this is that by an enumerated list term we denote the members of the union of the sets, the members of which we denote by its argument terms.

[9] If $t_1^{s_i}$ and $t_2^{s_j}$ are list terms of the sorts s_i and s_j respectively then

$$(\text{ET } t_1^{s_i}\; t_2^{s_j})$$

is a list term of the sort s_h iff

$$(s_i = s_h \wedge s_i \subseteq s_j) \vee (s_j = s_h \wedge s_j \subseteq s_i)$$

Example:

(12) (ET (LAMBDA x^{per} (FRIEND JOHN x^{per}))
(LAMBDA x^{per} (COLLEAGUE JAMES x^{per})))

'those being both friends of John and colleagues of James'.

The semantic explanation is that an ET-term denotes the members of the intersection of the sets whose members are denoted by its argument terms.

[10] If $t_1^{s_i}$ and $t_2^{s_j}$ are list terms of the sorts s_i and s_j respectively then

$$(\text{COMPL } t_1^{s_i} \ t_2^{s_j})$$

is a list term of the sort s_j iff $s_i \subseteq s_j$.

Example:

(13) (COMPL (LAMBDA x^{per} (FRIEND JOHN x^{per}))

(LAMBDA x^{per} (COLLEAGUE JAMES x^{per})))

'those colleagues of James that are not friends of John'.

The semantic explanation is that if we denote by $t_2^{s_j}$ the members of a set M and by $t_1^{s_i}$ the members of a set N, we denote by (COMPL $t_1^{s_i}$ $t_2^{s_j}$) the members of the set M-N.

[11] If t^{s_i} is a list term and *QU* is a quantificator of KS, then

$$(QU \ t^{s_i})$$

is a quantificational list term of sort s_i. Quantificators of KS are the natural numbers and the symbols:

ALL, SOME, SEVERAL, MANY, MOST
ATLEAST_n, ATMOST_n .

Example:

(14) (THREE (LAMBDA $x^{stuffcoll}$(SAMPLE G+L 76 $x^{stuffcoll}$)))

'three samples taken from the firm G+L in 76'.

(15) (ALL (LAMBDA $x^{stuffcoll}$(SAMPLE G+L 76 $x^{stuffcoll}$)))

'all samples taken from the firm G+L in 76'.

The introduction of the quantificator ALL may seem superfluous since the unprefixed list term itself represents the complete enumeration of the elements of the corresponding set. But, considering the context in which the corresponding natural language expressions occur, we observe a difference in the use of the definite plural article (KS: unprefixed list term) and the natural language quantifier *all* (KS: ALL-prefixed list term):

(16) *The samples contained arsenic and cadmium.*

(17) *All samples contained arsenic and cadmium.*

In (16) we do not postulate that every sample contains arsenic as well as cadmium, whereas we do so in (17). These differences - in part identifiable as scope differences - are handled by a context dependent interpretation of unprefixed and ALL-prefixed list terms.

The semantic explanation is that quantificational list terms denote the members of subsets of the set whose members are denoted by the quantified list term. The cardinality of the subset is either specified as in the case of natural numbers or vague as in the case of SOME, SEVERAL.

[12] If t^{s_i} is a list term of sort s_i, then

(RESPECTIVE t^{s_i})

is a list term of sort s_i.

RESPECTIVE-terms correspond to natural language reflexive or possessive pronouns as for instance in:

(18) *John and James love themselves.*

(LOVE (RESPECTIVE (LIST (JOHN JAMES))(RESPECTIVE (LIST JOHN JAMES))).

(19) *John and James wash their hands.*

(WASH (RESPECTIVE (LIST JOHN JAMES))(LAMBDA $x^{bodypart}$ (HAND (RESPECTIVE (LIST JOHN JAMES)) $x^{bodypart}$))) ,

where *their* is to be understood in the sense of *respectively*.

The prefixing of a list term by RESPECTIVE always concerns two or more identical list terms in a formula. It indicates that the formula becomes true only in the case of simultaneous instantiation of names of identical members of the sets denoted by the list terms.

Multiple LAMBDA-Abstraction

In KS it is possible to denote a function or a predicate in the usual way by LAMBDA-abstraction. As was shown in the section, Well-Formedness Conditions for Terms, in the case of LAMBDA-abstraction of one argument the resulting one-place predicate is used in an extensional sense as a term denoting a set of individuals. LAMBDA-abstraction of two or more arguments, can in the same way, be used to denote sets of pairs, triples, etc.

The well-formedness condition is:

If *A* is a LAMBDA-abstract, then

$(\text{LAMBDA } x^{s_i} A)$

is a LAMBDA-abstract.

LAMBDA-terms are LAMBDA-abstracts.

Example:

(20) $(\text{LAMBDA } x^{firm} (\text{LAMBDA } x^{int} (\text{SAMPLE } x^{firm} x^{int})))$

'those pairs of entities characterizing the samples of a firm at an interval of time'

The extension of that expression with respect to a particular data base can be represented in the schema of a relation in the sense of the relational model described by Codd [1970], e.g.,

SAMPLE (FIRM,	INTERVAL)
G+L	77/07/15
G+L	77/09/01
LAUXMANN	76/08/30
LAUXMANN	77/01/03

QUERY EVALUATION

Defining an Answer to a Query

A query to the system can be either a yes/no-question or a wh-question. Yes/no-questions are represented by KS-formulas prefixed by the pragmatic operator '?'. Wh-questions are represented by LAMBDA-abstracts. The answer to a yes/no-question is 'yes', 'no' or 'don't know', according to whether the truth value of the formula is T, F or 'undefined'. Under the 'closed world assumption'

(Reiter [1977]) the truth value of a wff is F, when it doesn't evaluate to T. The truth value of an atomic formula must be computed according to semantic interpretation rules for KS-terms. The truth value of a formula containing logical connectors is computed in the usual way from the truth values of the atomic formulas it contains. An answer to a wh-question is defined as the extension of an n-ary LAMBDA-abstract (viewed as an n-ary predicate), or it is computed if the body of the LAMBDA-abstract consists only of an atomic formula and the predicate of the atomic formula represents a computable function.

The Data Base

The PLIDIS data base contains ground atomic formulas without function symbols as well as axioms. In this paper we are concerned only with that part of the data base containing the atomic formulas. It can be viewed as a relational data base (Codd [1970], [1972]), the relations being the extensions of KS-predicates (under the 'closed world assumption'). They are all composed of simple domains only. As domains we can use the sorts of KS. Now the sorts of a KS-predicate are given in fixed order. Therefore the columns of a relation, which is the extension of a KS-predicate, cannot be interchanged, and the usual definition of union-compatibility must be restricted too.

<u>Definition:</u>

If s_1, s_2 are sorts of KS, then

$$sup(s_1,s_2)$$

is the least upper bound of s_1 and s_2 with regard to the relation $\subseteq$.

If we assume that the set of sorts in KS is a directed set, then for each pair s_1, s_2, $sup(s_1,s_2)$ exists.

Let P and Q be KS-predicates with sort-tuples $< s_1,\ldots,s_n >$ and $< r_1,\ldots,r_m >$ respectively. Then Ext$P$ and Ext$Q$, the extensions of P and Q respectively, are union-compatible iff

(i) $m = n$

(ii) $s_i \subseteq r_i$ or $r_i \subseteq s_i$ for all $i \in \{1,\ldots,n\}$

The relation Ext$P$ $\cup$ Ext$Q$ has the domains

$$sup(s_1,r_1),\ldots,sup(s_n,r_n)$$

The data base management allows as questions only expressions of the following kinds:

(a) < varlist > < atomic KS-formula > ,

where the atomic formula has as arguments only constants, variables, and enumerated list terms containing only constants, and the varlist contains all variables occurring in the formula. The semantics of such primitive formulas is well defined and therefore the data base management handling of such formulas can be separated as an independent component of the PLIDIS system.

(b) < keylist > ,

where the elements of the keylist must be constants which are elements of keys of any relations in the sense of the relational model (cf. Codd [1970],[1972]).

In both cases a list of ground atomic KS-formulas is returned.

Normalisation of Queries

Both, well-formed formulas and LAMBDA-terms, must be normalised. The aim of formula-normalisation is to remove quantifiers by means of term-embedding procedures. Normalisation of LAMBDA-terms involves normalising the formula contained in the term, so that it contains only the logical operators AND, OR and NOT which are replaced by their respective set-theoretic counterparts.

By this step, KS-expressions become more uniform, because a normalised KS-expression only contains KS-quantificators. Note that the quantificators are defined as the KS-counterparts of natural language-quantifiers and therefore they can also be generated by translation, not only by normalisation. By the normalisation-procedure we are able to handle all well-formed KS-expressions which can occur as queries. No restrictions are imposed on the use of logical operators as e.g. in ALPHA (Codd [1970]). For example,

(a) Negation may only occur together with conjunction, i.e., in formulas like

$F \wedge \neg G$

where F and G are formulas.

(b) Quantifiers are only allowed as 'range-coupled quantifiers', i.e., the existential quantifier may only occur together with conjunction, the universal quantifier only together with implication in formulas like

$\exists x\ (F \wedge G)$

$\forall x\ (F \rightarrow G)$

Formula-Normalisation

Definitions: In the following we use the letters F, G, H, K as variables for well-formed KS-formulas, A as a variable for atomic KS-formulas and negated atomic KS-formulas ('literals').

If F is a conjunction of literals, say

$$F \equiv A_1 \wedge \ldots \wedge A_n ,$$

then by $F - A_i$ $(i \leq n)$ we denote the conjunction,

$$A_1 \wedge \ldots \wedge A_{i-1} \wedge A_{i+1} \wedge \ldots \wedge A_n .$$

We define the symbols $\bigvee_{i=1}^{n}$ and $\bigwedge_{i=1}^{n}$ by

$$\bigvee_{i=1}^{n} F_i = F_1 \vee \ldots \vee F_n ,$$

$$\bigwedge_{i=1}^{n} F_i = F_1 \wedge \ldots \wedge F_n ,$$

where F_i are formulas.

The substitution of a symbol x occurring free in a formula F by a term t is denoted by

$$F^x_t$$

A symbol x occurs free in a formula F if it does not occur within the scope of one of the operators FORALL x, EXIST x, LAMBDA x.

Let F be a KS-formula, x^{s_i} a variable occurring free in F and T a LAMBDA-term of sort s_j, where $s_j \subseteq s_i$, which denotes the members of the set $\{a_1,\ldots,a_n\}$. Then

$$F^{x^{s_i}}_{(\mathrm{ALL}\ T)} :\equiv \bigwedge_{j=1}^{n} F^{x^{s_i}}_{a_j}$$

$$F^{x^{s_i}}_{(\mathrm{SOME}\ T)} :\equiv \bigvee_{j=1}^{n} F^{x^{s_i}}_{a_j}$$

Here e.g. $F^{x^{s_i}}_{(\mathrm{ALL}\ T)}$ is the formula which results from F by substitution of x^{s_i} by the term (ALL T).

The last definition is a first approach to the semantics of KS-formulas containing quantificational list terms. The problems resulting from it will be discussed below.

Let F be a formula. A formula G is a miniscope normal form of F if G is equivalent with F and the scope of each quantifier in G is as small as possible.

Example:

(21') is a miniscope normal form of (21):

(21) (EXIST x (OR (P x a)(Q x)))

(21') (OR (EXIST x (P x a))(EXIST x (Q x)))

Given a well-formed KS-formla, the first step we make is to put it into miniscope normal form. By this step the structure of the formulas within the scopes of quantifiers is simplified and the embedding step is defined for such simple formulas only. The miniscope normal form is achieved by the following algorithm which is based on well-known logical laws (cf. Kleene [1967]). (The sort of the variable is not important for the algorithm, therefore it is omitted.)

(a) Remove the junctors EQUIV and IMPLY using the following rules:

(EQUIV F G) ⇔ (AND (IMPLY F G)(IMPLY G F))

(IMPLY F G) ⇔ (OR (NOT F) G)

(b) Shift the quantifiers to the inner parts of the formula, thereby making their scopes smaller and smaller, using the following rules:

F ≡ (EXIST x A): Stop

F ≡ (FORALL x A): Stop

F ≡ (EXIST x (NOT G)): F ⇔ (NOT (FORALL x G))

F ≡ (FORALL x (NOT G)): F ⇔ (NOT (EXIST x G))

F ≡ (EXIST x (AND G H)):

If F' ≡ (AND G H) contains at least one OR, put it into disjunctive normal form,
else, if there are literals in F' not containing x,

rearrange F' in such a way that G' contains exactly the set of x-free literals, then

F ⇔ (AND G' (EXIST x H')) ,

else Stop.

F ≡ (FORALL x (AND G H)): F ⇔ (AND (FORALL x G)(FORALL x H))

F ≡ (EXIST x (OR G H)): F ⇔ (OR (EXIST x G)(EXIST x H)

F ≡ (FORALL x (OR G H)):

If F' ≡ (OR G H) contains at least one AND put it into conjunctive normal form,
else, if there are literals in F' not containing x, rearrange F' in such a way that G' contains exactly the set of x-free literals, then

F ⇔ (OR G' (FORALL x H')) ,

else Stop.

Clearly the algorithm starts with one of the innermost quantifiers and the next one is not taken until the algorithm reaches 'Stop'.

Having executed the algorithm with the whole formula we obtain a formula where the quantifiers can occur only in one of the following four positions (corresponding to the 'Stop'-condition of the algorithm):

(a) (EXIST x A)

(b) (FORALL x A)

(c) (EXIST x F), where F is a conjunction of literals and x occurs in all literals of F.

(d) (FORALL x F), where F is a disjunction of literals and x occurs in all literals of F.

In the next step, we remove the quantifiers according to the following theorem.

<u>Theorem:</u>

(a) $(\text{EXIST } x^{s_i} \text{ A}) \Leftrightarrow A^{x^{s_i}}_{(\text{SOME}(s_i))}$,

(b) $(\text{FORALL } x^{s_i} \text{ A}) \Leftrightarrow A^{x^{s_i}}_{(\text{ALL}(s_i))}$,

(c) $(\text{EXIST } x^{s_i} F) \Leftrightarrow (F - A)^{x^{s_i}}_{(\text{SOME}(\text{LAMBDA } x^{s_i} A))}$,

where F is a conjunction of literals all of which contain x^{s_i} and A is a literal in F. (A can be chosen heuristically so that the term (LAMBDA x^{s_i} A) denotes a set which is as small as possible.)

(d) $(\text{FORALL } x^{s_i} F) \Rightarrow H^{x^{s_i}}_{(\text{ALL}(\text{LAMBDA } x^{s_i} (\text{NOT } G)))}$,

where F ≡ (OR G H) and G and H correspond to one of the following forms, whereby $A, A_1, \ldots, A_n, B, B_1, \ldots, B_m$ are non-negated atomic formulas and $n, m \geq 1$:

(1) $G \equiv A$ and $H \equiv B_1 \vee \ldots \vee B_m$

(2) $G \equiv \neg A_1 \vee \ldots \vee \neg A_n$ and $H \equiv \neg B$

(3) $G \equiv \neg A_1 \vee \ldots \vee \neg A_n$ and $H \equiv B_1 \vee \ldots \vee B_m$.

Note that G has in most cases originated from the antecedent of an implication. Thus assume G ≡ (NOT K). Then

F ≡ (OR (NOT K) H) ≡ (IMPLY K H)

and

$$H^{x^{s_i}}_{(\text{ALL}(\text{LAMBDA } x^{s_i} (\text{NOT } G)))} \equiv H^{x^{s_i}}_{(\text{ALL}(\text{LAMBDA } x^{s_i} K))} .$$

In all cases (a) - (d) the term by which x^{s_i} is replaced should be prefixed by RESPECTIVE if x^{s_i} occurs more than once in the formula. By way of giving a semantic definition of such a formula the RESPECTIVE-operator guarantees the 'parallel' substitution of list terms prefixed by RESPECTIVE by their elements.

Example:

The formula (22) is equivalent to (22'):

```
(22)   (P (RESPECTIVE (ALL (LIST a b)))
          (RESPECTIVE (ALL (LIST a b))))
```

(22') (P a a) ∧ (P b b) ,

whereas the same formula without RESPECTIVE, namely (23), is equivalent to (23'):

```
(23)   (P (ALL (LIST a b))
          (ALL (LIST a b)))
```

(23') (P a a) $\wedge$ (P a b) $\wedge$ (P b a) $\wedge$ (P b b) .

Proof:

Assume $(s_i) = \{a_1, \ldots, a_n\}$.

(a) $(\text{EXIST } x^{s_i} \text{ A}) \Leftrightarrow \bigvee_{j=1}^{n} A^{x^{s_i}}_{a_j}$

$\Leftrightarrow A^{x^{s_i}}_{(\text{SOME}(s_i))}$

(b) $(\text{FORALL } x^{s_i} \text{ A}) \Leftrightarrow \bigwedge_{j=1}^{n} A^{x^{s_i}}_{a_j}$

$\Leftrightarrow A^{x^{s_i}}_{(\text{ALL}(s_i))}$

(c) Assume $(\text{LAMBDA } x^{s_i} \text{ A}) = \{a_{1_1}, \ldots, a_{1_k}\} \subset (s_i)$.

$(\text{EXIST } x^{s_i} \text{ F}) \Leftrightarrow \bigvee_{j=1}^{n} F^{x^{s_i}}_{a_j}$

$\Leftrightarrow \bigvee_{j=1}^{k} F^{x^{s_i}}_{a_{1_j}}$

because F is a conjunction of literals and therefore it does not hold for the elements $a_m \in (s_i) - (\text{LAMBDA } x^{s_i} \text{ A})$

$\Leftrightarrow \bigvee_{j=1}^{k} (F - A)^{x^{s_i}}_{a_{1_j}}$

because A holds for all elements of $(\text{LAMBDA } x^{s_i} \text{ A})$ and F is a conjunction

$\Leftrightarrow (F - A)^{x^{s_i}}_{(\text{SOME}(\text{LAMBDA } x^{s_i} \text{ A}))}$.

(d) Assume $(\text{LAMBDA } x^{s_i} (\text{NOT G})) = \{a_{1_1}, \ldots, a_{1_k}\} \subset (s_i)$

and $(s_i) - \{a_{1_1}, \ldots, a_{1_k}\} = \{a_{m_1}, \ldots, a_{m_{n-k}}\}$.

$$(\text{FORALL } x^{s_i} \ F) \Leftrightarrow \bigwedge_{j=1}^{n} F^{x^{s_i}}_{a_j}$$

$$\Leftrightarrow \bigwedge_{j=1}^{n} (G \vee H)^{x^{s_i}}_{a_j} \quad ,$$

by assumption on F,

$$\Leftrightarrow \bigwedge_{j=1}^{k} (G \vee H)^{x^{s_i}}_{a_{1_j}} \quad \wedge \quad \bigwedge_{j=1}^{n-k} (G \vee H)^{x^{s_i}}_{a_{m_j}} \quad ,$$

by assumption on (s_i), see above

$$\Leftrightarrow \bigwedge_{j=1}^{k} (\neg G \wedge H)^{x^{s_i}}_{a_{1_j}} \quad \wedge \quad \bigwedge_{j=1}^{n-k} (G \vee H)^{x^{s_i}}_{a_{m_j}}$$

because a_{1_j} are those elements of (s_i), for which G does not hold and therefore H must hold

$$\Leftrightarrow \bigwedge_{j=1}^{k} (\neg G \wedge H)^{x^{s_i}}_{a_{1_j}} \quad \wedge \quad \bigwedge_{j=1}^{n-k} G^{x^{s_i}}_{a_{m_j}}$$

because the a_{m_j} are those elements of (s_i), for which G holds

$$\Rightarrow \bigwedge_{j=1}^{k} (\neg G \wedge H)^{x^{s_i}}_{a_{1_j}}$$

weakening the conjunction

$$\Leftrightarrow \bigwedge_{j=1}^{k} \neg G^{x^{s_i}}_{a_{1_j}} \quad \wedge \quad \bigwedge_{j=1}^{k} H^{x^{s_i}}_{a_{1_j}}$$

by definition of $\bigwedge_{i=1}^{n}$

$$\Leftrightarrow \bigwedge_{j=1}^{k} H^{x^{s_i}}_{a_{1_j}}$$

because $\neg$ G holds for all elements of (LAMBDA x^{s_i} (NOT G))

$$\Leftrightarrow H^{x^{s_i}}_{(\text{ALL(LAMBDA } x^{s_i} \text{ (NOT G)))}} \, .$$

In case (d) we can only prove the implication. But under the 'closed world assumption', the equivalence can be proved because in this case, if $\neg$ G holds for the elements of a subset of (s_i), then G holds for the complement of the subset, and so

$$\bigwedge_{j=1}^{k} (\neg G \wedge H)_{a_{1_j}}^{x^{s_i}} \Rightarrow \bigwedge_{j=1}^{k} (\neg G \wedge H)_{a_{1_j}}^{x^{s_i}} \wedge \bigwedge_{j=1}^{n-k} G_{a_{m_j}}^{x^{s_i}} .$$

<u>Example:</u>

(24') and (25') are normalised forms of (24) and (25) respectively:

(24) (EXIST x^{s_i} (OR (NOT (P x^{s_i} a))
(Q x^{s_i} b))) .

(24') (OR (NOT (P (ALL(s_i)) a))
(Q (SOME(s_i)) b)) .

(25) (FORALL x^{s_i} (OR (NOT (P x^{s_i} a))
(Q x^{s_i} b))) .

(25') (Q (ALL(LAMBDA x^{s_i} (P x^{s_i} a))) b) .

It should be noted that a problem with the approach to the semantics of KS-formulas mentioned above is that different formulas of predicate calculus which are not equivalent have the same normalized form. So, e.g.,

```
F ≡ (FORALL x (IMPLY (Q a x)
                     (EXIST y (AND (R b y)
                                   (P x y)))))
```

and

```
G ≡ (EXIST y (AND (R b y)
                  (FORALL x (IMPLY (Q a x)
                                   (P x y))))) ,
```

have the same normalised form, namely

```
(P (ALL(LAMBDA x (Q a x)))
   (SOME(LAMBDA y (R b y)))) ,
```

but they are not equivalent; rather G $\rightarrow$ F, but the reverse does not hold! All refinements in the definition of KS-semantics involve the same problem. This is an interesting feature if one regards

KS as a semantic representation language for natural language. Here KS reflects the ambiguity of a natural language-formulation. But in our case we should be precise, and to overcome this problem we could index the quantificators. Thus,

$$(P\ (ALL_2(LAMBDA\ x\ (Q\ a\ x)))\ (SOME_1(LAMBDA\ y\ (R\ b\ y))))\ ,$$

is equivalent to F, while

$$(P\ (ALL_1(LAMBDA\ x\ (Q\ a\ x)))\ (SOME_2(LAMBDA\ y\ (R\ b\ y))))\ ,$$

is equivalent to G .

Term-Normalisation

Let T be the KS-term (LAMBDA x^{s_i} F) and F a KS-formula, then F is first normalised as described in the previous section, and then transformed into disjunctive normal form. F then has one of the following forms:

(a) $F \equiv (OR\ G\ H)$,

(b) $F \equiv (AND\ G\ H)$,

(c) $F \equiv (NOT\ G)$,

(d) $F \equiv A$.

Now the logical operators OR, AND, and NOT are replaced by their set-theoretic equivalents union, intersection, and complement respectively which are denoted in KS by LIST, ET, and COMPL. This can be done without any restrictions, because formulas embedded in a LAMBDA-term are now quantifier-free (cf. Reiter [1978]).

(a) $(LAMBDA\ x^{s_i}\ (OR\ G\ H)) = (LIST\ (LAMBDA\ x^{s_i}\ G)(LAMBDA\ x^{s_i}\ H))$,

whereby embedded list terms are brought to the top level according to

$$(LIST\ t_1\ \ldots\ t_{i-1}\ (LIST\ t_{i1}\ \ldots\ t_{ik})\ t_{i+1}\ \ldots\ t_n)$$

$$\equiv$$

$$(LIST\ t_1\ \ldots\ t_{i-1}\ t_{i1}\ \ldots\ t_{ik}\ t_{i+1}\ \ldots\ t_n)\ .$$

Note that a KS-list term is a 'heap', i.e. a commutative, associative and idempotent collection of individuals.

(b),(c) If F contains only positive literals, then no further normalisation is required.

If F contains only the negative literals $\neg A_1,\ldots,\neg A_n$, then

$$F \Leftrightarrow (\text{NOT } F')$$

whereby F' is a disjunction of the positive literals $A_1,\ldots,A_n$ and

$$(\text{LAMBDA } x^{s_i} (\text{NOT } F')) = (\text{COMPL } (\text{LAMBDA } x^{s_i} F')(s_i))$$

(COMPL A B) is defined as B - A.

If G contains only positive literals and H only negative literals, then

$$F \Leftrightarrow (\text{AND } G \ (\text{NOT } H'))$$

whereby H' is a disjunction of the positive literals in H, and

$$(\text{LAMBDA } x^{s_i} (\text{AND } G \ (\text{NOT } H'))) = (\text{COMPL } (\text{LAMBDA } x^{s_i} H') \ (\text{LAMBDA } x^{s_i} G)) .$$

(d) No normalisation is required.

The set equalities in (a) - (c) are easy to prove.

<u>Example:</u>

(26') is the normalised form of (26) (sort symbols are omitted):

```
(26)   (LAMBDA x (OR (AND (R a b c)
                          (AND (P a x)
                               (Q x b)))

                     (AND (R x c b)
                          (AND (NOT (S a x))
                               (NOT (Q x a)))))) .

(26')  (LIST (LAMBDA x (AND (R a b c)
                            (AND (P a x)
                                 (Q x b))))

             (COMPL (LIST (LAMBDA x (S a x))
                          (LAMBDA x (Q x a)))

                    (LAMBDA x (R x c b)))) .
```

The Interpretation of Queries

For the evaluation of the normalised query, a labelled cycle-free directed graph is constructed first according to the syntactic structure of the query, which is in the following so-called 'evaluation graph' (EG). Identical subexpressions of the query are represented only once in the EG. This minimizes the number of data base look-ups. Next the answer to the query is determined by evaluating the EG. Both the construction and the evaluation of the EG are straightforward. They are illustrated by means of an example. In clarifying the example the term 'n-th projection' is used in the following sense: Given the list of atomic formulas

(P a b m)

(P q r n)

(P d c h)

(P e f t)

the 'third projection' is the list (LIST b r c f).

Assume the following query was put to the system:

Give those plants in Stuttgart where Brecht took all samples in the year 1977.

The KS-representation of this query, after normalisation, would be

(LAMBDA $x^{plantnr}$ (AND (PLANT (SOME(firm)) STUTTGART $x^{plantnr}$)
(SAMPLER (ALL(LAMBDA $x^{stuffcoll}$
(SAMPLE x^{plantr} (IN-TEMP 77)
$x^{stuffcoll}$)))
BRECHT))) .

The EG shown in Figure 1 is constructed from this LAMBDA-term.

The value of the EG is the final value of N1. To compute this value we must first compute the values of its parent nodes N2 and N9. To compute the value of N2 we must find the values of N3 and N5. The value of N3 is a subset of the value of N4 because of the SOME-label, more specifically even a subset of the second projection of the value of N2. N4 is labelled by the sort predicate term '(firm)', therefore this sort is its value. N5 is labelled by a constant which is assumed as its value. Now we can determine the value of N2 by a data base query of the form

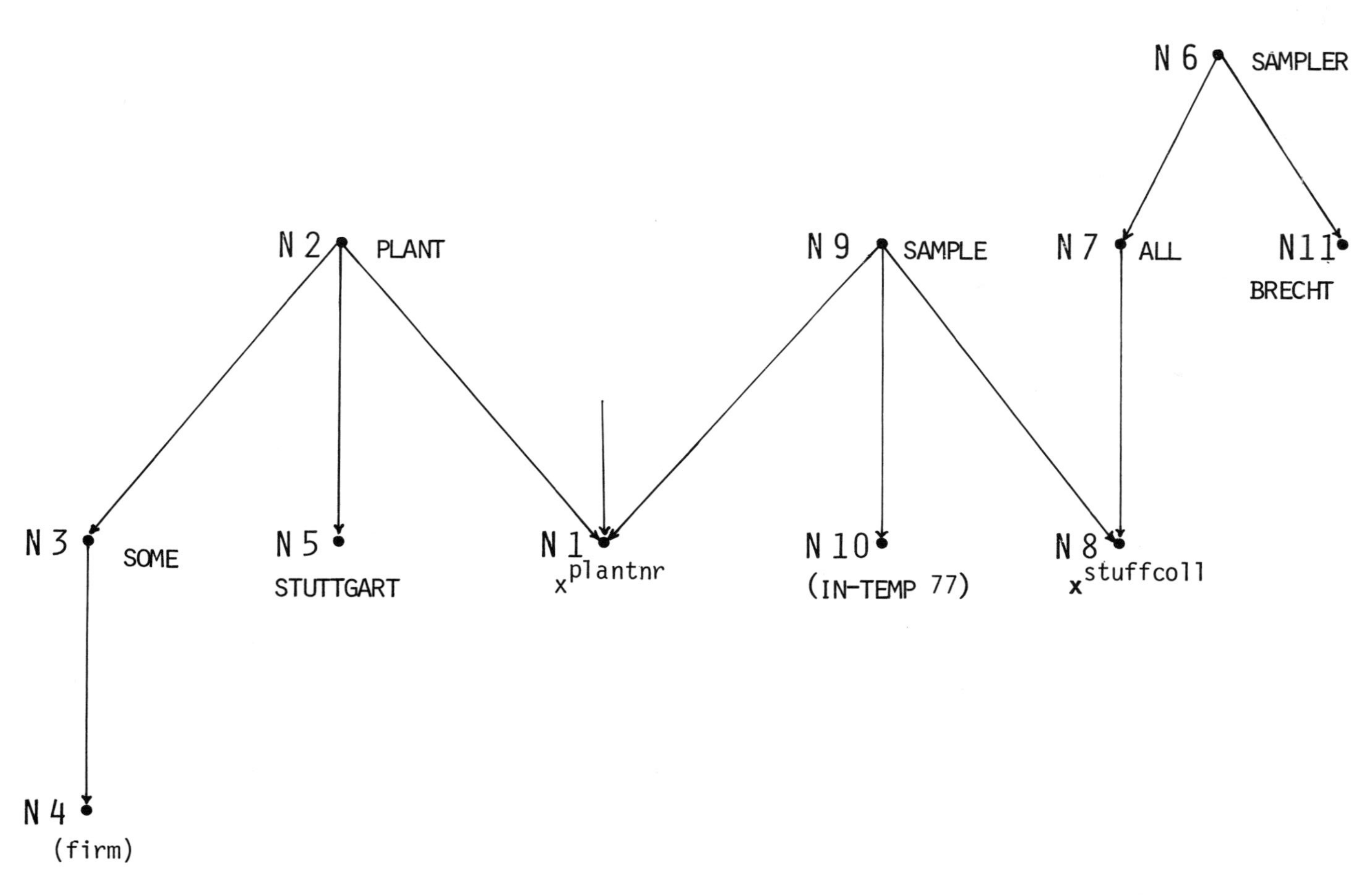

Figure 1. Evaluation Graph

(x y) (PLANT x STUTTGART y) .

Assume, this query yields the following list of ground atomic formulas:

(PLANT BOSCH STUTTGART \$1)

(PLANT LAUXMANN STUTTGART \$2)

(PLANT DMV STUTTGART \$5)

(PLANT DAIMLER-BENZ STUTTGART \$7)

Then the value of N1 at this stage of the query evaluation is the fourth projection of this list, i.e., the list

(LIST \$1 \$2 \$5 \$7)

The computation of the value of N1 is quite similar to Reiter's 'projection operator', applied twice to the list of argument triples of PLANT. The constant STUTTGART behaves like an existentially quantified variable. To determine the final value of N1 we have to take into account that an ALL-quantificator occurs in the second conjunct of the LAMBDA-term. If this had not been the case, we would only have to compute another value for N1 from N9 similarly as was done for N2, and to make the intersection of the two values. But now we have to investigate separately for each value of the list (LIST \$1 \$2 \$5 \$7) whether the second conjunct holds or not. Take for example the first value \$1. We must now compute the value of N8 for \$1 and then check, whether this value is a subset of the samples taken by Brecht or not. If so, \$1 is an answer to the question. This task can be reformulated as: We must compute the intersection of the fourth projection of the value of N9 with the second projection of the value of N6 as an 'intermediate value' of N8, say v. Then we must check whether the triple (\$1,t,a) for all a $\in$ v is an element of the SAMPLE-relation or not, where t is a date beginning with 77. If so, \$1 is an answer. This interpretation shows, that the handling of the ALL-quantificator is closely related to Reiter's 'division operator'. The main difference is, that for Reiter v constitutes the entire sort, whereas after term-embedding v is a subset of the sort, determined by a specific term, here the SAMPLE-term.

Now we will proceed with the evaluation of the graph. We need the value of N8 for \$1. This is the fourth projection of the value of N10. But N10 is labelled by IN-TEMP-term. IN-TEMP is a built-in function which computes from the third projection of the value of N9 the subset of those dates beginning with 77. Now the value of N9 is determined by the data base query

(x) (SAMPLE $1 (IN-TEMP 77) x) .

Assume we get the following atomic formulas as answers:

(SAMPLE $1 77/02/15 $111)

(SAMPLE $1 77/05/18 $112)

(SAMPLE $1 77/10/02 $113) .

Then we must check whether the term

(LIST $111 $112 $113)

represents a subset of all samples taken by Brecht, i.e. if all the three formulas

(SAMPLER $111 BRECHT)

(SAMPLER $112 BRECHT)

(SAMPLER $113 BRECHT)

hold. If the data base look-up is positive in each case, $1 is an answer. Proceeding with $2, $5, $7 in the same way as with $1 we get the final answer which is a subset of the first value of N1.

This example can also serve to illustrate our handling of existential presuppositions (see the section General Principles in Constructing KS). Assume there were no samples taken in 1977 from any plant in Stuttgart. Then if existential presupposition were not taken into account, the answer to the query could be the enumeration of all plants in Stuttgart. (For in a strictly logical sense Brecht has indeed taken all samples in 1977 of the plants in Stuttgart since this set is empty.) But this would obviously not be a desirable answer. Since the KS-terms involve existential presuppositions the system immediately reacts by an appropriate remark to the violation of existential presupposition expressed by the term

$$(\text{LAMBDA } x^{\text{stuffcoll}} \ (\text{SAMPLE } x^{\text{plantnr}} \ (\text{IN-TEMP } 77) \ x^{\text{stuffcoll}})).$$

If, after the evluation the whole graph is stored together with the values of its nodes, we can quickly answer such follow-up queries using some values of the first question, e.g.,

Which products were produced by those plants?.

This enhances the dialogue-quality of the question-answering system.

CONCLUSION

If KS were to be used directly as a data base query language, it might appear rather clumsy. There are redundancies in the notation of query-expressions and some constructions are difficult to read. But KS was not designed as a user-oriented query language, rather as an internal representation language standing on an intermediate level between natural language and the primitive operations on a data base. It is part of a question-answering-system which allows access to the data base by natural language questions. These are translated into KS-expressions the user is not confronted with. Therefore it is not necessary that KS-expressions be modelled on the natural language surface structure, for instance by avoiding as far as possible the use of variables as is done in the language ILL (cf. Lacroix [1978]). Because of the close relation of KS-expressions to predicate calculus-expressions, KS benefits from the advantages of predicate calculus, e.g. the usual deduction mechanisms defined for predicate calculus.

Under the aspect of a data base query language, KS can be compared with query languages such as SQUARE (Boyce et al. [1975]) especially with regard to wh-questions, which correspond to the 'mappings' of SQUARE. It can be shown that KS is 'relationally complete' (cf. Codd [1972]). No restrictions on the syntax of KS are required for the formulation of questions.

At the present stage only one data type is defined in KS, namely 'heaps' (see the section Term-Normalisation). Therefore no expressions involving other data types, e.g. bags, can be constructed and operations defined for such data types as 'average', 'count' etc. cannot be used in the present system.

ACKNOWLEDGMENT

The authors particularly wish to thank Genevieve Berry-Rogghe, who has closely collaborated with them and who has implemented the evaluation procedure.

REFERENCES

1. Berry-Rogghe, G. and Wulz, H. [1978] An Overview of PLIDIS, A Problem Solving System with German as Query Language, In *Natural Language Communication with Computers* (L. Bolc, Ed.), Springer, Heidelberg, 1978, forthcoming.

2. Boyce, R. F., Chamberlin, D. D., King III, W. F., and Hammer, M. M. [1975] Specifying Queries as Relational Expressions: The SQUARE Data Sublanguage, *CACM 11*, 18 (Nov. 1975), 621-628.

3. Chang, C. L. [1978] DEDUCE 2: Further Investigations of Deduction in Relational Data Bases, In *Logic and Data Bases* (H. Gallaire and J. Minker, Eds.), Plenum Press, New York, 1978, 201-236.

4. Codd, E. F. [1970] A Relational Model for Large Shared Data Banks, *CACM 13* , 6 (June 1970), 377-387.

5. Codd, E. F. [1972] Relational Completeness of Data Base Sublanguages, In *Data Base Systems* (R. Rustin, Ed.), Prentice-Hall, Englewood Cliffs, N.J., 1972, 65-98.

6. Hayes, P. J. [1971] A Logic of Actions, In *Machine Intelligence 6* (B. Meltzer and D. Michie, Eds.), Edinburgh University Press, Edinburgh, 1971, 495-520.

7. Kellogg, C., Klahr, P. and Travis, L. [1978] Deductive Planning and Pathfinding for Relational Data Bases, In *Logic and Data Bases* (H. Gallaire and J. Minker, Eds.), Plenum Press, New York, 1978, 179-200.

8. Kleene, S. C. [1967] *Mathematical Logic*, Wiley & Sons, New York, 1967, (see pp. 125-134).

9. Lacroix, M. and Pirotte, A. [1977] Domain-Oriented Relational Languages, *Proceedings International Conference on Very Large Data Bases*, Tokyo, IEEE, 1977, 370-378. Also *MBLE Report R-351*, April, 1977.

10. Landsbergen, S. and Scha, R. [1978] Formal Languages for Semantic Representation, In *Aspects of Automated Text Processing* (J. Petöfi, Ed.), Buske, Hamburg, 1978, forthcoming.

11. McCarthy, J. and Hayes, P. [1969] Some Philosophical Problems from the Standpoint of Artificial Intelligence, In *Machine Intelligence 4* (B. Meltzer and D. Michie, Eds.), Edinburgh University Press, Edinburgh, 1969, 463-502.

12. McSkimin, J. R. and Minker, J. [1978] A Predicate Calculus Based Semantic Network for Question-Answering Systems, In *Associative Networks - The Representation and Use of Knowledge* (N. Findler, Ed.), Academic Press, New York, 1978.

13. Minker, J. [1978] An Experimental Relational Data Base System Based on Logic, In *Logic and Data Bases* (H. Gallaire and J. Minker, Eds.), Plenum Press, New York, 1978, 107-147.

14. Pople, H. R. [1972] A Goal-Oriented Language for the Computer, In *Representation and Meaning* (H. A. Simon and L. Siklossy, Eds.), Prentice-Hall, Englewood Cliffs, N.J., 1972, 329-413.

15. Quine, W. [1972] *Methods of Logic, 3rd Edition*, Holt, Rinhart and Winston, New York, 1972, (see pp. 232-234).

16. Reiter, R. [1977] An Approach to Deductive Question-Answering, *BBN Tech. Report 3649*, Bolt Beranek and Newman, Inc., Cambridge, Mass., Sept. 1977, 161 pp.

17. Reiter, R. [1978] On Closed World Data Bases, In *Logic and Data Bases* (H. Gallaire and J. Minker, Eds.), Plenum Press, New York, 1978, 55-76.

18. Sandewall, E. [1971] Representing Natural Language Information in Predicate Calculus, In *Machine Intelligence 6* (B. Meltzer and D. Michie, Eds.), Edinburgh University Press, Edinburgh, 1971, 255-277.

19. Thomason, R. H. [1972] A Semantic Theory of Sortal Incorrectness, *Journal of Philosophical Logic 1*, 1972, 209-258.

20. Woods, W. A., Kaplan, R. M. and Nash-Webber, B. L. [1972] The Lunar Sciences Natural Language Information System, Final Report, *BBN Report No. 2378*, Cambridge, Mass., June 1972.

21. Zifonun, G. [1977] Die Konstruktsprache KS. Entwurf eines Darstellungsmittels für natürlichsprachlich formulierte Information, In *kasustheorie, klassifikation, semantische interpretation*, Papiere zur Textlinguistik 11, Buske, Hamburg, 1977, 305-322.

HIGH LEVEL DATA BASE QUERY LANGUAGES

Alain Pirotte

MBLE Research Laboratory

Brussels, Belgium

ABSTRACT

The paper presents a general framework for comparing high-level non-procedural query languages for the relational model of data. The principal language features are presented as modifications of operations in the first-order predicate calculus. These modifications suggest a classification of the retrieval operations of eleven existing relational languages (ALPHA, DEDUCE, DEDUCE 2, FQL, ILL, QUEL, QUERY-BY-EXAMPLE, SEQUEL, SEQUEL 2, SQUARE, TAMALAN).

INTRODUCTION

A recent trend in the studies about the architecture of data base management systems is the interest in providing data-independent interfaces for non-specialist users. Data independence implies that users may view the contents of a data base as constrained only by a logical formalism of data organization and not by its implementation on physical storage.

Another area of active work has been the study of data structures for expressing the user views of data bases. Ideally, such data structures must be simple to manipulate for the users while remaining powerful enough to allow a reasonably natural description of the information contained in data bases. At the same time, such data structures should be translatable into physical storage structures so that the performance of the data base systems which support them remains acceptable.

The relational model is a simple logical formalism for describing the organization of data. It views information contained in a data base as sets of objects and sets of relationships among these objects. Interactions of users with such data base descriptions can be independent of any physical representation, and user requests can be formulated in high-level non-procedural languages.

Most existing non-procedural languages for the relational model were more or less directly inspired by the first-order predicate calculus. This paper presents a general framework to relate the retrieval features of several languages to the calculus. It is a constructive survey of languages, which separates the superficial from the essential differences between languages. Thus, a comparison can be based on the aspects which are deeply rooted in the languages and it can leave aside those aspects which are easily changed.

The comparison is illustrated by several queries expressed in calculus formalisms which underlie constructions in eleven existing relational languages: ALPHA, DEDUCE, DEDUCE 2, FQL, ILL, QUEL, QUERY-BY-EXAMPLE, SEQUEL, SEQUEL 2, SQUARE, and TAMALAN.

RELATIONS AND RELATIONAL DATA BASES

A relational data base consists of a collection of domains and of a collection of relations.

A domain is a set of values, which represent relevant objects in the universe described by the data base. In the example used in this paper, the list of domains includes *employee names, salaries, department names, items, companies, floors, item classes, cities*. In general, data base domains need not be disjoint. The fact that two domains are not disjoint is a structural information that should be explicitly indicated.

A relation defined over n (not necessarily distinct) domains $D_1,\ldots,D_n$ is noted $R(A_1:D_1,\ldots,A_n:D_n)$. The attributes $A_1,\ldots,A_n$ are all distinct for a given relation R: they identify the roles played by the domains in the relation. At any given moment, the extension of relation R is a subset of the Cartesian product of its domains: $R \subset D_1 \times \ldots \times D_n$.

Relations represent various kinds of associations among the values in the domains of the data base. The extension of a relation is a set of n-tuples (also called simply tuples) of values from data base domains. Each such tuple $(d_1,\ldots,d_n)$ with $d_1 \in D_1,\ldots,d_n \in D_n$ may be viewed as expressing a predicate which holds for the values $d_1,\ldots,d_n$. An alternative view of a relation is in the form of a table where:

- the values in any given column belong to the same data base domain;

- no two rows (or tuples) are identical;

- the order of the rows is immaterial;

- the order of columns, considered with their associated attribute, is immaterial.

Each relational language has its preferred view of relations (Pirotte [1978]). In this paper, the following relations are used as an example:

EMP (EMPL:NAME, SAL, MGR:NAME, DEPT)

SALES (DEPT, ITEM)

SUPPLY (COMP, DEPT, ITEM)

LOC (DEPT, FLOOR)

TYPE (ITEM, CLASS)

ADDRESS (COMP, CITY)

When a data base domain participates only once in a relation, then the convention is made that the name of the domain and the attribute are identical and that only one of them is indicated. This notation clearly indicates that e.g. in the *EMP* relation, the *EMPL* and *MGR* attributes are defined on a common data base domain called *NAME* which represents a set of employee entities.

Relation *EMP* describes the fact that employees have a salary, work for a manager who is also an employee and work in a department. Relation *SALES* says that departments sell items, relation *SUPPLY* that companies supply items to departments. Relation *LOC* gives the floor of each department, *TYPE* the type or class of each item, *ADDRESS* the city where each company is situated.

DEFINITION OF AN APPLIED PREDICATE CALCULUS

Only a brief definition of an applied calculus is given here. Details can be found in any logic text as, for example, Reichenbach [1948] and Rosser [1953].

Syntax

The calculus makes use of the following kinds of symbols: variables, constants, logical connectives ($\neg$, $\wedge$, $\vee$, $\rightarrow$, $\leftrightarrow$), function symbols, predicate symbols, quantifier symbols ($\forall$, $\exists$) and parentheses.

The *terms* are defined as follows:

- a constant is a term;
- a variable is a term;
- if f is a function symbol of n arguments and if $t_1,\ldots,t_n$ are terms, then $f(t_1,\ldots,t_n)$ is a term.

The *propositions* are defined as follows:

- if P is a predicate symbol of n arguments and if $t_1,\ldots,t_n$ are terms, then $P(t_1,\ldots,t_n)$ is a proposition;
- if A and B are propositions, so $\neg A$, $(A \wedge B)$, $(A \vee B)$, $(A \rightarrow B)$, $(A \leftrightarrow B)$.

Instead of the fully parenthesized form, the following usual order of increasing priorities can be used for connectives: $\leftrightarrow$, $\rightarrow$, $\vee$, $\wedge$, $\neg$.

The *formulas* are defined as follows:

- propositions are formulas;
- if x is a variable, then $(\forall x)$ and $(\exists x)$ are *quantifiers* containing x. If A is a formula which contains x but no quantifier containing x, then $((\forall x)A)$ and $((\exists x)A)$ are formulas. A is the scope of the quantifier $(\forall x)$ or $(\exists x)$. Parentheses may be removed if the structure remains unambiguous. They are used freely in this paper.

A variable x is free in a formula A if A contains x and A does not contain a quantifier containing x. If A contains x and x is not free in A, then x is bound in A. Variables free for the whole formula are often called simply free variables.

Semantics

The calculus defined here is "applied" in the sense that its universe of discourse is finite and that its predicate symbols have a fixed interpretation in this universe. Therefore, given the universe of discourse D, the following mappings are known:

- a correspondence between constants of the language and elements of the universe D;

- a correspondence $D^n \rightarrow D$ for each function symbol of n arguments;

- a correspondence $D^n \rightarrow \{true, false\}$ for each predicate symbol of n arguments.

The truth value of a formula can be computed by the following algorithm:

(1) replace each formula of the form $\forall x\ A(x)$ by $A(a_1) \wedge \ldots \wedge A(a_m)$ where $A(x)$ indicates that x is free in A; $a_1, \ldots, a_m$ are all the elements of D and A(a) represents the result of substituting a for each free occurrence of x in A;

(2) replace each formula of the form $\exists x\ A(x)$ by $A(a_1) \vee \ldots \vee A(a_m)$;

(3) replace each remaining variable x_j, i.e. each free variable of the whole formula, by a constant a_j;

(4) apply functions to their arguments according to the mappings associated with function symbols;

(5) apply predicates to their arguments according to the mappings associated with predicate symbols;

(6) evaluate the resulting proposition, where the operands are truth values and the propositional connectives have their usual meaning. The value of the formula is the truth value eventually obtained.

TRANSFORMATION OF THE CALCULUS INTO A QUERY LANGUAGE

Two modifications are necessary before the applied calculus can be considered as a query language: give an interpretation to its free variables and link its universe D to a data base. Calculus functions are left out of the discussion until the penultimate section of this paper.

Free Variables

According to the semantic definition of the calculus, the truth-value of a formula depends on the value of its free variables, i.e. on the particular element of the universe picked for each free variable.

Only the formulas without free variables, sometimes called sentences, have a fixed truth value. Therefore sentences of the calculus are used to represent the "yes-no" queries.

To represent "list" queries whose answer is a set of elements or a set of tuples of elements of the universe, the calculus is extended as follows. A formula containing free variables has as value the set of all tuples of elements of the universe D such that each tuple makes the formula *true*, when the elements in the tuple replace in a specified order the free variables.

For clarity, the free variables of a formula which denotes a list query will be written in front of the formula in a *target list*. For example $\{(x,y) \mid F(x,y)\}$ denotes the set of pairs of elements from the universe D such that the formula F, with x and y as free variables, is *true* for each of the pairs, when the first element of the pair replaces the occurrences of x in F and the second element replaces the occurrences of y.

Universe

The universe of the applied calculus must be tied somehow to the relations of a particular data base. This can be done in two ways: (1) let the universe of the calculus correspond with tuples of relations and use *tuple variables* or (2) let the universe correspond with domains of the data base and use *domain variables*.

However, it is not very interesting to simply associate the universe of the calculus with the set of tuples from all relations nor with the union of all data base domains. For example, most formulas involving universal quantification will be meaningless if the range of the quantifier is the whole universe. Another undesirable example deals with negation: $\neg$ P is *true*, if P has one free variable, for all the elements of D for which P is *false* (if P has n free variables, for all the elements of D^n for which P is *false*). In general that can be a very large and meaningless portion of D (or of D^n).

Therefore, filters have been introduced to reduce the range of domain variables or of tuple variables to meaningful subsets of the universe D, which are linked to the structure defined by the data base relations.

This can be done in two ways: (1) force variables to have a unique type, defined by a data base domain or by a relation or a union of relations, or (2) provide special unary predicates, called "range predicates", each of which is *true* on a domain or on a relation, and require that every variable be used in at least one range predicate.

Having types allows type checking of the predicates. A predicate is no longer an application $D^n \rightarrow \{true, false\}$ but it becomes instead an application $D_1 \times \ldots \times D_n \rightarrow \{true, false\}$ where $D_1, \ldots, D_n$

are the subsets of D which define types $T_1,\ldots,T_n$. Only those predicates are syntactically correct for which the i-th term has type T_i, for $1 \leq i \leq n$. Using types requires that a type be assigned in some way or another to every variable (remember that calculus functions are not considered here), but this need not be done explicitly inside calculus expressions.

On the contrary, range predicates are ordinary predicates of the calculus and they imply nothing about type checking. Furthermore, simply providing range predicates in the calculus is not enough to preclude the meaningless queries produced by application of e.g. universal quantification and negation as indicated above. In addition to defining range predicates, a discipline must be imposed which makes sure that these predicates are used properly in the formulas of the calculus.

For example, if x has a type which corresponds to the subset D_x of D, then $\{x \mid \neg P(x)\}$ is equal to the set of elements in D_x for which P is *false*. On the contrary, in a typeless language, if RP is a range predicate associated with D_x (i.e. a unary predicate *true* on D_x and *false* elsewhere in D) then a query with the same value is written $\{x \mid RP(x) \wedge \neg P(x)\}$.

Choosing between types and range predicates is independent of whether tuple or domain variables are used. However a calculus with tuple variables must also provide operations to manipulate (i.e. retrieve, compare, etc.) elementary values in relation tuples, whereas on the contrary a calculus with domain variables need not necessarily have tuple operations. Therefore, the system of types to be defined for tuples variables is a bit more complex if it has to control all the operations on tuples and pieces of tuples.

Existing relational languages belong to families which can be defined by two characteristics: domain or tuple variables, and types or range predicates.

(1) The family characterized by tuple variables and range predicates is the basis for the ALPHA language (Codd [1971]). A few modifications show that QUEL (Held et al. [1975]) and a part of SQUARE (Boyce et al. [1975]) and SEQUEL (Chamberlin et al. [1974]) also belong to this family.

(2) The family characterized by tuple variables and types has not been studied in the context of data bases. A calculus where tuple variables have a type associated with one data base relation and an "indexed tuple" has a type associated with a data base domain is not very different in practice from its correspondent in the first family, but its definition is cleaner. The difference

is rather a difference in the emphasis put on domains in the data base description: if they are essential elements in the definition of relations, then it is natural to associate with them types for the indexed tuples.

(3) The family characterized by domain variables and types is the basis for FQL (Pirotte [1974,1976]). ILL (Lacroix and Pirotte [1977]) is a remote member of this family.

(4) The work of Kuhns [1967] and related work by Artaud and Nicolas [1973] provide a basis for defining languages with domain variables and range predicates. DEDUCE (Chang [1976]), DEDUCE 2 (Chang [1978]) and QUERY-BY-EXAMPLE (Zloof [1975,1977]), and also the mapping constructions of SQUARE, SEQUEL and TAMALAN (Nijssen and Vandijk [1975], Vandijk [1977]) are clearly domain-oriented with no introduction of types.

The next sections define calculus languages in the first and third families, and then show how they can be modified to describe other languages. A detailed comparison of actual relational languages may be found in Pirotte [1976,1978]. Many examples may be found in Lacroix [1976] which contains a list of 66 queries expressed in 10 languages.

TUPLE FORMALISMS

Tuple Relational Calculus

A tuple relational calculus (or TRC) has been defined by Codd [1972]. Besides tuple variables, it contains terms called *indexed tuples* which have the form r.N, where r is a tuple variable and N is an integer: r.N identifies the N-th component of a tuple r. TRC also has a constant terms which correspond to the elements of the data base domains.

The only predicates in TRC are:

(1) unary range predicates, whose argument is a tuple variable, and which are in a one-to-one correspondence with data base relations;

(2) binary comparison predicates =, $<$, $>$, $\leq$, $\geq$, $\neq$ whose arguments are indexed tuples and constants.

A binary comparison predicate with its two indexed tuple or constant arguments is called a *join term*.

Predicates with tuple variable arguments like comparisons are not defined. They would not be very useful.

A *proper range formula* over a tuple variable r is a formula which contains only range predicates involving r and which is *true* on a data base relation, or on a relation which can be obtained from "union-compatible" data base relations by applying set union, intersection and difference.

In the domain-oriented view of relations presented in this paper, two relations are said to be union-compatible if they have the same number of attributes and if these are two by two defined on compatible data base domains. Two data base domains are compatible either if they are the same domain or if one is contained in the other.

Range-coupled quantifiers are defined as follows:

$(\exists r \in P)\ Q(r)$ means $\exists r\ P(r) \wedge Q(r)$

$(\forall r \in P)\ Q(r)$ means $\forall r\ P(r) \rightarrow Q(r)$

where P is a proper range formula over r, r is among the free variables of Q and Q does not contain a range predicate for r.

If only range-coupled quantifiers are used, then the range of quantifiers is always a meaningful set of tuples.

Queries in TRC have the following form:

$$\{(t_1,\ldots,t_k) \mid U_1(r_1) \wedge \ldots \wedge U_n(r_n) \wedge V(r_1,\ldots,r_n)\}$$

where

- $k \geq n \geq 1$;
- $t_1,\ldots,t_k$ are tuple variables or indexed tuples which altogether contain n different tuple variables $r_1,\ldots,r_n$;
- $U_1,\ldots,U_n$ are n proper range formulas over n distinct tuple variables $r_1,\ldots,r_n$;
- V is either absent or it is a calculus formula without range predicates, with $r_1,\ldots,r_n$ as free variables and where all quantifiers are range-coupled.

In all the relational languages based on TRC, proper range formulas are simply range predicates. Then, indexed tuples can be written r.A where A is an attribute of the relation on which r ranges: the dependence on an order of the relation attributes is thereby removed.

Three examples are now given. Each range predicate is written as the associated relation name and, for clarity, its tuple variable argument is omitted.

(Q1) List the companies supplying SHOE items to departments on the second floor.

TRC: (Q1.1) {s.COMP ∈ SUPPLY | s.ITEM='SHOE' ∧
∃ l ∈ LOC (l.FLOOR='2' ∧ l.DEPT=s.DEPT)}

(Q2) List the companies which do not supply SHOE items to any department on the second floor.

TRC: (Q2.1) {s.COMP ∈ SUPPLY |
¬(∃ s1 ∈ SUPPLY ∃ l ∈ LOC
(s.COMP=s1.COMP ∧ s1.ITEM='SHOE' ∧ s1.DEPT=l.DEPT ∧
l.FLOOR='2'))}

TRC: (Q2.2) {s.COMP ∈ SUPPLY |
∀s1 ∈ SUPPLY(s1.COMP=s.COMP ∧ s1.ITEM='SHOE') →
¬(∃ l ∈ LOC(l.DEPT=s1.DEPT ∧ l.FLOOR='2'))}

Other TRC versions of Q2 can be written, which are not simpler than Q2.1 or Q2.2.

It is worth noting that both Q2.1 and Q2.2 require *companies* to supply something in order to be in the answer, whereas the English formulation of Q2 does not. To express the English meaning, the range predicate must be chosen in order that one of its projections is the whole domain of *companies*. Which predicate to choose depends on the particular integrity constraints of the relational data base. If no such predicate is available, then a proper range formula must be used which defines the whole domain of *companies*.

(Q3) List departments selling all the items that they are supplied.

TRC: (Q3.1) {s.DEPT ∈ SALES | ∀ sp ∈ SUPPLY
(s.DEPT=sp.DEPT → ∃ sl ∈ SALES (sl.DEPT=s.DEPT
∧ sl.ITEM=sp.ITEM))}

No type-checking is defined in Codd [1972] for the binary predicates of TRC (=, <, etc.): any constant or indexed tuple can be compared with any other, and therefore many meaningless queries can be formulated. In Codd [1974], Codd comes close to defining type checking for relational data bases when he writes that "it is normally (though not always) nonsensical to make comparisons" of values from different data base domains. In Pirotte [1976], a view of relational data bases is presented where domains are defined in such a way that it is always nonsensical to compare for equality values which do not belong to the same domain.

In order that TRC have the power of the relational algebra, the introduction of range predicates associated with projections of relations was considered (Codd [1972]). If that was done, then TRC would become very redundant. For example it would contain a domain relational calculus without types.

Set Tuple Relational Calculus

Quantifiers can be removed from TRC and replaced by operations on sets as follows:

$(\exists r \in P)\ Q(r)$ becomes $\{r \mid P(r) \wedge Q(r)\} \neq \emptyset$

$(\forall r \in P)\ Q(r)$ becomes $\{r \mid P(r)\} = \{r \mid P(r) \wedge Q(r)\}$

where $\emptyset$ is the empty set. Similarly

$(\forall r \in P)\ Q(r) \rightarrow R(r)$ can be written:

$$\{r \mid P(r) \wedge Q(r)\} \subseteq \{r \mid P(r) \wedge R(r)\} .$$

A calculus can be built on these well-known transformations. It will be called set tuple relational calculus (or STRC). It can be defined after TRC as follows:

- no quantifiers are available;
- the following binary predicates on sets are added to the predicates of TRC: $=$, $\neq$, $\subset$, $\subseteq$, $\not\subset$, $\not\subseteq$;
- sets are written $\{r \mid P(r) \wedge Q(r)\}$ where r is a tuple variable, P is a proper range formula over r and Q is an STRC formula with r (plus possibly other variables) as free variable; r is called a "set variable": it is bound in the set expression just as a quantified variable is bound to its quantifier;
- $\emptyset$ is a constant set: the empty set.

Thus, set expressions appear as queries nested inside queries, except that the set variables cannot be indexed tuples and that the set expressions can contain free variables. The generalization to several variables in the set header is obvious but not very useful.

(Q2) List the companies which do not supply SHOE items to any department on the second floor.

STRC: (Q2.3)
```
{s.COMP ∈ SUPPLY |
   {l ∈ LOC | l.FLOOR = '2' ∧
     {sp ∈ SUPPLY | sp.COMP=s.COMP ∧
       sp.ITEM='SHOE' ∧ sp.DEPT=l.DEPT}
     ≠ ∅}
   = ∅}
```

STRC: (Q2.4)
```
{s.COMP ∈ SUPPLY |
   {s1 ∈ SUPPLY | s1.COMP=s.COMP ∧ s1.ITEM='SHOE'}

 ⊆ {s2 ∈ SUPPLY |
       {l ∈ LOC | l.DEPT=s2.DEPT ∧ l.FLOOR='2'}
     = ∅}}
```

Further modifications will be made to the set tuple relational calculus after domain calculi have been defined.

DOMAIN FORMALISMS

Domain Relational Calculus

A domain relational calculus (or DRC) can be defined as follows. The universe D is made of all the data base domains. There is a constant in the calculus for each value in the data base.

The predicates are of two kinds:

(a) binary comparison predicates: =, <, >, ≤, ≥, ≠ (i.e. the same as in TRC) whose arguments are constants and variables;

(b) *model predicates*, which interact with data base relations; there are two possible definitions for model predicates:

   (b1) one n-place model predicate is defined for each relation with n domains; it is *true* when the tuple made of its n arguments taken in the textual order belongs to the associated relation; it is *false* otherwise;

   (b2) 2^n-1 model predicates are defined for each relation with n domains: they have between 1 and n arguments and correspond to all possible ways of selecting between 1 and n domains in the associated relation. A predicate is *true* if the tuple made of its arguments belongs to the associated relation projection; it is *false* otherwise.

Definition (b2) is adopted for the calculus defined in this section. However it is clear that both definitions are equivalent. With this notation, attributes are used to prefix arguments which need therefore not be ordered.

The following example is formulated in a domain relational calculus with representation (b1) as (Q4.1) and also with representation (b2) as (Q4.2).

(Q4) List departments which sell all items supplied by company X.

DRC: *(Q4.1)* $\{d \mid \forall i\ (\exists dt\ SUPPLY('X', dt, i)) \rightarrow SALES(d, i)\}$

DRC: *(Q4.2)* $\{d \mid \forall i\ SUPPLY(COMP{:}\ 'X', ITEM{:}i) \rightarrow SALES(DEPT{:}d, ITEM{:}i)\}$.

In (Q4.2), *SUPPLY(COMP: 'X', ITEM:i)* and *SALES(DEPT:d, ITEM:i)* are predicates associated respectively with the projection of relation *SUPPLY* on its *COMP* and *ITEM* attributes and with relation *SALES*. In order not to create a great number of predicate names, each model predicate is identified by a relation name and by attributes which define the projection associated with the predicate. Thus, for example, in *SUPPLY(COMP: 'X', ITEM:i)*, *SUPPLY(COMP: , ITEM:)* plays the role of a predicate name and its arguments are constant *'X'* and variable *i*.

A calculus could be defined in which restrictions are introduced in the use of model predicates, in a way more or less similar to the restrictions TRC puts on the use of range predicates.

Instead, DRC is defined as a many-sorted calculus by the introduction of *types*. A type is associated with each data base domain. Constants therefore have a type. Associating a type to variables can be done in several ways: by an explicit declaration as in most programming languages; by an implicit declaration i.e. by the use of a distinct notation for variables of each type; by a contextual declaration, as in FQL, where variables are associated with a type by their occurrence in model predicates. The latter convention is adopted for DRC.

When types are introduced, a predicate with n arguments is defined as an application: $C_1 \times \ldots \times C_n \rightarrow \{true, false\}$ instead of an application $D^n \rightarrow \{true, false\}$ where $C_1, \ldots, C_n$ are the domains associated with the types of the arguments.

The semantics of quantifiers is defined as follows:

$$\forall x\ P(x) \equiv P(a_1) \wedge \ldots \wedge P(a_n)$$

$$\exists x\ P(x) \equiv P(a_1) \vee \ldots \vee P(a_n)$$

where $a_1, \ldots, a_n$ are the elements of the domain associated with the type x.

A query in DRC is defined as:

$$\{(x_1,\ldots,x_n) \mid P(x_1,\ldots,x_n)\}$$

where $P(x_1,\ldots,x_n)$ is any formula in DRC which has $x_1,\ldots,x_n$ as free variables.

The mere definition of types and the introduction of type checking in DRC produces a language of the same level as TRC, but without the need to define proper range formulas, range-coupled quantifiers and restrictions on the form of allowed queries.

In effect, any formula $F(x_1,\ldots,x_n)$ with free variables $x_1,\ldots,x_n$ of types $T_1,\ldots,T_n$ is an application: $T_1 \times \ldots \times T_n \rightarrow \{\mathit{true}, \mathit{false}\}$ and it is syntactically incorrect if one of the arguments does not have the right type. It is equivalent to the formula:

$$\text{Domain}(x_1) \wedge \ldots \wedge \text{Domain}(x_n) \wedge F(x_1,\ldots,x_n)$$

defined in a language in which variables are not typed, and $\text{Domain}(x_1),\ldots,\text{Domain}(x_n)$ are predicates which are *true* on the domain associated in DRC with the type of $x_1,\ldots,x_n$ respectively and *false* otherwise.

The three examples formulated above in TRC are now expressed in DRC.

(Q1) List the companies supplying SHOE items to departments on the second floor.

DRC: (Q1.2) {c | ∃ d LOC(DEPT:d, FLOOR:'2') ∧ SUPPLY(COMP:c, DEPT:d)}.

(Q2) List the companies which do not supply SHOE items to any department on the second floor.

DRC: (2.5) {c | ¬ (∃d LOC(DEPT:d, FLOOR:'2') ∧ SUPPLY(COMP:c, DEPT:d, ITEM:'SHOE'))}

DRC: (2.6) {c | ∀d LOC(DEPT:d, FLOOR:'2') → ¬ SUPPLY(COMP:c, DEPT:d, ITEM:'SHOE')}.

Unlike the TRC and STRC formulations of Q2, Q2.5 and Q2.6 do not require *companies* to supply something in order to be in the answer, because variable c has a type associated with the domain of all *companies*. This agrees with the English formulation of Q2. If it is desired that all *companies* present in the answer supply something, then, for example, Q2.7 can be formulated:

DRC: *(Q2.7)* $\{c \mid SUPPLY(COMP{:}c) \wedge \forall d\ LOC(DEPT{:}d,\ FLOOR{:}'2') \rightarrow \neg SUPPLY(COMP{:}c,\ DEPT{:}d,\ ITEM{:}'SHOE')\}$.

(Q3) List the departments selling all the items they are supplied.

DRC: *(Q3.2)* $\{d \mid \forall i\ SUPPLY(ITEM{:}i,\ DEPT{:}d) \rightarrow SALES(DEPT{:}d, ITEM{:}i)\}$

The DRC formulations of Q2 and Q3 are remarkably simpler than their TRC and STRC correspondents. See also SDRC formulations of Q2 given later.

Modified Quantifiers

The range of DRC quantifiers is limited to domains of the relational data base. Many queries in natural language contain quantifiers whose range is further restricted to a fraction of a domain: this can be modelled in query languages by defining quantifiers whose range can be controlled in a general manner.

Natural language quantifiers syntactically appear as qualifiers of nouns. In general a noun is the central constituent of a noun phrase, where the noun is further qualified by adjectives, relative clauses, etc.

Semantically, quantifiers bear on the whole noun phrase: their range is the restriction, by all the qualifiers of the noun, of the set of objects denoted by the noun.

For example, in "*all the (items supplied by company A to departments on the second floor)*", the quantifier bears on the whole noun phrase between parentheses.

Restricted quantifiers (Reichenbach [1948], Rosser [1953]) have been defined as follows:

$(\forall x \in F)\ \ G(x)$ means $\forall x\ F(x) \rightarrow G(x)$

$(\exists x \in F)\ \ G(x)$ means $\exists x\ F(x) \wedge G(x)$

where $(\forall x \in F)$ and $(\exists x \in F)$ are restricted quantifiers in which F is a formula containing x as a free variable.

The range-coupled quantifiers of TRC are a simple case of restricted quantifiers in which F is a proper range formula over the quantified variable. However range-coupled quantifiers are a must in TRC to give a meaningful range to quantified variables. On the contrary, ordinary quantifiers with typed variables are sufficient in DRC to determine the range of variables, and modified quantifiers are only defined to improve the analogy with natural language.

In natural language, a presupposition is usually made that the range of a quantifier is not empty: there is a secondary meaning to a quantified expression which states that the quantifier is to be actually taken into account only if the range is not empty.

This presupposition is not well accounted for by the universal restricted quantifier, since its value is *true* if the range is empty. Hence, *extensional quantifiers* (Kuhns [1971]) have been proposed, which require the range to be non-empty in order to have the value *true*:

$(\forall x \text{ in } F)\ G(x)$ means $\exists x\ F(x) \wedge \forall y\ F(y) \rightarrow G(y)$.

$(\exists x \text{ in } F)\ G(x)$ means $\exists x\ F(x) \wedge G(x)$

i.e. $(\exists x \in F)\ G(x)$

The universal extensional quantifier has the value *false* when the restriction formula F defines an empty range. That may sometimes be an adequate answer to the natural language question "do all F's satisfy G?", although a fully explicit answer involves a refutation of the presupposition that there exist values for which F is *true*. These considerations led to the definition of the verification operation in FQL. For example:

(Q2) List the companies which do not supply SHOE items to any department on the second floor.

FQL: (Q2.8) *get (c) st*

for all (d) st LOC(DEPT:d, FLOOR:'2')

holds not SUPPLY(COMP:c, DEPT:d, ITEM:'SHOE') end

end

If there is no department located on the second floor, then the answer to Q2.8 will consist in an indication of this fact.

Several extensions of predicate calculus quantifiers fit naturally in the framework of FQL verification (Pirotte [1976]). Such quantifiers are (n being an integer): at least n, at most n, exactly n, only, all and only, no, not all. Some of them are more useful in practice than the universal verification in the process of querying a data base.

(Q5) List the companies that are the only supplier of at least 10 items.

FQL: (Q5.1) get (c) st

for 10 (it) st SUPPLY(COMP:c, ITEM:it)

holds for exactly 1 (cp)

holds SUPPLY(COMP:cp, ITEM:(it)

end end end

The recently defined DEDUCE 2 language (Chang [1978]) is a calculus with domain variables and restricted quantifiers and also several numerical quantifiers (at least n, etc.). However it has no types for variables and no restriction, similar to the definition of proper range formulas in TRC, on the use of negation. DEDUCE 2 can be seen as a simple version of FQL.

From a calculus point of view, QUERY-BY-EXAMPLE (Zloof [1975]) can be viewed as a language with domain variables and without types. Instead of having a type, each variable is associated with a relation attribute by a special graphical representation of queries. Quantifiers are similar to restricted quantifiers.

Set Domain Relational Calculus

Quantifiers in DRC can be replaced by set operations, in a way similar to the transition from TRC to STRC: thus, a set domain relational calculus (or SDRC) is obtained. However, "domain predicates" are needed if all quantifiers are eliminated from DRC: "Domain(x)" is *true* on the domain associated with the type of x and *false* on the other domains.

Remark that explicit domain predicates are unnecessary in DRC, and that the ordinary DRC quantifiers are equivalent to restricted quantifiers as follows:

$\forall x\ P(x)$ is equivalent to $(\forall x \in \text{Domain}(x))\ F(x)$.

The rules for eliminating quantifiers from a domain calculus with types follow:

$\exists x\ F(x)$ becomes $\{x \mid F(x)\} \neq \emptyset$

$\forall x\ F(x)$ becomes $\{x \mid \text{Domain}(x)\} = \{x \mid F(x)\}$

$(\exists x \in F)\ G(x)$ becomes $\{x \mid F(x) \land G(x)\} \neq \emptyset$

$(\forall x \in F)\ G(x)$ becomes $\{x \mid F(x)\} \subseteq \{x \mid G(x)\}$

$(\forall x \text{ in } F)\ G(x)$ becomes $\{x \mid F(x)\} \neq \emptyset \land \{x \mid F(x)\} \subseteq \{x \mid G(x)\}$

In all these transformations, F and G are any calculus formulas.

The SDRC formalism can be defined after DRC as follows:

- no quantifiers are available;
- the following binary predicates on sets are added to the predicates of DRC: $=, \neq, \subset, \subseteq, \not\subset, \not\subseteq$;
- a new unary predicate is defined: Domain(x), which is *true* on the domain associated with the type of x and *false* on the other domains (actually, there is one predicate per data base domain);
- sets are written $\{x \mid P(x)\}$ where P(x) is any DRC formula with x (plus possibly other variables) as free variable: x is bound to the set expression and is called a "set variable";
- $\emptyset$ is a constant set: the empty set.

The generalization to several variables in the set header is obvious: the corresponding expressions describe sets of pairs, triplets,...,n-tuples of values, but they are not frequently necessary.

(Q2) List companies which do not supply SHOE items to any department on the second floor.

SDRC: (Q2.9) {c | {d | LOC(DEPT:d, FLOOR:'2') ∧ SUPPLY(COMP:c, DEPT:d, ITEM:'SHOE')} = ∅}

SDRC: (Q2.10) {c | {d | LOC(DEPT:d, FLOOR:'2')} ⊆ {d1 | ¬SUPPLY(COMP:c, DEPT:d1, ITEM:'SHOE')}}

The DEDUCE language (Chang [1976]) is based on a set domain calculus without types. Q2 can be formulated as follows:

*DEDUCE: (Q2.11) query SUPPLY(*COMP:c)*

and subquery (SUPPLY(COMP:c,#DEPT:d,ITEM:'SHOE')

and LOC(DEPT:d, FLOOR:'2'))

and set (d) = ∅

The essential difference between (Q2.9) and (Q2.11), namely the presence of the predicate *SUPPLY(*COMP:c)* in (Q2.11), follows from the absence of types in DEDUCE. To be in the answer to (Q2.11) companies have to supply something, whereas, for (Q2.9), they have to belong to the data base domain of companies.

The latest definition of QUERY-BY-EXAMPLE (Zloof [1977]), where universal quantification is presented as a function, can be viewed as a set domain relational calculus.

Removal of Some Variables

In general, variables are used in languages to designate the same object in several places of an expression, program or query.

Variables are absent from the relational algebra, from simple queries in languages like SQUARE, SEQUEL, ILL, TAMALAN and also from natural languages.

In English, the possibility of referencing several times the same object is provided by various kinds of pronouns and adjectives. In addition, in many cases where calculus languages need a reference mechanism, English can do without it by describing objects with their properties by nested constructions: in many cases, the references can be expressed by textual contiguity.

This section shows how the mapping construct of SQUARE, SEQUEL and TAMALAN can be obtained by removing variables from domain calculus expressions. A similar reasoning can be applied to derive queries in the ILL language which is entirely based on a structure of nested expressions.

This section does not give a precise description of a translation algorithm: it would not be very interesting in practice since not all calculus expressions can be transformed, and since, in addition, the limits of the mapping are not very clear in SQUARE and SEQUEL, and not many queries can be expressed with the mapping construct alone.

The goal of this section is to investigate the relationships between existing languages by relating them to a common framework: the predicate calculus. Therefore, only simple forms of restricted quantifiers of a domain calculus like DRC will be considered and generalizations will be indicated:

$$(\forall y \in P(B1{:}y))\ Q(A{:}x, B2{:}y) \qquad \text{(a1)}$$

$$(\exists y \in P(B1{:}y))\ Q(A{:}x, B2{:}y) \qquad \text{(b1)}$$

The expressions (a1) and (b1) can be formulated as mappings in SQUARE as follows:

$$\underset{A\ \underline{B2}\ B1}{Q\ (\ P)} \qquad \text{(a2)}$$

```
 Q  (  P)
A B2 B1                                                    (b2)
```

The disappearance of variables can be explained in a few steps. Firstly, in the mapping, in ILL and in English, a quantifier is not in a prefix position: this is a typical calculus feature. Instead, it is nested with its range inside another expression. Thus, (a1) and (b1) are transformed into (a3) and (b3) respectively, without changing their meaning:

Q(A:x, B2:<u>all</u> y | P(B1:y)) (a3)

Q(A:x, B2:y | P(B1:y)) (b3)

The next transformations can be called "nominalization" and "pronominalization": the textually first occurrence of each variable is replaced by the attribute of the predicate domain in which it occurs ("nominalization"); "pronominalization" consists in replacing the other occurrences of variables by a reference (a "pronoun") to the corresponding "noun".

Thus (a3) and (b3) become:

Q(A, <u>all</u> B2 | P(B1 = <u>this</u> B2)) (a4)

Q(A, B2 | P(B1 = <u>this</u> B2)) (b4)

The references are written as '<u>this</u>' followed by the "noun" pointed at. This way of expressing references is a frequent source of ambiguity in English. It must be made more precise in a formal language when a reference to a "noun" follows more than one occurrence of that noun (Lacroix and Pirotte [1976b]).

The next transformation can be called "subject raising": one of the arguments of each predicate is extracted from the argument list and placed in the "subject" position, in front of the predicate name which may be seen as a verb. Hence (a5) and (b5):

A Q(<u>all</u> B2 | <u>this</u> B2=B1 P) (a5)

A Q(B2 | <u>this</u> B2=B1 P) (b5)

The last transformation consists in deleting the "pronouns" that immediately follow the "noun" they refer to:

A Q(<u>all</u> B2 | B1 P) (a6)

A Q(B2 | B1 P) (b6)

If, like (a6) and (b6), the expressions obtained after the last transformation do not contain references, then they are equivalent to a mapping expression. The following example is formulated in a domain calculus with restricted quantifiers, in SQUARE and in ILL:

(Q4) List the departments which sell all the items supplied by company X.

DRC: (Q4.3) $\{d \mid (\forall i \in SUPPLY(COMP\text{: 'X'}, ITEM{:}i))\ SALES(DEPT{:}d, ITEM{:}i)\}$

SQUARE: (Q4.4)

```
get(     SALES      (      SUPPLY      ('X')))
     DEPT       ITEM  ITEM        COMP
```

(ITEM after SALES is underlined.)

ILL: (Q4.5) <u>get</u> DEPT[SALES(<u>all</u> ITEM[SUPPLY(COMP='X')])]

If all references have not disappeared after the last transformation, then the query cannot be expressed as a mapping in SQUARE and SEQUEL. However it can be expressed in ILL, nearly as it is produced by the transformation. An example follows in a domain calculus with restricted quantifiers and in ILL.

(Q3) List the departments which sell all the items that they are supplied.

DRC: (Q3.3) $\{d \mid (\forall i \in SUPPLY(ITEM{:}i, DEPT{:}d))\ SALES(DEPT{:}d, ITEM{:}i)\}$

ILL: (Q3.4) <u>get</u> DEPT[SALES(<u>all</u> ITEM[SUPPLY(<u>this</u> DEPT)])]

The transformations described in this section are valid for more complex cases which produce mappings. A mapping with several arguments is produced by a calculus expression with a sequence of several restricted quantifiers. In this case, the order of quantifiers must be preserved by the first transformation which nests quantifiers and their range in a model predicate. A mapping embedded inside another mapping is produced by nested restricted quantifiers, as in the following example given in the domain calculus with restricted quantifiers, in SQUARE and in ILL:

(Q6) List departments selling all items supplied by companies situated in PARIS.

DRC: (Q6.1) $\{d \mid (\forall i \in (\exists c \in (ADDRESS(COMP{:}c, CITY\text{: 'PARIS'}) \wedge SUPPLY(COMP{:}c, ITEM{:}i))))\ SALES(DEPT{:}d, ITEM{:}i)\}$

SQUARE: (Q6.2)

```
get(     SALES      (      SUPPLY      (      ADDRESS      ('PARIS'))))
     DEPT       ITEM  ITEM        COMP  COMP         CITY
```

(ITEM after SALES is underlined.)

ILL: *(Q6.3)* get *DEPT[SALES (all ITEM [SUPPLY(COMP [ADDRESS(CITY='PARIS')])])]*

RELATIONSHIPS BETWEEN SET TUPLE AND SET DOMAIN FORMALISMS

An obvious generalization of STRC consists in allowing an indexed tuple as set variable. If, in addition, the proper range formula of the set expression reduces to a range predicate, then the calculus thus obtained will be called extended set tuple relational calculus (or ESTRC).

Many queries are simpler in ESTRC than in STRC. For example:

(Q7) List companies which supply all the items supplied.

TRC: *(Q7.1)* $\{s.COMP \in SUPPLY \mid (\forall s1 \in SUPPLY)\ (\exists s2 \in SUPPLY)\ s1.ITEM = s2.ITEM \wedge s.COMP{=}s2.COMP\}$

STRC: *(Q7.2)* $\{s.COMP \in SUPPLY \mid \{s1 \in SUPPLY\} = \{s3 \in SUPPLY \mid \{s2 \in SUPPLY \mid s3.ITEM{=}s2.ITEM \wedge s.COMP{=}s2.COMP\} \neq \emptyset\}\}$

ESTRC: *(Q7.3)* $\{s.COMP \in SUPPLY \mid \{s1.ITEM \in SUPPLY\} = \{s3.ITEM \in SUPPLY \mid s3.COMP = s.COMP\}$

In the tuple formalisms, the range predicates of the query are now written in the target and the range predicate of a set is written in the set header.

In the ESTRC formulation of (Q7), variable s2 has disappeared: it was necessary in STRC only because sets of tuples of SUPPLY had to be compared instead of sets of items.

The following formulation of (Q7) in SDRC is not very different from the ESTRC formulation given above:

(Q7.4) $\{c \mid \{i \mid SUPPLY(ITEM{:}i)\} = \{it \mid SUPPLY(ITEM{:}it,\ COMP{:}c)\}\}$

It is easy to imagine how the ESTRC formulation could be translated to SDRC, provided the difference between types and range predicates is disregarded. The ESTRC formulation for (Q7) yields:

(Q7.5) $\{c \mid SUPPLY(COMP{:}c) \wedge \{i \mid SUPPLY(ITEM{:}i)\} = \{it \mid SUPPLY(ITEM{:}it,\ COMP{:}x) \wedge x = c\}\}$

which is obviously equivalent to the preceding SDRC formulation (Q7.4).

Thus, there is a great variety of SDRC formulations since ESTRC contains STRC by definition and all SDRC queries can be translated into ESTRC in a straightforward manner. Consider the following example and its formulation in SDRC:

(Q8) List companies which supply every item of type A to some department.

(Q8.1) $\{cp|$
$\{d|$
$\{i|TYPE(ITEM{:}i,\ CLASS{:}'A')\} \subseteq$
$\{it|SUPPLY(COMP{:}cp,\ ITEM{:}it,\ DEPT{:}d)\}\}$
$\neq \emptyset\}$

It can be systematically translated in ESTRC by replacing each set variable in a set header by an indexed tuple and a range predicate, and by replacing each model predicate with n arguments by n-1 comparisons of join terms. Thus, the following ESTRC query is obtained:

(Q8.2) $\{cp.COMP \in SUPPLY|$
$\{d.DEPT \in SUPPLY|$
$\{i.ITEM \in TYPE|i.CLASS='A'\} \subseteq$
$\{it.ITEM \in SUPPLY|it.COMP=cp.COMP \wedge it.DEPT=d.DEPT\}\}$
$\neq \emptyset\}$

The reverse transformation from ESTRC to SDRC is not always so simple. For example, (Q8) also admits the following ESTRC formulation:

(Q8.3) $\{cp.COMP \in SUPPLY|$
$\{i.ITEM \in TYPE|i.CLASS='A'\} \subseteq$
$\{it.ITEM \in SUPPLY|it.COMP=cp.COMP \wedge it.DEPT=cp.DEPT\}\}$

In this formulation, there is a feature which has no correspondent in SDRC: there can exist indexed tuples, like *cp.DEPT* in this example, which are not used at the first level of the set expression in which the variable is bound but which are used in inner set expressions. This phenomenon is typical of all tuple formalisms and inexistent in domain formalisms: using tuple variables, even only in the form of indexed tuples, entails the possibility of indirect cross-references which can upset the meaning suggested by the superficial structure of a query (Pirotte [1976,1978]).

An algorithm which translates from ESTRC to SDRC must therefore create a predicate $\{...\} \neq \emptyset$ corresponding to each indexed tuple which appears in a query and which is not in a set header or in the target. This predicate must be nested at the first level inside the set expression where the corresponding tuple variable is bound.

The QUEL language (Held et al. [1975]) is of the family of the ESTRC calculus: it has set expressions and set operations, no universal quantifiers and implicit existential quantifiers. The bigger part of SQUARE (Boyce et al. [1975]) and SEQUEL (Chamberlin et al. [1974], Chamberlin et al. [1976]) uses variables, set expressions and set operations in a way similar to the ESTRC calculus.

QUEL: (Q8.4) *range cp* $\in$ *SUPPLY, i* $\in$ *CLASS;*

get cp.COMP where

set (i.ITEM where i.TYPE='A') $\subseteq$

set (cp.ITEM by cp.COMP, cp.DEPT)

SEQUEL: (Q8.5) *select COMP from SUPPLY*

group by COMP, DEPT

having set (ITEM) $\supseteq$ *select ITEM from CLASS where TYPE='A'*

FUNCTIONS

The term "function" in the present context refers to two different notions: predicate calculus functions and function routines.

Predicate calculus functions represent 1-n links between elements of the universe. In the relational model, such links are expressed by functional dependences inside relations. However instead of the usual data definition in terms of relations and functional dependences, another description, based on a domain calculus, can be imagined where predicates express the n-m links and functions the 1-n links (Meyer and Schneider [1975]).

That would be a clean presentation of a data model. However, a special treatment of 1-n links would reduce the symmetry of the relational model: a relation treats all domain alike whereas a function does not.

The second relevant meaning of "function" is that of function routines as they are defined in programming languages; these are needed to compute values which are not stored in the data base but can be obtained from stored values. Except for trivial cases, function routines cannot be expressed as predicate calculus functions. Many interesting functions (e.g. count, sum, average) have an argument which is a set and, in general, this argument has to be computed by an arbitrarily complex expression of the query language.

Function routines have been defined in a general manner for the FQL language. Other languages like ALPHA are explicitly presented as sublanguages, i.e. as languages to be embedded in a host language. Most computations are left to be performed by host language operations.

CONCLUSIONS

This paper presents a unifying theory which relates the retrieval operations of a number of relational languages to the predicate calculus. The presentation is not meant to suggest that all the languages were built by modifying the calculus. Rather, the calculus is a convenient underlying basis for a technical comparison: by reference to the calculus, interesting relationships between different constructions clearly appear.

The small number of underlying calculus formalisms and the clear correspondences between formalisms suggest that relational languages do not differ in an essential manner as to their possibility of being efficiently implemented.

As to the perception of languages by users, the essential result of the comparison is the contrast between two families of language constructions: those which can be traced back to a calculus with variables ranging on data base domains and those which correspond to a calculus with tuple variables. It appears that, as a fairly general rule, queries in domain languages are simpler, i.e. easier to read and to write, than queries in tuple languages. This point is illustrated with more detail in Lacroix and Pirotte [1976a,1977], and Pirotte [1976,1978]. The main reason for the relative simplicity of domain languages is that they directly manipulate domains and domain values and thereby interact more directly with the real world semantics expressed by the relations.

Often the predicate calculus is not considered as a suitable basis for user languages. This study suggests that the question of how users like calculus formalisms should be considered separately for domain formalisms and for tuple formalisms.

ACKNOWLEDGMENT

This paper is a slightly updated version of a paper with the same title presented at the International Seminar on Question-Answering and Data Base Systems held in Bonas (France), June 21-30, 1977, organized by J. -C. Simon and L. Siklossy. Proceedings of the seminar are available as a volume of the collection "Colloques IRIA" from IRIA, Domaine de Voluceau, Rocquencourt, BP 105, 78150 Le Chesnay, France. Permission to publish is gratefully acknowledged.

REFERENCES

1. Artaud, A., Nicolas, J. M. [1973] An Experimental Query System: SYNTEX, *Proceedings of the International Computing Symposium*, Davos (Sept. 1973), North-Holland, 1974, 557-563.

2. Boyce, R. F., Chamberlin, D. D., King, W. F. [1975] Specifying Queries as Relational Expressions: The SQUARE Data Sublanguage, *CACM 18*, 11 (November 1975), 621-628.

3. Chamberlin, D. D., Boyce, R. F. [1974] SEQUEL: A Structured English Query Language, *Proceedings ACM SIGMOD Workshop on Data Description, Access and Control*, May 1974, 249-264.

4. Chamberlin, D. D., Astrahan, M. M., Eswaran, K. P., Griffiths, P. P., Lorie, R. A., Mehl, J. W., Reisner, P., Wade, B. W. [1976] SEQUEL 2: A Unified Approach to Data Definition, Manipulation and Control, *IBM J. Res. Develop. 20*, 6 (November 1976), 560-575.

5. Chang, C. L. [1976] DEDUCE: A Deductive Query Language for Relational Data Bases, In *Pattern Recognition and Artificial Intelligence* (C. H. Chen, Ed.), Academic Press, 1976, 108-134.

6. Chang, C. L. [1978] DEDUCE 2: Further Investigations of Deduction in Relational Data Bases, In *Logic and Data Bases* (H. Gallaire and J. Minker, Eds.), Plenum Press, New York, 1978, 201-236.

7. Codd, E. F. [1971] A Data Base Sublanguage Founded on the Relational Calculus, *Proceedings ACM SIGFIDET Workshop on Data Description, Access and Control* (Codd and Dean, Eds.), ACM, San Diego, November 1971, 35-68.

8. Codd, E. F. [1972] Relational Completeness of Data Base Sublanguages, In *Data Base Systems* (R. Rustin, Ed.), Courant Computer Science Symposium 6, Prentice-Hall, 1972, 65-98.

9. Codd, E. F. [1974] Understanding Relations: Installment 5, *FDT Newsletter 6-4*, (1974), 18-22.

10. Held, G. D., Stonebraker, M. R., Wong, E. [1975] INGRES: A Relational Data Base System, *AFIPS Conference Proceedings, Vol. 44* (1975), 409-416.

11. Kuhns, J. L. [1967] Answering Questions by Computer: A Logical Study, *RAND Memo RM-5428-PR*, December 1967.

12. Kuhns, J. L. [1971] Quantification in Query Systems, *Proceedings ACM SIGIR Symposium of Information Storage and Retrieval* (J. Minker and S. Rosenfeld, Eds.), ACM, University of Maryland, April 1971, 81-93.

13. Lacroix, M., Pirotte, A. [1976a] Example Queries in Relational Languages, *MBLE Technical Note N107*, January 1976 (Revised April 1978).

14. Lacroix, M., Pirotte, A. [1976b] ILL: An English Structured Query Language for Relational Data Bases, *MBLE Report R334*, August 1976, *Proc. IFIP TC-2 Working Conference on Modelling in Data Base Management Systems* (G. M. Nijssen, Ed.), Nice, France, North-Holland, 1977, 237-260.

15. Lacroix, M., Pirotte, A. [1977] Domain-Oriented Relational Languages, *Proceedings International Conference on Very Large Data Bases*, Tokyo, IEEE, 1977, 370-378. Also *MBLE Report R351*, April 1977.

16. Meyer, B., Schneider, H. J. [1975] Predicate Logic and Data Base Technology, Presented at the advanced course on Data Base Languages and Natural Language Processing, Freudenstadt, August 1975.

17. Nijssen, G. M., Vandijk, E. [1975] Towards a simpler retrieval language, Unpublished Note, April 1975.

18. Pirotte, A., Wodon, P. [1974] A Comprehensive Formal Query Language for a Relational Data Base: FQL, *R.A.I.R.O. Informatique/Computer Science 11*, 2 (1977), 165-183. Also *MBLE Report R283*, December 1974.

19. Pirotte, A. [1976] "Explicit Description of Entities and Their Manipulation in Languages for the Relational Data Base Model," Thèse de doctorat en sciences appliquées, Univ. Libre de Bruxelles, Décembre 1976. Also, *MBLE Report R336*.

20. Pirotte, A. [1978] Linguistic Aspects of High-Level Relational Languages, *MBLE Report R367*, January 1978.

21. Reichenbach, H. [1948] *Elements of Symbolic Logic*, MacMillan, 1948.

22. Rosser, J. B. [1953] *Logic for Mathematicians*, McGraw-Hill, 1953.

23. Vandijck, E. [1977] Towards a More Familiar Relational Retrieval Language, *Information Systems 2*, 4 (1977), 159-169.

24. Zloof, M. [1975] QUERY BY EXAMPLE, *AFIPS Conference Proceedings, Vol. 44* (1975), 431-438.

25. Zloof, M. [1977] QUERY BY EXAMPLE: A Data Base Language, *IBM Syst. J. 4* (1977), 324-343.

AUTHOR INDEX

Abrial, J. R., 238, 256, 326, 342
Arnold, R. S., 234
Artaud, A., 52, 416, 434
Astrahan, M.M., 203, 215, 228, 230, 233, 434
Badler, N., 146
Basili, V.R., 108, 144
Battani, G., 347, 350, 375
Beeri, C., 16, 30, 50, 52
Bentley, J.L., 277, 287
Bergman, M., 87, 101
Bernstein, P.A., 208, 233
Bibel, W., 260, 287
Blasgen, M.W., 233
Bolc, L., 406
Boyce, R.F., 30, 202, 205, 233, 406, 415, 432, 434
Boyer, R.S., 302, 320
Bracchi, G., 238, 256-257
Bruynooghe, M., 275, 287
Burger, J., 199
Burstall, R.M., 252, 256
Cadiou, J. M., 12, 30, 234, 327, 343
Carnap, R., 111, 144
Carson, D.A., 200
Casey, R.G., 208, 234
Chamberlin, D.D., 12, 15, 28-29, 202, 233, 331, 343, 406, 415, 432, 434
Chang, C.L., 4, 18-19, 22, 25, 26, 29, 39, 51-52, 82-83, 101, 110, 142, 144, 172-173, 175-177, 202-203, 205, 219,
Chang, C.L. (cont'd) 224-225, 229, 233-234, 236, 282, 287, 297, 320, 328, 343, 378, 382, 407, 416, 425, 434
Chen, C.H., 52, 101, 233, 237, 256
Cholnoky, E., 29, 375
Clark, K., 23-24, 62, 76, 85, 95, 101, 174, 177, 203, 233, 261, 265, 274, 276-277
Codasyl, 237-238, 256
Codd, E.F., 12, 15, 17, 29, 42, 52, 65, 76-77, 79, 81, 90, 101, 140, 142, 144, 150, 155, 177, 201-202, 205-206, 208, 219, 231, 234, 237, 239, 243, 256, 282, 287, 294, 302, 321, 355, 375, 390-392, 406-407, 415-416, 418-419, 434
Colmerauer, A., 27, 49, 53, 260, 287
Colombetti, M., 20, 237
Dahl, V., 27, 29
Darlington, J.L., 83, 101, 140, 144
Darvas, F., 29, 101, 347, 370, 375
Date, C.J., 29, 43, 53, 327, 343
Davis, R., 183, 199
Deliyanni, A., 19, 29, 79-80. 101, 141, 144, 375
Delobel, C., 208, 234

deLong, S.P., 103
Demolombe, R., 34, 50, 52-54, 235, 331, 342-343
Dilger, W., 18-19, 26, 377
Diller, T., 199
Elliott, R.W., 184, 199
Elovitz, H.S., 140, 144
Emden, van, M.H. *see* van Emden
Enderton, H.B., 18, 49, 109, 144
Eswaran, K.P., 233, 331, 343, 434
Fagin, R., 30, 52, 208, 234
Fedeli, A., 238, 256
Findler, N., 30, 407
Fishman, D.H., 39, 53, 125, 144, 146, 177
Florentin, J.J., 53
Fogt, K., 199
Futó, I., 27, 29, 90, 101, 347, 375
Gallaire, H., 3, 16-17, 23-24, 33-34, 69, 76, 78, 84, 101-103, 177-178, 202, 213, 233-235, 282, 284, 287-289, 294, 321, 325-328, 331-332, 342, 344, 376, 401-402, 434
Gilchrist, B., 257
Gödel, K., 8, 29
Goguen, J.A., 20, 29, 239-240, 252, 256
Gotlieb, L., 228, 234
Gray, J.N., 233
Green, C.C., 134, 140, 144-145, 161, 172, 177, 204, 286-287
Griffiths, P.P., 233, 434
Guttag, J., 261, 287
Hall, P., 238, 256
Hammer, M.N., 326, 343, 406
Hayes, P.J., 261, 287, 382, 407
Hayes-Roth, F., 199, 234
Held, G.D., 238, 257, 415, 432, 434
Henschen, L., 74, 76
Hewitt, C., 62, 76, 284, 287 294, 321, 332, 343
Hill, R., 125, 145, 301, 315, 321
Hoare, C.A.R., 239, 257, 261, 288
Howard, J.H., 30, 52
Hubbard, G.U., 358, 376
IMS/360 -Application Description Manual, 257
Kanoui, H., 87, 101, 287
Kaplan, R.M., 408
Kellogg, C.H., 18-19, 22, 39, 53, 82, 102, 140, 143, 145, 172-173, 175, 177, 179-181, 199, 200, 202-203, 234, 282, 288, 378, 382, 407
King, J., 183, 199
King, III, W.F., 233, 406, 434
Klahr, P., 22, 53, 102, 140, 143, 145, 173, 177, 179, 181, 183, 186, 197, 199-200, 203, 234, 288, 407
Kleene, S.C., 53, 394, 407
Klein, M., 137, 143, 145
Klimbie, J.W., 256
Knuth, D., 261, 267, 270, 275, 282, 288, 302, 321
Koffeman, K.L., 256
Kowalski, R.A., 17-19, 25, 27, 29-30, 40, 53, 69, 76-77, 79-80, 89, 101-102, 125, 141, 144-145, 183, 199, 203, 235, 260, 269, 282, 288, 293, 297, 317, 320-321, 332, 343, 375, 376
Kramosil, I., 297, 321
Kuehner, D., 125, 145, 317, 321
Kuhns, J.L., 416, 424, 434-435
Lacroix, M., 202, 235, 382, 386, 406-407, 416, 428, 431, 433, 435
Lansbergen, S., 378, 407
Lee, R.C.T., 4, 29, 51-52, 110, 144, 203, 229, 233, 235-236, 297, 320, 328, 343
Levien, R., 12, 30
Liskov, B.H., 261, 288
Lochovsky, F.H., 12, 30

Lockemann, P.C., 199
Lorie, R.A., 233, 434
Loveland, D.W., 125, 145
Luckham, D., 134, 145
Maron, M.E., 12, 30
Mazurkiewiz, A., 30, 343
McCarthy, J., 261, 265, 286, 288, 382, 407
McJones, P.R., 233
McLeod, D.J., 326, 343
McSkimin, J.R., 19, 24, 30, 39, 53, 108-109, 116, 120, 130, 134, 141, 145-146, 153, 177, 184, 199, 203, 235, 272, 288, 378, 382, 407
Mehl, J.W., 233, 434
Melli, L., 146
Meloni, H., 347, 350, 375-376
Meltzer, B., 101-102, 177-178, 320, 407-408
Mendelson, E., 4, 30, 35, 53
Meyer, B., 432, 435
Michie, D., 101-102, 177-178, 320, 407-408
Minker, J., 3, 18-24, 30, 34, 39, 53, 76, 83, 101-103, 107-109, 116, 120, 127, 130, 134, 141, 145-146, 153, 157, 175, 177-178, 184, 199, 202-203, 231, 233-234, 236, 282, 287-289, 321, 332, 343, 375, 378, 382, 407, 408, 434-435
Minsky, M., 18, 30, 91-92, 94, 102
Moore, J.S., 302, 320
Mylopolous, J., 141, 146
Nash-Webber, B.L., 408
Neuhold, E.J., 199, 321
Nicolas, J.M., 3, 16-17, 23-25, 33-34, 36, 39, 44, 50, 52-54, 62, 69, 76, 84, 102, 140, 146, 202, 208, 213, 235-236, 282, 284, 288, 294, 321, 325-328, 331,
Nicolas, J.M. (cont'd) 332, 342-344, 416, 434
Nijssen, G.M., 256, 416, 435
Nilsson, N., 134, 145
Owlett, J., 238, 256
Palermo, F.P., 157, 178
Paolini, P., 237-238, 240, 243, 253, 256-257
Pasero, R., 287
Pelagatti, G., 237-238, 240, 253, 257
Pereira, F., 322
Pereira, L., 322
Perrault, R., 178
Petöfi, J., 407
Pirotte, A., 25-26, 83, 102, 202, 235, 407, 409, 411, 416, 418, 428, 431, 433, 435
Pople, H.R., 382, 407
Powell, P., 134-135, 140, 143, 146
Putzolu, G.R., 233
Quillan, M.R., 19, 30
Quine, W.V., 266, 289, 379, 408
Raphael, B., 140, 145
Raver, N., 358, 376
Rehert, M., 143
Reichenbach, H., 411, 423, 435
Reisner, P., 434
Reiter, R., 16, 18-19, 21-24, 26, 28, 30, 39, 54-55, 58, 74, 76, 82, 95, 103, 125, 142, 146, 149-150, 157, 161, 163-165, 172, 176, 178, 181, 199, 202-203, 213, 231, 236, 284, 289, 294, 319, 321, 378, 380, 382, 391, 400, 404, 408
Rissanen, J., 208-236
Robinson, G.A., 154, 173, 178, 200
Robinson, J.A., 9, 30, 74, 76, 124, 146, 183, 200, 268, 289, 349, 352, 376
Rosenfeld, S., 435
Rosser, J.B., 411, 423, 435

Roussopoulos, N., 146, 234
Roussel, P., 20, 30, 51, 54, 62, 76, 85, 103, 238, 254, 257, 262, 275, 287, 289, 294, 321
Rustin, R., 76, 101, 177, 234, 407, 434
Sandewall, E., 382, 408
Scha, R., 378, 407
Schneider, H.J., 432, 435
Schubert, L.K., 141, 147
Shapiro, S.C., 141, 147
Sickel, S., 183, 200, 203, 219, 236
Simon, H.A., 407
Siklossy, L., 407, 433
Slagle, J.R., 203, 219, 224-225, 229, 231, 233, 236
Stonebraker, M., 238, 257, 326, 344, 434
Syre, J.C., 36, 39, 53, 62, 76, 83, 140, 146
Szeredi, P., 101, 347, 375
Tarnlund, S-Å., 19-20, 95, 101, 259, 261, 265, 274 277, 281, 286, 289
Thatcher, J.W., 29, 256
Thomason, R.H., 382, 408
Thompson, P., 135, 140, 143, 147
Todd, S., 238, 256
Tou, J.T., 178
Traiger, I.L., 233
Travis, L., 24, 53, 102, 140, 143, 145, 173, 177, 179-180, 183, 199, 200, 234, 288, 407
Tzichritzis, D.C., 12, 30
Turner, A.J., 108, 144
VanderBrug, G., 332, 343
Vandijk, E., 416, 435
van Emden, M.H., 27, 30, 68-69, 76, 83-84, 102, 282, 287, 293, 320-321
van Heigenoort, J., 29
Wade, B.W., 233, 434
Wagner, E.G., 29, 238
Warren, D., 27, 30, 275, 289, 294, 303, 322, 350, 370
Waterman, D., 199, 234
Watson, V., 233
Wilson, G., 108, 123-124, 147
Winston, P., 30
Woden, P., 435
Wong, E., 434
Woods, W.A., 141, 147, 378, 408
Wos, L., 74, 76, 154, 173, 178, 200
Wulz, H., 377, 406
Yazdanian, K., 25, 33, 44, 53, 54, 235, 325
Yeh, R., 29, 256
Zadeh, L.A., 195, 200, 203, 231, 236
Zifonun, G., 18-19, 26, 377, 408
Zilles, S., 261, 289
Zloof, M., 83, 90, 103, 202, 236, 416, 425, 427, 435

SUBJECT INDEX

Abstract data types, 20, 29, 237, 239-240, 246, 256
Access Paths, 228
Action relations, 25, 336
Advice file, 185-186
Air pollution control data base, 356, 368
ALPHA language, 392, 409-410, 415
Ancestor resolution, 317
Answer literal, 161
Answer/reason extraction, 113-114, 134, 137, 143, 146, 188, 197
Answer to a query, definition of, 390
Antecedent, 12, 25, 183, 298, 319, 333, 348
  conditional, 186
Antecedent information, 333, 335
Antecedent theorem, 332
Approximate reasoning, 236
Argument placeholder, 116
Artificial intelligence, 20, 52-53, 101, 233, 407
Assertions, 12, 79-80, 88-89, 112-113, 117, 180, 349
Associative network, 407
Associative search, 270
Atomic formula, 204-205, 210
  definition of, 5, 348
  ground, 55-56, 74, 377, 391
  truth value of, 391
Atomic queries, 55-56, 64-66, 73, 75, 165
Atomic relations, 343
Attributes, 13, 51, 202, 204, 208, 229
Axiomatic data base theory, 259
Axiom schema, 7
  for lists, 98
Backtracking, 27, 85, 252, 254, 302, 317, 350, 353
Backward chaining, 11, 22, 186
Bags, 205, 207, 406
Balanced tree, 270, 275
Base relations, 22, 48, 141, 172, 201-202, 210, 213
BCE (*see* Boolean Category Expression)
Best projected merit, 132
Binary representation of n-ary relations, 79
Binary resolution, 11, 74
Binary tree search and insert algorithm, 274-275
Bit-mask technique, 352
BNF syntax of DEDUCE, 206, 231
Boolean Category Expression, 116-117, 119, 122-124
Boolean function (*see* Optimization problem)
Bottom-up search, 11-12, 87, 332-333
Built-in procedures, 350, 354
Cancellation law, 9
Case analysis, 316-317
Categories (*see* Boolean Category Expression)
C(B) (*see* Completed data base)

CDL (Complier Definition Language), 350
Clause,
  definition of, 9
  ground unit, 293
  "regular", 49
Clause interconnectivity graph, 200
Clause template, 117, 130
CLEAR language, 252
Closed formula, 15
Closed list, 132-133
Closed queries, 14, 37-38
Closed wffs, 6, 9, 51
Closed world, 35-36, 69, 167, 235
Closed world answers, 17, 56, 63
Closed world assumption, 16-17, 23-24, 39, 55-56, 59, 62, 64-65, 67-69, 71, 165, 172, 380, 390-391, 399
  answers, 60-62
  consistent under the, 69
  consistent with the, 66, 69, 73
  consistency, 68
  minimal, 70-71
  query evaluation under the, 63-64, 66, 75
Closed world data bases, 16, 55, 103, 178, 321, 408
Closed world model, 213
Closed world query evaluation, 55-56
CNF (Conjunctive Normal Form), 70, 195, 197
Compiler definition language, 350
Compiling the IDB, 164-165
Complete axiomatization, 52
Completed data base, 24, 293, 297, 299-300, 303-312, 314, 317-320
  definition of, 296
Complete inference system, 11, 21, 24, 163, 294, 297, 314, 317, 319-320
Complete inference system,
  definition of, 125
Completeness,
  answer extraction, 174
  derivational, 195, 197
  predicate calculus, 8, 18-19, 35, 44, 51, 163-164, 171, 175-176, 195, 200, 259, 321
  query evaluation, 175, 214
Completeness laws, 35-36, 39
Completeness results, 163
Completion law, 295-296, 303, 314
Congruence class, 248-251
Congruence relations, 241, 246
Conjunctive normal form, 70, 195, 197
Connection graph, 22, 183, 199, 220, 222-223, 233, 235
Consequent, 7, 12, 25, 183, 348
  conditional, 186
Consequent literal, 300
Consequent theorem, 332
Consistent data base, 67, 75
Consistent under the CWA, 24
Consistency,
  set of wffs, 37, 40, 44, 56, 64, 68, 71, 74-75, 78, 91, 93, 187, 202-203, 209, 215, 259, 312, 317, 319
  types, 74
Consistency auditing, 53
Control structure, 21, 125, 367
Convention for negative information, 17, 23
CONVERSE, 180, 199-200
Correctness, query evaluation, 305
Coroutine, 85
COUNT function, 202
Counting information, 119, 142
Counting predicates, 381
Counting relation, 119
Currency indicators, 238
CWA (*see* Closed World Assumption)
CYBER-EDMS, 375
DADM (Deductively Augmented Data Management) 184-185, 189

Data base,
  axiomatic, 259
  consistent with the CWA, 56
Data base access strategy, 187
Data base administrator, 183, 326
Data base completion (*see* Completed data base)
Data base interpretation, 344
Data base management systems, 30, 34, 39, 53, 101, 107-108, 237 239, 256-257, 343, 347, 350, 369, 391-392
Data base model, 282
Data base search, 188
Data base semantics, 189
Data base theory, 259, 282-283, 344
Data construction, 298
Data definition, 87, 343, 434
Data description and logic, 321
Data model, definition of, 237-238
Data semantics, 256, 342
Data structures, 19, 27, 88-89, 239, 260-261, 269-270, 277, 286
Data types, 239, 406
DB (Data Base), 55, 57, 59-60, 63-74
DBM (*see* Data Base Management System)
DC (Domain Closure), 154, 176
DEDUCE language, 42, 101, 201-236, 409-410, 416, 426, 436
DEDUCE 2, 22, 25, 144, 177, 201, 409-410, 416, 425, 434, 439
DEDUCE 2 syntax, 201, 231
Deduction,
  automatic, 53, 76, 102, 146, 173
  in information retrieval, 56, 69, 76, 149-150, 293, 321
  and logic, 3, 18, 30, 77, 143-144, 147, 177,
Deduction (cont'd)
  and logic (cont'd) 180-181, 202, 235, 262, 264, 282, 296
  and query languages, 52, 101, 201, 233, 434
  and question-answering, 30, 53-54, 62, 69, 75-76, 103, 144-146, 149, 153, 172, 177-178, 181, 186, 199-200, 234, 236, 321, 377, 408
  in relational data bases, 53, 112, 146, 177-178, 184, 201, 203, 230-231, 234-235, 325, 346, 407
  and search, 107-108, 113-114, 143, 181, 382
  and theory, 259, 261, 286
Deduction capability, 53, 120, 181, 378
Deduction completeness, 296
Deduction mechanism, 108, 125-134, 150, 170, 179, 181-182, 189-190, 192, 260, 301, 367
Deduction methods (plans), 144, 177, 179, 181, 183, 186, 187-189, 192, 195-199, 234, 407
Deduction rules, 8, 51, 117, 147, 181, 260, 262, 286, 293, 296-297, 321, 334
Deductively Augmented Data Management, 184-185, 189
Deductive pathfinding, 22
Definite answer, 58-59, 78
Definite clause, 24, 68
Definite CWA answers, 62, 73
Definite data base, 17, 56, 69, 75
Degree of plausibility, 180
Δ(DB), definition of, 68, 75
Dependencies, 14
Dependency links, 183
Dependency statements, 34, 50-51

Depth first search strategy, 252, 255, 347, 349, 367
Deque, 267
Derivation length, 264, 269, 282, 284, 285
Derivation program, 275, 285
Derivation rules, 24, 33, 40-41, 46-47, 325-326, 328-329, 331-332, 334, 342
Dictionary, 19, 107, 113-114, 117, 119
Difference list, 265-271
Discriminator, 277-283
Discriminator counter, 278-281
Discriminator number, 260, 279
Disjunction tuples, definition of, 153
Division operator, 154-155, 172, 404
d-list, 265-271
Domain calculus, 420, 429
Domain classes, 183, 198
Domain closure assumption, 154, 176
Domain closure axioms, 151-152, 154, 157, 176
Domain-oriented relational languages, 26, 435
Domain predicates, 425
Domain relational calculus, definition of, 420
Domain variables, 414-416
Double-ended queue, 267
DRC (Domain Relational Calculus), 420-427
D-RESTRICTION, 242-243, 245
Drug interaction data base, 27, 347, 356, 369, 371
d-rules (*see* Derivation rules)
EDB (*see* Extensional Data Base)
$\overline{\text{EDB}}$, 60-75
EG (Evaluation Graph), 302, 377, 402-403
Elementary facts (*see* Extensional data base)
Embedded list terms, 400
Empty clause (formula), 8-9, 75, 129, 252, 349
English question-answering system, 182, 202
Entity-relationship model, 237, 256
Enumerated list terms, 392
Equality, 28, 151-152, 154, 157, 163, 173-174, 176, 178
  built-in, 154
Equality axioms, 154
Equality relations, 304
Equality schemas, 296, 303
Equivalence relations, 241, 303
ESTRC (Extended Set Tuple Relational Calculus), 430-432
ET-term, definition of, 388
Evaluation graph (tree), 302, 377, 402-403
Evidence chains, 180
Existential closure, 38
Existential statement, 380
Expressional completeness, 195
Extended set tuple relational calculus, definition of, 430-432
Extensional clause, 132
Extensional data base, 16, 20-21, 23, 25, 59-61, 69, 107, 111-134, 142, 149-150, 152, 156, 159, 163-165, 172-173, 181, 189, 202, 294, 332
  definition of, 60
Extensional quantifier, 424
Extensional relations (*see* Extensional data base)
Extensional query evaluator (processor), 149-150, 156-157, 163, 165
Extensions of KS-predicates, 391
Factor, clause, 10-11
Facts, 114, 150, 182
Failure tree, 307-309
Finite search tree, 164, 302
First order data base, 69, 178

First-order deduction, 295
First-order logic (*see* First-order predicate calculus)
First-order predicate calculus, 3, 18, 33-34, 53-54, 107-109, 140-141, 144-145, 183, 195, 199, 203, 214, 219, 233, 235, 260, 262, 282, 286, 297, 318, 343, 349, 378, 405, 409, 410, 435
  applied, 411
  with description, 379
  functions, 432
  language, 37, 39, 108, 377
First-order theory, 7, 36, 44, 52, 101, 175, 178
  with identity, 260, 267
Formula-normalization, 292
Formulas, definition of, 412
Formal Query Language (FQL), 409-410, 416, 421, 424-425, 435
Forward chaining, 11, 22, 186
4NF, 14, 43
FQL (Formal Query Language), 409-410, 416, 421, 424-425, 435
Frame axioms, 90
Functional dependency, 24, 28, 49-50, 208-209, 233, 235
  definition of, 16
Fuzzy formulas, 203
Fuzzy intersection, 185
Fuzzy logic, 235-236
General axioms (laws, statements, rules), 34-35, 40, 46, 77-91, 107, 114, 116-117, 181, 293
General rules, drug interaction data base, 372-374
Goal tree, 21
Heap, 406
  definition of, 400
Herbrand interpretation, 298
Hierarchical constraint, 319
Hierarchical data base, 12, 36, 237, 318
Horn clause (set), 11-12, 16-17, 23, 67-68, 74-76, 85, 93-100, 111, 120, 123, 125-126, 132, 141, 172, 225, 252, 274, 297, 301, 311, 331, 347
  definition of, 11, 348
    if-half, 94, 99
  logic program, 97
  procedural interpretations, 12, 349
  refutation, 315
  theorem prover, 293, 314
Horn data base, 55-56, 67-69, 74-75
  consistent, 69
Horn formulas (*see* Horn clauses, definition of)
IDB (*see* Intentional Data Base)
IDB clause, 21
Identity theory, 305-306
if-and-only-if, definition of, 24, 85, 94, 96, 296
  if-half of the, 24, 85, 94-95, 99-100, 296, 299, 303, 311, 314
ILL language, 409-410, 416, 427-429, 435, 438
Implication chain, 186
Implication clauses, 328
Inconsistent data base, 37, 40, 55-56, 67, 74-75, 87, 91
Indefinite answer, 58, 153, 172
Indefinite CWA answers, 62
Indefinite data base, 17
Indexed tuple, 415-416, 419, 430-431
Indexing clauses in a logic data base (*see* Knowledge base index)
Inequality schemas, 295, 314
Inference (*see* Deduction)
Inference rules, 7, 11, 349, 365
Information structures (*see* Data structures)
INGRES data base system, 434

Input-output relation, 87
Insecticides data base, 356
Insert operation on queue, 267
Insert relationship, 272-273, 275, 280
Integrity constraints, 15, 40, 55, 69, 84, 87, 92, 107, 201, 203, 208, 215, 344, 418
Integrity, data base, 3, 4, 24, 39, 56, 107, 153, 343, 344
Integrity checking, 25, 33, 54, 235, 325
Integrity recovery, 329, 331-332
Integrity rules, 16, 33, 43-44, 46-47, 49, 325-333, 342
Intensional clause, 69, 132, 149-150, 174, 181, 189, 201
Intensional data base (file), 16, 20-23, 107, 111-114, 117, 120, 123-134, 142, 150, 152, 156, 159, 164-165, 167, 171, 173, 181, 202, 293
  compiled, 142
Intensional processor, 149, 163, 165
International phonetic alphabet, 140
Interpretation,
  first-order theory, 6, 33, 36, 41-42, 46, 51, 325, 341-342
  of queries, 402
Interpreting negation as failure, 23
Inverted index structure, 122-123
Iota-operator expression, definition of, 379
Irreducible model, 238, 343
I-rules (*see* Integrity rules)
Isa-predicates, 84
Joins, 206, 209, 228-229
Joins (cont'd)
  computing of, 234
  natural, 50-51
Join term, 416
Join variable, 206
k-dimensional tree, 270, 277, 300
key,
  primary, 42, 260, 277, 282, 286
  for a relation, 13, 238, 240, 249-251, 253, 270, 272, 278
  secondary, 261, 270, 277, 282, 284-286
Knowledge, about the domain, 60
Knowledge base index, 113-114, 120-124, 133, 142, 376
Knowledge representation, 18, 183, 343, 345, 407
Knowledge representation language, 377
König's lemma, 402
Konstruktsprache (*see* KS)
K-RESTRICTION, 242-244
KS (Konstruktsprache), 377, 381, 386, 390, 406, 408
  atomic formula of, 383
  formula, definition of, 383
  as a query language, 378
  as a semantic representation language for natural language, 400
  syntax of, 378, 381
KS-assertions, 382
KS-expressions, 392, 406
  normalization of, 392
KS-formula,
  normalization, definition of, 393
  semantics of, 399
KS-language, 27, 382
KS-list term, 400
KS-quantificators, 392
KS-predicates, 391
KS-terms, 381, 391, 400, 405
LAMBDA-abstraction, multiple, 390
λ-conversion, 251

LAMBDA-term, 384-385, 390, 392, 400, 402, 404
  normalization of, 392
language, internal representation, 406
Lemma formation, 127-128, 130
Letter-to-sound rules, 140, 144, 147
Linear resolution (refutation), 64, 67, 300, 301, 311
  with selection function (*see* SL-resolution)
  with unrestricted selection function for Horn clauses (*see* LUSH resolution)
Link array, 191
Linked plan, 225-227
LISP, 27, 88, 265, 322
LISP 1.5, 192
List, 20, 262-271, 278-280
List term, 386-387
  definition of, 385
  prefixed, 389
  unprefixed, 389
Literal,
  definition of, 5
  selected, 126
Literal template tree structure, 121, 123
Logical axioms, 7
Logical consequence, 7, 51, 93-94, 293
Logic programming (*see* Predicate logic as a programming language)
LUSH-resolution (Linear resolution with unrestricted selection function for Horn clauses), 115-117, 120, 124, 301, 321
Many-sorted algebra, 240, 243
Many-sorted domain, 377
Many-sorted logic, 18-19, 24, 108-110, 117, 134, 382
Mapping oriented languages, 14, 25
Maryland Refutation Proof Procedure System 3.0 (*see* MRPPS 3.0)
Mathematical logic (*see* first-order predicate calculus)
Mechanical theorem proving (*see* theorem proving)
Meta-language, 97-99, 331
Meta-level proof, 98-100
M.g.u., (most general unifier), 301, 306-307
Middle-term chaining generator, 22, 186-187, 190-197
Minimal answers, 153
  to a query, definition of, 58
Minimal model, definition of, 69
Minimization problem for a Boolean function, 229
Miniscope normal form algorithm, 394
Minsky's monotonicity assumption, 91
Model, 36, 44, 113, 211-212, 341
  definition of, 7, 420
  of a theory, 7, 34, 261, 282, 286
Modus ponens, 7-8
Monadic predicate, 151
Monotonicity criticism, 92, 94
Most general unifier, 301, 306-307
MRPPS 2.0, 108, 125, 142, 145-146
MRPPS 3.0, 19, 108, 111-112, 117, 123, 125, 127-128, 134-135, 140-141, 143, 235
  block diagram of, 114
MTCG (Middle Term Chaining Generator), 22, 186-187, 190-197
Multilevel data bases, 257
Multiple views, 240
Multivalued dependency, 16, 24, 30, 54, 234-235
  definition of, 51

Multivalued dependency statements, 33-34, 43, 49-50, 52
Multiway tree, 270
Natural language data management systems, 27, 95, 96, 199
Natural language answer/reason output, 107, 112, 137-139, 143, 146
Natural language proof, 113, 137
Natural language query, 26, 381, 406
Natural language question-answering, 29, 146
Natural language "set" descriptions, 381
Natural language spoken output for deductive systems, 112, 114, 135, 146
Natural language understanding, 100
Navigation, generalized, 189
Negated atomic formula (literal), 56, 183, 300
Negated question, 125
Negation, 64, 85, 97, 100, 294, 392, 415, 425
  as failure, 62, 76, 101, 177, 293-294, 296-297, 320, 325
  as failure inference rule, 293, 297, 314, 320
  set theoretical handling of, 382
Negative advice, 186
Negative clauses, 55-56, 68-69, 75
Negative facts (also negative ground literals, negative information), 16, 23, 33, 35, 42, 48-49, 59-60, 75, 295
Negative information, convention for, 39
Negative operators, 62
Negative premises, 321
Negative procedure calls, 85
Network data model, 12, 36, 237-238, 257
Node Generation, 127-128, 130-133
Nondeterministic language or program, 237, 248, 296, 300-302, 318
Non-logical proper axioms, 7
Non-procedural languages, 410
Non-terminal symbols, 223-224
Normal form, 43, 81, 183, 197, 251, 343
Normalized query, 377, 392
Normalized relation, 14, 201, 208
N^{th} projection, definition of, 402
NRL grammar for voice output, 140
Null clause (*see* Empty clause)
Numerical quantifiers, 25, 201-202, 209, 214, 219, 285
Ob-tree (*see* ordered binary tree)
Ok-tree (*see* tree, ordered k-dimensional)
1NF, 14
Only-if half of the definition, 94-100, 303
Open formulas, 15
Open queries, 14, 37
Open world, 17, 35
Open world answer, 56
Open World Assumption, 16, 55, 58-60, 63, 73, 165
  answer, 61
  atomic query evaluation, 67
  evaluation, 75
Open world evaluation, 55-56
Operator list (*see* OPLIST)
OPLIST (Operator List), 132-134
Optimization problem for Boolean functions, 23, 201, 203, 228-230, 233
Optimizing transformations, 170
Ordered binary tree (ob-tree), 271-283

OWA (*see* Open World Assumption)
Parallel search, 53, 144, 147
Paramodulation, 154, 178
Pathfinding, 145, 177, 179, 187, 407
Pattern-directed search, 127, 128, 133, 147, 199, 234
  control structure of, 146
  global, 129
Pattern matching (*see* Unification)
Pattern matching module, 134
Pattern recognition, 52, 101, 233
PCG (*see* Predicate Connection Graph)
Pesticides data base, 367
Π-clauses, translation into English, 145
Π-representation, 53
Π-σ clause, 117, 130
Π-σ literal, 124, 130
Π-σ notation, 108, 111, 115-117, 134-135
Π-σ resolution, 133
Π-σ sets, 116, 119, 124, 130
Π-σ substitution component, 119
Π-σ substitution sets, 114, 117, 119
Π-σ unification, 133
Placeholder variable, 119
Plan formation, 89-90, 187, 191, 198-199, 224-226, 228, 234
PLANNER language, 62, 76, 294, 332, 343
Plan review, 187
Plan selection, 187
Plan verification, 187, 191
Plausibility measures, 186, 195
Plausibility of the plan, 192
Plausible knowledge, 198
PLIDIS data base, 391
PLIDIS language, 27, 377-378, 392
Positive knowledge, 56
Positive ground literal (*see* Atomic formula, ground)
Positive unit (*see* Atomic formula, ground)
Positive unit refutation, 74
Postcondition, 240
PPG (*see* Proof Plan Generator)
PPV (*see* Proof Plan Verifier)
Preconditions, 89, 240
Predicate array, 189, 191
Predicate calculus (*see* First-order predicate calculus)
Predicate calculus languages, 14-15
Predicate connection graph, 183, 185, 190, 195
Predicate domain, 184
Predicate logic as a programming language, 30, 51, 76, 85, 94, 376
Premise array, 189
Premises used in proofs, 191
Prenex normal form, 110, 126, 214-215
Primitive categories, 118
Primitive conditional, 183, 189, 192, 195, 197
Primitive relations, 47
Problem solving, 29, 78, 82, 102, 147, 343, 345, 378, 406
Problem solving graph, 130
Procedural view of clauses, 349
Procedure body, 349
Procedure declaration, 349
Procedure head, 349
Production rules, 183
Production systems, 199
Program logic, 260-261, 263-264, 268, 272-278, 281, 284-285
PROgramming language based on LOGic (*see* PROLOG)
Projection operator, 50-51, 56, 65-66, 154-155, 165, 172, 205, 211, 228, 404

PROLOG (see PROgramming language based on LOGic), 20, 27, 30, 51, 54, 62, 85, 87, 90, 101, 103, 237-238, 249, 252-253, 257-258, 260, 262, 264, 267-268, 274, 282, 284, 286, 294, 302, 321-322, 347-377.
  Hungarian version, 346-376
PROLOG selection rule, 312, 315
Proof, failure to find, 55-56, 294-295, 308
Proof graph, 9, 113, 125, 134, 136, 156, 187, 192, 197
Proof plan generator, 183, 190
Proof plan verifier, 190
Proof procedure, 125, 199, 234, 262, 264, 268, 274-275, 283
Proof rule, 294
Proof tree, symbolic form of, 135
Proof theory, 34, 262
Proper axioms, 342
Proper range formula, 417-418, 422
Proposition,
  in clause form, definittion of, 347
  definition of, 5, 412
Propositional calculus, 6, 9, 234
Proving properties of logic programs, 78, 85, 87
QA systems (*see* Question-Answering systems)
Quantificators of KS, definition of, 388
Quantifier-free formula, 57
QUEL language, 409-410, 415, 432
Query-by-example, 83-84, 90, 103, 236, 409-410, 416, 427, 434
Query containing universal quantifiers, 194
Query-d-rules, 331, 335
Query evaluation, 58, 149-150, 293, 296-297
Query language, 27, 49, 56, 83, 90, 364, 377, 406, 409, 413
Query optimization, 178
Query refinement, 187
Query transformation, 203, 216, 217, 219, 228, 230
Question-answering systems, 33-34, 36, 53, 144-145, 177, 180, 199, 235, 347, 350, 353, 406-407
Queue, 263, 266-267
Range coupled quantifiers, 392, 417, 422-423
Range, domain variable, 414
Range predicates, 26, 414-415, 418
RDMS (*see* Relational Data Management Systems)
Reconciling inconsistency, 92
Record (fact) (*see* Extensional data base)
Recursive axioms (laws), 22, 28, 49, 142, 164, 171
Recursively defined relation, 90, 140-141
Recursive premises, 185
Refutation graph (*see* Proof graph)
Refutation proof procedure system, 9, 75, 125, 146, 158
Refutation search tree, 166, 169
Relation,
  definition of, 12, 410
  extension of, 16, 111, 410
  schema of, 390
Relational algebra, 14, 25, 56, 140, 165, 172, 205, 419, 427

Relational calculus, 10, 15, 17, 25, 83-84, 140, 234, 294, 299, 434
Relational completeness, 17, 29, 76, 101, 144, 177, 321, 406-407, 434
Relational data bases, 3, 21-22, 27, 33, 52, 79, 83, 85, 101-102, 107, 111, 120, 142, 145-146, 149-150, 177, 179, 199, 201-202, 204-205, 208, 228, 233-235, 294, 296, 391, 407, 410, 434
Relational data base management system, 29, 52, 163, 177, 180-182, 192, 198, 203, 226, 343
Relational data base schema, 207
Relational expressions, 406
Relational languages, 235, 409-436
Relational model of data, 3, 14, 25, 30, 43, 81, 83, 101, 204, 234, 237-239, 256, 321, 343, 390, 392, 407, 410, 432
Relational representation, 36
Relation placeholders, 116
RENDEZVOUS language, 233-234
Reorder relationship, 275-277
Resolution and paramodulation, 51
Resolution principle, 9, 30, 75-75, 144, 146, 161, 177, 200, 235, 252, 268, 297, 302, 310, 376
Resolution proof trees, extracting information from, 145
Resolved literal, 9-10, 158-159, 161, 306
Resolvents, 9-10, 74, 161
RESPECTIVE-operator, 396
RESPECTIVE-terms, 389
Restricted existentional quantifier, 151
Restricted quantifiers, definition of, 423
Restricted universal quantifier, 151
Restriction of variables, 26
Reverse list, 268-269
Reverse relationship, 269
Rewriting rule, 23, 201, 203 219-220, 222-223, 228, 230-231, 233
RIAD R22, 350
Right literal, 161, 220, 222
RP(*see* Range predicates)
Satisfiable set of formulas, 7-10
Scott's minimal fixpoint, 69
Scott-Strachey, 27
SDRC (*see* Set Domain Relational Calculus)
Search-compute plan, 22, 187
Search space, 300
Search strategy, 11, 125, 146
Search strategy control structure, 125, 127-129, 131-132, 134, 143
Search tree, 21
Selection of relevant premises, 181
Selection rule, 300, 315
Semantic actions, 127-130
Semantic advice, 185-186
Semantic antecedents, 189
Semantic categories, 113, 117, 119, 122
Semantic classes, 39-40
Semantic constraints, 119
Semantic domain restrictions, 185
Semantic form space, 19, 107, 113-114, 117, 119
Semantic graph, 107, 113-114, 116-118, 143, 382
Semantic implicaions, 189
Semantic information, 120, 145, 184
Semantic integrity, 343
Semantic network, 19, 27, 29-30, 53, 79, 101, 107, 112-

Semantic network (cont'd)
113, 115-116, 141-147, 177, 180, 182, 184, 199, 235, 375, 407
elements of the, 116
extended form of, 19
Semantic point of view, 69
Semantic relation, 19
Semantic representation language for German, 377-378, 407
Semantic theory, 408
Semantics,
of the data model, 240
of the domain, 170
of the extensional data base, 189
operational, 27
of predicate calculus, definition of, 412
of programming languages, 30
of quantifiers, 421
Semi-decidable proof system, 8
SEQUEL (Structured English Query Language), 30, 233, 409-410, 415-416, 427, 429, 432, 441
SEQUEL 2, 331, 343, 409-410, 434
Set domain relational calculus, 425-427, 430-431
Set intensions, 175-176
Set-of-support inference system, 197-198
Set-oriented query language, 56
Set tuple relational calculus, 12, 14-17, 22-23, 420, 422-423, 425, 430-431
definition of, 419
Set variable, 419
SIEMENS 7'755, 350
Σ-congruence relation, 241
Σ-equation, 241
Signature of a model, 20, 237, 241, 246
SIMPL language, 108
SIMPL-T language, 144
Skeletal derivations, 179, 183, 187
Skölem constants, 174
Skölem functions, 37, 51, 110, 173-174, 197
Skölemized quantifier free form, 176, 183, 328
SL-resolution (Linear resolution with Selection function) 125-127, 130, 134, 145, 317, 321
Sorted variables, 384
Sorts, 18-19, 40, 109, 113, 240, 246, 248, 382
of KS, 391
Sort symbols of KS, 386
Sound inference system, 320
definition of, 8, 18, 24, 125
Soundness,
of predicate calculus, 24
of resolution, 311
Specification list, 132-134
SPECLIST, 132-134
SQUARE language, 406, 409-410, 415-416, 427, 429, 432, 434, 438, 441
SSCE (Search Strategy Controller Executive), 128, 134
Stack, 263-264, 302
State laws, 325-327, 339, 342
State of the world, 34, 325-326
STRC (*see* Set Tuple Relational Calculus)
Structural induction, 71
Structured English Query Language (*see* SEQUEL)
Structure sharing, 302, 320
Subproblem selection, 125, 127-128, 132
Symbolic integration, 87-88, 100
Symmetric relationship, 268
Syntactic filtering, 127-130

SYNTEX system, 52-53, 102, 140, 146, 434
System R, 201, 203, 219, 233
T_{Σ}, 241
TAMALAN language, 409-410, 416, 427
Tautologies, 130
Template form (structure), 115, 119-120, 130, 134
Term,
  canonical, 248-253
  definition of, 5, 108, 204, 412
Terminal symbols, 223-224
Termination problem, 231
Term normalization, 400, 406
Theorem as program, 260-261, 263, 267-268, 272, 273, 276-281, 286
Theorem proving, 8, 21-22, 52, 99, 101-102, 107, 142, 144-145, 149-150, 156-157, 163, 165, 170, 172, 177-178, 183, 200, 203, 215, 233, 249, 297, 320-321, 343, 347, 349-350, 367, 371, 375, 378
Theory of Boolean switching functions, 234
Third normal form (Boyce-Codd Normal Form), 14, 42-43, 233
3NF(BCNF) (*see* Third normal form)
Top clause, 158
Top-down search (goal tree), 11, 21, 87, 252, 254, 332, 347, 349, 367
Transition laws (rules), 25, 325-326, 336-342
Transition rules, consistency of, 325, 340
Transitive closure, 117
Traverse a list, 265, 268
TRC (*see* Tuple Relational Calculus)
Trees, 20
  operations on, 272
  ordered k-dimensional (ok-tree), 20, 272, 278-281, 284, 288
Tree traversal, 285
Truth functional semantics, 62, 262, 294, 296, 378
Truth value of a formula, 413
Tuple oriented languages, 26
Tuple relational calculus, 416-425
Tuple variables, 414
Turing machine, 260
Twffs, (*see* Typed well-formed formulae)
2NF, 14
Type checking, 253, 418, 422
Typed domain-oriented language, 27
Typed positive unit refutation, 75
Typed resolution, 74
Typed unification algorithm, 156
Typed variables, 26, 57, 151-153, 158-159, 164, 167-168, 183, 185, 198, 240, 414-416, 421-422, 426
Typed well-formed formulae, 149-151
Type inconsistency, 168
Unary range predicates, 416
Unification, 10, 124, 131-134, 153, 183, 195, 197-198, 202, 252-253, 300-301, 306
Unification algorithm, 74, 127, 163, 268, 349, 352, 370
Unification array, 191
Unifying substitution, 22, 134, 302
Unit clauses, 302, 352, 355, 370
Unit fully instantiated clauses, 117
Unit refutation, 76

Universally quantified query, 285
Universal type, 167
Unnormalized relations, 43
Unquantified query, 283
Unsatisfiable set, 7-9, 75
Unstated only-if assumption, 96
Updating anomallies, 208
Validation of negation as failure, 305
Valid set, 7, 51
Verified plans, 187, 191
Verifying data base integrity constraints, 78
Views, 15, 230, 257, 344
Virtual attributes, 213
Virtual relations, 22, 111, 112, 120, 131, 134-135, 141, 172, 201-231
Voice proofs, 113, 138
Voice synthesizer (Votrax), 140
Votrax voice synthesizer, 140
Well-formed formula of predicate calculus, 4-5, 16, 34, 36, 40, 50, 107-108, 110, 204, 326, 328, 337
  definition of, 5
Well-formedness conditions, 383
Well-formedness of KS terms, definition of, 384
Well-formedness test on input, 113-114
Wffs (*see* Well-formed formula of predicate calculus)
Wh-question, 390
  answer defined, 391
Workspace controller, 127-128, 130
World model, 325, 382
Yes-No queries, 14, 390, 413

LIST OF REFEREES

The editors would like to thank the reviewers for their detailed reading and constructive comments. The quality of the articles has been enhanced due to their efforts.

C. L. Chang

K. Clark

R. Demolombe

H. Gallaire

C. H. Kellogg

R. A. Kowalski

M. Lacroix

J. Minker

J. M. Nicolas

A. Pirotte

R. Reiter

R. Scha

S-Å. Tärnlund

G. Zanon

ADDRESSES OF CONTRIBUTING AUTHORS

C. L. Chang
IBM Research Laboratory
Monterey & Cottle Roads
San Jose, Calif. 95193
USA

K. Clark
Dept. of Computer Sci. & Stat.
Queen Mary College
University of London
Mile End Run
London, E1 4NS, England

M. Colombetti
Politecnico di Milano
Istituto di Elettrotecnica ed Elettronica
Piazza Leonardo da Vinci, 32
20133 Milan, Italy

F. Darvas
SZKI
H 1052 Bp. V. Martinelli ter 8
Hungary

W. Dilger
Institut für deutsche Sprache
Friedrich-Karl-Strasse 12
D-6800 Mannheim
FRG

I. Futó
NIM IGUSZI
H-1134 Bp Lehel U.11
Budapest, Hungary

H. Gallaire
CERT-DERI
2, Avenue Edouard Belin
31055 Toulouse Cedex
France

C. H. Kellogg
System Development Corporation
2500 Colorado Avenue
Santa Monica, Calif. 94406
USA

P. Klahr
System Development Corporation
2500 Colorado Avenue
Santa Monica, Calif. 94406
USA

R. Kowalski
Dept. of Computing & Control
Imperial College of Science and Technology
180 Queen's Gate
London, SW7 2BZ, England

J. Minker
Department of Computer Science
University of Maryland
College Park, Maryland 20742
USA

J. M. Nicolas
CERT-DERI
2, Avenue Edouard Belin
31055 Toulouse Cedex
France

P. Paolini
Politecnico di Milano
Istituto di Elettrotecnica ed Elettronica
Piazza Leonardo da Vinci, 32
20133 Milan, Italy

G. Pelagatti
Politecnico di Milano
Istituto di Elettrotecnica ed Elettronica
Piazza Leonardo da Vinci, 32
20133 Milan, Italy

A. Pirotte
MBLE - Laboratoire de Recherches
Avenue Van Becelaere 2
B-1170 Brussels,
Belgium

R. Reiter
Department of Computer Science
University of British Columbia
Vancouver, BCV 67 1W5
Canada

P. Szeredi
NIM IGUSZI
H-1134 Bp. Lehel U.11
Budapest, Hungary

S-Å. Tärnlund
Computer Science Department
University of Stockholm
S 104 05 Stockholm 50
Sweden

L. Travis
Department of Computer Science
University of Wisconsin
Madison, Wisconsin 53706
USA

K. Yazdanian
CERT-DERI
2, Avenue Edouard Belin
31055 Toulouse Cedex
France

G. Zifonun
Institut für deutsche Sprache
Friedrich-Karl-Strasse 12
D-6800 Mannheim
FRG